Political Performances

Themes in Theatre

Collective Approaches to Theatre and Performance

4

Political Performances
Theory and Practice

Edited by
Susan C. Haedicke, Deirdre Heddon,
Avraham Oz and E.J. Westlake

IFTR/FIRT
Political Performances Working Group

Amsterdam - New York, NY 2009

Official Publication of the International Federation for Theatre Research/
Publication officielle de la Fédération Internationale pour la Recherche
Théâtrale

Cover photo: *Neighbours*, a Collage of Hanoch Levin Plays. Adapted by Tal
Itzhaki and Amit Gazit. Minor Latham Playhouse (Columbia University, New
York), 2004. Designer: Tal Itzhaki. Photograph by Ayala Gazit.

Cover design: Pier Post

The paper on which this book is printed meets the requirements of "ISO
9706:1994, Information and documentation - Paper for documents -
Requirements for permanence".

ISBN: 978-90-420-2606-3
E-Book ISBN: 978-90-420-2607-0
©Editions Rodopi B.V., Amsterdam - New York, NY 2009
Printed in the Netherlands

Printed by Printforce, the Netherlands

ACKNOWLEDGEMENTS

We would like to acknowledge Professor Ravi Chaturvedi, for inviting the Political Performances Working Group for and extra meeting in Jaipur, on January 2007, where the most recent papers included in the volume were given. We would also like to thank the editorial staff at Rodopi Press, especially Esther Roth, for their guidance and patience.

TABLE OF CONTENTS

PART ONE: QUERIES

PART TWO: TEXTS

PART THREE: CONTEXTS

PART FOUR: PRACTICE

MAPPING POLITICAL PERFORMANCES:
A NOTE ON THE STRUCTURE OF THE ANTHOLOGY

E.J. WESTLAKE

Political Performances: Theory and Practice emerges from our work together in the Political Performances Working Group of the International Federation for Theatre Research. Our group strives to interrogate and expand the boundaries of what we mean by political performance. Members of Political Performances are from around the world and so approach the intersection of politics and performance from very different perspectives. Some focus on socio-political context, others on dramatic content, and others on political issues and activism. We have tried to structure this book in a way that makes productive use of our diverse positions and highlights the variety of ways in which politics and performance converge. Each section frames this confluence according to certain common threads we saw emerging in our work.

When I first joined the Political Performances Working Group, I remember wondering why there had to be a group. It seemed strange to me that the study of political performances was segregated into a separate group. Aren't all performances political, I wondered, even if only to uphold the dominant culture? Even when artists set out to make "political" performances, aren't they always in danger of falling into the trap of creating art that ultimately reifies rather than transgresses, disintegrating into the self-congratulatory instead of inciting to action? And how can we, as scholars, even *begin* to negotiate the complexity of myriad starting points and obstacles and the unpredictable ways in which they are read?

But the members of Political Performances did not enter into their work lightly and were not oblivious to these same issues. Throughout our meetings, scholars and artists (and scholar-artists) continued to dig for ways to find some political traction in what was potentially a Foucaultian sea of relativism. Ultimately, the "political" in the performances we study springs from the new constellations of relationships we form; hinges on being able to locate ourselves and our work and our intended audience in a way that highlights our position on a map of political context and political action. The politics of representation is the politics of multiple relationships: of the character to the actor, the character to the person being represented, the history to the story, the place to the space of performance. Being able to see those relationships, and hopefully the possible consequences of forming them, leads to an opening where political change can take place.

As I look back over the work of our contributors and contemplate where the essays fall in relation to each other, I am continuously drawn back to the image of the map. This is not to say that we harboured any illusions that we would accurately and completely draw out a representation of a fixed terrain. We are not, through this collection, attempting to create a detailed atlas. On the contrary, the more we explore, the more we find that a complete representation is an impossible enterprise. But in keeping with the fourth order of Baudrillard's simulacrum (1993: 347), the map is its own reality, one on which several interlocking relationships are constituted. It is the map of a moment where we have found a series of useful coordinates.

More productively, perhaps, the map might reveal our own relationships as contributors: to each other, to our political contexts, and to the subjects of our essays. In "Geographies of Learning," Jill Dolan noted in 1993 the emergent use of the "location" metaphor in both scholarly and political discourse. In her discussion of positionality, the act of locating oneself in relation to one's subject, Dolan contends that it is: "a gesture toward placing oneself within a critique of objectivity, but at the same time stopping the spin of post-structuralist or postmodernist instabilities long enough to advance a politically effective action. A position is an unstable but effective point of departure" (417). Through stopping long enough to make note of our positions on our shifting landscape, we were able to draw some of the Cartesian equations that make up our years-long debates on political performances. We drew these along the axes of Queries, Texts, Contexts, and Practice.

These sections are prefaced by an introductory essay from our working group convenor, Avraham Oz. Oz uses examples from both classical and contemporary drama to define the role of political performances as a catalyst for political change. It is followed by *Queries*, the first section of our book, which contains five essays that raise crucial questions when considering the role of performance in the political process. These essays form the foundation of many of our debates about politics and performance and serve as a springboard into some of the more specific essays that follow. In her essay on the Public Sphere, Paola Botham seeks to redefine political theatre, moving away from the teleological Marxist paradigm, in danger of being undermined by late capitalism. The Habermasian concept of the Public Sphere, she argues, could offer insight into the efficacy of verbatim theatre, specifically "tribunal theatre" performances such as Tricycle Theatre's *Bloody Sunday*. Tribunal theatre goes beyond mere dramatic presentation of opposing perspectives in that the testimonies of the participants are replayed on stage. Botham examines how this level of recreation interacts with the audience members' perceptions of veracity.

David Grant takes up the concept of orality in the next essay as he considers the ways in which the spoken, embodied word translates into written text. Taking his cue from Walter J. Ong, he interrogates the authority attributed to writing in our culture and engages the question asked by William B. Worthen: "Is it possible to understand performance through the scripted form of dramatic texts? […] Is the form of a printed book an adequate delivery system for plays? Is it a delivery system at all" (2006: 213)? Grant examines the creation and publication of performances such as *The Wedding Play* and posits that an orality paradigm can aid in the understanding of "rules of engagement" for community-based and collaborative projects. He poses questions about the politics of ownership and authenticity in the collection of a community's oral history.

In her article on Ariane Mnouchkine, Bérénice Hamidi-Kim grapples with the definition of political theatre. She follows the evolution of the performances of Théâtre du Soleil as the company transitions from performing "people's theatre" to performing "citizen theatre." Hamidi-Kim examines the current role of Théâtre du Soleil in addressing political issues and discusses Mnouchkine's commitment to art that is also political as opposed to art as a means to a political goal. This transition to "citizen theatre," she argues, constitutes an adaptation in the face of the shifting political landscape of the 21st century.

Censorship is the subject of Tal Itzhaki's essay on Israeli theatre. Itzhaki examines government censorship and the play by Itzhak Laor that lead to the lifting of government restrictions in 1984. However, Itzhaki notes, censorship in the form of self-censorship continues. While there are no forbidden subjects, she argues, certain images remain unseen. While calling attention to the disappearance of war imagery from the Israeli stage, Itzhaki explores the complex relationship of audience to artist and the persistent modes of erasure and denial.

The last essay in our section on queries raises questions of the uncertain ethical implications of performing biography and autobiography. Framed by her own biographical narrative, Deirdre Heddon considers a range of political issues that arise when the words of living people are performed publicly. Following Paul John Eakin's assertion that interconnectedness should make writers aware of their responsibility to others when writing about themselves, Heddon proceeds to explore the myriad forms this responsibility takes in the wide range of biographical and autobiographical performance. Different questions emerge as she takes a critical lens to verbatim performances from Liverpool Everyman's *Unprotected* to Lisa Kron's *Well*. In her discussion of *Well*, Heddon notes the ways in which Kron attempts to highlight her role in the construction of her mother as a character in her performance, inviting the audience to reflect on the autobiographical performer's subjectivity.

The section on *Texts* deals with the texts of political performances, from examinations of the plays of dramatists who write for social change to performers who rework texts to highlight pressing current issues. The first essay in this section by Carl Lavery sifts through the debates over the political significance of Jean Genet's later plays. Using Genet's long-absent preface to his play *The Blacks*, Lavery demonstrates that Genet was indeed creating political theatre, one that eschews the liberal and humanist approach, which is an approach that ultimately fails in the impossible enterprise of speaking for another, in favour of an approach of "betrayal." Lavery employs the ideas of Situationist Guy Debord to posit that Genet's work places the spectator in a position where passive consumption of spectacle is replaced by experience, by an encounter with the actors on stage.

The next essay deals with a recent mise-en-scène of *The Persians*, the Greek tragedy by Aeschylus. Sydney Cheek O'Donnell describes Waterwell's 2005 production of *The Persians…a Comedy about War with Five Songs*. Waterwell's performance is a radical reconfiguration of the play and a critique of the Western chauvinism at the root of both Aechylus' characterization of his adversaries and of the attitudes of modern Westerners toward the Middle East. Cheek O'Donnell focuses on the performance of gender in the production. She observes that the performers use of Brechtian acting points to the construction of identity and to the role such constructions play in shaping U.S. foreign policy.

Tom Maguire turns his attention to stereotypes in his article on the contemporary political performances of Northern Ireland. Writing about plays that have been performed both in Ireland and elsewhere, Maguire questions the political efficacy of portraying Loyalists and Republicans in ways that reinforce established caricatures. He notes that this merely upholds the dominant culture and makes work for peace all the more difficult. It also allows spectators abroad to further distance themselves from what can be too easily dismissed as foreign madness.

Using Melchinger's definition of political theatre, Sanja Nikčević follows the development of dramatic writing in Croatia, from the protest plays written in the former Yugoslavia to the current work of Miro Gavran. As Nikčević points out, if the function of political drama is to show the social and political forces that destroy the individual, then political theatre died out with Communist censorship and has only recently re-emerged on the Croatian stage. Beginning with Gavran's 2004 production of *How to Kill a President*, the new political drama addresses issues of globalization, terrorism, and the fear that comes with the new era of alienation.

In the face of the growing popularity of verbatim theatre, David Watt seeks to trace a genealogy of scripted drama created from interviews and individual testimony. The form, he argues, was first named by Bertolt Brecht in 1926 and put to use by practitioners such as Erwin Piscator to provide the audience with an opportunity to objectively analyze the actual material of history. As verbatim theatre became fashionable, Watt observes, theatre practitioners lost sight of

its history, specifically its history as community-based theatre as it
was developed by early pioneers of the form, such as Charles Parker
and Peter Cheeseman. This loss, he claims, could come at the expense
of the political efficacy of a form intended to generate dialogue within
communities from which these performances spring.

It is here that we turn from *Texts* to *Contexts* in order to
understand the function of political performances in the broader
political arena. How do political performances prompt or inform
political action? How do we move spectators to feel, to think, and
most importantly, to act? How are political events constructed in
political performances and how are these constructions read or
deployed? Shimon Levy examines the play *Plonter*, the film *Arna's
Children,* and the work of the Ruth Kanner Group and notes their use
of different self-referential methods to construct or represent the
Israeli occupation of the Palestinians.

The historical emplotment of Algeria's independence from
France and the ensuing civil war are the subject of Susan C.
Haedicke's essay as she discusses *Such a Great Hope* by Franco-
Algerian dramatist Noureddine Aba. In the play, she argues, Aba
negotiates the blurred distinctions between fiction and history in order
to grapple with the conflicting interpretations of Algeria's "invisible"
war. Haedicke suggests that this radical exploration of the themes and
ideas that make up an historical account can potentially offer a new,
more hopeful, vision of an Algerian political future.

While Haedicke seeks to define the relationship of political
performance to history, Wendy Clupper examines the role of the
spectator versus the role of the performer in the making of a political
performance. Through her participation in the *Critical Tits* bicycle
ride of the Burning Man festival, Clupper muses about the level of
agency of the performer in establishing a performance as ultimately
empowering when the performer is in danger of being objectified.
While the women of the ride attempt to create a space of freedom and
solidarity, the gaze of the male spectators mitigates this agency.
Clupper reads the ride and her participation in it through the context
of the festival and its web of performance installations.

E.J. Westlake, in her essay on the Nicaraguan dance-drama *El
Güegüence*, follows the characters of the drama and their complex
signification through the Nicaraguan political process. While the title
figure has become a national symbol in the last century, she observes,

the characters have more recently come to stand for events and dynamics in electoral politics. Westlake argues that these political metaphors have the potential to either reify or to resist the dominant political power.

In *Practice*, the last group of essays address the process of making political performances. These four essays of Practice examine the issues practitioners encounter as they engage with a community in the process of generating creative dialogue. Beverly Redman recounts her struggle to create meaningful political theatre with the "citizen artists" who were in residence at the Union Station Foundation homeless shelter and treatment program. She examines the reasons why both she and participants felt unable to sustain their work. Ultimately, Redman concludes that the cross purposes of the foundation's need to use a final product as a fundraising tool and Redman's desire to create community-based work that addressed the needs of the community caused the project to fail.

Seizing on Jan Cohen-Cruz's observations that community-based theatre can facilitate the exploration of "a common concern" (2005: 3) among participants with diverse and diverging perspectives, Kerrie Schaefer discusses the Birabahn/Threlkeld project in Lake Macquarie, New South Wales to open a forum on the shared history between aboriginal and non-aboriginal Australians. Understood against a backdrop of an incomplete and imperfect reconciliation, Schaefer explores the dynamic relationship between Taylor's archive and repertoire, the understanding of the fluid nature of history and the ways in which the embodiment of history informs its essence.

Lloyd Peters and Sue Becker consider the nature of political theatre though the involvement of young people in Peters' production of *E to the Power 3 – Education, Education, Education*. Peters hoped, in the course of the project, not only to examine British educational policies, but to find a way to engage the young participants in investigating the attitudes and ideas about education and the ways in which they are affected by them. To that end, Peters also attempts to gain an understanding of the performance tools best suited to address political themes.

We conclude this collection with an essay by Sonja Arsham Kuftinec as she explores the limits of community-based theatre. These limits, Kuftinec argues as she departs from Dolan's concept of performative utopias, are not negations of hope, but rather opportunities for "productive dissent—ruptures that make systems of difference and exclusion visible but also potentially allow for their renegotiation" (349). To examine these renegotiations and understand their productive potential, she discusses the actions of two participants in recent Cornerstone productions. Through this understanding, Kuftinec seeks a way beyond the static extremes of "enforced consensus or mere co-existence" toward an alternative that is more dynamically democratic (369).

It is worth it to note that while we have chosen the frames of "Queries," "Texts," "Contexts," and "Practice," there were any number of maps we could have made of the terrain that rises along the horizons of politics and performance. As with any map, the boundaries are not entirely arbitrary, nor are they set into the landscape. The explorations of the working group continue to generate new maps based on newly-created visions of what the landscape might be. And a rereading of the work of our contributors by the editorial team continued to reveal new connections and open possibilities.

While the current road might take the reader from thought to word to place to action, other paths might be found along landmarks such as verbatim theatre, the subject of the essays by Botham, Heddon, Grant, and Watt. Collectively, this group of essays raises questions about the politics of representation in terms of who can speak for whom (Heddon), ownership of personal stories (Grant), and the political effectiveness of veracity (Botham, Watt).

The politics of the representation of history formed another opening though which many contributors read their subjects. While Haedicke discussed the ways in which the creative reworking of history could fashion a productive understanding of the future, Schaefer envisioned an embodied history as a means of opening dialogue and building connections. Others, such as Watt and Hamidi-Kim felt that political performances could be reenergized through an understanding of the history of the forms of political performances themselves.

We were also deeply conscious of our own starting points in our own political processes and our relationships to the art, the artists, and the communities in which they are situated. Additional questions arose about the ethics of representing vulnerable communities such as students (Peters/Becker), prostitutes (Heddon), and the homeless

(Redman) and of the politics of the gaze (Clupper). Can a political performance adequately represent vulnerable groups, or facilitate their self-representation? Can it do so without also facilitating voyeurism on the part of the spectator? Does the spectator's role really matter in the course of the empowerment of the participant? Several of the authors (Peters/Becker, Lavery, Cheek, Maguire) attempt to find performance strategies that might circumvent the expectations of the audience and push them to contemplate, in ways that are both critical and moving, how their own attitudes and actions are part of a broader terrain of social issues.

There has been, in our group, an energetic discourse about the ability of political performances to represent atrocity, and several of the following essays grapple with this issue. The possibility of representing war or genocide is taken up by Haedicke, Itzhaki, Levy, and Nikčević. Both Itzhaki and Nikčević deal with censorship and self-censorship and the evolution of political performances in the face of both. Haedicke and Levy examine alternative strategies to try to represent the unrepresentable, to inspire deeper understanding in the audience about something that is impossible *to* understand.

There are countless other maps, with innumerable paths between as-of-yet undiscovered landmarks. We have generated here a small travelogue on a journey that continues. It is the fruit of our short time together and the discussions and debates we have had along the way.

REFERENCE
Baudrillard, Jean. (1993) "The Precession of Simulacra," in Joseph Natoli and Linda Hutcheon, eds. *A Postmodern Reader*. Albany: SUNY Press.
Dolan, Jill. (1993) "Geographies of Learning." *Theatre Journal*. 45 (4): 417-441.

INTRODUCTION

PERFORMANCE AS SEPULCHRE AND MOUSETRAP: GLOBAL ENCODING, LOCAL DECIPHERING

AVRAHAM OZ

Political performances have served as common companions to political events and moves since ancient times. Revolutions, crises, and wars are commonly anticipated, accompanied, and accounted for by performance to various degrees of distance, from "a living paper" to a fable remote in time and place. As the present volume may show, the term "political performances" embraces a large variety of theatrical phenomena, profusely aggregating throughout our cherished rites of leisure and self-interrogation. They range from a direct reflection of the collective conduct of a given community undergoing change, to a multi-layered depiction of communal activity whose currents turn awry under the burden of ideology; from a utopian order representing an idealized society to an ironic nightmare of allegorical hell on earth; from a solidly constituted representation of the hierarchy and genealogy of political reality, to the dynamics of a Deleuzian war machine, extending outside the parameters encoded within the consistent order professing constancy, transforming the latter into the nomadic historicity of permanent change. It is the latter move which often makes for the genuine substance and velocity of political performance. For it is the ever-leaping gaze of the political performer, that deliberate *zoon politikon* premeditating the revolution of the times, who extricates the linear movement of history from the engulfing embracement of myth, which transforms hierarchy into rhizome, and process into nomadic migration: through lack of reverence towards the informing structures of political conduct, sometimes verging on deploying anarchy, political performance offers to shake ideological certainties and substitute. All this performative activity, through which reality is closely observed, dynamically scrutinized, and ritually dramatized and commented upon, seems to entail an analysis of that relation it bears to real life's prerequisites and ethos: to what extent do the latter apply to the fictional construct of political reality? How is the course of performance, often governed by what seems to be aesthetic formations, related to political concepts taken from the world of reality and what is their status within the aesthetic discourse generating and surrounding them? Are political performances conducted and governed by some specific laws of genre? Does the catharsis they may induce and effect represent a political move, or is it merely a product of yet another manipulative fictional ruse? Yet, crucial as such interpretive considerations may be for the practice of theatre research, the formal act of revisiting such political performances in the attempt to capture, retrieve, and account for in writing the very process and core of their nomadism may readily turn upon itself; since all these mock microcosms of change contract an inevitable, yet infamous distortion, often verging on travesty, when undergoing the solidifying procedures of written documentation and academic analysis. Thus this volume, while saving from a possible oblivion a selection of performative moments, or enterprises deserving commemoration, at the same time condemns its objects of observation to the festering, polluted stasis of a permanent, often irrevocably displaced representation.

Key phrases in the project of political performance are observe, witness, and rehearse; all to do with shedding light on communal activity which begs interpretive visibility. Its reception by those who are being observed is often dialectical, sometimes to the point of an oxymoron: for it has always been the urge of communities a one and the same time to encode the experience of their communality as a global expression through ritual and performance, and at one and the same time undermine such processes under the threat of dangerous deciphering of local meanings, bringing censorship into play. The emblem of this dialectics may be seen in Claudius' dual response to Hamlet's producing of *The Mousetrap*, in which Hamlet employs the band of wandering actors to encode and uncover political truths. At the crucial moment, in Act 3 Scene 2, when Claudius rises and uses his prerogative of censorship to interfere with the performance of the play within the play, Hamlet, either gleefully or desperately, but certainly in great excitement, blurts: "What, frighted with false fire?" This line, which is in the Folio, but omitted in the second Quarto, has given rise to much speculation among commentators. "False fire" is usually related to the real or metaphorical shooting with blank cartridges, an alarm without substance. Charles Edelman, in *Shakespeare's Military Language*, has related Hamlet's response to his statement in his second soliloquy, accounting for his projected use of the play as a subversive means of interrogating the conscience of the king, "if 'a do blench, I know my course." Edelman intriguingly argues that Hamlet likens the Danish King to the raw recruits of Queen Elizabeth's army, who would regularly flinch, or close their eyes, when firing their calivers, which is why it was recommended "that the first training bee made with false fyer,' saving the expense of shot until the soldiers had learned to keep their eyes open when firing their weapons." Now Claudius, of all people, should know that a theatre performance is nothing but a "false fire." He who, from his very first appearance on stage, is conducting a well-orchestrated one man show; in which Voltimand and Cornelius, his two ambassadors to Norway, are summoned to perform a ceremonial dumb show, as if their missions were not already sealed, is well aware of the added value mimetic rituals lend to the operation of power systems. Yet his success as a performer depends on his being observed:

> let thine eye look like a friend on Denmark.
> Do not for ever with thy vailed lids
> Seek for thy noble father in the dust. (*Hamlet*, I.2.69-71)[1]

Here, however, we find him surprised: Hamlet's eye does look at him, but hardly as a friend. Appropriating the range of his vision, he renders the king an observer kept in the dark, rather than the panopticon coercing the performer into the cheer and comfort of his eye. By flinching, he admits a weakness, curbing his control. Edelman's speculation may be reinforced by the King's immediate demand for "some light." It is the house light he seeks, which he controls, unlike the false fire, whereby he now realizes he has been manipulated. What made him jump may have been Lucianus' black thoughts, endorsed by Hecat's ban where "else no creature seeing." To be sure, Claudius has no misgivings about keeping others in the dark, as long as he is the one in control of the performance. For Claudius, who insists on keeping his nephew "in the cheer and comfort of [his] eye," to learn that the black thoughts of the mimetic "nephew to the King" are passing show is reason enough to stop the performance of the theatrical show. His suspicion may have been aroused earlier, when he enquired of Hamlet whether there was no offence in the argument of his play. To his question, Hamlet bluntly tells him the name of the play was *The Mousetrap*, a title which does not contribute, as we may gather, to pacify the King's discomfort with it. Like Shylock, for whom "goodness" consists exclusively of financial sufficiency, Claudius reads "offence" exclusively as appropriating his patent control on the gaze informing the performance. The King, who would have his realm as his theatre, would not allow performance which excludes him from the position of the absolute viewer. Prospero, another producer of political performance, will similarly stop his own show, upon realizing that his control of the global narrative involving kings, princes and universal spirits is threatened by a local native of the island, a creature of darkness subversively leading his mock army of plebeian clowns into the devious paths of his alternative narrative.

As mentioned above, political performance is committed to observing and witnessing reality. In this, it goes back to the very core of theatrical activity. There is a Gordian knot binding the theatre, from its very beginning, to panopticon. Its famously etymological source, a house of seeing, deploys the histrionic necessarily within the domain of vision. The charged semantic tension between *theatron* and *theoria* suggests a potential conflict between the seeming gaze offered the allegedly clear-sighted, yet indeed manipulated spectatorship and the unified perspectives, emanating from a single source, namely, the party in charge of performance. There is an inherent conflict between the allegedly innocent promotion of theatre as extending literary mimesis into the field of vision, and the limits of speculum, ascribed to the theatre's either faulty or morally misguided vision which may furnish anything from censorship to total anti-theatricalism. Whereas love's capability of transposing "things base and vile, holding no quantity… to form and dignity" may be read both from pejorative and ameliorative perspectives, the magic ring whereby Gyges, the mythological Lydian shepherd of whom Glaucon tells his master in Plato's *Republic*, acquires invisibility, obviously turns him into a plotting villain. Justice, with which the newly celebrated tragic vision is allegedly blessed, gives way to rational manipulation, for who will not seize the opportunity offered by invisibility? In adopting this suspicion of *theatron*'s pretension to appropriate *theoria*, Platonian Glaucon anticipates a Nietzschean scepticism of the infiltration of a local Socratic dialectics into the global domain of Apollinian vision. Unaccountable to words subservient to the global idea, *theatron*, the house of vision, left to its unguided devices of loose visibility, which, from the point of view of hegemony may easily turn misguided, is to be either censored, or totally rejected. Mimetic vision, uncontrolled by the same hegemony that feeds it, becomes an independent broker of vision, implicating hegemony with fallibility, or, worse still, questioning its integrity.

Claudius' act of censorship belongs to a long lasting continuity whereby *theatron*, fostered by hegemony as a visionary instrument for distributing its global *theoria*, betrays its ascribed vocation by manipulating local visibility. Ever since the advent of Western theatre in fifth century BC Athens, communities and hegemonies celebrated the global meaning of their communal existence through political representation in performance. However, the urge to encode the experience of communality as a global expression through performance, is prone, sooner or later, to encounter the undermining of such processes under the threat of dangerous deciphering of local meanings, when a licensed Thespis gives way to a local Gyges. The story of medieval theatre is a case in point. The traditional suspicion of the theatrical exercised by Tertulian and other early church fathers gave way in the height of the Middle Ages to the didactic use of performance at the altar (representing the sepulchre); yet as soon as its putative potency was revealed as deciphering the structure of power underlying authority, the sepulchre, enshrined by performance, gave way to the multifarious perspectives of a menacing mousetrap. Claudius' censorial response to Hamlet's production of *The Mousetrap* becomes the fictional emblem of this dialectic. The material equivalent of such a dialectic visibility may be epitomized by case of Phrynicus' *The Fall of Miletus*. Originally designed, possibly, to enshrine, at the Dionysian altar of *theatron*, the collective empathy of the Athenian community with the wreckage and disaster inflicted by Artaphernes on its neighbouring town, which totally quenched the Ionian revolt, betrays its vocation by uncontrolled visibility. What may have been designed as a celebration of the newly risen mimetic mode of tragedy, codifying global meanings, was transformed by the intensity of spectacle to a local picture of shame, conceived by many as indicting the Athenian community for not joining in with Miletus' campaign against the Persians. Phrynicus was heavily fined and his tragedy banned, but his play may have contributed to the initiation of the Persian wars.

A more recent example, remote from the former in time and place, may exemplify this dialectical mechanism in briefly reviewing a local instance, problematizing hegemonic vision both in reality and performance. Written in 1984, three years before the first Palestinian *Intifada*, Yitzhak Laor's play *Ephraim Goes Back to the Army* was scheduled to be produced at the Haifa Municipal Theatre. It never happened, though. The Israeli government's official arm of civil censorship, the Council for Controlling Films and Plays, operating under the auspices of the Ministry of the Interior, banned the play from being produced, grounding their objection on two particular moments in the play: one was the scene of oral sex carried out between military governor Ephraim and his subordinate, a young

Figure 1. *Ephraim Goes Back to the Army*, a play by Yitzhak Laor. Tzavta Theatre (Tel Aviv). Directed by Etty Resnik. Design and photograph by Tal Itzhaki.

female soldier; the other, a story beaten to boredom by Ephraim, in which a fellow officer, a holocaust survivor, proved smart enough during the 1967 war to guess that the innocent schoolbag carried by a small Palestinian child in occupied Nablus (or Qunaitra, or El-Arish, in later repeated versions of the story, where the child is Syrian or Egyptian respectively) contained the family jewels, since he himself used the same ruse as a young child under the Nazis.

The first moment was obviously considered by the authorities a practice unbecoming an Israeli high-ranking military commander. They labelled it pornography, in the common censorial sense of the term. Even if this were the case, reproaching a work of art for excessively "exciting" its audience by excessive visibility seems at best anachronistic in the second half of the twentieth century. "Pornography is one of the branches of literature—science fiction is another—aiming at disorientation, at psychic dislocation," says Susan Sontag. "Pornography that is serious literature aims to 'excite' in the same way that books which render an extreme form of religious experience aim to "convert" (Sontag 1970: 144). The concept of pornography implied here is however much more comprehensive. In fact the scene is pornographic mainly in the general sense used by Fredric Jameson in relation to film, namely that:

> the visual is *essentially* pornographic, which is to say that it has its end in rapt, mindless fascination; thinking about its attributes becomes an adjunct to that, if it is unwilling to betray its object; while the most austere films necessarily draw their energy from the attempt to repress their own excess (rather than from the more thankless effort to discipline the viewer). Pornographic films are thus only the potentiation of films in general, which ask us to stare at the world as though it were a naked body. (Jameson 1992: 1)

The censors' intent was directed against the pornographic in this wider sense (at the price of betraying the object), rather than exercising (as they seem to profess) the morally anachronistic, "thankless effort to discipline the viewer."

The other dramatic moment having contributed to the ban the production was perceived as drawing a defaming analogy between the conduct of the IDF and that of Nazi troops. Apart from the damaging implications of banning an image that is central to the integral meaning of the play (the shifting *loci* and national identity of the child turn him into an emblem, an iconic representation of an idea), the

Figure 2. *Ephraim Goes Back to the Army*. Photograph by Tal Itzhaki.

censors' judgment tellingly marks the full-ranged trajectory of the ideological bias informing its censorial guidelines. "It is not so much judgments as it is our prejudices that constitute our being," Gadamer argues (Gadamer 1976: 9); the censor's learned readings of the text may serve as a radical parody of his hermeneutic contentment. Rather than passively abiding by their prejudices, they activated their judgments in order to exert their power on knowledge and block any visibility of evidence contradicting their fetishist image of the Zionist hero, allegedly represented by Ephraim, to the extent that not only conflicting images, but visibility itself is declared the enemy of truth. In doing so, not only do they alienate themselves from the world, "now mostly a collection of products of our own making," as Fredric Jameson tells us, offered us by society "as just such a body, that you can possess visually, and collect the images of" (Jameson 1992: 1), but they thus unwittingly situate themselves in the voluntary blindness to which Ephraim, Laor's chief character, commits his own judgments, and whereby his physical existence is confined. For in that narrated image forbidden by the censors, the hero of the Zionist ethos is positioned in the ambiguous fetishist *gestalt* that it both desires (as the icon of vigour negating its allegedly impotent diasporic *alter-ego*) and rejects (as the eternal victim, a status providing him with the rationale for acting out aggression against enemies threatening to devour its very existence). The iconic child carrying his schoolbag all over the map of the occupied territories becomes a fetish for Ephraim, obsessively repeated and informing his constant, though passive repulsion towards his self-image as an occupier: fetishist "as a form of regression—not a return to childish innocence, but rather a resurfacing of knowledge repressed in the transition to adulthood" (Krips 1999: 23). It is associated with, and enacts, a reversed Oedipal desire of a childless man who trades *coitus* for *cunnilingus*; a death-wish of one who feels himself responsible for the killing of a child, who symbolically blinds and buries himself in his room, while fiercely and obsessively denying his action to the point of mixing guilt with fantasy.

Although residing on the same continuity, the consensual image of the Israeli war hero has undergone a significant transformation since its inception in the pioneering (pre-1948) era, when the desired figure of the native Israeli was ideologically constituted. Its historical icon is ironically revived within the blinding closure of Ephraim's room, when a fragile subordinate soldier ironically called David, allegedly gay, a favourite victim/chastiser of the military governor, whose choric wise-fool presence offers throughout souvenirs-memories such as those informing commodity in the Benjaminian arcades (Friedberg 1993: 49), creates a parodic dimension of history, visibly invoking the familiar khaki-clad figure of late 1940s heroic Israeli warriors. Now, however, the "collection of products of our own making" that Ephraim (as well as his spectators) is prone to see outside his office's window may amount to stones thrown by kids at soldiers, demolished buildings, or even disjointed human limbs (like that of the dead boy killed in a Palestinian demonstration, the inquiry into whose death underlies the action of the play), when mass demonstrations join those "big parades and monster rallies, in sports events, and in war, all of which nowadays are captured by camera and sound recording," where, Walter Benjamin prophetically observes, "the masses are brought face to face with themselves" (Benjamin 1968: 251). All these belong to that family of images "that the visionary Hieronimus Bosch has fixed, for all time, in painting, in their ascent from the fifteenth century to the imaginary zenith of modern man" (Lacan 1977: 4-5). And since Ephraim's room is physically bolted against the scenes occurring outside its window, it is David's choric vision that provides the closured space of the stage, representing with his imaginary visibility.

This is an image that the censors would not have the audience watch, since indeed it is "of our own making," compromising the desired agenda of constructing the Zionist subject as simultaneously "an enlightened victor" or "constructive colonizer," bringing redemptive peace and progress to a savage domain on the one hand, and an inherent victim of terrorist acts defending itself by denying the occupied other its right to a recognized political identity on the other.[2] In both his opposite functions, the Zionist subject is revealed to himself as partaking in a discourse of profound religiosity: the colonialist redeemer of the promised land, a modern version of the medieval crusader, meets the ancient Abel-like scapegoat, whose inherent sacredness has been noted by various influential anthropologies, from Frazer's, Bakhtin's, or Lévi-Strauss', to Girard's attempt to transcend "objectivist" structuralism in his theory of violence and the sacred. Tracing the origin of the sacrificed victim back to primal phases of culture, Girard notes that "the sacrificial process requires a certain degree of *misunderstanding*. The celebrants do not and must not comprehend the true role of the sacrificial act. The theological basis of the sacrifice has a crucial role in fostering this misunderstanding. It is the god who supposedly demands the victims..." (Girard 1977: 7). Whereas the authentic function of sacrifice, namely saving the community from directing their violent aggression at each other by instead inflicting violence "on a surrogate victim," was protectively repressed, it was manipulatively accorded an illusory aura of sacredness. Thus "a deliberate act of collective substitution performed at the expense of the victim and absorbing all the internal tensions, feuds, and rivalries pent up within the community... designed... to restore harmony to the community, to reinforce the social fabric" (7-8), was sublimated into an inevitable ritual of elated nature.

The modern consciousness, adopting a more liberal ethos, in which nation often substitutes for god, cannot absorb this primary rationale without further sublimation; it thus often goes beyond the original rationalization suggested by Girard in resorting to a more complex move, where consciousness is proclaiming itself simultaneously both sacrificer and victim. Thus Shakespeare's Caesar, having just been likened to a menacing "serpent's egg," is to be eliminated by Brutus and his fellow plotters as "sacrificers but not butchers" (2.1.32, 165). In a similar vein, the post-holocaust "new Jew" at once dissociates itself from the diasporic weakling going like sheep to the slaughter and embraces the role of the eternally endangered victim. What we have here is an ideological trap, a paradoxical situation, where, as Slavoj Žižek puts it, "the mask is not simply hiding the real state of things; the ideological distortion is written into its very essence." Thus visibility itself is seen as a threat for the guardians of ideology, since we have here "a being which can reproduce itself only in so far as it is misrecognized and overlooked: the moment we see it 'as it really is', this being dissolves itself into nothingness or, more precisely, it changes into another kind of reality" (Žižek 1989: 28).

Excessive visibility may attack Ephraim's consciousness with a rain of unequivocal facts, which shower down on him (and on his audience on stage and beyond) like the shower of stones thrown at charismatic soldiers by the fragile hands of little children, soldiers whose heavy armour leaves them devoid of a visible face. Exposure to excessive visibility may harm, think the censors. This, of course, cannot be gauged: it is indeed a charismatic visuality, gazing at the desiring subject behind a veil of authenticity. Norman Holland cites a rare comment by Kafka on motion pictures, from a conversation with Gustav Janouch: "Sight does not master the pictures, it is the pictures which master one's sight. They flood the consciousness" (Holland 1968: 65-66). To employ Anne Friedberg's useful terms, once the cinematic and TV camera enhanced the influence of the visual by combining the *mobilized gaze* with the *virtual gaze* (Friedberg 1993: 2-3), the effect of the visual must be curbed, think the censoring protectors, and they operate their jurisdiction on the *virtual gaze* appropriated by the stage. In thus exerting their radical sanction on the visual, they ironically exercised their own panoptic privilege over both playwright and audience, effecting "a brutal dissymmetry of visibility," in Jacques-Allain Miller's phrase: "the *seer* with the sense of omnipotent voyeurism and the *seen* with the sense of disciplined surveillance" (17).[3] The censors are satisfied with Ephraim's voluntary self-confinement to the blindness of his room, but add to the

deal their own panoptic surveillance over his vision. Ephraim is thus
committed to a double imprisonment, one conscious, and one directed
at his audience. At the same time, this blocking of visibility is
consonant with a sanction on temporal orientation, of the kind
Jameson ascribes to the postmodern condition: "the disappearance of a
sense of history, the way in which our entire contemporary social
system has little by little begun to lose its capacity to retain its own
past, has begun to live in a perpetual present" (Jameson 1985: 125).

This tense closure and lack of visibility informing the text of
Ephraim Goes Back to the Army gained another dimension, however,
when a private production of the play, if short-lived, was put on
during the first *Intifada*, which the play had prophetically anticipated.
In the hands of director Etti Resnik and designer Tali Itzhaki, the
battle for perspectives took a significant turn on stage. Beyond the
closed room of Ephraim's office, where the action takes place, a huge
painting of the *Intifada* demonstrations dominated the scene,
branching slightly into the room itself. Thus a level of visibility was
silently recaptured, in a similar vein ascribed by Jameson to
postmodern specularity, "where the psychic subject disappears
altogether... and along with it, the process by which looking is
specifically foregrounded as a privileged element and a psychological
motive *within*... Postmodern specularity needs no motivation since it
has become its own reason for being" (Jameson 1992: 217). This was
the first time that a view of the *Intifada* invaded the actual theatrical
space of the Israeli stage; but rather than true-to-life photographic
images, it offered its presence as a visual icon of a painted reality,
borrowed from the Benjaminian mediating TV camera, and
"cannibalized" by the spectator as "'a work of art' designed for that
very purpose in a random—but highly visual—appropriation of its
various 'bonuses of pleasure" (217).

Dominating visibility, yet not seen or motivated, it invited the
gaze in an almost pornographic manner, but being iconic rather than
illustrative, it presented voyeurism as a kind of intended fetish, "as a
specular structure divorced from human pleasure and desire" (Krips
1999: 173). The panoramic painting mainly consisted of children
throwing stones—an iconic materialization of the literal reality as
conveyed and mediated to the average Israeli by the printed and
electronic media. For most Israelis, confined to their home towns and
totally separated from the occupied territories, the first *Intifada* was a

televisual *simulacrum*, in the same sense in which the Gulf War was later accounted for by Baudrillard to the rest of the world. In this context, the stage realization of *Ephraim Goes Back to the Army* exposed, indeed, the information crisis that worried the censors of the play: in losing control of the visual perspectives of the occupation, the iconic presence of the victims threatened the fragile balance whereby history was being written by the victors, rewriting their role as the actual victims. If nothing else, that production of *Ephraim Goes Back to the Army* vividly anticipated the explicit battle of perspectives that, while these lines are being written, still continues, where a major energy on both sides, fully conscious of the effect of a world subjected to privatized modes of visibility, is invested not only in the act of subjectively recording the revolution of the times, but often in actually creating it by the subjective use of ideologically charged speech-acts and image-acts that write and rewrite reality.

Prophetically, political performance has always predicted the crisis erupting today, where the revolution in the economy of knowledge substitutes former revolution to converge the practice of government and means of material production. The role of political performance as representing an external control over reality, once matched with and often drawing on the means of the new economy of visibility is thus enhanced as never before. I have divided elsewhere the political attitudes of theatre and performance towards reality into three, namely: the theatre of containment or prejudice, the theatre of protest, and the theatre of prophecy (Oz 1999: 56-60). Whereas the first, mainly referring to the a-political Bourgeois theatre, accepts the dominant ideology at its face level, and the second often attempts to substitute the totality of the latter by an alternative totality, the prophetic theatre assumes perpetual nomadism. Its constantly shifting gaze adopts a strategy remindful of Žižek's fantasy, which masks (temporarily) the antagonistic fissure: "fantasy is a means for an ideology to take its own failure into account in advance" (Žižek 1989: 126). As dramatists such as Bertolt Brecht knew but too well, the political society consciously constructs its representations, the state structures its citizens, and since these are never completely obtainable, integrity requires the constant acknowledgement of lack, an acknowledgement which does not necessarily contradict satisfaction. In the realm of the genuine political performance, which hardly pretends to present its project as a circular mythical entity which breaks down the boundaries of reality, the lack is expressed through the fictional prophecy, never totally fulfilled, but its existence as a prophecy which aims at its fulfilment on the experiential level of the theatrical show is totally concrete, and may even, surprisingly, please, through a kind of cathartic pleasure.

The project of the prophetic theatre may thus be summarized as undermining, through prophetic vision, the totality informing ruling ideology. We can therefore say, that the political theatre uses the conventions of a chosen theatrical form to emphasize, reveal, and criticize the ideology serving as the social background of human actions or situations, to locate alternative discourses to the one preferred by the ruling ideology, and to liberate human consciousness from its circular binding to mythical formations (Oz 1999: 61). The political performance does not seek to make the audience forget the fact that they are taking part in a ritualistic event, subject to conventions of form; rather it emphasizes its dependence upon such conventions, as well as its deliberate use as visible constituents of stereotypes and agit-prop. The exposure of these formations often comes at the expense of focusing on the psychological motives of individuals. Yet the well-rounded circularity offered by the bourgeois theatre at the expense of genuine visibility, does not provide, in the long run, any better satisfaction for the theatrical project, even on its aesthetic levels. It is here where political performances may be taken to represent the true core of genuine dramatic art.

This collection of essays on political performance stems out of the work of the FIRT-IFTR working group on political performance. Its distinction among other working groups of the federation for theatre research was manifested from its very outset, when its initial gathering, at Jaipur, India, in 2003, was opened by an impressive dramatic presentation of a paper on political performance on the small outdoor amphitheatre at the Jaipur Arts Centre, thus laying the ground for its constant exchange between academics and practitioners (often residing in the work of one and the same person). This tradition was continued in its following meetings (eight to-date) spanning from Maryland to St Petersburg, from Helsinki to Stellenbosch, and from Jaipur to Seoul, and a good selection of its fruitful discussion is hereby presented.

NOTES

[1] All Shakespearean quotations are cited from the Arden editions.

[2] Of the many publications analyzing Israel's ambiguous policy towards the occupied territories see, eg: Shlomo Gazit (1995) *The Carrot and the Stick: Israel's Policy in the Administered Territories, 1967-68*. New York: Bnai Brith Books; Alouph Hareven (1989) *Israel and the Palestinians: Wars and Peace*. Tel Aviv: Dvir.

[3] Cf Gilles Deleuze: "the subject who sees is himself a place within visibility, a function derived from visibility (as in the place of the king in classical representation, or the place of any observer in any prison system)." (1988) *Foucault*. Seán Hand, trans. and ed. Minneapolis: University of Minneapolis Press, 57.

REFERENCES

Benjamin, Walter. (1968) *Illuminations*. Harry Zohn, trans. New York: Schocken.

Friedberg, Anne. (1993) *Window Shopping: Cinema and the Postmodern*. Berkeley, Los Angeles, and Oxford: University of California Press.

Gadamer, Hans-Georg. (1976) *Philosophical Hermeneutics*. Berkeley: University of California Press.

Girard, René. (1977) *Violence and the Sacred*. Patrick Gregory, trans. Baltimore and London: Johns Hopkins University Press.

Holland, Norman N. (1968) *The Dynamics of Literary Response*. New York: Oxford University Press.

Jameson, Fredric. (1985) "Postmodernism and Consumer Society." in Hal Foster, ed. *Postmodern Culture*. London and Sydney: Pluto Press.

———. (1992) *Signatures of the Visible*. New York and London: Routledge.

Krips, Henry. (1999) *Fetish: An Erotics of Culture*. Ithaca and New York: Cornell University Press.

Lacan, Jacques. (1977) *Écrits: A Selection*. Alan Sheridan, trans. London: Tavistock.

Oz, Avraham. (1999) *Political Representations in the Theatre: Prejudice, Protest, Prophecy*. Tel Aviv: Zmora-Bitan & Haifa University Press.

Sontag, Susan. (1970) "The Pornographic Imagination," in Douglas A. Hughes, ed. *Perspectives on Pornography*. New York: Macmillan St Martin's Press.

Žižek, Slavoj. (1989) *The Sublime Object of Ideology*. London and New York: Verso.

PART ONE: QUERIES

WITNESSES IN THE PUBLIC SPHERE: *BLOODY SUNDAY* AND THE REDEFINITION OF POLITICAL THEATRE

PAOLA BOTHAM

"It's almost like the old days. Political theatre has started popping up everywhere," proclaimed critic Michael Billington in February 2001, perhaps with a mixture of nostalgia and disbelief. Dramatist Carl Miller was nearly convinced a year later (post-9/11, pre-Iraq), when he declared: "After more than a decade in which the death of political drama was loudly mourned or celebrated [...] the body has started twitching. Could it be heading for resurrection?" Since then, to acknowledge a revival of political theatre in Britain has become a truism, making the premature epitaphs all but redundant. However, as Billington himself puts it, it is only *almost* like the old days. New political plays have indeed multiplied on the British stage, yet customary definitions of political theatre have been historically and theoretically destabilised. David Edgar, a veteran playwright of the so-called counterculture, admits that in the 1970s and the 1980s "we confidently expressed, 'this is the way you should look at the world' [...] Now, we are challenged to validate our political work because political theatre is on the defensive" (2004: 48). It is in this context that verbatim drama, constructed using direct quotations from testimonies and documents, has become "the most striking feature of political theatre practice in Britain over the past decade" (Megson 2005: 370).

Following the revitalisation of British political theatre in general and the rise of verbatim forms in particular, an alternative theoretical framework is needed to interrogate the residual functions of this type of drama, one that avoids in equal measure the groundless confidence of the past and the hopeless resignation of some recent analyses. I have suggested that Jürgen Habermas' notion of the "public sphere" can provide such a framework (Botham 2008).

Conceptualised historically as the locus where private people come together to discuss matters of common concern and normatively as a site for critical debate, the public sphere encourages a sensible interpretation of the scope (and limits) of contemporary political theatre. Habermas reminds us that the vitality of autonomous public spheres is still essential in maintaining and extending democracy, but that it does not necessarily translate into social change (1996: 371-372). Drama as a cultural artefact and the theatre as a meeting point were already at the core of the historical public sphere. This article concentrates on the link between the theatre and the tribunal, using the concept of "witnessing" (Peters 2001) to explain how current tribunal plays—a distinctive strand within verbatim drama—operate in the public realm to promote collective responsibility.

The tribunal plays produced by the Tricycle Theatre in Kilburn, North London, have been based scrupulously on transcripts from high-profile inquiries—national and international—and are set in a faithful reproduction of the courtroom environment.[1] They recreate a public occasion that "happened" and was purposefully fashioned to find the "truth" about controversial events. This endorses their accounts with a factual import that places them apart from verbatim texts assembled from a collection of interviews (e.g. *The Permanent Way*, *Talking to Terrorist*) or a compilation of diaries or personal letters (e.g. *Guantanamo*, *My Name is Rachel Corrie*). What makes it to the stage is in all cases heavily selected, but the claims of multiple voices in the tribunal need not be juxtaposed by the craft of playwriting; they offer themselves in the already dramatised process of cross-examination.[2] Tricycle artistic director Nicolas Kent and journalist Richard Norton-Taylor—the editor of all the tribunal plays but one (*Srebrenica*, compiled by Kent himself)—take the medium extremely seriously: "words are not changed from the source documents, the chronology is maintained and answers to one question are not put against another" (Wroe 2004). Focusing on *Bloody Sunday: Scenes from the Saville Inquiry* (2005), I would argue that their method of making live performance effectively transforms spectators into conscious witnesses, extending the scope of the public sphere.

The Tricycle's *Bloody Sunday* was a highly successful production. Critically applauded in London, it also played in Belfast, Derry and Dublin, and won an Olivier Award for "Outstanding Achievement." At the same time, it constitutes one of the company's most complex projects. The events examined by Saville—the deaths of thirteen civilians shot by the British Army during a civil rights demonstration in Derry, Northern Ireland[3]—occurred in 1972, but were obscured by a very partial original inquiry. This first tribunal, conducted by Lord Widgery, exonerated the soldiers declaring that, even though "[n]one of the deceased or wounded is proved to have been shot whilst handling a firearm or bomb [...] there is a strong suspicion that some others had been firing weapons or handling bombs in the course of the afternoon and that yet others had been closely supporting them." While the report, published less than three months after the shootings, acknowledged that in some cases "firing bordered on the reckless," it shifted the blame away from the army. Its first conclusion reads: "There would have been no deaths in Londonderry on 30 January if those who organised the illegal march had not thereby created a highly dangerous situation in which a clash between demonstrators and the security forces was almost inevitable" ("Widgery Report," 1972). While Widgery's pronouncement has long been discredited,[4] it remained the official version until former British Prime Minister Tony Blair announced a second inquiry in January 1998 (the 26th anniversary of the killings) on the basis of "new evidence." It would take seven more years until the last witness was heard, making Saville the longest and most expensive judicial process in Britain. Around 2500 people provided statements; 922 of them were called to give oral evidence, including 245 from the military and 505 civilians (The Bloody Sunday Inquiry). First predicted for 2005, the outcome of Saville is still awaited at the time of writing.

Bloody Sunday is considered "a watershed in the collective memory of 'The Troubles, the 30-year campaign of violence and murder carried out by loyalist and republican paramilitary organizations and the state over competing claims to the territory of Northern Ireland" (Conway 2007: 120, n.3). In the decades gone between the incident and its reassessment, several books, fictional plays and films have tackled the subject.[5] After so many years and so many layers of representation—two inquiries, media coverage, artistic interventions—the restraint of the Tricycle's approach, limited to representing Saville's oral evidence, offered an opportunity to look at the events anew. Writing from the Irish Republic in anticipation to the production's visit to the Dublin Festival, Patrick Lonergan reflected on how *Bloody Sunday*, "designed with a British rather than an Irish audience in mind" (2005: 32), achieved something that had eluded previous plays about Ireland: British engagement with the Troubles.[6]

> What makes *Bloody Sunday* stand out is that it doesn't attempt to explain Ireland [...] Nor does it use exoticised language or rural settings to mark out Irish characters as different from the English audience. Rather, the play argues forcefully that Bloody Sunday is not just about Ireland, but that it also goes to the heart of British society: its army, its legal system, its government. (31)

This is realised by keeping a narrow, almost surgical focus on the incidents of that Sunday in 1972, a strategy that permits to step back from partisan sympathies into the consideration of issues of justice and the accountability of the state. Yet objectivity, as in all political theatre, is not the right measurement to use. In the play's selection of "five civilians and five soldiers," Lonergan perceived "a clear 'for' and 'against' argument" (2005: 30). However, as activist Eamonn McCann (2005) noted after seeing the production in Derry: "None of the five soldiers whose evidence is covered [...] emerges with [his] reputation intact. All of the civilians depicted [...] came across as credible." McCann also reported the reaction of John Kelly, whose brother was shot on Bloody Sunday: "It was completely balanced, completely objective [...] Anybody watching that play can see we were right."[7] Although this latter statement may seem contradictory, a detailed consideration of the public sphere and how both the tribunal and the theatre operate in it can illuminate the matter.

THE PUBLIC SPHERE, THE THEATRE, AND THE TRIBUNAL
In *The Structural Transformation of the Public Sphere* (first published in German in 1962), this seminal concept appears as both a historical category and a theoretical tool (Habermas 1989). Historically, it designates the bourgeois public sphere which emerged in Europe from the late seventeenth century, mediating between the newly separated domains of public authority (state and court) and private realm (civil society and family). Theoretically, it serves as an ideal case, "a normative category for political critique" (Hohendahl 1979: 92). In its historical evolution, the public sphere was a cultural phenomenon before turning into a political one. It belonged initially to what Habermas identifies as "the world of letters," whose rules were rational argumentation, openness, and inclusion (Habermas 1989: 36-37). In principle, "[a]nyone with access to cultural products—books,

plays, journals—had at least a potential claim on the attention of the culture-debating public" (Calhoun 1992: 13). In reality, the bourgeois public sphere, especially in its later political form, restricted itself to educated male proprietors. Habermas recognises an ideological equation of *property owner* and *human being* that determined the exclusion of women and the underprivileged (1989: 56). At the same time, and consistently with his normative project, he describes the bourgeois public sphere as "more than mere ideology" (88).

In the 1990s, as a response to developments in historiography and cultural studies, Habermas amended his original conception of the public sphere. He now recognises "the coexistence of competing public spheres" and "the dynamics of those processes of communication that are excluded from the dominant public sphere" (Habermas 1992: 425). His revised blueprint also addresses implicitly the concerns of media academics who had perceived an obsolete privileging of face-to-face communication in the initial scheme (Dahlgren 1991; Garnham 1992; Thompson 1993). By contrast, the updated model of the public sphere encompasses a variety of publics, characterised as *episodic* (in taverns, coffee houses, on the streets), *occasional* (in theatre performances, rock concerts, party assemblies, church congresses) and *abstract*, geographically dispersed but gathered through the mass media (Habermas 1996: 374). This is doubtless a welcome expansion, yet—as I hope to demonstrate in the next section—there are certain intrinsic features important to discriminate in each case.

Habermas also stresses that in the complexity of the contemporary public sphere, its participants are "furnished with unequal opportunities for exerting influence" (1996: 364). On this basis, a distinction can be made between actors who simply utilise the existing structures of the public sphere and those who "at the same time interpret, defend, and radicalize their normative content" (369-370). It is within this latter function that political theatre retains its agency, both by offering alternative interpretations to public events and—in the specific case of verbatim forms—by providing marginal voices with access to the public realm. Thus, it can be said that the Tricycle's reputation is based not on a pretence of balance but on its ability to extend the public reach of certain demands for justice. In this sense, the tribunal plays continue a strong historical tradition that has connected the law courts and the theatre since the birth of the public sphere.

As an institution, the judiciary is a branch of state power and its decisions (except in the case of trial by jury) are self-determining. Nevertheless, the introduction of modern court proceedings—and their later publication—created a space for public interaction in legal matters. Historian David Bell highlights that the idea of a tribunal was the most common metaphor among French eighteenth-century authors to describe the then budding notion of "the public" (1992: 913) and that the court system in this pre-revolutionary phase constituted "the principal arena for legally expressing social and political claims" (919).[8] In addition, the publication of *mémoires judiciaries* established a strong association between legal, literary, and theatrical discourses. According to Sarah Maza, these trial briefs had a crucial political function: they were "the main bridge between the courtroom and the street" at a time when trials were secret (1989: 1253). They were built however not on rational debate but on "emotional persuasion" (1256) and the successful ones "read like works of fiction" (1255). In the popular story of Count de Sanois, published in 1786 by defence lawyer Pierre-Louis de Lacretelle—who would later take to playwriting—Maza identifies the conventions of melodrama,[9] a form that created a reciprocal influence between the courtroom and the theatre:

> If trial briefs borrowed from the new "bourgeois" drama its tears and tirades, dramatists, in turn, began to consider the courtroom an important source of inspiration for their plays. The playwright Mercier suggested in his treatise *Du Théâtre* (1773) that great judicial cases be replayed on stage and that spectators confirm the verdict of the law by cheering the resolution of the case. (1989: 1258)

As it has been noted, the already dramatised dealings of the court are an obvious attraction to the theatre. But more importantly, the link with the tribunal can supply theatre audiences with an opportunity for considering issues of common concern (even if not as directly as Mercier envisaged). Although such consideration always requires reflection, it is never purely rational.

In the nineteenth century, Dublin-born dramatist Dion Boucicault caused admiration with *The Trial of Effie Deans; Or, The Heart of Midlothian* (1863), a fictional play that nonetheless included a convincing representation of the protagonist's court case. Regarding this show as a prime example of sensation theatre (the type of melodrama that dominated the British stage in the 1860s), Lynn Voskuil maintains that "[i]n their shared, somatic responses to sensation plays, Victorians envisioned a kind of affective adhesive that massed them to each other in an inchoate but tenacious nineteenth-century incarnation of the English public sphere" (2002: 245).[10] Like Maza, Voskuil emphasises emotional and bodily aspects of public life that Habermas tends to ignore. She also draws attention to the paradoxical "blend of apparent authenticity and self-conscious theatricality" upon which sensation theatre depended (250). These tensions—between the rational and the affective; between the authentic and the theatrical—are certainly still at work in contemporary tribunal theatre. Moreover, as Gregory Mason indicates, they are the root of the two lines of development taken by documentary drama since Brecht and Piscator:

> Brecht differed from Piscator in wanting above all to maintain an aesthetic distance between the stage and the audience; he strove to provoke the audience to rational reflection, rather than to draw it into emotional involvement. Piscator, however, sought to further a theatre of involvement through documents, a goal which resulted in the evolution of a clear distinction between these two elements: on the one hand there is theatre as revolution, which proposes to spill over into direct action; and on the other there is theatre as theatre, with less immediate agitational goals. (1977: 267)

Mason argues that Brecht saw in the tribunal form a chance "for a systematic presentation of evidence" and that "[t]he public nature of the trial also enhanced the alienation effect [because] the tendency to see characters as 'cases' rather than private individuals lessened identification" (1977: 269). In Mason's terms, the redefinition of political theatre I am proposing follows the sobering view of "theatre as theatre," a theatre that recognises its limitations in the world beyond the stage and values rational debate over emotional propaganda. Yet, as the historical origins of the tribunal genre reveal, its affective component should not be disregarded. Brecht's intentions notwithstanding, a duality of rational reflection *and* emotional involvement seems to be inherent in audiences" responses to trials, whether in the courtroom or in the theatre.

Graham White, who has explored the performative aspects of Bloody Sunday both as an inquiry and as a play, cautions against "the

affective impact of courtroom testimony" (2006a: 174), particularly
when—as in this case—material evidence is scarce and immunity
from prosecution not guaranteed.[11] "In such circumstances the
witnesses who testify to protect themselves against serious accusations
may be engaged in a performed enactment of truth [...] which
achieves an effect of veracity that the law then fixes as the truth it
seeks" (177). According to White, the same risk of deception is then
replicated by the realistic style of the Tricycle's production, which, to
"confirm its mimetic accuracy and convince of the verisimilitude of its
project", offers "a—however revealing, stringent and powerful—
necessarily mythologising narrative distillation of the event" (2006b:
84).

          White's analysis is insightful but partial. It is indeed ironic that,
coming from what Mason accurately portrays as the Brechtian side of
documentary drama, best represented by non-naturalistic efforts such
as Peter Weiss' *The Investigation* (1964), contemporary tribunal
theatre would exhibit "a general orientation towards hardcore
illusionism" (Megson 2007: 116).[12] However, this is automatically
tempered by the constraining task of representing the trial situation
itself. In this respect, Mason's description is still valid for the current
tribunal form, which—as the term *verbatim* makes clear—relies "at
times excessively on the spoken word" and suffers "a restriction to the
telling rather than the showing of events in a defined, confined
setting" (1977: 273). The paradox of the tribunal play in its latest
incarnation is well captured in Lonergan's comments about *Bloody
Sunday*: "the aesthetic at work here is that there are no aesthetics—the
production's creators do all they can to maintain the illusion that
we're not in a theatre. Which is of course highly theatrical" (2005:
30). And, perhaps, dangerous. In Carol Martin's words,
"[d]ocumentary theatre is an imperfect answer that needs our
obsessive analytical attention especially since, in ways unlike any
other form of theatre, it claims to have bodies of evidence" (2006: 15).
While White's and Martin's warnings are not without justification,
they overlook the resources that both the law and the stage possess to
counter excessive claims of veracity.

THE QUESTION OF AUTHENTICITY
White derives his conception of testimony as the "performance of
memory" from Philip Auslander's influential piece *Liveness:*

Performance in a Mediatized Culture (1999). Auslander's argument is relevant to the present analysis in two counts: first, in terms of the relationship between "liveness" and the law; second, in its attempt to blur ontological distinctions between live and mediatised events. By demonstrating that "[l]ive performance is [...] essential to legal procedure" (1999: 113), Auslander productively questions the political claim advanced by performance theorists such as Peggy Phelan that "performance's disappearance and subsequent persistence only in memory makes performance a privileged site of resistance to forces of regulation and control" (112). At the same time, Auslander insists that in law as well as in performance theory, "this respect for liveness is ideological and [...] rooted in an unexamined belief that live confrontation can somehow give rise to the truth in ways that recorded representations cannot" (128-129). In his view, the live and the mediatised are embedded in the same cultural economy and mirror each other to the point of dedifferentiation (39).

Auslander's case against the customary mystification of the live event is a healthy reminder that an assessment of the political value of performance cannot rely on liveness per se, disregarding "intentions and contexts" (1999: 47). However, he shares with Phelan and other performance theorists a Foucaultian prejudice about legal discourses, in which an indeterminate notion of resistance is advocated in response. As Best and Kellner emphasise (1991: 69), "[Habermas] has correctly observed that Foucault describes all aspects of modernity as disciplinary and ignores the progressive aspects of modern social and political forms in terms of advances in liberty, law, and equality." In this particular context, a Foucaultian approach neglects both the historical contribution of the courts towards the creation of an independent public sphere (as discussed in the previous section) and the democratic potential still present in the link between the theatre and the tribunal. The complex conception of law developed by Habermas is more fruitful in order to understand the collective importance of public inquiries such as Saville, despite the inevitable shortcomings rightly identified by White. For Habermas, the law exists in a tension between facticity (its actual power to restrain and punish) and validity (its claim to legitimacy): "Legal norms [...] make possible highly artificial communities, associations of free and equal legal persons whose integration is based simultaneously on the threat of external sanctions and the supposition of a rationally motivated agreement" (Habermas 1996: 8). This tension is especially acute in a divided society like Northern Ireland's, where the authority of British law has been historically contested.

The legitimacy issues surrounding the Derry march on 30 January 1972 are intricate to say the least. On the one hand, the demonstration was an *illegal* protest against the *legal* introduction of internment, even though both detention without trial and the banning of demonstrations (despite their lamentable prevalence) are now almost impossible to defend.[13] On the other hand, the Widgery Inquiry's ludicrous failure to restore confidence in the rule of law supplied a recruiting ground for the IRA. Still, as legal scholar Angela Hegarty emphasises, the bereaved families' lengthy campaign for a second inquiry epitomises the conflicting qualities of law: "Law may be capable of delivering the accountability and truth sought by victims of human right violations, but it is also often the tool employed by states to avoid or deny responsibility" (Hegarty 2004: 200). In the case of Bloody Sunday, "victims are both suspicious of the legal process and yet also demand from it an outcome that validates their experience" (203). Whilst Hegarty is sceptical about whether the outcome of Saville will effectively challenge the state's "official denial," she values the artistic interventions in the public sphere created during its progress.

> As the Saville Inquiry continued its hearings, two new films dramatising the events of Bloody Sunday were made. The production of these two films has driven the debate about what happened about Bloody Sunday back onto the mainstream agenda in Britain in a way that the Inquiry's proceedings, reported sporadically in the British media, has not. Arguably these two films—and the poems, songs and plays about the events—have had a far greater impact upon public consciousness than the Inquiry's proceedings. (220)

Although Tricycle's *Bloody Sunday* was produced after the publication of Hegarty's essay, the play shares with the films the fact that their political gravity does not come from a position of resistance to the law as represented by the second tribunal. On the contrary, these works rely on Saville's copious release of information and create awareness of the need for a just conclusion.[14] Their version of events is however independent from the still awaited tribunal's report, typifying the position of the public sphere as a site that is distinct, and potentially critical, from both state and market. Contrasting with the earlier plays about Bloody Sunday, the Tricycle's belongs, like the films, to the genre of "documentary drama," yet its strategies of construction are widely divergent. Martin complains that "[d]ocumentary theatre's blurring of the real and the represented is just as problematic as television's ambiguous 'reenactments,' 'docudramas,' and 'reality' shows" (2006: 13). I believe tribunal plays at least escape this accusation. Using similar source material in a dissimilar medium, the two films on Bloody Sunday had to "reenact" the day itself, while the Tricycle offered instead a live "distillation"[15] of the court proceedings that was as dramatic and, judging from its reception, much more credible. Significantly, the *Daily Mail* and the *Daily Telegraph*, two British newspapers that had been hostile to the inquiry and particularly negative about the films,[16] joined in the general acclamation of the play. Writing for the former, Quentin Letts confessed: "For any patriot it is painful to hear the ropey evidence of senior Army officers. Yet this is not a one-sided account" (quoted in *Theatre Record* 2005: 470).

The production's credibility is of course a result of its claim to authenticity, to its scrupulous closeness to the actual inquiry in both Norton-Taylor's editing and Kent's staging. Yet the effect is not a blurring of reality and representation. Quite the reverse: the strength of tribunal theatre comes from a respect to the real as ontologically different, albeit linguistically mediated. The words of the tribunal refer back to the painful and unspoken truth of those who died in 1972. The play's author admits to this: "'If you look carefully / You will see the impression / Of a body in the concrete,' wrote Zephaniah in his poem Derry Sunday. Listening to the evidence and reading the words of the Saville Inquiry is a reminder that we are still haunted by the ghosts of the people who were killed that day" (Norton-Taylor 2005b). In other words, while the tribunal is a kind of reality susceptible to be distilled and represented in detail, Bloody Sunday's *bodies of evidence*—to paraphrase Martin—are elsewhere.

However important it is for academics to treat verbatim theatre with vigilance, its impact cannot be attributable to simple deception or a *post*-postmodern desire to reconnect with "reality." Chris Megson perceptively explains audiences' investment in this type of drama as a consequence of its power to facilitate "a collective act of bearing witness" (Megson 2007: 123).[17] I will build on this insight to suggest—*pace* Auslander—that tribunal theatre gains its vigour from being experienced as live performance. An appropriate definition of witnessing can be found in the work of John Durham Peters,[18] in which the witness is acknowledged as "the paradigm case of a *medium*: the means by which experience is supplied to others who lack the original" (2001: 709). Peters distinguishes four basic modes of relating to an event, of which the first three correspond—in different degrees—to the idea of witnessing:

> To be there, present at the event in space and time is the paradigmatic case. To be present in time but removed in space is the condition of liveness, simultaneity across space. To be present in space but removed in time is the condition of historical representation: here is the possibility of a simultaneity across time, a witness that laps the ages. To be absent in both space and time but still have access to an event via its traces is the condition of recording: the profane zone in which the attitude of witnessing is hardest to sustain. (Peters 2001: 720)

In this scheme, "being there" covers theatre, concerts, and sport; live transmission in radio, television or the web constitutes the second mode and museums, memorials and shrines, the third. Finally, books, video and CDs are examples of the fourth type. The tribunal plays could be characterised as a valuable hybrid. As theatre performances they belong to the first order, but they bring to this realm words from the inquiries (once also public live performances) which, because *recorded*, would not otherwise grant a witnessing experience.

Like Auslander, Peters avoids presenting the live and the mediatised in a binary opposition. Yet unlike Auslander, Peters recognises that witnessing, in any of its forms, "actually carries weighty baggage, if not ontological, at least historical." Furthermore, "this baggage is not only a burden, but also a potential treasure, at least since it makes explicit the pervasive link between witnessing and suffering" (2001: 708). The historical sources of the bulky heritage of witnessing are, according to Peters, law (the witness as a core for judicial decisions), theology (the witness as a martyr) and atrocity (the witness as a survivor of the Holocaust). Indeed, as Peter Buse observes in a different context, the recently developed field of "trauma theory'—where the concepts of witnessing and testimony have been researched for the most part—did arise from the larger area of Holocaust studies (2001: 175).[19]

A thorough consideration of trauma would certainly exceed the scope of this article, but certain key elements are relevant to the present discussion of tribunal theatre, which can be said to focus, like trauma theory, on "the complex and often painful and distorted ways in which the past continues to haunt and affect the present" (Buse 2001: 176). Peters stresses this point by noting that, because witnesses "are elected after the fact [...] [t]estifying has the structure of repentance: retroactively caring about what we were once careless of" (2001: 722). In trauma, however, the process of recalling the past is extremely difficult, and so trauma theory is as much about witnessing as it is about its crisis (Buse 2001: 181-183). It would be fair to say that witnessing is always—as White has rightly pointed out with respect to the Bloody Sunday tribunal—riddled with uncertainty. "The whole apparatus of trying to assure truthfulness, from torture to martyrdom to courtroom procedure, only testifies to the strange lack at its core," insists Peters (2001: 713), who attributes this lack to the epistemological gap between private experience and its articulation in public discourse (710). Nevertheless, trauma theory demonstrates that the precariousness of the private-to-public trajectory involved in witnessing must not deter from its importance.[20] In the words of Barbie Zelizer,

> The act of bearing witness helps individuals to cement their association with the collective as a post hoc response to the trauma of public events that, however temporarily, shatter the collective. By assuming responsibility for the events that occurred and reinstating a shared post hoc order, bearing witness thus becomes a mark of the collective's willingness to move toward recovery. (Zelizer 2002: 698-699)

Drawing on Peters and Zelizer among others, Carrie Rentschler (2004) regards witnessing as a political act: "Witnessing constitutes a form of selective attention to victims—and sometimes identification with victims—in ways that often make invisible citizen's own participation in state violence against others" (296). Writing in the US, Rentschler is concerned in particular with the way in which the memory of the victims of 9/11 has been used as justification for the so-called war on terror, but she could have been talking about Northern Ireland's Bloody Sunday, where "British military authorities have always maintained [...] that firing by the army was in response to a sustained attack upon them by the IRA" (Hegarty 2004: 210). The success of the Tricycle's production lies in inviting the audience to understand that even in such a climate, state violence is inexcusable.

What convinced the *Daily Mail* critic about the neutrality of the play was the testimony placed right at the end, in which Official IRA's quartermaster Reg Tester says that he could not deny that shots were fired from his side on Bloody Sunday. His words however are preceded by Counsel to the Inquiry Christopher Clark QC acknowledging Tester's argument that to have admitted this in 1972 "was thought to distract attention from what it is said really to have happened, that the soldiers had killed and wounded a number of civilians without justification" (Norton-Taylor 2005a: 96). This is a reverberation of one of Bernadette McAliskey's eloquent speeches earlier in the play:[21]

> I actually do not care, and I do not think that it matters if the entire Brigade of the Provisional IRA, aided and abetted by the Official IRA and anybody else that they could gather up for the occasion were conspiring to take on the British Army on that day, even if that—which I do not believe—even if any of it and all of it were true, it did not justify the Army opening fire on the civilian population on that demonstration (30-31).

Although McAliskey is a recognised figure in the republican camp, her words here are emblematic of the play's focus on the claim of the innocent victims against the state, a justice claim that does not depend on anybody's position on the Irish conflict and that could even find echo within supporters of the establishment's case. The Tricycle's productions do not take sides but neither do they operate under a false pretence of objectivity. As Norton-Taylor implies in the statement quoted above, the company's ethos is to support those who have suffered. To be "on the right side," as Peters bluntly puts it (2001: 714), is part and parcel of witnessing.

In conclusion, it is my contention that tribunal theatre contributes to the public sphere by making available a collective experience that, because it occurs as live performance, corresponds to the first order of witnessing. As a new breed of political theatre (although with deep historical roots), the work of the Tricycle permits its audience *to be there*, offering the simultaneity in space and time that encourages public responsibility. To be sure, what spectators see and hear is not the "real" inquiry, not even a copy; rather, a highly edited version of it. Yet if one accepts, with Peters, that witnessing is always already a case of mediation, there is no reason to disqualify Norton-Taylor and Kent as legitimate witnesses (to the tribunal) who have taken enormous care in transmitting the words of witnesses (to the event) as uttered in the courtroom. By allowing the grieving voices from the past to be heard again, tribunal theatre makes them part of our present and incorporates them into a more radical public sphere.

NOTES

[1] The list of verbatim work at the Tricycle includes *Half the Picture: The Scott Arms to Iraq Inquiry* (1994), *Nuremberg: 1946 War Crimes Trial* (1996), *Srebrenica: UN War Crimes Tribunal* (1996), *The Colour of Justice: The Stephen Lawrence Inquiry* (1999), *Justifying War: Scenes from the Hutton Inquiry* (2003), *Guantanamo: Honour Bound to Defend Freedom* (2004), *Bloody Sunday: Scenes from the Saville Inquiry* (2005) and *Called to Account: The Indictment of Anthony Charles Lynton Blair for the Crime of Aggression against Iraq – A Hearing* (2007). In the first tribunal play, *Half the Picture*, transcripts were mixed with fictional material written by the late John McGrath. *Guantanamo* and *Called to Account* are not tribunal plays as such: the former made the case for the British detainees in Guantanamo Bay using interviews, letters and statements; the latter recreated a "hearing" organised by the Tricycle itself.

[2] "Since cross-examination follows direct examination and the rules of evidence prohibit the introduction of new material by means of this type of questioning, it is often the goal of the cross-examiner either to subvert the testimony which the witness has previously given or to offer an alternative interpretation of that testimony [...] or both" (Harris 2001: 70).

[3] Another fourteen civilians were wounded, one of them died months later. No soldiers were injured. Derry's official name is Londonderry, "but the addition of the prefix "London" in 1613 has never been accepted by the majority nationalist population of the city" (Hegarty 2004: 209, n.37).

[4] For instance, a memorandum made public in 1997 revealed that the then British Prime Minister Edward Heath had instructed Widgery to "never forget it is a propaganda war we are fighting" (quoted in Hegarty 2004: 214). In a letter sent to former Derry MP John Hume in 1993, former Prime Minister John Major refused to hold a second inquiry but stressed: "The government made clear in 1974 that those who were killed on Bloody Sunday should be regarded as innocent" (quoted in Bew 2005: 115).

[5] White (2006a: 185, n.3) provides a comprehensive list of works produced prior to the closing of Saville. Most recently, another play, *Heroes with Their Hands in the Air* (2007) gave a verbatim account by survivors and relatives of the inquiry itself. It was based on Eamonn McCann's book of interviews *The Bloody Sunday Inquiry: The Families Speak Out* (2005).

[6] By comparison, when Brian Friel's play *The Freedom of the City* opened in London in 1973, "there were bomb scares at the theatre, accusations that the play was IRA propaganda, and many other difficulties" (Lonergan 2005: 30). According to Tom Maguire, "the first production of *The Freedom of the City* ... was panned by the critics as an exercise in propaganda both in London and New York. ... Arguably the reviews were a complete misreading of the complex dramaturgical structures within

the play which with the passing of time have become more generally recognised"
(2006: 48-49). The play was revived in London in December 2005.
[7] McCann's article calls attention to the fact that the BBC (which has broadcasted all
the other Tricycle tribunal plays and contributed funds to the development of this one)
has not televised *Bloody Sunday*: "To many in the audience it seemed obvious that
here was another example of the media glancing at Bloody Sunday and then averting
its eyes from the clear truth emerging, and that the appropriate reaction was to fetch
out the placards".
[8] Bell builds on the work of Keith Michael Baker (1990). Both historians are critical
of Habermas' supposed overplaying of economic factors in the emergence of the
public sphere.
[9] The melodramatic conflict between good and evil is used in this story to portray
Sanois' wife in a negative light, underlining for Maza "[t]he association between
"bad" femininity and corrupt despotism [which] was also one of the commonplaces of
polemical literature in the 1780s" (1989: 1260). Maza follows Joan Landes' feminist
historiography. Landes contends that the bourgeois paradigm was "essentially, not
just contingently, masculinist" (1988: 7) and that "the [French] Republic was
constructed against women, not just without them" (171). Landes promotes a
"multidimensional", "embodied" and "gendered" model of the public sphere and
judges as misleading Habermas' strong emphasis on language (Landes 1995: 92, 107).
In a similar vein, Garnham has charged Habermas with neglecting "the rhetorical and
playful aspects of communicative action", which would have led him to overlook the
important connection "between citizenship and theatricality" (1992: 360).
[10] Sensation theatre – as opposed to the early (popular) melodrama – arrived with
consumer culture, a development linked in Habermas' original account to the
historical decline of the public sphere. Voskuil nonetheless defends this theatre's
power to produce a revitalised public.
[11] Even though the Saville Inquiry is "not a trial," it "does not rule out the possibility
of future criminal proceedings." The witnesses' own evidence cannot be used against
them, but could incriminate third parties (The Bloody Sunday Inquiry).
[12] Despite their different emphases, Mason (1977), White (2006b), and Megson
(2007) employ Weiss as a reference point.
[13] Submissions to the Saville Inquiry on behalf of NICRA suggest that there is
sufficient ground for the tribunal to declare both measures retrospectively unlawful
(Blom-Cooper 2006).
[14] Both films were shown on British television in 1992, the 20th anniversary of the
event. Jimmy McGovern's *Sunday* is based on his own interviews with eye-witnesses
(including soldiers) and the bereaved families, plus material from the Inquiry. Paul
Greengrass' *Bloody Sunday* relies entirely on the latter. Greengrass writes: "There
was no need to go out and interview people. It was just a matter of patiently reading
the thousands of statements and documents gathered by the Saville inquiry, both
military and civilian". He also observes that after the screening of his film in Derry,
the spirit was "a cautious sense that perhaps at last the Saville inquiry may yet redeem
the stain on our judicial system of Lord Widgery's dishonourable conclusions"
(Greengrass 2002).

[15] Norton-Taylor (2005b) uses this term himself.

[16] This is a summary offered in the *Financial Times*: "*Daily Mail* headlines over articles about [Greengrass'] *Bloody Sunday* included "Bloody fantasy" and "Just a pack of lies', and the *Daily Telegraph*'s account of both programmes said "Shocking depictions that do nothing to help 30-year search for the truth'" (Dunkley 2002: 14).

[17] A similar claim is advanced by Hesford (2006: 35).

[18] I have discussed Peters' differences with Habermas – which echo Garnham's critique (see n. 9) – elsewhere (Botham 2008: 311).

[19] There is also a connection to be made here with tribunal theatre in Germany in the 1960s (Hochhuth, Weiss) and to the Tricycle's second tribunal play, *Nuremberg.*

[20] Writing on the theatre of Northern Ireland – including Friel's play *The Freedom of the City*, which, although fictional, can be said to employ documentary conventions – Maguire (2006: 54-59) uses the idea of witnessing to advocate a different notion of authenticity that depends not on the factual but on the authority of the tellers.

[21] McAliskey (nee Devlin) had become the youngest woman to be elected MP in 1969 and was one of the speakers in the Bloody Sunday march. Lonergan comments that the choice of McAliskey as the voice of republicanism allows *Bloody Sunday* to undermine and transform stage stereotypes of republicans as "barbarous psychopaths" (2005: 32).

REFERENCES

Auslander, Philip. (1999) *Liveness: Performance in a Mediatized Culture*. London and New York: Routledge.

Baker, Keith Michael. (1990) *Inventing the French Revolution: Essays on French Political Culture in the Eighteenth Century*. Cambridge: Cambridge University Press.

Bell, David A. (1992) "The 'Public Sphere,' the State, and the World of Law in Eighteenth-Century France." *French Historical Studies* 17 (4), 912-934.

Best, Steven & Douglas Kellner. (1991) *Postmodern Theory: Critical Interrogations*. Basingstoke and New York: Palgrave Macmillan.

Bew, Paul. (2005) "The Role of the Historical Adviser and the Bloody Sunday Tribunal." *Historical Research* 78 (199), 113-127.

Billington, Michael. (2001) "Theatre of War." *Guardian*, 17 February, 4.

Blom-Cooper, Louis. (2006) "Bloody Sunday: Was the NICRA March Illegal or the Ban on Marches Unlawful?" *The Political Quarterly* 77 (2), 227-237.

"The Bloody Sunday Inquiry." <http://www.bloody-sunday-inquiry.org> [Accessed 27 November 2008].

"Bloody Sunday: Scenes from the Saville Inquiry" [Reviews]. (2005) *Theatre Record*, 9-22 April, 469-473.

Botham, Paola. (2008) "From Deconstruction to Reconstruction: A Habermasian Framework for Contemporary Political Theatre." *Contemporary Theatre Review* 18 (3), 307-317.

Buse, Peter. (2001) *Drama + Theory: Critical Approaches to Modern British Drama*. Manchester and New York: Manchester University Press.

Calhoun, Craig. (1992) "Introduction: Habermas and the Public Sphere" in Craig Calhoun, ed. *Habermas and the Public Sphere*. Cambridge and London: MIT Press, 1-48.

Conway, Brian. (2007) "Moving through Time and Space: Performing Bodies in Derry, Northern Ireland." *Journal of Historical Sociology* 20 (1-2), 102-125.

Dahlgren, Peter. (1991) "Introduction" in Peter Dahlgren and Colin Sparks, eds. *Communication and Citizenship: Journalism and the Public Sphere in the New Media Age*. London: Routledge, 1-24.

Dunkley, Christopher. (2002) "Never Mind the Style, See the Truth." *Financial Times*, 16 January, 14.

Reinelt, Janelle. (2004) "'Politics, Playwriting, Postmodernism:' An Interview with David Edgar." *Contemporary Theatre Review* 14 (4), 42-53.

Garnham, Nicholas. (1992) "The Media and the Public Sphere," in Craig Calhoun, ed. *Habermas and the Public Sphere*. Cambridge and London: MIT Press, 359-376.

Greengrass, Paul. (2002) "Making History." *Guardian*, 11 January, 4.

Habermas, Jürgen. (1989) *The Structural Transformation of the Public Sphere: An Inquiry into a Category of Bourgeois Society*. Thomas Burger and Frederick Lawrence, trans. Cambridge: Polity.

——. (1992) "Further Reflections on the Public Sphere." Trans. Burger, Thomas in Craig Calhoun, ed. *Habermas and the Public Sphere*. Cambridge and London: MIT Press, 421-461.

——. (1996) *Between Facts and Norms: Contributions to a Discourse Theory of Law and Democracy*. Trans. Rehg, William. Oxford: Polity.

Harris, Sandra. (2001) "Fragmented Narratives and Multiple Tellers: Witness and Defendant Accounts in Trials." *Discourse Studies* 3 (1), 53-74.

Hegarty, Angela. (2004) "Truth, Law and Official Denial: The Case of Bloody Sunday." *Criminal Law Forum* 15 (1-2), 199-246.

Hesford, Wendy S. (2006) "Staging Terror." *TDR: The Drama Review* 50 (3), 29-41.

Hohendahl, Peter Uwe. (1979) "Critical Theory, Public Sphere and Culture. Jürgen Habermas and his Critics." *New German Critique* 16, 89-118.

Landes, Joan B. (1988) *Women and the Public Sphere in the Age of the French Revolution*. Ithaca and London: Cornell University Press.

——. (1995) "The Public and the Private Sphere: A Feminist Reconsideration" in Johanna Meehan, ed. *Feminists Read Habermas: Gendering the Subject of Discourse*. New York and London: Routledge, 91-116.

Lonergan, Patrick. (2005) "Speaking Out." *Irish Theatre Magazine* 4 (23), 26-34.

Maguire, Tom. (2006) *Making Theatre in Northern Ireland: Through and Beyond the Troubles*. Exeter: University of Exeter Press.

Martin, Carol. (2006) "Bodies of Evidence." *TDR: The Drama Review* 50 (3), 8-15.

Mason, Gregory (1977). "Documentary Drama from the Revue to the Tribunal." *Modern Drama* 20, 263-277.

Maza, Sarah. (1989) "Domestic Melodrama as Political Ideology: The Case of the Comte de Sanois." *American Historical Review* 44, 1249-1264.

McCann, Eamonn. (2005) "Why Isn't This Shown on the BBC?" *Guardian*, 19 September, 22.

Megson, Chris. (2005) "'This Is All Theatre:' Iraq Centre Stage." *Contemporary Theatre Review* 15 (3), 369-386.

——. (2007) "'The State We're In': Tribunal Theatre and British Politics in the 1990s," in Daniel Watt and Daniel Meyer-Dinkgräfe, eds. *Theatres of Thought: Theatre, Performance and Philosophy.* Newcastle: Cambridge Scholars, 110-126.

Miller, Carl. (2002) "Goodbye Cats... Hello Kabul." *Observer,* 5 May, 7.

Norton-Taylor, Richard, ed. (2005a) *Bloody Sunday: Scenes from the Saville Inquiry.* London: Oberon Books.

——. (2005b) "Fourteen Million Words Later..." *Guardian,* 30 March, 12.

Peters, John Durham. (2001) "Witnessing." *Media, Culture & Society* 23 (6), 707-723.

Rentschler, Carrie A. (2004) "Witnessing: US Citizenship and the Vicarious Experience of Suffering." *Media, Culture & Society* 26 (2), 296-304.

Thompson, John B. (1993) "The Theory of the Public Sphere." *Theory, Culture and Society* 10 (3), 173-189.

Voskuil, Lynn M. (2002) "Feeling Public: Sensation Theater, Commodity Culture, and the Victorian Public Sphere." *Victorian Studies: An Interdisciplinary Journal of Social, Political and Cultural Studies* 44 (2), 245-274.

White, Graham D. (2006a) "'Quite a Profound Day': The Public Performance of Memory by Military Witnesses at the Bloody Sunday Tribunal." *Theatre Research International* 31 (2), 174-187.

——. (2006b) "Compelled to Appear: The Manifestation of Physical Space Before the Tribunal" in Thomas Rommel and Mark Schreiber, eds. *Mapping Uncertain Territories: Space and Place in Contemporary Theatre and Drama.* Trier: Wissenschaftlicher Verlag Trier, 73-86.

"Widgery Report." (1972) <http://cain.ulst.ac.uk/hmso/widgery.htm> [Accessed 27 November 2008)].

Wroe, Nicholas. (2004) "Courtroom Dramas." *Guardian,* 24 July <http://books.guardian.co.uk/print/0,3858,4976948-110738,00.html> [Accessed 24 September 2004].

Zelizer, Barbie (2002). "Finding Aids to the Past: Bearing Personal Witness to Traumatic Public Events." *Media, Culture & Society* 24 (5), 697-714.

ORALITY AND THE ETHICS OF OWNERSHIP IN COMMUNITY-BASED DRAMA

DAVID GRANT

When Northern Ireland's Community Arts Forum produced the *Wedding Community Play Project*, or *The Wedding Play* as it is generally known, as part of the Belfast Festival in 1999, just five years after the first IRA Ceasefire began a protracted "Peace Process," it attracted high praise. The critic, Mic Moroney's response (2001: 272) was typical when he described it as "one of the most moving pieces I've ever seen about Belfast." Yet, in 2004, reassessing the experience of coordinating the event, Gerri Moriarty (2004a) expressed profound unease at the way in which the authentic "voice" of the local participants had been compromised once the writers assumed ownership of their ideas. This example illustrates a central tension in the practice of community drama that I propose to examine here in the context of the relationship between orality and literacy. These terms are intended to denote much more than the simple difference between the spoken and the written word. As I will seek to show, each stands for a whole set of associations – distinct literacy and orality paradigms underpinned by their own presuppositions. Thus, "orality" is used here to connote the broader idea of the "embodiment" of language as distinct from its representation in writing.

The Wedding Play was the culmination of more than two decades of developmental community drama work in Northern Ireland.[1] In *Playing the Wild Card* (1993), a comprehensive report on community-based drama published by the Northern Ireland Community Relations Council, I recorded brief histories of a range of community drama companies throughout Belfast. Most of these operated almost exclusively within their own social and geographical environment which, in terms of the city's demographic segregation into Protestant and Catholic areas, meant that in the euphemism used by the Community Relations Council, they were "single identity" groups. I was careful in my conclusions to acknowledge the value of such projects in helping enhance community confidence and argued that this was an essential prerequisite for the logical next step of an integrated community drama initiative. I pointed to the need for an umbrella group to coordinate the interests of the community arts sector and was pleased to see soon afterwards the establishment of the Community Arts Forum which, within six years, was to bring about the first truly cross-community drama venture in the form of *The Wedding Play*.

Our Wedding Video, a video documentary about the overall project, which ran throughout most of 1999, records the first residential encounter between members of the participating groups which included the Stone Chair Community Theatre, Tongue´n Cheek Theatre Company, and Dockward Community Theatre (all based in Catholic areas of the city) and Ballybeen Community Theatre and Shankill Theatre Company (from Protestant areas). Real World Theatre Company, whose membership included people with disabilities, completed the partnership. The membership of Real World comprised people from both sides of Northern Ireland's political divide and it would be misleading to suggest that the other groups had had no prior contact. Just as the members of Real World were brought together through a connecting concern to provide access to creative activity for people with disabilities, so the other groups had built up strong links through their work with the Community Arts Forum. But the fact that the proposed cross-community production would inevitably advertise these connections to the wider world required careful reflection. Implicit in the extract from the residential workshops featured in the documentary, which addressed the potential sensitivity of an actor from one tradition representing a character from the other, was the anxiety about the viability of such cross-community engagement at all. Presumably for this reason, the facilitator of the workshops, Gerri Moriarty, began the process in advance of the residential with a number of "single identity" sessions. Despite this understandable caution, by her own account: "The residential workshop in which the two groups first came together was, I think the most electric and voluble I have experienced in twenty years of drama work" (2004a: 17).

Moriarty has since articulated a clear ethical basis for such work, which I believe stems in part from her experience of *The Wedding Play*:

> At the core of a community play should be a unique voice – content or forms of expression which could only be brought to the surface by this group of people, living, observing, struggling in this specific socio-cultural context. That is what authentic authorship means [...]. At the same time, not every idea conceived in the workshop is interesting, not all will translate into a dramatic medium [...]. In the search for a conventional definition of quality, it can be easy for the artist to wield knowledge and power dictatorially, ignoring the previous search in workshops for dialogue and understanding [...]. I have sometimes found difficulty achieving this level of negotiation and balance when working with a writer and a group to develop a community play; a writer is more accustomed to taking an individual route and can find it difficult to develop an approach which is more transparent and shared. (Moriarty 2004b: 151)

In the case of *The Wedding Play*, although it was to be "co-written" by two leading local dramatists, Marie Jones and Martin Lynch, the expectation of the community-based performers was that the material they were to perform would meaningfully reflect the content of preliminary workshops with which the project began. According to Moriarty's later account, many of the participants felt that this expectation was not realised:

> Participants noticed that although the writers came to some workshops, they spent a great deal of time talking to each other outside the workshop area, rather than watching the improvisational process. Participants reported in the final evaluation that they believed more of this [improvisation] material would be reflected in the script. (Moriarty 2004a: 18)

The Protestant participants expressed particular dissatisfaction as they felt that they had been represented in Marie Jones' sections of the script in a stereotypical way.

Jones, coming from a working class Protestant background herself, seemed at the outset of the project to be the obvious counterpart to the Catholic dramatist, Martin Lynch. Both had an impressive track record in supporting community drama. Indeed, in *Playing the Wild Card* I found very few initiatives that had not been inspired or influenced by one or other writer. While it is certainly arguable that Marie Jones' political position has moved some way

from her East Belfast roots (a predominantly Protestant quarter of the
city), as evidenced, for instance by the play *A Night in November*
(1996) in which a Protestant clerk rediscovers his Irishness, Lynch's
politics are also far from typical of the majority of Belfast's
Nationalist community where he grew up. It is the contention of this
article that the crucial clash in *The Wedding Play* process was not so
much political, as between the oral assumptions that underlay the
project's initial devising workshops and the literary assumptions that
governed the intervention of the two writers.

Those familiar with the work of Jones and Lynch may be
surprised at their designation as "literary." Both write in a strongly
vernacular style, often rendering the dialogue phonetically on the
page. For much of their writing careers, their work could be accessed
only in performance. Indeed, it wasn't until I included Jones' *The
Hamster Wheel* in *The Crack in the Emerald* (1990) a collection of
new Irish drama, that any of the plays of either writer was available in
published form. The oral qualities of Jones' writing were especially
evident in the use of the ellipsis as the predominant method of
punctuation throughout the typescript – a convention both the
publisher and I were quick to retain.

Marie Jones' style of writing owes much to her early work with
Charabanc Theatre Company, whose collaborative methodology was
firmly founded on oral principles. The company's first two plays, *Lay
Up Your Ends* in 1983 and *Oul' Delf and False Teeth* in 1984, were
based on exhaustive tape-recorded interviews with local women about
their experience of the local linen industry and Belfast's experience of
the wartime "Blitz," respectively. The relationship between research
and script was mercurial and plays changed substantially through the
course of each tour, with the result that the performance on the final
night differed significantly from that seen at its opening. In her
introduction to the published version of *Lay Up Your Ends,* Brenda
Winter, another founder-member of Charabanc, recalls frequent script
meetings with Pam Brighton, the director of the production:

> A veteran in devising drama she soon imposed a routine. A scene would be
> discussed by the whole group and revisions agreed upon. Either Jones or
> Lynch would then take the scene away to rewrite, usually overnight. The
> scene would then be returned to the group for further discussion and further
> revision if this was thought necessary [...] the process could and did continue
> right into performance. (2008: 28)

Martin Lynch worked closely with Charabanc on *Lay Up Your Ends* and the title page of the published edition preserves the original billing, crediting authorship to "Martin Lynch and The Charabanc Theatre Company." But as Helen Lojek (1999: 90) concludes in an apt metaphor for a play about the Linen industry, "the threads of contribution are so tangled that it is impossible to sort them out precisely." I am reminded of Tiffany Stern's description of early modern English drama as "patchwork" and the playwright (a term, as she points out, probably itself pejorative, with its hint at artisanship) as "play-patcher" (a phrase of the Jacobean dramatist, Dekker):

> Theatre histories often explore the context surrounding the creation of the play. Was there one author or many? Did the physical make-up of the theatre or the company shape the production of the work? [...] But despite the huge interest in what shaped the play, the nature of the play itself is less often questioned. The unity of a play is often taken as a given. But "play-patcher" [...] points in the direction of a truth about theatre [...]. Plays had the bit, the fragment, the patch in their very natures. (2004: 154-155)

As Martin White reminds us:

> Although levels of literacy improved markedly during the [early modern] period, the transition from an oral culture to one dominated by the written word was still far from complete [...] plays were generally viewed by their creators as scripts for theatrical production, to be heard rather than seen. (1998: 3)

Charabanc's methodology fits well this sense of oral dramaturgy – a conclusion supported by Lojek's comment on the experience of the director of the American premier of *Lay Up Your Ends* which "illustrates the difficulty of re-creating Charabanc plays without authoritative text: she relied on personal connections with Charabanc company members and a typescript replete with errors and omissions." (1999: 93) For her part, Marie Jones appears to have relished the immediacy of the early Charabanc writing process, telling *The Irish Times*: "Because we're writing our own stuff, it's never finished. We're always striving to make it better – to perfect it. It's a good opportunity that actors don't normally get" (29 December 1987). Interviewed by Imelda Foley in 2002, she remarked:

It was years before I would even call myself a writer. Even though I was penning all the material and I loved doing it, it was very much a function in order to allow me and the company to perform material that was real and important to us as actresses in Northern Ireland at that time. (Foley: 30)

Ostensibly, Jones brought a similarly open approach to *The Wedding Play*. In her first appearance in *My Wedding Video* (2000), she comments: "I just personally love being involved in a collaborative process." But it is my contention that by that stage in her career she had begun to internalise a literary rather than an oral approach to her creativity. Not only was she a published playwright, but she also had a growing international reputation, due not least to the success in the West End and on Broadway of the Olivier Award-winning and Tony-nominated *Stones in his Pockets*. Later in *My Wedding Video*, she refers to unspecified difficulties in the *Wedding Play* process. Moriarty's analysis of these difficulties is persuasive:

My view now is that deeply entangled within *The Wedding Community Play* Project were two fundamentally different models of community theatre. One model sees community theatre as a collaborative process, owned by all those who agree to participate in it... The second model is predicated more on creating theatre *about* communities, using material such as testimony and research... The outcomes can more easily be predicted; for professionals it feels less risky. (Moriarty 2004a: 20)

Though Marie Jones' writing was now subject to the combined artistic and commercial pressures of her burgeoning reputation, it is my contention that developing technology further served to mask the "oral" origins of the drama. The printouts from her computer were a far cry from the manuscripts of an earlier age. Typescripts from the 1950s held by Belfast's Linen Hall Library, for instance, reveal much explicit evidence of editing. That of Gerald McLarnon's *The Bonfire* (the play selected to represent Northern Ireland at the 1958 Edinburgh Festival),[2] includes alterations fixed with tape over the original text. The word-processed script produced by Jones would have been closer to palimpsest than patchwork, concealing more seamlessly the working processes that have informed the writing.

When Marie Jones severed her links with Charabanc in 1990, she set up the Dubbeljoint Theatre Company with Pam Brighton, who proceeded to direct a series of new Marie Jones plays and adaptations. These included the first production of *Stones in his Pockets* which, when it was revived in 1999 by Belfast's Lyric Theatre, went on to tour widely to international acclaim. A subsequent, unsuccessful legal action by Pam Brighton, claiming part authorship of the play, served to underline the difficulties of defining ownership of any theatre process, but especially of one grounded in such a collaborative methodology. The case rapidly entered the legal textbooks as a key precedent in the common law governing joint authorship. Lior Zemer (2007: 212-213) takes issue with the findings of the trial judge that Brighton's contribution was insignificant, citing the earlier case of *Cala Homes* which had established:

> that a person might be a joint author, even if he had not himself put the pen to paper and another had effectively written what he had created. In the light of this ruling it was wrong to measure Brighton's contribution on the basis of whether or not she had pushed the pen onto the paper [...]. *Brighton v Jones* is a notorious example of a situation in which without the contribution of the party who was not recognised as a joint author, the work under dispute would not have come to fruition... There is no doubt that the creative act is socially and culturally constructed, there is also no dispute that every author's dependence on and consumption of collectively produced and owned properties is what makes the creative impulse successful. However, copyright law consistently denies this contribution.

In *Brighton v Jones*, although the judge acknowledged Pam Brighton's important contribution to the script, the case turned on Marie Jones' explicit contractual claim to authorship.

Similar uncertainties have dogged the publication of the early Charabanc plays. A 2007 edition of four plays edited by Claudia Harris all date from the second half of the 1980s, by which time Marie Jones' contractual claim to authorship had become clearer. In relation to the subsequent publication of *Lay Up Your Ends* (2008), Brenda Winter notes:

> The reason for the long delay in getting this text from stage to page has its source in the politics of publishing and in Charabanc's origins as a theatre collective... They were too busy getting the next show on the road on a shoestring budget to enter into negotiations with a publisher [...]. Besides, "joint efforts" were not perceived then to be as worthy of note as the single authorial voice [...]. Publishers have traditionally been wary, sometimes with just cause, of the complex copyright wrangles posed by devised or collaborative playscripts. (2008: 34-35)

Mic Moroney (2001: 253) has described *Stones in his Pockets*, which recounts the experience of two Irish extras on a Hollywood film shoot in County Kerry, as "a curious reappraisal of the little people of Irish history and the way their stories are invisibly subsumed into the making of it." According to Moriarty's account of *The Wedding Play*, in that production, a similar process would seem to have been at work. Against the background of contentious ownership disputes outlined above, it might seem hardly surprising that when asked to script sections of *The Wedding Play*, both Jones and Lynch should fall into an authorial rather than a collaborative mode; but viewed in terms of literacy and orality, this process should not be seen to have been a conscious appropriation by Marie Jones and Martin Lynch. Instead, I would argue that it was the inevitable consequence of the implicit status of the written over the spoken word. As Walter J. Ong (1988) has shown, the authority of writing has long been internalised by humanity. However committed they may have felt to an oral process, once dialogue took on the mantle of typescript, the performers felt much less empowered to challenge it.

Ong challenged many of the assumptions that govern our understanding of the relative positions of the written and the spoken word and demonstrated how our thought processes have been systematically influenced by the exposure of countless generation after generation to the effects of literacy. In general, this has been a benign trend, extending our intellectual capacity for sustained thought: but there has also been a cost in the form of our reduced sensitivity to the purely oral (if, indeed, such a thing can still be said to exist at all). This argument has profound significance for practitioners of drama. It reminds us constantly to question the extent to which our practice is influenced and conditioned by the written word. It allows us to see writing itself as a transitory medium between the original oral expression of dramatic ideas and their representation in the relived orality of performance.

To this extent, writing can be seen as a kind of scaffolding, and as Erving Goffman (1959: 15) has observed in another context, "scaffolds, after all, are to build other things with and should be erected with an eye to taking them down." This principle applies to all drama, but it has become easier to expound with the emergence of more obviously oral forms of theatre practice in recent decades. For instance, the insightful analysis of William B. Worthen in *Print and the Poetics of Modern Drama* (2004) of the part played by typography in our understanding of the printed playtext, draws attention to the work of Anna Deavere Smith (1993: xxiii), whose self-declared goal has been "to find American character in the ways that people speak." To this end, she makes use of audio (and sometimes video) recordings of real subjects and the printed versions of her performances include a range of unusual typographical conventions aimed at providing a fuller sense of the oral sources.

Such a predominantly oral approach highlights the function of the written text as simply a temporary means of transmission, which is disregarded once the performers assume ownership of the language. As Michael Goldman (2000: 52) puts it: "Memorizing a part is actually a means of freeing oneself from its mere textuality." Worthen provocatively asks: "Is it possible to understand performance through the scripted form of dramatic texts? [...] Is the form of a printed book an adequate delivery system for plays? Is it a delivery system at all" (2006: 213)?

My own accumulative experience as a director leads me to share these doubts, in chief because the hegemony of the printed text in theatre denies the predominant orality of performance. This predominance became clearest to me when I directed a Hungarian language production of Brian Friel's play *Translations* in Transylvania in September 2001. I have written elsewhere (2004) about this production and how the process of directing through the medium of an interpreter paralleled many of the ideas in the play. Of central relevance to my current argument, however, is how my almost total ignorance of the Hungarian language opened my ears to the complex web of phonic signals which accompany the dictionary meaning of language. This idea is familiar to phoneticists such as Kenneth Pike who comments:

> An extraordinary characteristic of intonation contours is the tremendous connotative power of their elusive meanings... we often react more violently to the intonational meaning than the lexical one... In actual speech, the hearer is frequently more interested in the speaker's attitude than in his words. (1972: 56)

The experience for me as a director of working through a language I didn't understand has profoundly changed my understanding of the drama process. The bi-lingual production of Stravinsky's *The*

Soldier's Tale at London's Old Vic theatre in 2006 also evidenced the expressive power of performance in an unfamiliar language. In this case, the language was rendered alternately in English and Arabic. For a non-Arabic speaker like myself, this allowed me to appreciate the additional layers of experience provided by the Arabic sounds while cross-relating them with the English meaning.

Just as the voice teacher Stewart Pearce (2005: 122-125) identifies vowels with feelings and consonants with facts, so in my own directorial practice, I often find myself discussing with actors the expressive differences between light, energised unvoiced consonants and their solid, weighty voiced counterparts. Seamus Heaney captures the expressive capacity of phonemes well in his poem *Anahorish*, when he speaks of the evocative sounds of that Irish placename - "soft gradient of consonant, vowel-meadow" (1998: 46). And in relation to Marie Jones' own work, Imelda Foley notes that in Jones' 1986 play, *Somewhere Over the Balcony*, which is set within the "Troubles"-torn Divis Flats in the Catholic Falls Road area of Belfast:

> Males, young or old, are named "Tucker," a pet name for Thomas, but, according to Marie Jones, used constantly in the text to suggest the alliterative effect of the constant *tuc tuc tuc* of overhead British army surveillance helicopters. (2003: 43)

The phenomenological contribution of sound and rhythm to our construction of theatrical sense can thus be seen (or rather heard) to fulfil an important complementary role to the semiotic function of the lexical meaning of language. Bert O. States has a vivid way of explaining the complementary relationship between the semiotic and the phenomenological:

> If we think of semiotics and phenomenology as modes of seeing, we might say that they constitute a kind of binocular vision: one eye enables us to see the world phenomenally; the other eye enables us to see significatively [...]. Lose the sight of your phenomenal eye and you become a Don Quixote (everything is something else). Lose the sight of your significative eye and you become Sartre's Roquentin (everything is nothing but itself)." (1985: 8)

Extending the image to the aural, it can be argued that while our "significative ear" may respond to the lexical aspects of language, our "phenomenological" ear derives equally important meaning from the purely phonic aspects of language. While acknowledging the close interdependence of these two modes of perception, I would go further and suggest a series of "predominant associations" in relation to the ear and the eye as set out in the table on the following page:

	Predominant Associations		
	EAR	EYE	
ORALITY	Phenomenology	Semiotics	**LITERACY**
	Actor	Writer	
	Performer	Character	
	Embodiment	Text	
	Interiority	Exteriority	
	Phonetic	Lexical	
	Lore	Law	

In bringing together such a diverse range of concepts, I am seeking to convey the wider metaphorical possibilities of the literacy-orality debate. Having already suggested a connection between orality and phenomenology on the one hand, and semiotics and writing on the other, I am interested in exploring other parallel relationships. States (1985: 126), in his chapter on the actor and the text cites Kierkegaard (1967: 77) imagining the actor to be saying to the writer – "Here is the original you were trying to copy" evoking the actor's phenomenological embodiment of the writer's semiotic imagination. Elsewhere, States distinguishes between the actor as performer and the actor as character, recalling Meyerhold's famous equation $N = A_1 + A_2$ (where N is the artist, A_1 the material the artist organises and A_2 the artist as organiser of the material) (Hodge 2000: 39). A helpful way of thinking about this distinction is in terms of Phillip Zarrilli's idea of "interiority" (a way of avoiding traditional Cartesian notions of a psycho-physical divide) and the "exteriority" of what the audience perceives. In this way, we move beyond the simplistic distinction between the phonic and the lexical and can begin to understand the "eye" and "ear" to represent a whole matrix of alternatives. The eye inevitably looks outwards, whereas the ear absorbs vibrations from within the body. States argues that: "in the theatre [...] the eye awakens and confiscates the image. What the text loses in significative power in the theatre it gains in corporeal presence, in which there is extraordinary perceptual satisfaction" (1985: 29). But from the performer's standpoint, in a contest between the eye and the ear, the ear has the prior claim.

The final line of the table relates to the earlier discussion of *Brighton v Jones*. The law, as we saw, preferred the clarity of the written contract to distant memories of the oral process. Ong cites many such examples, his account of colonial experiences in Nigeria being particularly resonant with the above argument:

> Some decades ago among the Tiv people of Nigeria the genealogies actually used orally in settling court disputes have been found to diverge considerably from the genealogies carefully recorded in writing by the British forty years earlier... The later Tiv have maintained that they were using the same genealogies as forty years earlier and that the earlier written record was wrong. What had happened was that the later genealogies had been adjusted to the changed social relations among the Tiv... The integrity of the past was subordinate to the integrity of the present. (1988: 47-48)

As artists, we have much to learn from the Tiv. The written word is not the only story.   One   way   of   demonstrating   the   wider "embodied" application of an orality paradigm to the theatre is by reference to two episodes in which dance has been used in recent Irish drama. In *Dancing at Lughnasa* by Brian Friel (1990: 21-22), the pivotal scene in which the five Mundy sisters shake off their degradation in a Dionysian display of Irish dancing is meticulously described in nearly two pages of detailed stage directions. Just as memorable, is the scene in Marie Jones' *Stones in his Pockets* (2000: 41), in which the two actors portray between them an entire *ceilidh* set dance, evoking the presence of a score of characters. The stage direction consists of just nine words – "*Charlie and Jake dance as if with other people.*"

In an interview with Irene White in 2003, Conleth Hill, a cast member in both the 1999 revival of *Stones in his Pockets* and the original Dubbeljoint production, which had included no dance sequence, recalled:

> We were dealing with clichés of Irishness but we didn't have a dance and we felt that because of *Riverdance* and *Dancing at Lughnasa* the Hollywood film producers would want to put a dance in there... So that's where the dance came from and Sean [Campion, the other actor] and I choreographed it in half an hour. (2003: 41)

Just as the first American director of *Lay Up Your Ends* relied on direct contact with Charabanc members to recreate the play, a vital component of *Stones in his Pockets* cannot be reproduced by reference to the published text alone. This anecdote graphically illustrates the importance of an oral understanding of the drama process.

Ruth Finnegan's 1980s study of music-making in Milton Keynes (1988: 123-138) provides an illuminating analogue for this discussion. She identified three "modes" of activity which she defines in terms of literacy and orality in the same broad metaphorical sense that they are being used here. The "classical" mode (where musicians were formally trained, music was seen as finite and transmission was understood by the practitioners themselves to depend entirely on the written score) she deemed to be the most literary. The "jazz mode" (where musicians learned "by doing," and improvised freely around a received set of models) was deemed the most oral. But she also distinguished a third "rock" mode, where self-taught musicians engaged in a high level of original composition, preparing in advance fixed performances through a fluid process of experiment. Applying these models to drama, we might see the established, mainstream, literary theatre culture to belong to the "classical mode"; the "jazz mode" to represent the growing interest in improvised and interactive theatre forms (best exemplified by the work of Augusto Boal); and the community theatre tradition as exemplified by *The Wedding Play* and Charabanc's early work as falling within the "Rock mode" – where the oral gives rise to the written.

Finnegan's taxonomy shows that although grounded mainly in theatre, the oral paradigm put forth in this article has wider applications. But it has a special cogency in the field of community-based arts, particularly given the increasing use of verbatim techniques in drama. When embarking on collaborative projects, it is important for all participants, but particularly for writers and directors to have a clear and explicit understanding of the "rules of engagement" and how these are framed in terms of literary and oral assumptions. Both the collaborative and authorial models of community drama distinguished by Gerri Moriarty can be valid, but problems arise where there is an ambiguity of intention. This ambiguity is invariably associated with a denial of the oral origins of the drama process. Because literacy is so internalised within the modern human mind, directors and writers alike need to train themselves to counteract its influence.

NOTES

[1] The term "community drama" is used throughout this article to denote work aimed at achieving social as well as artistic goals. I am aware in the United States, for instance, it is used as a synonym for amateur drama.

[2] Unpublished, but an extract and background details can be found in Byrne (2001: 42-45).

REFERENCES

Byrne, Ophelia, ed. (2001) *State of Play*. Belfast: Linen Hall Library.

Claudia Harris, ed. (2007) *Four Plays by Charabanc Theatre Company*. Oxford: Oxford University Press.

Finnegan, Ruth. (1988) *Literacy and Orality: Studies in the Technology of Communication*. Oxford: Basil Blackwell.

Foley, Imelda. (2003) *The Girls in the Big Picture*. Belfast: Blackstaff Press.

Friel, Brian. (1992) *Dancing at Lughnasa*. London: Faber.

Goldman, Michael. (2000) *On Drama: Boundaries of Genre, Borders of Self*. Anne Arbor: University of Michigan Press.

Goffman, Erving. (1959) *The Presentation of Self in Everyday Life*. New York: Doubleday. Quoted in States. (1996)

Grant, David, ed. (1990) *The Crack in the Emerald*. London: Nick Hern Books.

——. (2004) *The Stagecraft of Brian Friel*. London: Greenwich Exchange Books.

Harris, Claudia, ed. (2007) *Four Plays by Charabanc Theatre Company*. Oxford: Oxford University Press.

Heaney, Seamus. (1998) *Opened Ground*. London: Faber.

Hodge, Alison. (2000) *Twentieth Century Actor Training*. London: Routledge.

Jones, Marie. (1996) *A Night in November*. London: Nick Hern Books.

——. (2000) *Stones in his Pockets*. London: Nick Hern Books.

Kierkegaard, Soren. (1967) *Crisis in the Life of an Actress and Other Essays*. Stephen Crites, trans. London: Collins.

Lojek, Helen. (1999) "Playing Politics with Belfast"s Charabanc Theatre," in John P. Harrington and Elizabeth J. Mitchell, eds. *Politics and Performance in Contemporary Northern Ireland*. Amhurst: University of Massachusetts Press, 82-102.

Moriarty Gerri. (2004a), "The Wedding Community Play Project: a cross-community play project in Northern Ireland": in Richard Boon and Jane Plastow, eds. *Theatre and Empowerment: Community Drama on the World Stage*. Cambridge: Cambridge University Press, 13-32.

——. (2004b), "Community Arts and the Quality Issue," in Sandy Fitzgerald, ed. *An Outburst of Freshness: Community Arts in Ireland – A Reader*. Dublin: New Island, 148-156.

Moroney Mic. (2001) "The Twisted Mirror: Landscapes, Mindscapes, Politics and Language on the Irish Stage," in David Bolger, ed. *Druids, Dudes and Beauty Queens.* Dublin: New Island, 250-275.

Ong, Walter J. (1988) *Orality and Literacy.* Oxford: Routledge.

Our Wedding Video. (2000) Directed by Gerard Stratton. Belfast: Northern Visions [Video: VHS].

Pearce, Stewart. (2005) *The Alchemy of Voice.* London: Hodder Mobius.

Pike, Kenneth L. (1972) "General Intonation," in, Dwight Bolinger, ed. *Intonation.* London: Penguin.

Smith, Anna Deavere. (1993) *Fires in the Mirror: Crown Heights, Brooklyn and Other Identities.* New York: Anchor.

States, Bert O. (1985) *Great Reckonings in Little Rooms.* Berkeley: University of California Press.

———. (1996) "Performance as Metaphor." *Theatre Journal* 48 (1), 1-26.

Stern, Tiffany. (2004) "Repatching the Play," in *From the Script to the Stage in Early Modern England.* Peter Holland and Stephen Orgel, eds. Houndmills: Palgrave Macmillan, 151-177.

White, Irene. (2003) *Building with Stones: Marie Jones' Stones in his Pockets in the context of recent developments in Physical Theatre in Ireland.* M.A. thesis, Queen's University, Belfast.

White, Martin. (1998) *Renaissance Drama in Action.* London: Routledge.

Winter, Brenda. (2008) "Introduction," in Palmer, Richard, ed. *Lay Up Your Ends.* Belfast: Lagan Press, 17-39.

Worthen, William B. (2006) *Print and the Poetics of Modern Drama.* Cambridge: Cambridge University Press.

Zarrilli, Phillip B. (nd) "body, breath, activation, performance." < http: //www.phillipzarrilli.com/trainapp/index1.html> [Accessed 7 January 2009].

Zemer, Lior. (2007) *The Idea of Authorship in Copyright.* Aldershot: Ashgate Publishing.

THE THÉÂTRE DU SOLEIL'S TRAJECTORY FROM "PEOPLE'S THEATRE" TO "CITIZEN THEATRE:" INVOLVEMENT OR RENUNCIATION?

BÉRÉNICE HAMIDI-KIM

In 1995, at the 49th Avignon Festival, the company Le Théâtre du Soleil was hailed as the emblem of "citizen theatre," a phrase publicly used by Ariane Mnouchkine, which gained official status as a concept in theatrical criticism following two events: the first one was the alternate running by the theatre company of two plays, *Tartuffe* and *La Ville Parjure ou le Réveil des Erynies*, and the second one an exhibition coinciding with the publication of a book both entitled *Le Théâtre Citoyen du Théâtre du Peuple au Théâtre du Soleil*[1] (Ory 1995). In this book, theatre historian Pascal Ory retraces the genealogy of the concept of "citizen theatre," which grew out of "Le Théâtre du Peuple" ("the people's theatre"), citing Ariane Mnouchkine's company as the most accomplished incarnation. The phrase "people's theatre" refers both to the project launched in 1896 by Maurice Pottecher and to an essay by Romain Rolland first published in 1903 (Rolland 2006). That expression, or its synonym "théâtre populaire"[2] as in Jean Vilar's "Théâtre National Populaire," was then used all through the twentieth century by artists as well as by critics and public authorities. My project is to scrutinize the concept of "citizen theatre" as defined by Ory by focusing on the Théâtre du Soleil which supposedly constitutes its best illustration. Does this notion throw greater light on the trajectory of the company than that of "people's theatre," of which it would constitute an improved, more contemporary version? To answer this question, I shall first explore the historical and semantic contradictions inherent in the expression "people's theatre." I shall then go on to chronologically retrace the changing discourse and practice of Théâtre du Soleil and especially of director Ariane Mnouchkine, from the late 1960s to this day, which will reveal that Ory substituted "citizen theatre" for "people's theatre" not out of a need for scientific precision but on account of ideological motivations which go beyond a mere analysis of this company, as they interrogate the current status of the concept of "people" in the theatrical world and more generally in the French public space.

THE COMPLEX NOTION OF "THE PEOPLE'S THEATRE"

Whereas Pascal Ory posits a filiation between the "people's theatre" and "citizen theatre," and consequently focuses on their similarities, I will choose a diametrically opposed route, exploring the differences between the two concepts and starting with this initial question: what prompted him to replace the project's original name ("people's theatre") with an anachronistic concept ("citizen theatre") when he could have regarded Mnouchkine as the heiress of Pottecher's *People's Theatre* and therefore of a "people's theatre?" A first answer could be that Ory rejects a word laden with too many acceptations, as two contradictory meanings are attached to the word "people." (Robert and Tartakowsky 2000). It is therefore necessary to distinguish between two conceptions of "people's theatre" ever since the phrase was first used in the late nineteenth century, as the shift from one meaning of "people's theatre" to the other is reflected in the trajectory of Théâtre du Soleil.

Two historical circumstances accompanied the early stages of the debate about the "people's theatre" in France at the end of the ninetienth century: the strengthening of the republican model in the shape of the Third Republic and the expansion of the socialist movement. These two societal models were fairly close for the better part of the nineteenth century. But after the 1860s a rift developed between them, each with its own definition of "the people" (Pessin, in Robert and Tartakowsky 2000: 131). First, the concept of people may embrace all social classes, the communal sense of belonging to the republican Nation then transcending social differences. In this case the "people's theatre" comes to designate a theatre intended for all and not just for the poor, true to the idea upheld by the actual founder of the National People's Theatre. Indeed, Firmin Gémier set out to promote a "theatre which could be accessible to all social classes" (Gémier 1920, in Meyer-Plantureux 2006: 142) and would allow to "build bridges between the nation's various trends and schools of thought, until they merged, suffused as they would be by the same emotion and carried away by a unanimous enthusiasm." (Gémier 1920, in Meyer-Plantureux 2006: 142). This conception of "people's theatre" does not call into question the economic and political system currently in place but intends to integrate all those that are excluded from it by means of a cultural re-appropriation, theatre thus truly fulfilling a public utility mission. This perfectly reflects the meaning of the undertaking launched with the full approval and support of public authorities, during the Popular Front and after World War II by Jean Vilar and the advocates of theatrical decentralization.

But in the second half of the 1960s, the unanimistic conception of "the people's theatre" came under fierce attack, in the context of "the 1968 decade" (Dreyfus-Armand, et. al. 2008), but also from the increasingly influential Marxist sociologists. (Bourdieu and Darbel 1961: 151)[3] Gémier's or Vilar's ambition to have "the shopkeeper from Suresnes, the high-ranking magistrate, the factory-worker from Puteaux, the stockbroker, the poorman's postman and the highly-qualified teacher all receive the dramatic communion in the auditorium" (Vilar, in Abirached 1993: 15), was shattered by the realization that there existed a "non-public," a category that became the emblem of economic, social and cultural exclusion. In the "Déclaration de Villeurbanne" on May 25th 1968 (Abirached 1994: 195-197), the younger generation of directors working with publicly-funded theatres (Planchon, Chéreau, etc.) implicitly challenged Vilar's model, outflanking it in the left; later that year, Vilar himself was heckled at the Avignon Festival. The theatre critics, who were also Marxist, also contributed to questioning this model of a national-republican "people's theatre" (Copfermann 1965 and 1969: 5-29) and to promoting instead a class war people's theatre. The second conception of people's theatre thus came to be in the front of the stage again at the time. This conception of the "people's theatre," underpinned by a definition of the people understood as the working class (*plebs*), was already at work among some pioneers of French "people's théâtre;"[4] it later informed the Soviet agit-prop theatre in the 1920's (Bablet 1978) or Piscator's work in Germany (Piscator 1962). Thus defined, the people's theatre is intended for a particular social class to the exclusion of any other. Its ambition may be translated into a protest against the current political system and the ruling classes,

and it aims at widening existing social divisions so as to make them
still more unbearable and to stir spectators to revolt.

THE THÉÂTRE DU SOLEIL, FROM CLASS-WAR THEATRE TO REPUBLICAN THEATRE?

Created in 1964, the Théâtre du Soleil company, organized as a
workers' cooperative, was first influenced by the current debate about
redefining the "people's theatre." At the time, the company advocated
a class war theatre, in the wake of the revolutionary impetus of May
1968, which far from stitching up society's divisions, strove to widen
them:

> I share Planchon's view that if you are to woo working-class audiences into
> theatres you have to make their access difficult to other social-classes.
> Anyway segregation within theatre audiences is an actual fact and currently it
> operates to the sole benefit of the upper classes. (Mnouchkine 1968: 124)

Such a conception of the "people's theatre" translated into Théâtre du
Soleil's active involvement not just on the theatrical stage, but also in
various fights on the political stage proper. The practice of the
company at the time bore all the hallmarks of "activist theatre"
defined as "any theatrical form taking part in a struggle which it
wishes to contribute to, as auxiliary, instrument or as a moment of this
struggle." (Neveux 2004: 11). That was a time when Théâtre du Soleil
was aiming at preparing for the Revolution and the advent of a theatre
truly of the People, an ideal which can only come true in a classless
society:

> You are activists, critical of this society and yet you depend on its subsidies
> for your livehood.

> All of us live in a world steeped in contradictions and our own way of
> reconciling them is to retrace the events of *1789* rather than produce a
> beautiful Shakespearian play. We certainly refrain from gloating and we know
> that Revolution won't happen in a hurry. We are only preparing the ground for
> this future Revolution… by which we are likely to be swept away once a truly
> popular art is born. But of course we are well aware that the play loses part of
> its edge because we have to tread carefully in certain matters. If *1789* had
> been a flop, we should have had FF 80 million to pay back. So there are
> contradictions, that's for sure. But what were we to do? Give up staging *1789*?

> You draw in mostly intellectual audiences.

Yes, that's right. Despite our efforts to produce a piece which is within the reach o everyone, very few workers have watched it. There cannot be any such thing as a true "people's theatre" under a capitalist system, so it is no wonder workers should be few and far between in auditoriums; actually, they will only gain full access to life after the Revolution. (Mnouchkine 1971a)

At the time the Soleil was therefore inextricably mingling artistic and political practices and did not hesitate to exploit its art for political ends. For example, during the Summer of 1968, their show *The Kitchen* was performed during the sitdown strikes at Citroën, Renault, Kodak, and SNECMA plants, at the request of the "Groupe d'Intervention dans les Prisons." In the same way, the company took part in the festivals of the Communist Party and of Lutte Ouvrière (an extreme left-wing party) all through the 1970s. "The Cartoucherie was then the venue of a great many meetings and political demonstrations in connection with all the protest movements of the time: Women's rights, campaign against the Vietnam war, or for Chile's return to democracy." (Labrouche 1999: 22). As a result, relationships with public authorities were somewhat strained throughout the decade, as can be seen from *L'enterrement de la liberté d'expression*, an occasional play first performed in May 1973 to scoff at Valéry Giscard d'Estaing's Minister for Arts, Maurice Druon who had voiced his exasperation at "those who hold out the begging bowl with their left hand while clutching a Molotov Cocktail in their right one" (Labrouche 1999: 21). In its early days Théâtre du Soleil distanced itself from the ideal of a national republican "people's theatre" embodied by Vilar is an understatement indeed. When questioned in the early Seventies about her stance on Vilar's notion of celebration-theatre which reunites a divided society, Mnouchkine gave the following answer:

On this point I disagree with Jean Vilar. On the contrary, my own belief is that the function of theatre is to widen these divisions [...] There is no doubt that it has to divide but it also has to "reenergize" the spectator, to infuse him with new strength. (Mnouchkine 1971b: 118)

And yet, beyond the apparent opposition to Vilar's model, this quote expounds the principle which can lead to a rapprochement. For the concept of energy constitutes a point of entry into a wholly different aspect of the conception of drama implemented and theorized by Mnouchkine. And it contains the explanation for her shift from a divisive, class war "people's theatre" to an oecumenical "people's theatre." To be more exact, this notion of energy in its potentially religious dimension (etymologically, the Latin verb "religere" meaning "to link") is proof that as early as in the late 1960s, Mnouchkine did not conceive a "people's theatre" only as class war theatre. According to her, the theatre had to widen social divisions and at the same time must not be content with this role. To begin with, from 1968 onwards, the producer would already warn against one of the risks inherent in this kind of "people's" theatre intended for one social class against another, but produced and watched precisely by the latter, the bourgeoisie:

> Proletarians are few and far between in theatres: who are the regular theatre goers? members of the lower and upper middle-class, both recent and long time. And being into "people's theatre" consists in aiming for a proletarian audience - which sounds somewhat patronizing and turns out to be as dangerous as persisting in trying to make other people happy against their will. For proletarians do not mind being deprived of theatre, they do quite well without it and are not clamouring for it and rightly so! [...] Being unfamiliar with it, they cannot feel any need for it and whenever their tastes are being surveyed, they turn out to incline towards the second rate. So the next question is, how can this need be aroused and more importantly, why should it be? A play is somehow more than just a show, it has to assume a social function which consists in broadening people's minds [...] Let me repeat once more that there is no such thing as a popular audience. (Mnouchkine 1968: 122)

Therefore, while proclaiming that she was in the theatre in order to "change the world" (Mnouchkine 1968: 119), Mnouchkine kept her distance from a whole aesthetic and political conception of avant-garde theatre of the 1970s (Biet and Neveux 2007) as exemplified by playwrights such as Fernando Arrabal, an in-yer-face theatre which can only persuade those "who are already convinced beforehand." (Mnouchkine 1968: 120.) She would thus declare herself cut off from "a large part of contemporary playwriting," (Mnouchkine 1968: 121) opposing its "aggressiveness," (Mnouchkine 1968: 120) convinced as she was by her own experience as a spectator, that aggressiveness can only bring rejection. Mnouchkine has always held the opinion that theatre is like a space-time of sharing and communion, a view which can be traced back to Rousseau's definition of theatre as a popular celebration.[5]

With a determination to divide and a commitment not to antagonize anyone, the Soleil's position in the 1970s eventually appears to be somewhat ambiguous, compared with its present day position, characterized by a much more consistent and indeed humble ambition: "We will decide to put on a play because [...] it moves on, upsets us, constrains us to change. Does it have the same effect on others? Truly I don't know." (Mnouchkine 2004b.) This change of course accounts for a certain uneasiness about the ideas the company used to uphold in its early days, an uneasiness apparent in the contradictory reinterpretation of the past: on the one hand, Mnouchkine regrets the "silly views" (Mnouchkine, in Mnouchkine and Pascaud 2005: 27) voiced on occasion by the company following the events of May 1968, but on the other hand, she strongly denies the company having ever been "leftist" or "sectarian." When she lays stress on the fact that Théâtre du Soleil was created before and not in the wake of 1968, her intention is to contrast the "idealistic commitment" (Mnouchkine, in Mnouchkine and Pascaud 2005: 26) of her company with the "ideological" (27) theatre which prevailed at the time. In the same way, today "the people" to her no longer equates with the working-class and the Soleil's practice seems to fit into the national republican "people's theatre" Commentators will indeed refer to her as "Vilar's spiritual daughter" (Pascaud, in Mnouchkine and Pascaud 2005: 82) and Mnouchkine considers this as an honour. It is now time to examine first in what respect Théâtre du Soleil truly deserves to be classified as "people's theatre" in the national republican sense of this phrase, and then to understand what prompted Ory to replace this phrase with the notion of "citizen theatre" even if the Soleil's theory and practice doesn't completely fit this model.

THE THÉÂTRE DU SOLEIL TODAY AND THE AMBIGUITIES OF "CITIZEN THEATRE"

Beyond a rejection of all ideologies and any kind of subjection to any political allegiances whatsoever, what characterized the discourse and practice of Théâtre du Soleil today is an unfailing championing of democratic and republican principles. Mnouchkine thus holds the view that in the current debate about immigration and the opening up of all frontiers, one should never lose sight of the fundamental republican values, namely the motto "Liberty, equality, fraternity" and the principle of secularism:

> If we did defend our principles with greater determination, if we did not have
> any undue qualms and misgivings about upholding secularism, sexual
> equality, equal access to education, health, housing and justice; in short, if we
> upheld the laws of democracy more firmly – especially against those who very
> cleverly manipulate them against democracy itself – we would not have to
> worry so much about our frontiers. I am convinced that French people would
> be more hospitable if they felt that nobody, be they French citizen or
> foreigners is allowed to infringe these fundamental, non-negotiable and to me
> cross-cultural principles. (Mnouchkine, in Mnouchkine and Pascaud 2005: 61)

This explains why Mnouchkine's positions, including the stands she
takes in her productions may shock some people due to their seeming
lack of tolerance for all that contravenes these humanist principles,
which in her view, should be shared universally and on which she
adamantly refuses to compromise. In 1995, at the Avignon Festival
where Théâtre du Soleil was officially hailed as the emblem of
"citizen theatre," her production of Molière's play T*artuffe* thus
exposed the "dangerous abuses of Islamic fundamentalism"
(Mnouchkine, in Mnouchkine and Pascaud 2005: 97) and resolutely
championed the cause of secularism, knowingly incurring the risk of
shocking the proponents of radical tolerance in the name of
multiculturalism:

> And some people made a wry face. How dare I attack Islam! Well exactly as
> Molière dared to attack our own national brand of bigotry three centuries ago!
> [...] We were all the more sensitive on this subject as some Algerian exiled
> artists who for their part make no bones about attacking bigotry, were telling
> us bluntly tall that had been inflicted on them. [...] I am revolted by the
> duplicity of Western countries when they continue to negotiate in the name of
> economic and political realism with all those states all over the world that
> assume the right to enslave woman, to kill intellectuals, artists, students,
> journalists, all the mouthpieces. Western countries are all so many Tartuffe
> and Orgon! (Mnouchkine, in Mnouchkine and Pascaud 2005: 27)

Mnouchkine gave still another instance of this republican activism in
2004 when she justified endorsing the "Appeal against the war on
intelligence" launched that year by the *Inrockuptible* magazine.
According to her, despite its "somewhat elitist" (Mnouchkine, in
Mnouchkine and Pascaud 2005: 153) character, and a certain degree
of confusion, this appeal was necessary nonetheless: "at least the
Inrockuptibles' appeal had the merit of uniting researchers, teachers,
hospital workers and of exposing an overall plan for the destruction of

the commongood." And it is because the French Nation is the embodiment of republican values that Mnouchkine finds it indispensable to defend it away from any kind of chauvinism. This was her answer to the theatrical critic Fabienne Pascaud who wondered why the French flag was flying over the pediment of the Théâtre du Soleil alongside the republican motto "Liberty, equality, fraternity" and accused Théâtre du Soleil of "laying on thick" (Pascaud, in Mnouchkine and Pascaud 2005: 103):

> We decided to hang the flag out in 1995 precisely during the epic of the undocumented immigrants[6] who were constantly telling us about the ideal France. Besides, it is a very beautiful flag which I certainly will not allow Le Pen to confiscate![7] As soon as I saw it flying proudly I felt the need to add the motto "Liberty, equality, fraternity" as on any self-respected public building. (Mnouchkine, in Mnouchkine and Pascaud 2005: 103)

Quite unlike nationalism, her intention when sporting these symbols, was to reassert the ideal embodied by the French Republic, so as the better to criticize any infringement of its principles of which any one government might be guilty:

> I do not approve unreservedly of France as it is. But if one finds fault with it, then one has to fight to make it a better place. If you keep repeating to people that the country they live in is the worst place on earth they will end up believing it and making it worse. It is not the worst place on earth, not by a long shot! Simply, one has to work so that the unacceptable, the base, the petty occur as seldom as possible. Sneering that France is a pathetic, hopeless place is not enough to make it better. (Mnouchkine, in Mnouchkine and Pascaud 2005: 104)

Not only does she criticize actual France in the name of its republican ideal but she also strives to positively uphold its principles against the adversaries of the republican model. When Pascaud asked her to sort out the republican principles in order of importance, this was Mnouchkine's answer:

> Right now? Sexual equality. I am revolted to see that unacceptable practices are being tolerated. I see that concerning women, in many fields, the French State does not carry out its mission of protection. What I see today is that if when she comes back home a little girl is not allowed to say to her dad or her brother 'Dear Daddy, I wish I could wear it, but we are not allowed to wear a veil at school by law', she will end up being constrained to wear a veil [...] There is something warm, reassuring about a community, provided it does

mean prison, exclusion, separation. When you arrive in a country, you have to treasure and keep memories, but you have to give up a number of things – even though your accent will forever reveal your foreign origin, you have to prepare your children for becoming citizens of this country. (Mnouchkine, in Mnouchkine and Pascaud 2005: 62)

Beyond human rights, Mnouchkine now fights for women's rights but also secularism, the common good and the principles summed up by the French Republic's motto "Liberty, equality, fraternity" in her public discourse, in her productions, as well as in her extra-theatrical activities. Therefore what justification can be provided for Ory's view when he describes Théâtre du Soleil as the product of a historical and genetic mutation of the national republican "people's theatre?" Two distinct factors account for it: first, a number of signs seem to point to a departure of Théâtre du Soleil from the model of republican theatre and then there is the way public opinion and more particularly the political and cultural elite imagines the people and the "people's theatre."

The most crucial way in which Mnouchkine currently differentiates herself from the tradition of the "people's theatre" has to do with her present conception of political commitment. Unlike Vilar himself, that icon of the national republican "people's theatre" who people either loved or hated for his "elective affinities" (Lambert and Matonti 2001: 381) with the Communist Party, or one of his well-known followers Antoine Vitez, that proponent of a universal culture who was a member of that same Party, Mnouchkine rejects the very notion of a long-term activist commitment, opting instead for one-off commitments. This change of mind regarding commitment is in keeping with a less divided perception of social relationships. Mnouchkine presently refuses to have her theatrical or extra-theatrical practices dubbed "activist" first because she feels she is not enough of an activist:

I resent being called an activist. The word refers to a form of commitment which I personally reject. Taking a stand, campaigning for ideas, for an ideal is one thing. Being a activist is another thing. It is a full-time activity, almost like a job. Well, it is not my job. I regard myself as a person who intends to take part in current events, by making use of primarily artistic means. (Mnouchkine, 1998b)

A distinction must therefore be made between two different spheres of activity: the artistic sphere proper (the productions) and the civic sphere (the various causes the company occasionally supports). Of these two spheres the first takes priority in Mnouchkine's life, which to her is a way to remain faithful to the specificity of artists for whom, according to her, artistic commitment comes and has always come before political commitment:

> Zola made no secret of the fact that if he had been busy writing a novel when he was asked to come to the rescue of a Jewish officer by the name of Dreyfus, he would not have committed himself and would not have written "J'Accuse."[8] He was being honest and speaking in the name of all artists. By the way, seasoned activists are well aware of this. They don't resent it when we say to them: "Well, look, right now, I can't. We are rehearsing a new production." They know they can rely on us to give them a hand on many occasions but not all the time. (Mnouchkine, in Mnouchkine and Pascaud 2005: 101)

And although her productions of course tell us about the current state of the world, Mnouchkine will never allow artistic meaning and quality to take second place, on the contrary. That is why she rejects activist aesthetic, which, according to her, dooms theatre to sink into realism:

> The function of theatre is to bring people pleasure. It is also moral, educational. It must lead people to think. This is not to say you have to embrace documentary or militant theatre. The point is to embody in poetic form a current, contemporary fact, giving it sufficient weight after the manner of a metaphorical fable. (Mnouchkine 1994)

What separates the theatrical sphere of action from the political one is first the aesthetic dimension, but it is also the kind of discourse specific to each sphere. For the productions of Théâtre du Soleil aim at promoting the idea that fraternity may be achieved through a universal communion in aesthetic emotion whereas its political commitments aim at helping to solve practical problems arising in specific contexts:

> The two things are different. I believe that the kind of political actions we can engage in as citizens are immediate actions. [...] The political weight of a play will not prompt the audience to leave the theatre and start a Revolution overnight [...] As a consequence the theatre has a civilizing, educational role

> to play [...] Political action for its part is not civilizing in any way. It aims at
> stopping or triggering something. (Mnouchkine, in Féral 1998: 38)

The company has not altogether given up all forms of commitment on the political stage proper; what can be observed is rather a change in nature and in the target of its commitment. Mnouchkine thus embodies the figure of the "committed" artist whom the French philosopher Daniel Bensaïd (Bensaïd 2006: 21-31) contrasts with that of the "activist." The latter is an insider, not a simple ally but a full member of the fighting group and as such, has to account for the statements (s)he makes and for his/her actions which will be praised in terms of effectiveness. The activist artist is therefore defined first and foremost as an activist who campaigns with his own means. (S)he thus accepts outright that his/her art should be used for political ends, art being conceived not as an end to itself but as a mere means at the service of an extra-theatrical cause, a political cause. Conversely, the "committed artist" is a friendly outsider who only takes part in the struggle and in political organization on occasions. The committed artist defines himself primarily as an artist, who will occasionally involve himself in a particular fight and decide to support a particular cause, these involvements always remaining of secondary importance. This change in nature of commitment also affects the chosen target. As a matter of fact, since the end of the 1970s, "the Cartoucherie has progressively stopped housing all the meetings or political events it had willingly hosted until then [...] A page was then turned" (Labrouche 1999: 22).

From that moment on, the company has been dedicating its efforts to causes which have nothing to do with an apprehension of society in terms of antagonistic classes. First, the company is concerned with defending artists, especially when they are denied freedom of expression. In 1979, Mnouchkine founded AIDA (Association Internationale de Défense des Artistes) whose mission consists of providing at least moral support for artists suffering from persecution or censorship in totalitarian countries, by sensitizing public authorities and Western opinion. Then, in the 1990s, the company took up two new causes, this time campaigning as artists but not for artists: on one hand, the fight "to put a stop to barbarity in Bosnia"[9] and on the other hand, the campaign in support of undocumented immigrants in France. In both cases, Théâtre du Soleil's committed itself away from any political party, in the name of humanism and human rights. But what is most striking about these new commitments is the fighting method used. Indeed it would seem that what accounts for the highly spectacular, highly symbolical nature of their mobilization is the refusal of Mnouchkine and the other artists involved to define themselves as activists or more exactly their contention that it is their artistic identity which confers meaning on their commitment. The protest against the role played by France in the former Yugoslavia conflict and to save Bosnia after the fall of Srebrenica in the summer of 1995 consisted of two forms of action taken not only as artists, but also in a specifically artistic way. To begin with, at the Avignon Festival, a group of choreographers and stage directors, including Mnouchkine, made a public appeal to French and European governments:

> We, theatrical people gathered in Avignon, taking account that this Festival is also that of public discourse and *civic demands*,[10] refusing to be resigned to the desertion of democracies in the face of the worst, hereby read the Avignon Declaration publicly. The large scalee ethnic cleansing operation launched by the fascistic regime of the " self-proclaimed Republic " of Bosnian Serbs is in full swing. [...] In the face of such an emergency, *as citizens privileged to be able to publicly address other citizens*,[11] we know take a common public stand. It has been years since the unacceptable mistakes made by UNO and our governments regarding Bosnia have caused us to lose all trust in their policy. [...] If democracies fail to react promptly we shall have a new Munich; if these crimes remain unpunished, this will result in a much worse disaster which will spread an acceptance of horror all over the world. For this will indeed amount to forsaking the principles of the United Nations Charter and of Law itself. This will signal the triumph of barbarity. ("Déclaration d'Avignon," 1995)

This Declaration is not simply a condemnation of "Serbian militias," through the choice of words it also offers an actual definition of the citizen artist: a "citizen, " just like any other, but apart from the citizenry in that (s)he enjoys the privilege of "being able to address other citizen" and of taking a public stand and by so doing of influencing public opinion and of acting as a pressure group to which the government is liable to pay heed. And it was precisely because the government seemed to turn a deaf ear to them that the artists later decided to take their politico-artistic action one stage further. In August 1995, they started a hunger strike – which some commentators did not hesitate to dub "an artistic gesture" (Pascaud, in Mnouchkine and Pascaud 2005: 99) - arguing that "it was essential artists should manage to leave the realm of the symbolic" (Mnouchkine, in Saison 1998: 20)[12] and that a hunger-strike was "the only way" (Mnouchkine, in Mnouchkine and Pascaud 2005: 99) for them "to involve" themselves "physically as well as morally." This symbolic physical strength also enables Mnouchkine and her colleagues to compensate for the lack of an activist competence which results from their status of citizen artists affiliated to no political parties. But at the same time it raises a new question: isn't this commitment truly more "moral," not to say Christ-like than civic? Historically, hunger-strike has been used in France as a weapon either used by those political players who are farthest removed from the public space, who have no command of verbal eloquence, or by players acting in the name of moral, if not religious principles (Siméant 1998: 59-85). "Citizen artists" occupy a prominent place in public life as citizens and as orators but they literally sympathize (from the Greek word συμπάθεια which means to suffer with) with suffering victims to the point that they make their own bodies experience the same suffering; more than mouthpieces, they become resonance chambers for the victims' suffering. In Mnouchkine's case[13] this paradox probably stems from her religious faith. This Christian as well as "citizen" dimension is quite apparent not only in the event staged for Bosnia, a period of fast to atone for the sins of Western Countries but also in the campaign in support of undocumented immigrants (Mouchard 2001), a cause Théâtre du Soleil has been championing since the mid 1990s. Indeed, in 1996, Mnouchkine (with Olivier Py again) took part in the sit-in at the Parisian church of Saint-Ambroise to protest the expulsion of undocumented immigrants. When the refugees were evicted from the Church they first took refuge in the Théâtre Du Soleil at the Cartoucherie of Vincennes. Then when they left to hold a sit-in in Saint-Bernard Church, Mnouchkine went with them and she took them in again at the Cartoucherie when they were evicted once more:

> Léon Schwarzenberg called me one evening in June: " Ariane, could you accommodate 382 undocumented immigrants for a few days? [...] The following day, the exodus were there. We were playing Tartuffe. First they stayed for a month. Then they held a two-month sit-in at Saint-Bernard Church. When they heard they were about to be evicted, we joined them for a week to support them. [...] Then, the notorious axe fell on the Church door on the orders of notorious Juppé. We were all kicked out. Back here they came. This did pose a number of problems. The Cartoucherie must not become a place of confrontation. It was a shelter, a sanctuary where they could perk up

and work on new strategies. Once they felt ready they would leave to launch another attack. Some blamed me for this, they wanted me to confront public authorities." (Mnouchkine, in Mnouchkine and Pascaud 2005: 101)

Théâtre du Soleil claims to be there to help, to offer support and protection, and not take a direct part in conflicts. Mnouchkine contributes to giving causes media coverage. The specificity of the help provided but also of the way the problem of undocumented immigrants is apprehended is apparent in the above quotation. Quite revealing is the biblical (religious as well as mythical) vocabulary, the notion of "exodus," the metaphor of the Cartoucherie as a "sanctuary." For Mnouchkine, the undocumented immigrants are both Historical characters and characters in a story and it is on these two accounts that she campaigns for them. Hers is therefore more a symbolic than a political approach. It was in support of this cause that Théâtre du Soleil staged two productions, one in the late 1990s, *Et Soudain des Nuits d'Eveil*, and the other in the first decade of the twenty-first century, *Le Dernier Caravansérail*. And from one to the next the shift from activist to "citizen theatre" is confirmed.

Et Soudain des Nuits d'Eveil is the only production of Théâtre du Soleil after the 1990s that could rightly be termed "activist," both in terms of its aesthetic choices and of the performance itself. This play is a transcript of the experience undocumented immigrants went through when they were expelled by police from the Saint-Bernard Church and then taken in by the company in the summer of 1997. The structure of the play is quite explicit: a Tibetan theatre company that has been invited by the Théâtre du Soleil, asks for political asylum at the end of a performance, in the presence of two hundred fellow Tibetans who have tried to talk the French Government out of selling a hundred fighter planes to China. A general conversation ensued between the Tibetans, the actors, and members of the public who are also determined to stay in the theatre. This autobiographical play was born from the company's involvement:

> Obviously the experience is nurturing our play. Complete with what it revealed about our faintheartedness, our fears, our laziness. How we can be both happy to be doing something and complain about the trouble it occasions to us. But had we been talking about Africa, we would have lacked the necessary distance the metaphorical minimum necessary for theatrical art to exist. (Mnouchkine, 1998a)

And yet, despite this use of metaphorical and indirect means, the company then faced mostly ironic, amused criticism. *Le Monde* ran the following headline: "The bizarre journey of the Théâtre du Soleil on the steep mounts of activism" (Salino 1998), following with this comment on the play: "At times, *Et Soudain des nuits d'éveil* goes as far as to give weapons to those who stupidly mock the Soleil's civic and political action." For others, the fact that the play was a flop once again attests to "the limitations of activist theatre" (AFP 1998). Even Fabienne Pascaud, who has always been an unfailing supporter of the Soleil, deplores the fact that "a number of scenes are marred by activist preachifying" (Pascaud, 1998, January 14) and to avoid pulling the play to pieces she is careful not to describe it as an activist piece, emphasizing the fact that "citizen Ariane and her Théâtre du Soleil avow quite frankly how difficult it is to be a committed artist." Conversely, *Le Dernier Caravansérail*, which premiered in 2003 to unanimous critical acclaim, can be considered as an emblem of "citizen theatre" on account of its aesthetic choices and also because of the function assigned to the performance. *Et soudain des Nuits d'Eveil* worked as an artistic trace of an actual political experience, namely the difficulties encountered by the company when it shared its living quarters with undocumented immigrants:

> Our territory was invaded, our place of work was completely disrupted, our sense of hospitality was seriously put to the test. Our high opinion of our patience, tolerance and generosity came out somewhat diminished. There had been moments when we had been neither patient, nor tolerant nor generous. But we had not given in. We wanted to talk about this: real life putting our ideals to the test. (Mnouchkine, in Mnouchkine and Pascaud 2005: 102-103)

> Conversely, the approach underlying *Le Dernier Caravansérail* is of a theatrical nature outright. It has no link with any political commitment, and does not constitue the artistic trace or development of any political action:

> Was *Le Dernier Caravansérail* inspired by a political motivation?

> Well, yes and no. It was inspired first by a theatrical urge. I always submit to actors the kind of play I would be happy to watch. If they agree to my proposal it is for exactly the same reasons. (Mnouchkine, in Mnouchkine and Pascaud 2005: 62)

At first, it was Mnouchkine's intention to explore the notions of journey and of encounter: "the starting-point would consist of people meeting as if it were a crossroads and then there would be flashbacks to various events in their personal lifestories" (Mnouchkine 2004b). It was only at a later stage that the figure of the refugee came to be associated with the notion of journey. It was because, according to her, Sangatte is "a metaphor of the whole world" (Mnouchkine, in Sellès-Fischer 2003). During the summer of 2001, she recorded hundreds of hours of testimonies at the place. In this case, it twas a theatrical move that led to a subsequent extra-theatrical commitment. For a number of the refugees she had interviewed during the preparatory stage later became members of the company. Some of them were professional actors already, like Sarkaw Gorany (Bédarida 2003) who by the way prefers to be known as a "traveller rather than as a refugee," others became actors, still others "simply stayed at the Cartoucherie" (Mnouchkine 2004), taking part in the company's life in a different way, for example by helping with the cooking or other chores. Again, it was as an artist (and in this instance mostly in support of other artists) that Mnouchkine became involved in a political fight, her celebrity helping to sort out a number of administrative problems so that refugees obtained papers faster than would have been the case without her intervention. Finally this play presents what paradoxically seems to be a characteristic of "citizen theatre," namely the fact of originating from a moral, even religious, rather than political commitment. In this play indeed, the unfathomable nature of human actions is echoed by the impenetrability of the ways of a Lord who, for all that he is unfathomable is nevertheless always fair and good: "God is eternal, God is pure, God is beautiful [...] God is words and whispers [...] The God of wrath is not God. He is the Devil. He is the Devil! It was Satan who cut our friends' throats."[14] In order to describe what prompted her to produce this play, Mnouchkine, in one of the many interviews she gave to catholic and protestant reviews, mentions "compassion," in the etymological meaning of the word, namely "sharing somebody's passion, or suffering" (Mnouchkine 2003).

Ory's change in terminology to describe the Soleil's trajectory can therefore be justified in part by Mnouchkine's current rejection of activism and of partisan theatre. Indeed, if the notion of "people's theatre" necessarily raises the question of the relations between an artist and the people, that of "citizen theatre" gives prominence to the individual-artist's political commitment, a commitment which is quite specific: indeed, the artist is not a member of any political party, (s)he is a member of the citizenry but his/her special status enables him/her to act as a spokesperson for other members of the citizenry. But the point is that Ory goes beyond the bounds of a mere analysis of the company's history to embrace that of the "people's theatre" throughout the twentieth century. In order to explain why this "citizen" rhetoric has found such favour not only with Ory but also with so many critics and theatrical people it is therefore necessary to interrogate the evolution of the significance of the reference to the people and consequently to the people' theatre on the theatrical scene but also more generally on the political scene.

"CITIZEN THEATRE" AS A SIGN OF
AN IDEOLOGICAL WATERSHED

To grasp what lies behind the reference to "citizen theatre," one has to examine how the word "citizen" made its entry on the public scene. The main reason why the term became popular is that the word "people" progressively fell into disfavour. One striking fact since the 1980s has been he ideological semantic layer added again to the word "the people" on the French political scene. It has been scrapped along with the notion of revolution by the Socialist Party, the incarnation of the left-when-in-the-Government (Conan 2004).[15] Actually, only right-wing parties currently refer to the word "people" (the UMP, formerly headed by Nicolas Sarkozy is the "Union pour une Majorité Populaire" – Union for a Popular Majority). Conversely, the craze for the "citizen theatre" should be put into the current political as well as theatrical context as theatre is of the only field in which "the citizen" is currently fashionable:

> In the past few years, the word "citizen," which had already been used by the French Revolution with great enthusiasm and indeed sometimes with excess, has become fashionable again in democratic countries in an insistent not to say obsessive way. As an adjective the word is currently used in conjunction with all sorts of nouns. For example some people will currently talk about "citizen meetings," "citizen action" or even "citizen cafés." (Schnapper 2000: 9)

But the more widely used the word is, the less political its meaning becomes and "in this very broad acceptation, it simply means 'non-professional', 'social' or even just 'friendly' or 'pleasant'. This is a far cry from the proper definition of the noun 'citizen', meaning 'a member of an autonomous political community, defined by his rights and duties'" (9). This trend is exacerbated in the theatrical sphere. Since the 1990s, the phrases "citizen theatre" and "citizen artist" have been going around among artists, critics,[16] and public authorities in charge of the theatre.[17] But once more it is primarily the reluctance to use the embarrassing notion of "people" which accounts for the success of the word "citizen." A distinction has to be made between two factors: first came the realization that the "non-public" whose existence was revealed in 1968 is no longer restricted to the victims of social exclusion but currently comprises the overwhelming majority of the French population (Coulangeon 2005: 106)[18] which raises an agonizing question is it still justifiable to have the taxpayers subsidize a very elitist cultural practice? Clearly theatre artists have no ready answer to the question put by Olivier Py, director of the Odeon Theatre: "How can a theatre which concerns only a minority of the population remain a 'people's theatre'?"[19] The question just makes French artists feel guilty. But another factor can account for the popularity of the word "citizen": this time having not so much to do with the sociological composition of theatre audiences as with the way cultural elites imagine the people and as a consequence, the "people's theatre."

Two distinct elements are at work. First, the switch from "people's theatre" to "citizen theatre" coincides with an ideological watershed, or rather, the theatrical community is simply taking account on a smaller scale of the transformations we have described on the political scene. It is increasingly wary of everything "populaire," which it tends more and more to equate with "populism"[20] and of the national republican model which equates with a potentially nationalist model. This rejection can in part be accounted for by historical events in the twentieth century: indeed, there were times when the model of a supposedly republican "people's theatre" actually flirted with a nationalist, xenophobic, not to say anti-Semitic theatre. In the 1930s and 1940s, some of the icons of the national-republican "people's theatre" made highly ambiguous statements about the religious identity of the French People. Far from including the whole of the national community, the "people's theatre" they advocated focused on the Christian people. Jacques Copeau, supported by l'Action Française, used the same rhetoric as that extreme right-wing group when he upheld the principle of a national regeneration through the theatre in 1941: "What we need is a Nation's Theatre. Not a class war theatre or a protest theatre. What we need is a theatre fostering union and regeneration." (Copeau, in Meyer-Plantureux 2006: 240). Similarly, another icon of that theatre, Léon Chancerel, wrote at the time (albeit under a pseudonym) an illustrated children's book singin the praises of Marshal Pétain which at one point reads:

> And then the Marshal said: "First, we have to restore order, separate the wheat from the chaff. And as he was speaking, one could see all the creeps, all the spiders, all the termites, all the vermin that had done such harm to France leave the native soil in a hurry. For the Marshal had taken hold of a broom to sweep them away. (Chancerel 1941: 4)

The spectre of a nationalist conception of the people and of the theatre may explain why Ory refuses to use the phrase "people's theatre." His rejection of the phrase involves a rejection of the "three romantic assumptions underlying this concept: first that there is such a thing as a People, then that there is such a thing as a popular form of theatre and finally that should such a form exist, it deserves to be used as a point of reference by the City" (Ory 1995: 13). To put it in a nutshell, he rejects this notion on account of its idealistic and therefore potentially normative, not to say totalitarian nature. Ory substantiates his choice of the phrase "citizen artist" arguing that this theatre "is aiming for the human being in his/her full autonomy [...] to give him/her access to a communion with the social group on which the emphasis is laid - be it the Nation of the Théâtre National Populaire for instance or the working class of the Bolshevik agit-prop in 1930." (Ory 1995: 13-14). Ory also considers the agit-prop theatre as a forbearer of "citizen theatre." The "agit-prop theatre" can hardly be reconciled with the integration into society and political power that is associated with the word "citizen." Unless the word "citizen" is used only to refer to an official propaganda theatre praising a regime, which using this kind of method would be bound to have an undemocratic conception of the State and to leave very little room for autonomous citizenship. On the other hand, French citizens who, since the Revolution of 1789, have been "born free and equal by right" do not have the same inducement to rebel as a working class feeling oppressed and deprived of all rights. So the two notions truly seem to me irreconcilable, so that "agit-prop" theatre cannot possibly be regarded as an ancestor of "citizen theatre."

This shift in meaning is part of a change in the definition of politics: the notions of struggle, of opponent are now absent from the concept and have been replaced by consensual protest. The citizen no longer refers to Aristotle's political animal but to an individual who has inherited the Declaration of Human Rights and the revolutionary struggle, and is therefore capable of becoming indignant in the name of these values. Political struggle becomes absorbed into moral indignation. It is indeed especially significant that as the conception of "citizen theatre" is gaining ground, other phrases such as "agit prop theatre" are increasingly working as foils. Sociologist Vincent Dubois (Dubois 1999: 273-274) has analysed the changing social and ideological background of cultural officials since the 1980s and has observed a definite swing away from the left and to the center of those responsible for selecting plays and allocating subsidies. It is in this context that the reference to "politics" as a divided social space, composed of potentially or actually conflicting classes has given way to an emphasis on the "civic" in the discourse of public authorities. It would be interesting to carry out a similar survey of theatre artists and critics from a quantitative angle. However a qualitative analysis of the views expressed by today's leading directors of subsidized theatres[21] or companies like Olivier Py or Ariane Mnouchkine but also by some researchers such as Pascal Ory seems to point to a similar change in ideological paradigm: "citizen theatre" has taken over from a "people's theatre" whose feasibility and indeed validity are now being radically called into question.

NOTES

[1] The translation of this quote and of all subsequent over is mine.

[2] In French, both terms share the same ambiguities and can refer either to the national community as a whole (in which case, "popular"/"people" are synonymous with "citizen"), only to those in the lower income bracket who constitue the bulk of the population (what sociologists call "catégories populaires"), sometimes even further reduced to the proletarian class fighing for its rights, in a Marxist conception of society. Bearing this in mind, I shall use the term "people" throughout this essay for convenience sake.

[3] In 1966, Pierre Bourdieu published with Alain Darbel a highly successful essay in which he presented works of art as so many codes which have to be broken by the public before they can be enjoyed. This undermined the two pillars sustaining the

policy of cultural democratization implemented since the creation of the Ministère des Affaires Culturelles in 1959: the sacred conception of works of art compelling immediate recognition, even from untrained and uneducated eyes on the one hand and on the other, the notion that to promote culture it is enough to bring the people into contact with the world's greatest artistic masterpieces.

[4] Romain Rolland thus holds the view that the growing popularity of socialism has drawn the attention of artists to the new sovereign" and has caused them to "discover the people." (Rolland, in Meyer-Plantureux 2006: 7) According to him, "the people's theatre […] is the forceful expression of a new society, its voice and thought and it is […] an instrument of warfare against an aged, obsolete society." (Rolland 2006: 27)

[5] Proof of this is the very layout of the premises at La Cartoucherie, as well as the way the evenings would unfold, both dictated y a desire to create a friendly, cosy atmosphere. Remarkably, Mnouchkine would personally usher the spectators into the auditorium and during the intervals those who left hungry would be served affordably priced hot meals by the actors themselves.

[6] See below my analysis of the show *Et Soudain des nuits d'éveil.*

[7] Jean-Marie Le Pen, head of the extreme-right party Le Front National (National Front), arrived in the second round of the 2002 presidential election.

[8] "J'Accuse" is a text published in the daily L'Aurore on January the 13th 1898, in which the famous novelist defended the reputation of Captain Dreyfus, wrongly accused of having betrayed his country, just because he was a Jew. Because of this involvement, Zola is considered as the first French "intellectuel." (Winock, 1997).

[9] Maguy Marin, Ariane Mnouchkine, Olivier Py, François Tanguy, Emmanuel de Véricourt, François Verret, *Déclaration d'Avignon*, 12 juillet 1995.

[10] My italics.

[11] My italics.

[12] Olivier Py is even more explicit when he explains that "there comes a moment when writing or making statement is no longer enough. When the artist's very body has to be involved." (Py, in Saison, 1998: 20)

[13] The same remark applies to Olivier Py.

[14] Quote from the play.

[15] After the 2002 presidential campaign, the socialist candidate Lionel Jospin was blamed by some left-wing commentators for never once using the word "le peuple" and not addressing the concerns of the "catégories populaires," i.e. employees and factory workers.

[16] In two leading articles written in 2006, Jean-Pierre Engelbach, director of the prestigious "Editions Théâtrales," established a link between the "social malaise" and a renewed citizen commitment of theatre actors. Engelbach, Jean-Pierre, "Brûlent les planches," *Dernières nouvelles,* brochure published by the Éditions Théâtrales, Paris, janvier 2006, and "Lectures citoyennes," *Dernières nouvelles*, brochure published by the Éditions Théâtrales, Paris, Mars 2006.

[17] In this respect, the various surveys of French people's cultural practices carried out at the request of the Ministère de la Culture since the 1980s have contributed greatly to making the artists working with publicly-subsidized theatres distance themselves from the ideal of a "people's theatre" which they knew was becoming ever more impossible to achieve.

[18] Indeed only 17% of the French population went to the theatre in the year 2001.

[19] Introduction to the discussion led by Olivier Py at the Théâtre du Rond Point in Paris on May 22nd 2006 within the festival "La Grande Parade d'Olivier Py."
[20] The followers of this current of thought were particularly vocal during the controversy over the choice of plays selected for the 2005 Avignon Festival. Jan Fabre's supporters inveighed against "the worm of populism" that had insinuated itself in the minds of French theatre-goers. (Tolochard 2005: 97).
[21] See the introduction to my PhD thesis (Hamidi-Kim, 2007).

REFERENCES
Abirached, Robert, ed. (1993) *La décentralisation théâtrale. 1. Le premier âge, 1945-1958*. Paris: L'Arche.
———. (1994) *La Décentralisation théâtrale. 3. 1968, le tournant*. Arles: Actes Sud.
Bablet, Denis. (1978) *Le Théâtre d'agit-prop. 1917-1932*. Lausanne: La Cité/L'Age d'Homme.
Bédarida, Catherine. (2003) "Sarkaw Gorany, kurde voyageur." *Le Monde*. (1 April)
Bensaïd, Daniel. (2006) "Clercs et chiens de garde," in *Clercs et chiens de garde. L'Engagement des intellectuels, Contretemps* 15. (February), Paris: Textuel, 21-31.
Biet, Christian and Olivier Neveux. (2007) *Une Histoire du spectacle militant. (1966-1981)* Montpellier : L'Entretemps.
Bourdieu, Pierre and Alain Darbel. (1966) *L'Amour de l'art. Les musées d'art européens et leur public*, Paris, Minuit.
Chancerel, Léon. (1941), *Oui, monsieur le maréchal! ou le Serment de Pouique le glouton et Lududu paresseux*. Grenoble, B. Arthaud/La Gerbe de France.
Conan, Eric. (2004) *La Gauche sans le peuple*. Paris : Fayard.
Copeau, Jacques. (1941) *Le Théâtre populaire*. Paris : Presses Universitaires de France.
Copfermann, Emile. (1965) *Le Théâtre populaire, pourquoi?* Cahiers libres 69. Paris: Maspero.
———. (1969) "Quelque chose a changé." in *Théâtres et politique. (bis) Partisans* 47, 5-29.
Coulangeon, Philippe. (2005) *Sociologie des pratiques culturelles*. Paris: La Découverte.
Dreyfus-Armand, Geneviève, Robert Franck, Marie-Françoise Lévy, and Michelle Zancarini-Fournel. (2000) *Les années 1968: Le temps de la contestation*. Bruxelles: Complexe.
Dubois, Vincent. (1999) *La Politique culturelle: Genèse d'une catégorie d'intervention publique*. Paris, Belin.
Féral, Josette. (1998) *Trajectoires du Soleil*. Paris : Editions Théâtrales.
Gémier, Firmin. (1920) *L'Ere Nouvelle du théâtre*. Paris: La Petite République socialiste.
Grelet, Stany. (2002) "Brûler ses vaisseaux - sur la grève de la faim. Entretien avec Johanna Siméant." *Vacarme* 18. (Winter) <http://www.vacarme.eu.org/article229.html> [Accessed 4 March 2009].
Hamidi-Kim, Bérénice. (2007) *Les Cités du théâtre politique en France de 1989 à 2007*. Ph.D. thesis. Université Lyon 2.

Labrouche, Laurence. (1999) *A. Mnouchkine: Un parcours théâtral.* Paris: L'Harmattan.

Lambert, Benoît and Frédérique Matonti. (2001) "Un théâtre de contrebande. Quelques hypothèse sur Vitez et le communisme," in Benoît Lambert and Frédérique Matonti, eds. *Artistes/Politiques. Sociétés et représentations.* 11. Paris: CREDHESS, 379-406.

Marin, Maguy, Ariane Mnouchkine, Olivier Py, François Tanguy, Emmanuel De Véricourt, and François Verret. (1995) *Déclaration d'Avignon. (extraits).* (12 July) <http://www.stoprenvoi.ch/archives/pdf/avignon.pdf> [Accessed 4 March 2009].

Meyer-Plantureux, Chantal. (2006) *Théâtre populaire, enjeux politiques.* Bruxelles: Complexe.

Mnouchkine, Ariane. (1968) "Une prise de conscience" *Le théâtre* 1, 119-126.

——. (1971a) "A. Mnouchkine, animatrice du Théâtre du Soleil à l'Université." *Ouest-France.* (March 27), 15.

——. (1971b) "L'Exemple: conversation with Françoise Kourilsky." *Travail Théâtral* 5. (automn), 117- 118.

——. (1994) "Interview." *La Croix.* (4 June)

——. (1998a) "Ariane au Tibet," Interview with Quirot, Odile, *Le Nouvel Observateur.* (1 January)

——. (1998b) "Interview." *Le Journal du théâtre,.* (9 February)

——. (2003) *Réformes,.* (26 July)

——. (2004a) *Le Dernier Caravansérail. (Odyssées)* "Programme de toutes les Odyssées." Paris, Éditions Théâtre du Soleil.

——. (2004b) "A conversation with Mnouchkine and the Soleil's company" transcribed immediately after a performance of *Le Dernier Caravansérail.* Transcription by Claire Ruffin. Theatre du Soleil, Archives. (7 April), np.

Mnouchkine, Ariane and Fabienne Pascaud. (2005) *L'Art du présent.* Paris: Plon.

Mouchard, Daniel. (2001) *Les exclus dans l'espace public: Mobilisations et logiques de représentation dans la France contemporaine.* Ph.D. thesis. Institut d'Etudes Politiques. (Paris)

Neveux, Olivier. (2004) *Esthétique et dramaturgie du théâtre militant.* Ph.D. thesis. Université Paris X-Nanterre.

Ory, Pascal. (1995) *Théâtre citoyen : du Théâtre du peuple, au Théâtre du soleil.* Avignon : Association Jean Vilar.

Pascaud, Fabienne. (1998) "Le Soleil en éveil." *Télérama.* (14 January)

Pessin, Alain. (1992) *Le Mythe du peuple et la société française du XIXe siècle,* Paris, Presses Universitaires de France.

Piscator, Erwin. (1962) *Le Théâtre politique.* Arthur Adamov and Claude Sebisch, trans. Paris: L'Arche.

Robert, Jean-Louis and Danielle Tartakowsky. (1999) *Le Peuple en tous ses états. Sociétés et représentations* 8. Paris: CREDDHESS.

Rolland, Romain. (2006) *Le Théâtre du Peuple.* Bruxelles, Complexe.

Saison, Maryvonne. (1998) *Les Théâtres du réel.* Paris, L'Harmattan.

Salino, Brigitte. (January 9th, 1998.) "L'Etrange voyage du Soleil sur les monts escarpés du militantisme." *Le Monde,* 28.

Schnapper, Dominique. (2000) *Qu'est-ce que la citoyenneté?* Paris, Gallimard.

Sellès-Fischer, Evelyne. (2003) "Sangatte sur scène," *Réforme.* (24 July)

Siméant, Johanna. (1998) "L'efficacité des corps souffrants: le recours aux grèves de la faim en France." *Sociétés Contemporaines* 31, 59-85.

"Théâtre du Soleil: *Et soudain des Nuits d'éveil* et les limites du théâtre militant.". (1998) Agence France-Presse. (9 January) AFP FSR FRA/ AFP-IR29. (0023)

Tolochard, Jean-Pierre. (2005) "Le ver du populisme," in Georges Banu and Bruno Tackels, eds. *Le Cas Avignon*. Vic La Gardiole: L'Entretemps, 97-118.

Winock, Michel. (1997) *Le Siècle des intellectuels*. Paris: Seuil.

WAYS OF UNSEEING:
GLASS WALL ON THE MAIN STAGE

TAL ITZHAKI

In the 1970s and 1980s, the familiar uniforms of Israeli soldier characters profusely crowded the Israeli stage, both in contemporary Israeli plays (such as *Platoon 3 Unit 1*; *Attrition*; *Sanjer*; *Fog*; and many others), and in modern interpretations of classical drama, from *Trojan Women* to *The Comedy of Errors* or *The Merchant of Venice*. To these one should add, of course, topical satires such as Hanoch Levin's *The Patriot*. The theatres' props and costume departments routinely stocked a host of uniforms and military weapons. Some Israeli actors used to claim they were spending more time in uniform on stage than during their active military service. *Murder* by Hanoch Levin (1998) must have been the last play to have been presented on the main stage (that of the Cameri theatre) in which one could watch a theatrical representation of Israeli soldiers killing a Palestinian, and Palestinians killing Israelis. Except for nudity or explicit sexuality, the theatrical treatment of the Israeli army's dignity and morality proved a favorite target of censorship. The banning of Itzhak Laor's *Ephraim Returns to the Army* (1984), and the subsequent celebrated court case, led to the official abolishment of censorship of stage plays in Israel (1991). The play concerned itself with IDF soldiers in the occupied territories: now it is probably the only play every first year law student can quote, but no theatre student has ever read.

Throughout the *intifada* (the Palestinian uprising) and since, even though official censorship was abolished, the local war and the occupation progressively disappeared from the main stages of the Israeli theatre. Themes of war were still there, but not their visual image: the familiar images of the local, recognizable war have almost totally disappeared from the dramatic visual culture. At the same time, one could hardly see, for a long period of time, any Arabs on the

Israeli stages, either as dramatic characters or as actors performing them. With a few exceptions, this is an ongoing predicament on the main stage of the established Israeli theatre.

This brief account is an attempt to understand the position of the mainstream theatre at this time and place as a manifestation of a cultural choice: of things we (namely, the wide audience of the Hebrew theatre) want to see, and others we do not care to look at. This situation has developed a complex system of self-censorship imposed by degrees and hierarchies. We have no officially forbidden themes or privileged information prevented by law from frequenting the public stage, yet certain issues or images have gradually become marginal, unimportant, insignificant, and finally invisible. There does not exist any longer an official censorship on stage plays in Israel. We experience a golden age of documentary Israeli and Palestinian films (commonly accounted for by film makers as "a heaven for documentaries, since we live in hell"). And yet we manage not to see the concrete images of war, the suffering, the pain. We know they are there, somewhere, but we don't care to watch it on stage.

The wall we keep building up to these very days between ourselves and the Palestinians forms the ultimate image, following years of unseeing. Photographers, artists, designers, have all reacted *en masse* to this monstrous monument of alienation. My personal feeling has been for some time now that the wall should be the only proper set for any play we present – particularly as political performances are concerned – until the real one is demolished. And still, I can state with confidence that most Israelis have never seen, nor are able to draw, the outlines of the wall on the Israeli map.

Speaking of the country map, a central icon and constituent of our national identity, let one enquire how many Israelis have seen, over the last decades, the pre-'67 borders map? The pre-'48 map, or our country map in Arabic, is something most of us have never seen, at least those of us who were born after 1948, the year the State of Israel was established. In his excellent, low-keyed and moving documentary film about the lost houses of Israeli Palestinians, *The Key*, actor-director Salim Daw stops his car for a moment beside the road, to consult the map. The camera wanders in to a close up on the map. This, I think, was the first and last time I have ever saw "our" road map in Arabic. I still wonder where he got it.

In his "Very Short Tale from Across the Wall" Alex Epstein, a Russian born Israeli author, writes as follows:

> In old history books you'll find that the wall was built many years ago, in order to separate us from the madman who stood there painting graffiti messages in the air. After the wall was erected, our forefathers couldn't see what happened to him. Maybe he abandoned the place. Maybe he continued his craft for many years. (Those who want to frighten their children at bedtime locate him on the other side of the wall even now: his palms have grown paintbrushes, he moves them at the speed of a demon, etching into the wall, writing, scratching, writing…). And of course, those who claim the wall has only one side to it, abuse logic and law. (2005: 2)

There is an image hidden behind the wall: a painting, a photographic image, a play. I am dealing here with the disappearance of the war image from the stage for the simple reason of its direct impact, because of the concentrated power visual images carry, which is far different from the power of words. One can easily demonstrate that the denial of present events on the Israeli theatre over the last twenty years or so is almost total; but I'll stick here to the absence of visual images; for visual images have a way of haunting our imagination, and having a grip on our minds for long. They have in them the power to vanquish and override our defense mechanisms and become icons. A compelling example is provided by the Austrian artist Gottfried Helnwein.

In 1979, Dr. Heinrich Gross became Head of the State forensic psychiatry in Vienna. The same Dr. Gross had been in charge of a mental hospital during the Nazi period, admitting now to have killed a host of children whose life "were not worth living." In an interview with Brendan Maher in *Start Magazine*, Helnwein reported that he was shocked to read:

> [A]n interview with him where a reporter asked him if he did in fact kill so many children, and he said, "Yes, that was the way we operated, but things were different then". He had no regrets, and he couldn't be more relaxed about it. He pointed out that he actually killed the children in a very humane way: "We put poison (Luminal) in their food, so they were not aware that they were going to die." My problem was not so much that somebody was insane enough to do something like this. My problem really was that nobody had a problem with it. Gross, who was still the leading forensic psychiatrist at that time in Vienna, openly admitted that he killed hundreds of children. People read it. No reaction. Not one letter of protest. At the same time the public sent 3,500 letters of protest to national television because for the first in Austrian

television history a presenter had appeared on air without a tie. That was
unheard of at the time. So for many people, the world ended right there.
People freaked out. I thought, "Maybe it's just because they can't read and
they didn't understand what the guy said in the interview." So I called the
leading news magazine, "Profil," and asked them to give me a page for an
open letter, and then I just painted what the doctor had described: a dead little
girl with her head in a plate of food.[1] And this did cause a reaction. People
were suddenly very upset. It triggered a discussion that finally, after years, led
to the dismissal of that guy. So it seems that pictures sometimes reach much
deeper than words. (Helnwein, as quoted in Maher 2004)

The wall we are building looks different from our perspective than
from the Palestinian one. From the Israeli side, it suggests safety (like
the end of busses blowing up), a necessary evil, a hurdle and an
obstacle preventing terror. From the Palestinian side, it invokes the
Warsaw ghetto, suggesting the end of hope, a stifling and terrible
despair that can only lead to hatred and perpetuation of the horrors.
There is another crucial difference: We Israelis, most of whom are
living at some distance from the border areas, may afford not to see
the wall; the Palestinians cannot ignore it: it is built right down their
throats. How is it that we manage not to see it?

Research recently published manifests how *The New York
Times* buried the holocaust in the centre pages of the paper. It shows
how hundreds of news items concerning the concentration camps and
the extermination were published during World War II in *The New
York Times*, almost every single week; but not even a handful of those
made the front-page headlines.[2] The point of this research is an
attempt to account for the true fact that most Americans failed to be
aware of the holocaust while its direct effects were occurring. At the
same week in which that research was announced, the front page of
the weekly magazine of *Ha'aretz*, the most serious Israeli daily paper,
was devoted to an amazing discovery regarding the late Naomi
Shemer, a popular song writer having become a national icon, who
admitted on her deathbed that the hymn that became the almost
official anthem of the sixty-seven war, written and composed by her,
"Jerusalem of Gold," was indeed plagiarized from a Basque popular
tune. On the same day, like every other day, two demonstrations
against the Wall were violently dispersed by the army, two
Palestinians killed, some others injured, and so on. It was the
plagiarized tune which made the main headline (Avrahimi and
Wurgaft 2005).

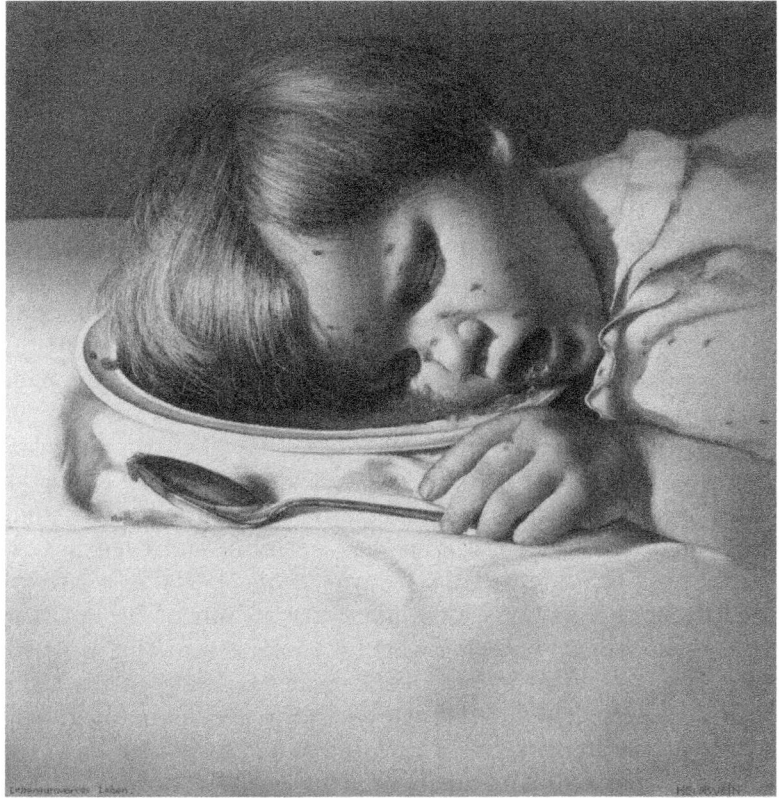

Figure 1. *Lebensunwertes Leben* (1979). Gottfried Helnwein. 72 cm x 72 cm, watercolor on cardboard.

In Israel of the new *intifada* information is current and available, protest exists, political theatre occurs; and yet a glass ceiling, or rather a glass wall is keeping those disturbing images, that would keep us awake for nights, out of the public eye and, of course, conscience. Anywhere in Tel Aviv, like in walking from my home to the national theatre, a fifteen-minute walk, one may notice at least thirty different anti-occupation graffitis. At least once a week I bump into a "woman in black," or any other anti-occupation piquet. People are injured while demonstrating against the fence (as the monstrous Wall is still commonly belittled and dubbed: a fence seems less offensive than "a wall"). They hardly make the news. The national

share of empathy to pain and suffering is currently focused on the pain
of the few settlers about to be evacuated from the Gaza strip (or, in
perspective, since this paper was presented a couple of months prior to
their evacuation, for that matter, their mourning of that evacuation).
Any other pain, the pain of the unemployed, the poor and the hungry,
the foreign workers and Palestinians, does not count. Censorship is
arranged by hierarchies.

One interesting theatrical example is *The Car*. Te Ortoda
theatre group and their artistic leader, director Amir Orian, are well-
respected theatre creators on the Israeli fringe scene. Their messages
are pointed, sharp, and heavily political, but their performances are
minor by definition. Their "Room Theatre" holds a maximum
audience capacity of 20 people per show. They have been widely
appreciated and invited to all possible festivals as long as they
complied with the fringe unwritten rules: play for extremely small
audiences or be a failure or keep message so "artistically" to the point
of being incomprehensible by the majority of your audience. As long
as you abide by these rules, you may perform, and even represent
Israel in any given international festival. *Plonter* (2005), a later play
by Yael Ronen, produced by the mainstream Cameri Theatre, a rare
and rather exceptional occasion where the wall is centrally depicted in
context, is a case in point: it is kept in the repertory of the Cameri
Theatre, sent persistently to international festivals, but in the repertory
of the theatre at home is rarely performed, and even then only at the
smallest auditorium of the Cameri complex.

For the Acco 2004 festival, this group attempted to break the
ideological siege informing political performance in Israel. Their *The
Car* street performance created a "straight in your face" image of war,
with pails of blood and body bags, and was performed not within the
confines of a closed room but rather on a main street for the large
public. At once the censorship apparatus was mobilized to stop them.
At one city (Bat-Yam), the police banned the performance. On the
very same day, the Acco festival artistic committee withdrew their
invitation for them to participate in the festival. In the 1980s and
1990s, any such act of the government's appointed censor, would have
raised immediate protest by theatre people, the left, and freedom of
speech defenders. Now, since censorship is unofficial, it passed almost
unnoticed: difficult to detect and hard to prove. You can't enlist
masses against an artistic committee allegedly exercising its artistic

Figure 2. *Plonter*, a play by Yael Ronnen. The Cameri Theatre (Tel Aviv), 2005. Designer: Einat Palgi. Photograph by Gadi Dagon. Published though special arrangement with the Cameri Theatre.

judgment. As a veteran of the Acco festival, I can vouch such an occurrence has never happened before. Shows were never canceled after having been accepted by the festival. If the artistic committee had reservations, they would try whatever it took to help improve the performance. It was clear this time that they felt the performance of *The Car* could cast a shadow on the festivity and growing respectability of the Festival, celebrating then its 25th year. Since it was the chief of police in the town of Bat Yam who banned the show in the first place, I remembered our fierce demonstrations days, when we, political activists, used to negotiate with the police for demonstrating licenses. I thus called Amir Orian, and suggested they applied to the Acco police for a license to hold a political demonstration. On such a request, the police authorities have no artistic judgment, nor a legal jurisdiction to prevent it: provided all security demands are met, they must grant a license. They may only make technical demands, like exacting the number of ushers and requiring the presence of ambulance. Ironically, on the same day I called Amir, the group was away, representing Israel in some festival abroad. Upon their return, however, they discussed my suggestion, voted in favor, and still had enough time to apply for the license. I was out of the country myself that year when the Acco festival took place, and thus I will quote reviewer Zvi Goren's reporting the event:

> *The Car*, for better or worse, is the only work of art in this year's festival which dares looking at ourselves, even though through a set of distorted and deformed mirrors. *The Car* is far from being a great work of art that could undermine the solid bases of the society it attacked, and I don't think the creators thought it would, they defiantly had hoped to shock, to make noise, to antagonize with the loud exaggerated use of blood and rain of photos, using the picture of the little boy in Warsaw ghetto. Policemen who were posted there to keep public order, in case of a riot, remained idle, except for one of them who was diligently reporting the description of the event to the police headquarters. (Personal communication, October 2005)

This example sheds light on the mysterious, hard to detect ways this obscure censorship is deployed: One enjoys complete freedom of expression, as long as one confines it to the fringe, out of the country, or to the lunatic extremes of the artistic zones. At the same time the main stages, successful and communicative like all commercial television channels, will carry on fostering ways of unseeing, informed by total escapism.

Our own experience at the Haifa University Theatre was a similar one. Once we reached the decision that, although the official tuition language of the University was Hebrew, the Department of Theatre consisting of 24% Palestinian students could allow itself to conduct one out of its several annual student production in Arabic (which is one of the two official languages in Israel according to law). A strong political play in Arabic, *Men in the Sun*, by major Palestinian writer Ghassan Kanafani, passed safely with the University authorities when performed in a small University studio holding sixty spectators. A much less controversial play, Hanoch Levin*'s Luggage Packers*, the *pièce de résistance* of Israeli drama, when it was performed in Arabic, for a mixed Jewish and Arab audience and became a huge success, caused eventually the closure of the theatre. Apparently we, as well, broke some rules by achieving, or even pursuing successful, communicative political theatre. In terms of the visual themes, the Kanafani play was more powerful, and extremely Arab. In the *Luggage Packers* there was no conspicuous threat, except for the success of the show and the mixed audience. It proved enough of a menace to cause the closure of the University Theatre (never having re-opened ever since).

One last example was *Les Paravents* (*The Screens*) by Jean Genet, directed by Ofira Henig, and designed by Miriam Guretzki. It was, in my opinion, a most prominent design, of local Mediterranean shape, with powerful stage images of refugees, war and death. The cast included, among others, a group of excellent Arab actors. In spite of the abstract, non-realistic design, the production had a distinct "Arab look." At the Israeli exhibition in the Prague Quadrennial, which I later curated, it was to occupy a central place.

The director of the show, Ofira Henig, is as mainstream as they come. At that time, she was the artistic director of the prestigious Israel Festival. The show was produced by the Habima National Theatre, but ran in exile, in a fringe venue which the National Theatre had never used before. It was to be closed, or turned into TV studio, shortly after the very brief run of the Genet play. With very little publicity, a very long artistic show, it was considered a failure in terms of communicability and audience rating, and was taken offstage shortly after having opened. Ofira was to become the director of a Jerusalem fringe theatre, "The Laboratory." The Israeli Palestinian actors are these days mostly unemployed, or occasionally produce films, which win quality prizes all over the world.

In IFTR's "political performances" working group 2004 meeting in St. Petersburg, I vowed to include the wall in my next project, *Neighbors*, a play I adapted and designed, with director Amit Gazit, from plays by Hanoch Levin. In the Theatre Department of Barnard College at Columbia University in New York, where Amit and I were invited as resident artists at the Fall term of that year, the play opened to the background of a very colorful Israeli urban view, modeled on Tel Aviv, a view which served the backdrop for domestic neighborhood scenes from several plays by Levin, interwoven together, interrupted and intruded again and again, like real life in Israel, by war scenes, mainly out of Levin's late play *Murder*.

Toward the end of the play, the black wings were turned around and became segments of the wall. The wall pieces moved forward until they have entirely covered the stage, stifling and blocking the proscenium. Our sensitivities were a little different from those of our US actors. For me, the wall image was very sad; the American actors were moved and reacted to the murder images, the uniforms, and guns. We ended the play with a touch of optimism: Suzanna, as the charming bride who was brutally raped and killed just a few scenes before, delivered a short speech about the future, probably the only one in the entire body of work by Levin, and stuck a flower in a bullet hall in the wall. Then all the other actresses in the cast came in, with flowers in hands, stuck them in the wall, and manifestly pushed the wall back.

Figure 3. *Neighbours*, a Collage of Hanoch Levin Plays. Adapted by Tal Itzhaki and Amit Gazit. Minor Latham Playhouse (Columbia University, New York), 2004. Designer: Tal Itzhaki. Photograph by Ayala Gazit.

Will the play ever be produced in Israel? I am not sure. I hope it will.

In representing Israeli art and theatre in the world, we have a completely different image. We overlook the main stages, and represent our country by presenting what we think "the world" may find interesting about us, the craziness we live in. We are allowed, even encouraged to do so abroad, and thus we represent democratic Israel very successfully. Fringe theatres like the Acco theatre group or the Jaffa Hebrew-Arab Theatre, are valuable assets in that way, forming great export vehicles. Back at home, however, our large theatre audience does not care too much to see what they offer. We go

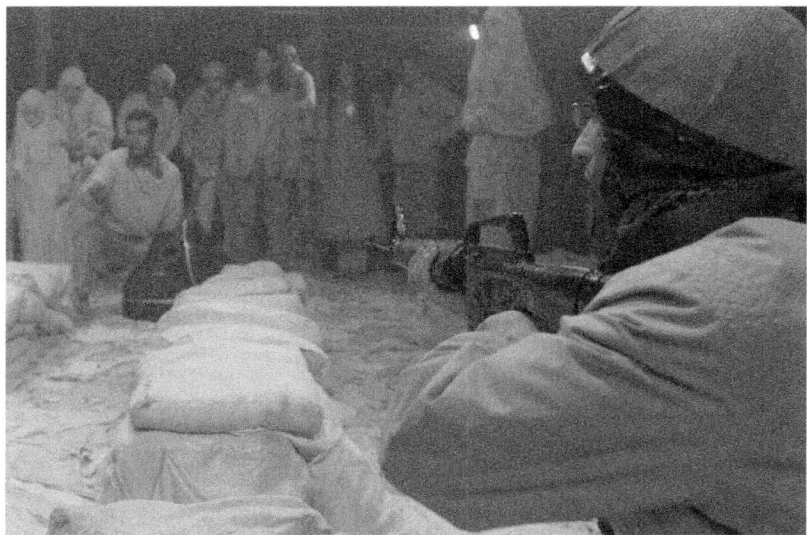

Figure 4. *Winter at Qalandia* after the book by Lia Nirgad. Adapted by Nola Chilton. The Arab-Hebrew Theatre (Jaffa), 2004. Designer: Miriam Guretzky, Chaya Biran, Irena Gluzman. Photograph by Eyal Landsman.

to the theatre for fun, we want to be entertained, and we have enough war throughout our daily realities. These statements are all true. The public does not want to see any of that. It is also true that detachment from the real world one lives in is a kind of madness.

Art has a real need to deal with real issues. Heiner Müller says about Helnwein: "How can a friendly person like Helnwein stand making his excellent painting into a mirror of the terrors of this century? Or is it that he can't stand not doing it? Does his mirror just reflect the attitude of the century?" (1986). How can we stand not to? It is not easy: if you look around, you feel the need to shout; in order to avoid it we need to train ourselves in unseeing. And we are successful it takes over. We lose our sensibility, we become numb, and then we become cruel. It does not stop with war, we tolerate all kinds of violence and corruption, and we cripple ourselves. It is a painful price we pay.

I would like to end this essay with a poem by Palestinian poet Mahmoud Darwish:

Our losses are between two and eight a day.
And ten are wounded.
Twenty homes are gone.
Forty olive groves destroyed,
in addition to the structural damage
afflicting the veins of the poem, the play,
and the unfinished painting. (Darwish 2002)

AFTERTHOUGHTS FOR 2009

In the years that have elapsed since this paper was written and presented, we in Israel have undergone more political violence. We witnessed the "Disengagement," the evacuation of Jewish settlers from the Gaza strip and two wars.

The "appearance," or visual images of those events, has yet to be seen on our main stages, in sharp contrast to their impact on Israeli films *Bil'in Habibti* and *Waltz with Bashir* are just two out of many.

In the fringe theatre—there was one very strong visualization of the road blocks situation—in *Winter in Qalandia*, directed by Nola Chilton and designed by Miriam Guretzki. The Wall as well as the lifesize figures of *Winter in Qallandia* served as the framework of the Israeli show at the Prague quadrennial stage design exhibition, 2007.

On the mainstream stages—not only the war visuals are missing in action. It would more and more seem nowadays that the entire visual aspect of theatre is becoming redundant. Thinking of those amazingly similar and inspiring phrases—used by Peter Brook as a definition of "Holy Theatre," and Merleau-Ponti's in regards to the purpose of art—"To make the invisible visible"—and without belittling drama or acting, it seems that losing the visual power of theatre is putting at risk the very essence of live performance.

NOTES

[1] The author would like to extend a special thank you to Gottfried and Renate Helnwein, for their kind permission and help in reproducing Helnwein's work.
[2] See Laurel Leff, *Buried by the Times: The Holocaust and America's Most Important Newspaper*, 2005.

REFERENCES

Avrahimi, Idit and Nurit Wurgaft. (2005) "Naomi Shemer had no reason to feel bad, says Basque singer." *Haaretz.com*, (6 May)

<http://www.haaretz.com/hasen/pages/ShArt.jhtml?itemNo=573295>
[Accessed 10 April 2009].

Darwish, Mahmoud. (2002) *A State of Siege*. Ramsis Amun, trans.
<http://www.arabworldbooks.com/Literature/poetry4.html#top> [Accessed 10 April 2009].

Epstein, Alex. (2005) *Blue Has No South*. Tel Aviv: Am Oved. English translation by the author. <http://iwp.uiowa.edu/writers/sample/Epstein_Alex_sample.pdf > [Accessed 10 April 2009].

Leff, Laurel. (2005) *Buried by the Times: The Holocaust and America's Most Important Newspaper*. Cambridge: Cambridge University Press.

Maher, Brendan. (2004) "Interview with Gottfried Helnwein." *Start Magazine*. (24 November) <http://www.gottfried-helnwein-interview.com/brendan_maher.html> [Accessed 12 April 2009].

Müller, Heiner. (1986) "Black Mirror/For Helnwein,"
<http://museum.helnwein.com/helnwein/print/texts/mueller.html> [Accessed 10 April 2009].

Orian, Amir. (2005) Personal communication (October). Conversation with the author.

TO ABSENT FRIENDS:
ETHICS IN THE FIELD OF AUTO/BIOGRAPHY[1]

DEIRDRE HEDDON

PERFORMANCE PROLOGUE

[*Dee, standing in front of an assembled "audience," pours out a glass of whisky and holds it up for a toast.*]

"Scotch Courage." I suspect you suspect this is cold tea or something —an old stage trick.

[*Dee takes a "nip." Removes tumblers from out of bag and proceeds to fill these too.*]

Is it ethical to bribe your audience?

[*Passes round the glasses of whisky.*]

A couple of years ago, I decided I would make a performance piece with my two brothers. We would return to all the places we had lived as children and as research we would re-walk the habitual walks we used to take on a daily basis: from home to school; from home to lochside; from home to sea. We would video the routes, tape our memories, rake over the forgotten past, and no doubt invent, embellish, and argue over versions. The performance itself would be made later out of whatever we gathered, fabricated, experienced— though I recognised that it would probably be me who devised and performed it.

And so it is that I arrange for my younger brother, who at 30 is not so young, to fly from, let's say Exeter, in the South of England to, let's say Glasgow, in Scotland, where I will meet him. From there we

will travel by train to join my older brother in—Argyll, the region of
our shared childhood. (Admittedly, the five-year age gap between me
and my younger brother proposes that it is perhaps less of a shared
childhood than I like to imagine.)

At about 11am I receive the first call from younger brother
informing me that he is at Exeter airport (phew—I thought he might
sleep in). But—my brother then goes on to tell me that the plane is an
hour delayed (sinking feeling in my stomach). At 11:45ish I receive
the next phone call. The plane is still further delayed. I'm not to
worry, though, he tells me, because he's in the airport bar waiting.
And having a drink to steady his pre-flight nerves. (The sinking
feeling is becoming more pronounced; but I reprimand myself for
being the bossy, controlling big sister.) At 1pm I receive the third
phone call. No sign of plane. Brother still in bar. "But stop worrying,"
he tells me, "it'll all work out fine, stop being so anxious, chill out,
big sis." My stomach has now sunk to my feet. By 3pm, of course, the
plane has come and gone, and he is not on it because airport security
has declared him unfit to travel. "They're wrong," he slurringly tells
me, "I'm absolutely fine." He is also, by this time, unable to
comprehend that there is only one plane a day from Exeter to
Glasgow, and that he is not on it. "I'll catch the next one," he says
repeatedly. "I'll catch the next one." I repeatedly tell him to go home.
Sleep it off. In the end, the police very obligingly give him a lift,
which I suppose saved him the £15 taxi fare.

So, after weeks of planning and not inconsiderable financial
cost to me (wasted plane tickets and empty hotel beds) the three
became two, which didn't quite work out, and I'm left with a vastly
different story to the one I anticipated. But is this a story about me?
About my younger brother? About me and him? Or me, him and my
older brother? About family relationships? About stupid, unrealistic
ideas (whose family did I think this was?)? About a genetic
predilection to alcohol? Or a fear of flying? Or about a story I have no
right to tell? Is this a story about ethics? A story unethically used to
discuss ethics? Of course, there's always the possibility that I'm
making the whole thing up.[2] [*Sip glass of whisky.*]

ETHICS
Ethics in the field of autobiographical performance has many points of
potential reference, including an "ethics of remembering," or an

ethical obligation to "history," to people who were there and the events that took place; or even an ethical responsibility, on the part of the spectator, to perform as a reliable witness and listen well and then to deliberate action. My concern here, however, is to think about the question of, or problem posed by, ethics in the relations between, and representations of, self and other.

The "self" is always relational. It is not only a historical and cultural construct but is imbued with, and indeed is inseparable from, others. Such inseparability does not refer only to the psychoanalytic understanding of the self as being dependent, structurally, on the other, but rather points also to more material connections between subjects. Our actions and experiences are never isolated; our stories are intertwined. As Nancy K. Miller asks, can autobiography ever be a story "separate from the significant others—parents, lovers—with whom we continually make and remake ourselves?" (2000 (1996): 123).[3] The question that I want to ask here is whether this unavoidable relationality of selves brings with it, for the autobiographical performer, a burden of responsibility? I am prompted in this exploration by Paul John Eakin's confident insistence that "Because our own lives never stand free of the lives of others, we are faced with our responsibility to those others whenever we write [perform] about ourselves. There is no escaping this responsibility" (1999: 159). What might such a "responsibility" mean in the field of autobiographical performance? This article engages with the question of responsibility by turning first to "verbatim theatre," a form explicitly dependent on re-presenting others' stories. Whilst recognising the political potential of verbatim drama to give theatrical space to untold stories, processes of verbatim practice and its various outcomes also allow me to identify some of the ethical difficulties that adhere to telling others' stories (and therefore telling other's selves, since our selves are inseparable from the stories told of/by them). The power implicit to "storying" another is then discussed in relation to Lisa Kron's latest auto/biographical work, *Well*, a performance that not only tells stories of Kron and her mother but which engages self-reflexively with the ethics of its own practice. Kron's ethical practice, I argue, lies in her strategically explicit articulation that, in the end (and, indeed, at the outset), it is not the other that is represented, but the self (the author/performer). This "absenting" of the other is unavoidable in acts of re-presentation—but rather than denying it, there is value to be found in admitting that the other is not, cannot be framed.[4]

In what follows, I intend to propose neither a moral theory nor ethical principles that then prescribe an ethical model of autobiographical performance. I come to the question of ethics not as a moral philosopher, but as a practitioner and spectator, and the questions I ask here have announced themselves in the auditorium and in the practice studio where I have experienced ethical challenges. My application of the term "ethics" is anchored within this lived space, and not in the realm of abstraction. Nevertheless, I do want to take seriously Eakin's insistence on "responsibility" in order to consider the ethical dilemmas that arise in the unavoidable practice of representing others when performing autobiography, or more accurately, performing auto/biography.

Though G. Thomas Couser's monograph, *Vulnerable Subjects: Ethics and Life Writing* (2004) refers exclusively to written texts, the series of questions he poses translate into the performance realm and are worth quoting at some length:

> Where does the right to express and represent oneself begin to infringe on another's right to privacy? How shall the desires of the self be weighed against the demands of another, concern for aesthetics with concerns for ethics? Is it necessary, or at least desirable, to obtain consent or permission from those to be represented? [...] Are autobiographers obliged to 'do good' —or at least to do no harm—to those they represent? Can harm to minor characters in one's autobiography be dismissed as unavoidable and trivial? If life writing necessarily involves violating the privacy of others and possibly harming them, what values might offset such ethical liabilities? Further, since published life writing is, after all, a commodity—in today's market, often a valuable one—is it necessary, or at least desirable, to share any proceeds with one's subject? What constitutes appropriation or even expropriation of someone else's story? (2004: x-xi)

The ethical models that Couser presses into service here are utilitarianism, where individual desires are set beside a concept of social (that is majority) "good;" and Kantian-based libertarianism, where individuals exist as ends-in-themselves and rationally perceive others as equal ends-in-themselves (rather than "means"). Whilst these dominant models have increasingly come under criticism from many feminist moral philosophers, they undoubtedly continue to hold considerable sway in general debates concerning ethical practice, and are still used to "weigh-up" choices.

VERBATIM THEATRE

In thinking about ethics in the field of auto/biographical performance, a useful starting point has been the debates around and practices of "verbatim theatre."[5] The term, first published by Derek Paget in 1987, refers to a form of theatre which places interviews with people at the heart of its process and product, since such interviews provide a foundation from which a script is developed that is then performed by actors. The term auto/biographical is entirely apt here since the words spoken are taken from people's reflections on events connected with their own lives (their *auto*biographies, then), whilst the representation of these by writers/actors casts the process as *bio*graphical. Moreover, in some examples of verbatim theatre the performers also incorporate elements of their own lives into the production, employing a self-reflexive mode.

Practiced in the UK since the 1970s, the past decade has seen a remarkable increase in—or at least public recognition of—performances that might also be called performances of solicitation and/or appropriation. Britain has recently experienced a flurry of highly visible verbatim performances, including works by Tricycle Theatre, Out of Joint, 7:84 Theatre Company, and Liverpool Everyman.[6] Though there are wide variations in terms of form and practices, a point made forcefully by playwright David Hare who reminds us that we would be "silly" to think that the performances had "a single, common character" (2005: 112), I would, nevertheless, argue that many productions do share a dramaturgical structure. Typically, they create a collage that enables multiple points of view, represented through multiple voices, but anchor this to a single or central storyline or thematic, offered up "for social deliberation" in an "alternate public sphere", thereby creating a "theater of public dialogue" (Jackson 2005: 52). Though these voices remain those of individuals, in many examples such a structure allows the spectator to "shift their discursive conceptions of the subject from the single protagonist to the greater community" (Claycomb 2003: 95). Verbatim plays, whilst consciously nodding towards a mode of realism, place people and their spoken thoughts side by side in order to imagine or stage conversations that have not yet happened. In this sense, we might consider them aspirational and even inspirational. As Della Pollock writes, these performances offer "less an alternative recording of the past than an ethical imaginary of a future" (2005: 7). Her use of the word "ethical" is to be noted here.

Hare describes verbatim drama as giving "a voice to the voiceless," and this seems to be a recurring rhetorical trope used in relation to the form, often coupled with an associated duty (for writers/performers—and arguably spectators) to "listen." The programme note to Liverpool Everyman's *Unprotected* (2006) is typical when it explains that "Verbatim Theatre enabled us to go to the heart of the issue, giving a voice to those most involved with and affected by street sex work" (Wilson *et al.* 2006). Both Hare and writer Rony Robinson actually align verbatim drama with a practice of democracy (Hare 2005: 112; Paget 1987: 317). Given that verbatim dramas often represent untold stories, this positioning is understandable; it also implicitly signals the fact that theatre is not usually the site for these stories (the marginalised), and the verbatim model might therefore itself be perceived as a democratising force within the theatre industry. Practitioners solicit the unsolicited, giving those unheard voices a public place, and perhaps then rewriting the dominant narratives in the process (narratives of history, social justice, community).[7]

Recognising the political motivation behind much verbatim work, we might nevertheless want to ask whose voice is spoken in verbatim productions and with what other potential effects? The typical process of creating verbatim dramas causes me to think that Hare's formulation might more accurately be phrased as "voicing the voiceless," since talking out is replaced in this act of ventriloquism by talking for or talking about. Linda Alcoff's insights resonate here: "Who is speaking, who is spoken of, and who listens is a result, as well as an act, of political struggle" (1991-2: 15). Exploring the politics of process, I want to engage a little more with the practices and implications of performances considered "verbatim" in an attempt to get under the rhetorical clichés of empowerment and liberation. Here, again, I am guided by Alcoff who recognises that "the problematic of speaking for has at its center a concern with accountability and responsibility" (16). When we take up the voice of someone else and inhabit their life-story, where does our responsibility lie? To the "owner" of the story? To the "story" that was passed to us (often with trust)? To the wider "act" in which we are involved? To our "art"? Such questions—their multiplicity—

render the "problem" or challenge of ethical practice in the field of auto/biographical performance transparent.

CONSTRUCTING THE OTHER

The practical methodology of verbatim performance, though it might vary in detail, generally includes the conducting of interviews by performers, which are often recorded. These are then used as the basis of the performed script (sometimes composed by a playwright and/or dramaturges), with performers taking on the words of the interviewees, and often key physical characteristics or what might be thought of as *gestus*. The process of interviewing is not at all accidental. Rony Robinson, for example, admits to Derek Paget that his "samples" were far from random. Reflecting on one interviewed subject, he reveals that he "actually knew of her and interviewed her. Because I wanted [...] that kind of voice" (Paget 1987: 324). Anna Deveare Smith similarly searches for specific kinds of people to interview (Martin 1993: 46). Undoubtedly, such selection is motivated by political agendas (in Smith's case, the desire to represent an often racially charged event from different perspectives). This might nevertheless be considered problematic because the use of the term "verbatim" serves to align it with some notion of the "authentic" and "truthful." [8] "Verbatim," and indeed "documentary," or even "autobiography," operate as signifiers that propose a relationship of veracity to the supposed facts and it is this relationship to "truth" that makes these performances so potentially powerful.

In addition to sourcing and selecting interviewees, verbatim practitioners also construct the questions that are then posed, thereby prompting certain answers. Finally, more people are interviewed than can possibly be included in a single performance. For *Unprotected*, 1000 pages of transcripts were transformed into a sixty page script. Having decided who to interview, then, the practitioner also decides which interviewees to represent. Some characters, producing what are considered "key interviews," are given "starring roles" in the productions and the burden of becoming in some way representative of an event, a perspective, a place or an issue, whilst others become mere one-dimensional "soundbites" (see Baglia and Foster 2005; Paget 1987). Still others, however, remain invisible, having been cut from the script. In such instances, then, these real people are doubly "voiceless," having been initially courted, but then passed over in

favour of other voices who are given time in the spotlight. This
reiteration of invisibility might be considered less than empowering.
As James Thompson insists, theatre practitioners who solicit stories
are witnesses to those stories; which then begs the question of
whether, "by asking to hear, must we retell?" (2005: 25).

Verbatim plays do not, typically, provide us with the contextual
information of the interviewing process itself; speech is lifted out of
context and used within a different context. Feminists have long
insisted, particularly within the realm of ethnographic and oral history,
that interviews and what they reveal must be treated with caution; as
Joan Sangster advises, "interviews must be carefully contextualised,
with attention to who is speaking, what their personal and social
agenda is, and what kind of event they are describing" (1998: 88).
Where they are speaking, when and to whom is also surely significant;
as is the act of listening. These are the "conditions of speaking"
(Alcoff and Gray 1993). As the interviewer is most often invisible in
the subsequently represented interview, we are not able to witness the
extent to which the speech statements are jointly authored, the
creation of a collaborative or interactive process (Sangster 1998: 94)
rather than unprompted and unmediated reflections. Where an address
to the interviewer is included within the performed text, this seems
only to increase the appeal to "veracity" rather than provide any actual
contextual information regarding the interviewing process and the
dynamics that structured it or indeed the process by which the
recorded interview was subsequently edited and restructured. In David
Hare's *The Permanent Way*, "David" is mentioned frequently, as in
this extract that we presume is from an interview with the Vicar of
Hatfield:

> David, I would like to see a drama of people who make things work. If
> Hatfield is in a play, I'd like it to be mentioned as a town of determined
> people. The town will regenerate and rebuild and rise up out of all this. (2003:
> 59)

"David" might be referenced, but as I recollect, we never actually see
him in the production; he is always out of view, a silent participant,
which diminishes any sense of him as a "controlling" presence in the
interview (or indeed in the play—he is actually credited as the
playwright). Rather, we might be inclined to think David is simply
recording and then reporting what he heard. In fact, as Hare states in

interview with British academic Richard Boon, while some of the speeches are reported directly as spoken, others are penned by Hare based on what he thinks "the person wanted" but failed to say. Hare admits bluntly that "The illusion is that I'm not present, but it's an illusion. I work like an artist, not like a journalist."[9]

Tectonic Theater Project's *The Laramie Project* (2000) does draw attention to the making process since the opening lines, spoken by a "narrator," inform us that

> On November 14, 1998, the members of Tectonic Theater Project travelled to Laramie, Wyoming, and conducted interviews with the people of the town. During the next year, we would return to Laramie several times and conduct over two hundred interviews. The play you are about to see is edited from those interviews, as well as from journal entries by members of the company and other found texts. (Kaufman *et al.* 2001: 5)

Such meta-theatrical gestures are now common in verbatim plays. *Unprotected* contains a similar moment at its opening, when Andy, an outreach worker speaking to a client, references some people in the drop-in centre (who are not represented by actors on the stage): "Have you heard about the project that these're doing? [...] They're doing a project about managed zones." Ali, a sex worker, asks him what happens, to which he replies: "Well they're gonna get actors and actresses to portray your words" (Wilson *et al.* 2006: 2). Ali then asks the invisible writers

> My face isn't gonna be on that is it? It's just using the voices, isn't it? Okay. That's cool. Alright. Cool. Cool.

We hear Ali give her consent.

The inclusion of such direct references to the process appears to make the mechanisms of that process more transparent. However, even in such examples we are rarely told or shown *how* or with what agenda the play is made, nor are the interviewing conditions ever made transparent. At the risk of dealing a no-win hand to verbatim practitioners, I share Ryan Claycomb's sense that these rhetorical appeals to "fairness" serve to further mask the playwrights' power (2003: 112). Meta-theatricality does not lessen the appearance that stories are simply being told and simply being "caught." As Julia Baglia and Elissa Foster conclude, "the audience is enticed to 'forget' that this play is constructed as an artistic representation" (2005: 134-5).

While some productions, such as *The Permanent Way,* do acknowledge the playwright's power in relation to representation, the actual mechanisms of that power, its deployment in the creative act, remain veiled. For Couser, "when mediation is ignored, the resulting text may be (mis)taken for a transparent lens through which we have direct access to its subject (rather than to its author)" (2004: 38). This, to me, is a key observation. Rather than showing their processes of creativity, the choices made and the reasons why, verbatim dramas, like other auto/biographical modes, more typically strategically deploy their closeness to the signifiers of "truth" and "authenticity." Particular devices are employed for rhetorical, persuasive effect, such as the use of the actual recorded interviews, or the projection of video recordings or photographs of the interviewed subjects.

Taking a moment to consider more fully the incorporation of such texts, the complexity of ethical practice in the field of theatre is made clear; arguably, intercutting the "real" with the "theatrically re-presented" *does* potentially serve to make transparent that what we are witnessing *is* a theatrical representation. The difference between the enacted voice and the recorded voice is undeniable. Second, by placing this actual recorded voice within the theatrical scene, that voice *is* given a literal place and is not being appropriated. Third, bringing the "real" onto the stage serves as a powerful reminder that outside the theatre the real world, in all its inequality and violence, continues unabated. In *Unprotected*, for example, near the end of the performance we learn that Anne Marie Foy has been murdered. We then hear the actual recorded interview of her:

> You're never safe. Ye know out there, ye—it's it's—it is—like every car you
> get into ye don't know whether ye gonna get out of it. It's it's dangerous all
> the time, ye don't realise how dangerous. And me of all people do realise 'cos
> I have been in situations where I've nearly died. (Wilson *et al.* 2006: 67)

Hearing Foy's voice, having just learnt of her death, is shocking, particularly given her prophetic vision. This appeal to the real is precisely the powerful potential of auto/biographical performance; but such close proximity to the real also encourages a realist mode of representation (including the recordings, videos and photographs) which risks masking mediation and construction. Though the real voice may be heard, or the real photo projected, the image may nevertheless be the *playwright's* (and surely the fact that these plays carry playwrights' signatures is clear evidence of this). Also, what agency does Anne Marie Foy have here? Is she used, even in death, for emotional effect and impact?

Not only are subjects (people and topics) selected from the range available, but those interviews that are used are subsequently subjected to further editing since interviews are rarely replayed in their entirety. Alecky Blythe, artistic director of Recorded Delivery, informs us that it is during the edit that she tries to "distil the characters and the key moments for dramatic effect. This is where you can control the story by being selective over what parts of the interview to present" (2005: 103). Blythe is, of course, right since this is, after all, *theatre*, not a moment of reality. Derek Paget, like David Hare, is blunt in his recognition of what takes precedence in the process of creating docudrama: "the end in view in a verbatim show is very different from a sociological survey, since an awareness of *theatricality* is ultimately informing the whole operation" (1987: 324).

That the people represented in verbatim dramas are theatrical constructions, characters rather than "real" people, is probably accepted by the majority of spectators. In most performances, alongside rhetorical appeals to "truth," there are also clear signals of the "play" that is involved. The impressive ensemble work that opens *The Permanent Way*, for example, signals clearly that this a creative (and collaborative) endeavour. The construction of a train setting, produced entirely from the physical movements conducted in unison by the cast, and the various tableaux created, places theatricality at the centre of the experience. Perhaps, then, my anxiety regarding the representation of others fails to do justice to either the spectators or the complex modes of address in operation in the actual performances.

Perhaps, also, my concern with ethics is naïve and misplaced since it assumes the existence of some "original" or "authentic" self that can be enacted, remaining "truthful" to the "source." In reality, the "self" is a historical, cultural and social construct. However, as Linda Alcoff recognises, whilst the self *is* a construction, every act of representing an other participates in that construction and as such extends beyond the theatrical frame, having a potential impact on the represented subject (1991-2: 9-10). Richard Kearney importantly reminds us of this when he insists that, "if at the epistemological level it is often extremely difficult to establish clear referential relations between narrative and world, this does not mean, especially from an ethical point of view, that there is no distinction whatsoever" (1999: 21). Laramie resident Harry Woods admitted to Amy Tigner that he found the experience of witnessing "himself" on stage "troublesome" since it reduced the complexity of his real life and his multiple subjectivity into a distilled extract, fixed in time (2002: 152). Harry, the real person, is inevitably reduced to a character in a play, with a limited number of thoughts, existing in one defined moment. The flux of life is erased. While *The Laramie Project* does attempt to represent the shifts that some people experienced over the eighteen-month period of its making, living subjects are, nevertheless, turned into stage characters, destined to repeat the same lines over and over every time the play is staged.[10]

An awareness of responsibility, often linked to notions of trust, does not go unmarked by practitioners of verbatim theatre. As Hare reflects, "with this particular material, there is a clear moral obligation which is quite complex, particularly when you're dealing with the suffering that people have been through."[11] In the programme for *Unprotected* we read that "With the trust that was developing between writers and sources, many of whom were sharing intimate and sometimes harrowing stories for the first time, came a grave sense of responsibility" (Wilson *et al.* 2006). In many examples "responsibility" seems to be linked to unproblematic notions of truth. In *The Laramie Project*, only one interview is repeated throughout the production, thereby offering itself up as a guiding *leitmotif*.

> Father Schmit: And I will speak with you, I will trust that if you write a play of this, that you say it right. You need to do your best to say it correct. (Kaufman 2001: 101)

Given the polyvocality of the "community" that is Laramie, and the varying perspectives and opinions offered by its residents, what would constitute saying it correctly or saying it right? To whom is one responsible or accountable? To the people interviewed? To the murdered Matthew Shephard? To his parents, who repeatedly, throughout the play/in real life, make a plea to the media to respect their privacy? To the bare facts (as if these could be known)? To the past (as if this could be fixed)? To the people involved in the event? Must one behave with equal responsibility to all the people of this story, including the two young men who murdered Shephard? Or is the company responsible to a wider community—of gay men and lesbians? Or to the wider historical moment in the USA—in which case Laramie and its inhabitants might matter less than this greater objective? Is it possible to be responsible to all these different needs?

In the majority of verbatim dramas, the performers are located as "outsiders," which seems to translate into being able to take a different, and arguably more distanced, objective perspective on an event (see also Dolan 2005). In Rony Robinson's words, the verbatim play is able to deliver the event "back with a bit of *light* on it to the people who have experienced it" (in Paget 1987: 317). Amy Tigner, who has connections with the city of Laramie, makes a similar claim for *The Laramie Project*, arguing that the production "had become a mirror in which the town people could view itself and could be used as a tool for Laramie to alter the way townspeople thought" (2002: 153). The dramaturgy of the play enabled "a community to talk to itself" (Kelley, in Fousekis 2005: 181), or at least to do so in the world of the play. The effect of this rhetoric of "light" and "visibility" is that it suggests that something already exists (albeit in the dark) and is simply waiting to be found. What all of this denies is that any so-called "reflection" is a creative construction and that what is reflected or made visible is the practitioners' perspective. Alcoff warns that often the act of speaking for another is "born of a desire for mastery, to privilege oneself as the one who more correctly understands the truth about another's situation or one who can champion a just cause and thus achieve glory and praise" (1991-2: 29). Inscribed in verbatim dramas are claims of gratitude. As a "Bereaved Mother" in *The Permanent Way* states:

> I'm grateful to you. You've let me come in and talk about something serious. I don't want to be gobby. I don't want to go on being gobby for the rest of my life. (Hare 2003: 38)

Always remaining off-stage, so to speak, are the potential "gains" and benefits to be had for companies (rather than participants) who devise such projects.

None of this is intended to deny that the stories told in verbatim dramas have social significance and are politically timely; rather, it is to question the location and structural condition of that telling and to challenge the assumptions that are generated through rhetorical gestures, in relation to whose story is being performed.

PERFORMANCE RIGHTS

If every self is necessarily relational then appeals to "autonomy," or the "rights" of individuals, such as I am proposing above, are surely problematic? To take just one example, while Couser might ask, "to what extent [...] is our freedom to narrate our own lives restricted by the rights of others to privacy?" (2004: 7), Eakin might respond that a relational model of identity "makes it more difficult to demarcate the boundaries of self upon which a privacy-based ethics can be founded" (1999: 160). Recognising that "autonomy" (alongside the disembodied subject of philosophy) is a problematic concept, some feminist philosophers now place stress on relationships of interdependence and contexts, or an "ethics of care," also arguing that understanding morality as codifiable is misguided (see Gilligan 1982; Walker 1998). Margaret Walker, for example, criticises the juridical-theoretical model for its inability to recognise particular bonds, histories, and expectations that exist between people (1998: 51); universal moral codes leave no space for the specific. Walker reminds us that:

> Ours is a society pervasively segmented and stratified by gender, class, race, age, education, professionalization, sexual practice, and other hierarchies of power and status. [...] Differently situated people may face different moral problems or experience similar ones differently. They will have reasonably different understandings of costs, risks, and relevance. They will see different responses realistically open to them in responding to these problems, and find different ways of resolving them to be successful or sane. They may well grasp their responsibilities as different in scope, content, kind, or stringency from those of others differently placed and experienced. (Walker 1998: 50)

Whilst we might be tempted to regard Walker's proposed ethical stance as being dangerously relativist, in fact we need to recognise her sensitivity to contextual determinants. It is not, then, that "anything goes," but that each situation is located within a matrix of determining conditions, and that each of these conditions makes a decision more or less likely to be ethical. This is the distinction, then, between "indeterminate" and "undecidable." Derrida clarifies,

Undecidability is the competition between two determined possibilities or options, two determined duties. There is no indeterminacy at all [...]. When I say that there is nothing outside the text, I mean there is nothing outside the context, everything is determined. (1999: 79)

Feminist philosopher Diane Elam, embracing the concept of undecidability within the field of ethics and ethical activism, similarly insists that we look for "the rule that may do justice to the case," rather than simply applying pre-existing rules. For Elam, "we must judge where we are, in our pragmatic context, and no transcendental alibi will save us" (1994: 108). Operating in the domain of the undecidable, a decision has to be made each and every time. To apply accepted knowledge is, on the contrary, a refusal to accept ethical responsibility since no decision is required. As Derrida writes, "if we knew what to do, if I knew in terms of knowledge what I have to do before the decision, then the decision would not be a decision" (1999: 66). Whilst every decision must of course be grounded in and informed by knowledge, "the moment I take a decision it is a leap, I enter a heterogeneous space and that is the condition of responsibility" (73). Taking responsibility means to make a decision, and to make it every time.

Cognisant of the importance of context, in place of the juridical-theoretical model Walker instead proposes an "expressive-collaborative" model, placing at its centre the practice of negotiation between people in deciding appropriate ethical behaviour. For Walker, "determining responsibilities in the concrete usually involves grasping histories of trust, expectation, and agreement that make particular relationships morally demanding in particular ways" (1998: 69). Surveying auto/biographies, Couser similarly constructs something of a moral continuum when he concludes that in "intimate life writing—that done within families or couples, close relationships," the degree of vulnerability between people is greater and therefore the "ethical stakes" are higher (2004: xii). A sense of betrayal is, perhaps, also greater, given that trust is a key component of most intimate relationships and it is within such relationships that one can arguably become most exposed and therefore "known" (see Baier 1994). In the remainder of this article, I want to explore a performance that negotiates this "betrayal," Lisa Kron's *Well*.

NEGOTIATING BETRAYAL

Lisa Kron's auto/biographical show, *Well,* premiered in 2004. Kron, a lesbian performer from the USA, has had a long career of making auto/biographical performances. The play that preceded *Well*, *2.5 Minute Ride*, a solo show written and performed by Kron, was first presented in 1996, but in fact Kron continues to perform it to this day. *2.5 Minute Ride* recounts the story of Kron and her father visiting Auschwitz together. Kron's father is a Holocaust survivor, a child of the kindertransport system. His parents, however, did not survive the Holocaust. In between the story of this return, Kron also weaves stories about her family's annual trip to a tacky theme park. The entire performance is both humorous and painful, switching emotional register and pace suddenly. Experiencing the show is akin to being on a roller-coaster—hence the production's title.

If Kron's father was a key reference point in *2.5 Minute* Ride, in *Well*, her mother takes on that role. Notably, where *2.5 Minute Ride* was a solo show, *Well* represents many characters, performed by actors (including, in its première, Kron, who plays "Lisa").[12] Though *Well* is not, as Kron herself says at the start of the production, about her or her mother, or indeed about their relationship, it is also not *not* about them; or rather, it is about them, but not simply nor singularly. The storyline of *Well* addresses the fact that both Kron and her mother, Ann, have experienced ill health related to allergies; however, where Kron got well again, her mother never did. At the heart of the play lie questions significant to this general discussion of ethics: how to experience or practice empathy without judgement or appropriation. In the play, one of the performers/characters advises Kron to stop "trying to make sense of her [mother] through your experience" and instead to "try just listening to her directly."

In order to write *Well*, Kron did, in fact, interview her mother about certain events, and according to Kron, a lot of the words in *Well* are her mother's (Kron 2004). Throughout the writing process, Kron would have frequent discussions with her mother about the play, giving her drafts of the text to read. Kron admits to having to confront her mother's terror in order to reassure her that the portrayal would not be negative. She also had to remind her mother that she was not the "Lisa" represented in the play (who is distinctly lacking in empathy) but was, in fact, the whole play (Kron 2004)—a point I will return to shortly.

Whilst we do not know Kron's particular history with her mother, we do know that she has been making solo, autobiographical work for many years and that *Well* is not a new or surprising departure. Moreover, *Well* follows on from *2.5 Minute Ride* and within this familial, historical trajectory might then be perceived as a balancing of eulogies rather than an act of appropriation or exploitation. While Ann Kron was reportedly "terrorized" by the process of producing *Well* (Kron 2004), is it possible that she would have felt under- or unvalued if her daughter had chosen only to pay tribute to her father? Thinking of Gilligan's "ethics of care," perhaps *Well* might be thought of precisely as a performance of Kron's responsibility to her mother, a responsibility of recognition discharged in the collecting of her mother's personal history. Whether it is appropriate for this history then to be made public of course begs another question. But there is no doubt that the making of this work would entail very specific collaboration with her mother, revolving around discussion and negotiation. Sensitive to hers and her mother's shared history but also to their shared future, the narrative of which was in some senses being written during the process of playmaking, Kron would have had to decide what was appropriate within this context. We might imagine that such an embedded relationship would make it impossible to ignore questions of responsibilities. While we must not forget the wider cultural-structural daughter/mother relationship that presses its own demands and expectations into service, *Well* addresses such relations and their negotiation explicitly, making it impossible for us to forget the power and privilege that enables one person to "story" another.

"STORYING" THE OTHER

Just as the disembodied subject of philosophy has been critiqued, so has the conception of the "self," a critique with wide ramifications for the practice of autobiography since autobiography has traditionally been understood as an unearthing or revealing of the deep, singular (and typically internal or hidden) self. Ethical appeals to "tell the truth," or to "say it correct," are appeals to this knowable, fixed subject; and such a subject, the "I," speaks with authority. This is, indeed, the power and appeal (and also danger) of autobiographical performance. Yet such a "self"—the individual, autonomous subject—is, as we have noted, itself a discursive and historical construct. In place of the singular self, there is a multiplicity of shifting selves—a multiplicity that can be harnessed and represented in performance since here there are always, at least, two subjects on view: the subject spoken and the speaking subject. We might think of this as an autobiographical "doubling." Gerry Harris's quote about British performer, Bobby Baker, is one that resonates helpfully here:

> Baker performs a subjectivity which is at the same time not Bobby Baker and not not Bobby Baker, both a hyperbolic, theatrical character and the 'real thing,' an ideological construct and a situated historical object, both entirely socially constructed and unique. (1999:137)

For Harris, this "doubled" positioning results in a "hiatus in iterability" which produces a moment and space of agency for Baker. How might such doubled gestures, a "self-consciousness" which works with and against the power and authority of the speaking "I," signal in relation to the ethics of representing others? Such doubling, when explicit, might offer one way to resist the appropriation, exploitation or mis-representation of others.

A larger theme of Kron's performance, *Well*, precisely concerns the ethics of representing others in the moment of self-representation. Adopting a self-reflexive, meta-theatrical dramaturgical structure *Well* aims to show the process by which an "other" becomes subjected, appropriated, interpreted and constructed—or "storied." At the beginning of the play, the character of Kron's mother, "Ann," presses "Lisa" to admit that she is undertaking a "theatrical exploration of issues of health and illness both in an individual and in a community." Asked which individual she is using to do this, "Lisa" replies testily, "I don't know what you mean by 'using'?" and then,

> Okay. Look. It's not ABOUT either one of us. I work using autobiographical material but ultimately this is a theatrical exploration of a universal experience. So it does utilize details about you. But it's not that big of a deal. I mean, I certainly wouldn't be the first person to write a play about her mother. I'll tell you, I wish I was that original.

Ann replies that though she does not like it, she can deal with it. However, Ann thwarts Lisa's attempt to tell the auto/biographical story by continuously disrupting and disputing her facts and memories of events, as well as her perspective and conclusions. *Well* could, of course, be considered a double bluff—a clever mimicking of agency on the part of the other. In the play, Kron's mother is allowed to disrupt and rewrite the script, and, in fact, to tell her own story. Nevertheless, ultimately, this *is* still a play, written by Kron. Ann is a representation, her interruptions and disputations created by Kron, and acted by another. In this, *Well* is perhaps not so far from the verbatim dramas discussed earlier. However, that this *is* Kron's story is something we are not allowed to forget and it is in this "not being allowed to forget" that an essential difference is inscribed. I end by returning to Couser's fundamental insight: "when mediation is ignored, the resulting text may be (mis)taken for a transparent lens through which we have direct access to its subject (*rather than to its author*)" (2004: 38; emphasis mine). Mediation, the processes and powers involved in—and reasons for—mediating an other's history, is magnified rather than ignored in this production. In a key line, as Lisa admits that Ann does not "make any sense as a character," Ann—or is it the actress playing her (Jane Houdyshell)?—replies, "Well, I guess that's the problem with using someone else's real life for your play." As Sarah Lansdale Stevenson puts it in her review of the show, by the end of the performance "Kron is destabilized, questioning her very right to tell her mother's story, questioning her ability to tell the story, her reasons for telling it" (2004: 674). Ann/"Ann"/Houdyshell (and, indeed, "Lisa"/Kron), continuously shift in and out of focus, making it impossible for me to ever really know who it is that is speaking when "Ann" supposedly speaks. This is Kron's/"Lisa"'s view of Ann/"Ann"; this is Ann's view of Ann/"Ann"; this is Kron's view of Ann's view of "Ann"; this is Houdyshell's rendering of Ann/"Ann" (or of Kron's view of Ann/"Ann", or of Ann's view of "Ann"...)? I am unable to find a stable viewing point as the frames of reference keep slipping and colliding.

Importantly, at the end of the production, it is literally and undeniably the "author" that is posited centre stage. As all the actors angrily walk off, refusing to play their parts, Kron is once again the solo autobiographical performer. The actress, Houdyshell, walks off stage too, refusing to even pretend to be Lisa's mother any longer. But this exit, this refusal is, of course, also carefully scripted by Kron. Kron's mother is precisely not there in the end—and has never been there. Absent from the theatrical frame, we (spectators) cannot presume to know her; nor can we consume her. Left alone on stage, Kron (as "Lisa") is performing the part of an author blatantly in search of her characters. The "own story" is, in the end, wholly—and self-consciously—hers.

Dee: A toast then. [*All raise glasses*] To absent—and to (strategically) absenting—friends and family.

NOTES

[1] An earlier version of this article was first presented at FIRT South Africa, 2006. A longer version has been published in Deirdre Heddon, *Autobiography and Performance* (2008), although here I introduce the idea of strategically "absenting" the other.

[2] Though, if I wasn't making it up, I would ensure that my younger brother had at least given me permission to share this story (acknowledging that the granting of such permission does not, in the end, resolve the ethical problems that I am about to recount).

[3] Indeed, as G. Thomas Couser notes, parents in fact may "make" us in more ways than one, given that they "serve as informal oral biographers," providing the details of our early lives which are beyond our own access or recall (2004: 57).

[4] Though my focus here is on representing others, the act of representing the "self" is also, arguably, an act of "absenting" the self since, firstly, there is no stable self to be represented and, secondly, even if there were, there is an unavoidable gap between any self and its representation. The impossibility of representing the "other," however, has different political implications than the impossibility of representing the "self." See Heddon (2008).

[5] The genre is also popular in the USA, where it may be called theatre of testimony or documentary theatre.

[6] Tricycle Theatre's *Guantanamo: Honour Bound to Defend Freedom* (2004), has become an international success. Out of Joint has staged a number of verbatim dramas recently, including *The Permanent Way* (2003), which explored the relationship between rail privatisation and passenger safety (see Hare, (2003)) and *Talking to Terrorists* (2005) which used interviews with "terrorists" as source material (see Soans (2005)). 7:84's *Private Agenda* (2004) was created from interviews with those working in the public sector, including teachers and nurses while *Tipping Point* (2005), written to coincide with the G8 Summit in Gleneagles, explored local responses to global issues, setting these beside politicians' empty rhetoric. Liverpool Everyman's *Unprotected* (2006) was created by a team of writers from interviews with sex-workers, their "clients," the mother's of two prostitutes who had been murdered and various government and social agency workers (see Wilson *et al.*, 2006). Closely related to the verbatim drama form, and sharing a genealogy with docudrama, are "tribunal plays." Described by Chris Megson (2004) as "forensic documentary 'replays,'" their primary (and in many cases only) source materials are the transcripts of official trials or enquiries. Examples include Tricycle Theatre's *Half the Picture* (1994), a restaging of the Scott Arms-to-Iraq Inquiry, followed by *Nuremberg* (1996), *Srebrenica* (1996), and *The Colour of Justice* (1999), which re-enacted the inquiry into the police response to the death of the young black youth, Stephen Lawrence; and *Justifying War: Scenes from the Hutton Enquiry* (2003).

[7] The restorative or interventionary potential of verbatim dramas should not, though, be simply assumed. As Alisa Solomon (2002) notes in relation to *The Laramie Project*, it failed to engage with disturbing facts, including that Matthew Shepard's parents were given overall power in the prosecution, that McKinney was not found guilty of first-degree murder, and that McKinney and Henderson were served with a gagging order. Solomon reads *The Laramie Project* as (perhaps unwittingly) contributing to the swell for "victim rights" and "vengeance."

[8] I am aware that such a "snapshot" of "verbatim drama" is, itself, unethical in that, as warned by David Hare, it fails to recognise or do justice to the specificities of different practices, in terms of aims, processes and outcomes. Anna Deavere Smith's work, for example, in that she conducts and performs all of the interviews herself, is far removed from *The Laramie Project* or *Unprotected*. My thanks to EJ Westlake for reminding me of this. My critical engagement with ethical practice in this field is also not predicated on any empirical study of what, precisely, practitioners do in terms of soliciting consent from interviewees, agreeing rights, terms and conditions, etc.

[9] David Hare in interview with Richard Boon, Cottesloe Theatre, 27 January 2004; <http://www.nationalthatre.org.uk/> [accessed 15 March 2007]. Hare's blunt statement here signals yet again the danger of collapsing practices into one broad category. The single term "verbatim" fails to capture the diversity of approaches.

[10] The fact that a play text is often published means that anyone (if they attain the rights) can mount it. When interviewees give their consent to allow their words to be used, do they realise what they are consenting to, in the long term? The play script of *The Laramie Project*, like any other script, is open to any interpretation that companies want to make of it. How does this sit with the much-circulated statement by practitioners that they must "honour" the people they interview? Watching a performance of *The Laramie Project*, produced by Fitchburg State College (Edinburgh Fringe, 2006), was something of a surreal experience. In the "original," the performers acted not only those they interviewed, but also represented themselves, sharing reflections from their journal entries. When they enacted residents from Laramie, they would also be drawing on the primary experience of having interviewed those people. In the Fitchburg State College production, the performers have no direct connection with the interviewees. There is also a "trippling" effect here, as they play the original performers playing those who were interviewed. Perhaps such restagings as this one are in fact *less* ethically problematic in that their distance from any supposed or rhetorical "real" is, from the outset, much greater?

[11] David Hare in interview with Richard Boon, Cottesloe Theatre, 27 January 2004; <http://www.nationalthatre.org.uk/> [accessed 15 March 2007].

[12] *Well* was produced in London in 2007/8, with an entirely new cast. The character of "Lisa" was also played by another performer, not Kron. Having not seen this restaged production, I do not know what impact such recasting might have on the discussion that follows.

REFERENCES

Alcoff, Linda. (1991-2) "The Problem of Speaking for Others." *Cultural Critique* 20, 5-32.

Alcoff, Linda and Laura Gray. (1993) "Survivor Discourse: Transgression or Recuperation?" *Signs* 18 (2), 260-290.

Baglia, Jay and Elissa Foster. (2005) "Performing the 'Really' Real: Cultural Representation, and Commodification in *The Laramie Project.*" *Journal of Dramatic Theory and Criticism* 19 (2), 127-145.

Blythe, Alecky. (2005) "[…] on verbatim theatre," in Robin Soans, *Talking to Terrorists.* London: Oberon Books Ltd., 101-103.

Claycomb, Ryan M. (2003) "(Ch)oral History: Documentary Theatre, the Communal Subject and Progressive Politics." *Journal of Dramatic Theory and Criticism* 18 (2), 95-121.

Couser, G. Thomas. (2004) *Vulnerable Subjects: Ethics and Life Writing.* Ithaca: Cornell University Press.

Derrida, Jacques. (1999) "Hospitality, Justice and Responsibility: A dialogue with Jacques Derrida," in Richard Kearney and Mark Dooley, eds. *Questioning Ethics: Contemporary Debates in Philosophy.* London: Routledge, 65-83.

Dolan, Jill. (2005) *Utopia in Performance: Finding Hope at the Theater.* Ann Arbor: University of Michigan Press.

Eakin, Paul John. (1999) *How Our Lives Become Stories: Making Selves.* Ithaca: Cornell University Press.

Elam, Diane. (1994) *Feminism and Deconstruction: Ms. En Abyme.* London: Routledge.

Fousekis, Natalie M. (2005) "Experiencing History: A Journey from Oral History to Performance," in Della Pollock, ed. *Remembering: Oral History Performance.* New York: Palgrave Macmillan, 167-186.

Gilligan, Carol. (1982) *In a Different Voice.* Cambridge, MA: Harvard University Press.

Hare, David. (2005) "[…] on factual theatre," in Robin Soans, *Talking to Terrorists.* London: Oberon Books Ltd., 111-13.

———. (2003) *The Permanent Way.* London: Faber and Faber.

Heddon, Deirdre. (2008) *Autobiography and Performance.* Basingstoke: Palgrave Macmillan.

Jackson, Shannon. (2005) "*Touchable Stories* and the Performance of Infrastructural Memory," in Della Pollock, ed. *Remembering: Oral History Performance.* New York: Palgrave Macmillan, 45-66.

Kaufman, Moisés. (2001) *The Laramie Project.* New York: Vintage Books.

Kearney, Richard. (1999) "Narrative and ethics of remembrance," in Richard Kearney and Mark Dooley, eds. *Questioning Ethics: Contemporary Debates in Philosophy.* London: Routledge, 5-11.

Kron, Lisa. (2006) *Well.* New York: Theatre Communications Group.

———. (2004) Interview with the author (14 October). New York.

———. (2001) *2.5 Minute Ride and 101 Humiliating Stories.* New York: Theatre Communications Group.

Martin, Carol. (1993) "Anna Deavere Smith: The Word Becomes You, An Interview by Carol Martin." *The Drama Review* 37. (4), 45-62.

Megson, Chris. (2004) "'Though Shall Not Be Fount Out:' Documentary Theatre as Political Intervention at the Tricycle Theatre. (1994-2003)." Unpublished paper.

Miller, Nancy K. (2000, [1996]) *Bequest and Betrayal: Memoirs of a Parent's Death*. Bloomington and Indianapolis: Indiana University Press.

Paget, Derek. (1987) "'Verbatim Theatre:' Oral History and Documentary Techniques." *New Theatre Quarterly* 3 (12), 317-336.

Pollock, Della, ed. (2005) *Remembering: Oral History Performance*. New York: Palgrave Macmillan.

Sangster, Joan. (1998) "Telling our stories: Feminist debates and the use of oral history," in Robert Perks and Alistair Thomson, eds. *The Oral History Reader*. London: Routledge, 87-106.

Smith, Anna Deavere. (1994) *Twilight Los Angeles, 1992*. New York: Anchor Books, Doubleday.

Solomon, Alisa. (2001) Irony and Deeper Significance: Where Are the Plays? *Theater* 31 (3), 2-11.

Stevenson, Sarah Lansdale. (2004) "*Well* Review." *Theatre Journal* 56 (4), 672-4.

Tigner, Amy L. (2002) "The Laramie Project: Western Pastoral." *Modern Drama* 45 (1), 138- 156.

Thompson, James. (2005) *Digging Up Stories: Applied Theatre, Performance and War*. Manchester: Manchester University Press.

Walker, Margaret. (1998) *Moral Understandings: A Feminist Study in Ethics*. London: Routledge.

Wilson, Esther, John Fay, Tony Green, and Lizzie Nunnery. (2006) *Unprotected*. London: Josef Weinberger.

PART TWO: TEXTS

READING *THE BLACKS* THROUGH THE 1956 PREFACE: POLITICS AND BETRAYAL

CARL LAVERY

It is becoming increasingly apparent that Jean Genet's small body of work dating from the mid-1950s to the early 1960s—*The Balcony*, *The Blacks* and *The Screens*—is one of the most politically astute theatres that we possess. Unlike the plays of Jean-Paul Sartre, Genet's earliest biographer, and, to a certain extent, those of Bertolt Brecht, a playwright whose work he detested, Genet's influence has grown to the point where he is now considered, by some, as the most politically sophisticated dramatist of his generation.[1] According to the French writer Marie Redonnet, for instance, "Genet is very much our contemporary. He's the only one who saw with lucidity what the new face of the enemy would look like" (2000: 156).[2] Redonnet is not alone in her claims. In a recent article, the theatre theorist Rustom Bharucha argues that the geo-political tensions produced by 11 September 2001 have finally disclosed the profound political significance of Genet's theatre:

> [...] to process [Genet's] radical insights into our own practice today [...] we have to find the courage to betray him imaginatively, not to disprove his politics and reject its anarchist affinities, but rather to test these affinities within the interruptions of the 'real' in the global terror of our times. Genet challenges us to spell out our politics in relation to where he stands. (2003: 24)

Redonnet's and Bharucha's observations are ostensibly based on three aspects of Genet's theatre. First, its critique of the conservativism inherent in national-liberation movements in Africa and the Arab world in the 1950s and 1960s; second, its suspicions about the effectiveness of committed art; and third, its preference for raising uncomfortable questions rather than providing simple solutions. This last point is particularly important to Bharucha. According to him, the political potential of Genet's theatre is found in its anarchic refusal to side with any form of established social order. By breaking with the "false sentimentality" of community, Genet, claims Bharucha, "articulate[s] a new risk-taking in performance" and allows spectators to "open [themselves] to new alliances that challenge the comfort of old solidarities" (27). In this way, he offers, Bharucha believes, the possibility of transcending the "terror of the times" which is increasingly based on essentialized notions of collective identity.

While there is much to admire in the readings of Bharucha and Redonnet, it is strange that they should refuse to negotiate with Genet's difficult (and, at times, contradictory) theory of political performance.[3] Although Bharucha and Redonnet would surely respond that Genet's personal endorsement does not harm the validity of their insights, their silence is problematic. Not only does their attempt to 'read against the grain' overlook Genet's sophisticated brand of political theatre, but it leaves the field open for right-wing critics who, for the lack of any evidence to the contrary, continue to argue that his drama is nihilistic, fascistic and anti-Semitic.[4] As a way, then, of basing the study of Genet's politics of theatre on solid foundations, it seems important to return to empirical sources.[5] The 1956 "Preface to *The Blacks*" has an absolutely vital role to play in this project. For, as Michel Corvin points out, this text is "absolutely unique in [Genet's] critical writing because of its length, seriousness, rigour, and the clarity and lucidity with which he reflects on his own political engagement" (2002: 1329).

To a certain extent, the failure of critics to cite the 1956 "Preface to *The Blacks*" is understandable,[6] for although the text was written between 1955 and 1956, it did not appear in full-length form until 2002 when it was finally published in Michel Corvin's and Albert Dichy's edited volume *Jean Genet: Théâtre complet*.[7] Despite its obscurity, "The Preface to *The Blacks*" nevertheless provides privileged access to Genet's unorthodox model of political theatre. For Genet, the notion of political theatre was neither straightforward nor self-evident. To be effective, political art needed to find a way of catching the audience off-guard. As was so often the case in Genet's work and life, betrayal was his favoured technique for subverting expectations.[8] For the rest of this essay, I will endeavour to explore how, in the "Preface to *The Blacks*," betrayal transcends its usual negative sense and exists as a positive and progressive principle. Or, to express this differently: betrayal is what allows us to approach what, for me, is the defining feature of Genet's concept of political performance as it relates to *The Blacks*: the attempt to combine a concern for alterity (respecting the otherness of the other) with a desire for concrete action in performance.

In the "Preface to *The Blacks*," Genet is sensitive to—perhaps even obsessed by—issues of representation. Discussing the background to *The Blacks*, he is at pains to point out that it was not his idea to write a play about black experience: he was commissioned to do it:

> Towards the end of last December [1954], Raymond Rouleau told me that he wanted to create a black acting company. I didn't know what his motives were. To tell the truth [...] I thought he wanted to exploit the actors, seeing them primarily as a novelty act for European audiences. When he asked me to write a play for the company, I accepted [...] "Yes," I said to myself, "the Blacks will go on stage. But I'll organize a spectacle that will be a trap for the spectators." (2002: 836)

Reflecting on the process behind the work, Genet explains that the eventual "point of departure" for his play was provided by an eighteenth-century "musical box," on which four "negro valets were bowing in front of a small, white porcelain princess" (839). The mention of the word "valet" is vital in this context: it establishes an immediate and intimate relationship between black identity and performance. According to Genet, it is impossible to write a naturalistic play for black actors in the West, since, he argues, black experience in a colonized society is inherently theatricalized. In a language that owes much to the existential vocabulary used by early anti-colonial thinkers such as Frantz Fanon and Albert Memmi, Genet claims that the colonized subject is forced to adopt an identity which s/he has not forged herself/himself. In other words, the colonized Black is, and can only ever be, a performer, an actor who, in order to survive, has to identify with a pre-established set of characteristics and stereotypical roles: "I'm not saying that Blacks are natural actors; on the contrary, they become actors as soon as they encounter the white gaze. They will remain actors as long as we, the white spectators, observe them before seeing them and think about them in terms of [stereotypical] categories" (840).

Genet's response to the ontological predicament confronting the black subject is to write a play that deliberately betrays the living reality of black experience by presenting it as it appears in white culture: that is to say, as something fake, performative and clichéd. According to Genet, the fact that he is constrained to write in French, the language of domination and oppression, disqualifies any authentic representation of black identity. In French, as in English, the meaning of blackness has been decided upon in advance. Discourse has colonized experience:

> The figures that surge out of this language, can they be anything other than the onstage projections of phantoms in whose ghostly image I wanted to transform real Blacks? This play is written in a bourgeois world. It indicates what that world has obtained from a race that has been put in contact with it. (841)

From this perspective, Genet's betrayal of his black collaborators in the play is not an expression of some deep-seated nihilism on his part; on the contrary, it is an attempt to protect the alterity or otherness of black experience, a quest to negate the negation of a racist world. Importantly, though, the extreme "cruelty" of *The Blacks* is intended to work dialectically: "Let's not speak too badly of evil, or rather cruelty [...] for, more effectively than a well-meaning intention, it can be at the origin of a generous work of art" (843).

Genet's interest in what we might call a "betrayal of betrayal" is caused by his vociferous rejection of liberal theories of artistic commitment which, he claims, let white society off the hook. In Genet's view, political art that celebrates black experience in a colonized society misses the point. Instead of accusing the oppressor and/or "inciting" the oppressed to "actively revolt" (837), it merely shows that racism has not altered the life-affirming joy of the black population, and thus was not so bad after all. This line of thinking accounts for Genet's angry attack in the "Preface to *The Blacks*" on Katherine Dunham's Afro-Cuban ballets of the 1950s, which, for him, are decidedly disingenuous and hypocritical:

> Where did [Dunham get her Blacks]? Whose ambassadors were they? What sovereign empire did they represent? Pale, discoloured, they emanated from an unearthly and unreal world, a world without roots, without suffering, without tears [...] Not from them would we ever know the pain of a black world [...] No sense of its rage, misery, anger or fear would ever be

> communicated [...] On the contrary, everything in [these performances] sang about what is called the joy of life and consoled us [...] by telling us that nothing could profoundly wound the Blacks, since their joy was so great. (836; translation modified)

Rather than liberating the black performer as they claim to do, performances like Dunham's merely satisfy their own desire for a clear conscience. For Genet, white liberal artists are profoundly disingenuous in their attempts to show to "hostile or indifferent Whites that a [Black] is 'a man just like another'" (837). Not only does this humanist mode of performance transform the black actor into a slave (a performer for Whites), but it allows the white liberal artist to absolve herself/himself of all racial responsibility, since s/he erroneously thinks that s/he has made a stand on behalf of the oppressed: "To want to write for Blacks could only be motivated by that form of moral abjection, which consists in leaning forward generously, with comprehension, towards the weak, in an attempt to clear one's conscience and to absolve oneself from any type of effective action" (838).

If the black population is to express itself, Genet argues that it needs to produce its own revolutionary writers, artists and spokespeople. For him, the task facing white writers is completely different: they need to betray their own culture:

> Minorities need to conquer their own freedoms. [As white writers] we need to mistrust our enthusiasm for noble causes: it quickly becomes an attitude of ethical self-satisfaction [...] I am not saying that we should systematically refuse to support the oppressed, but that it would be useless if, at the same time, we did not betray the dominant society which we are a part of: We have to betray ourselves. (838)

Genet's quest to betray himself—and by extension, western culture— accounts for his reluctance to speak positively on behalf of the black population in *The Blacks*. For while he knows how to speak to an individual Black, he has no idea how to address the black community as a collective body:

> Faced with them [the black population], I would have the painful sense that Whiteness was trying to speak to Negritude. You would have to be either a madman or a coward to accept such a dialogue [...] And anyway, to speak to them in this way would mean nothing; where could I find the depth of emotion necessary to express the myth that would ignite them? (835)

Like later post-colonial theorists such as Edward Said (1995), Genet realizes that to speak for someone invariably negates his/her difference and perpetuates colonialism in a new, more insidious form. In order to circumvent the dangerous hypocrisy of the liberal aesthetic, Genet insists that his "play is not written *for* Blacks but *against* Whites" (2002: 842; original italics). Genet's hyper-awareness makes the objections raised by black writers and academics in the United States during the New York premiere of the play in 1961 appear hopelessly naïve. Genet is not interested, as Ossie Davis and Lorraine Hansberry claimed, in using black experience as a pretext for his own ends. On the contrary, he used his experience as an outsider to further black ends, a pattern he repeated in the 1970s when he exploited his celebrity status to support the Black Panthers and Angela Davis.[9]

Given Genet's sensitivity to the danger or *leurre* of representation, it comes as little surprise to find deconstructionist readers such as Laura Oswald (1989) and Hédi Khélil (2001) arguing that the political significance of *The Blacks* stems from its capacity to represent blackness as a mythology, a mere nexus of signs. According to this interpretation, Genet is primarily a playwright of resistance, a dramatist whose political value resides in his ability to disrupt language and to destabilize essentialist notions of racial identity. While this deconstructionist interpretation of Genet's work certainly has currency, it nevertheless fails to address the more active and affirmative impulse inherent in his theory of political performance. A closer reading of the "Preface to *The Blacks*" shows that Genet is not simply interested in suspending identity; his real goal is to change identity by provoking a sudden transformation of the world in the spectator's consciousness. Crucially, this is to be achieved experientially through the "poetry" of theatre:[10]

> Theatrical expression is not a discourse. It does not address itself to man's rational faculties. It is a poetic act that imposes itself as a categorical imperative. Confronted by such an imperative, reason, although it does not disappear altogether, has to accept its subservience. I believe it is possible to find the unique expression that all men would understand. But the metamorphoses of history, instead of leading different societies towards a greater mutual understanding, have hardened the shell of their singularity, to the point that our primary occupation has to be focused on breaking open that shell, and in the process liberating a subject, who is impatient to experience his freedom. (2002: 835-6)

In the 'Preface to *The Blacks*', Genet intends "to break open" the "shell of singularity" in quasi-Artaudian fashion by overwhelming the spectator with painful affect, what he refers to as "wounding:"

> I had the opportunity to wound the white audience and, by doing so, to allow doubt to enter its consciousness. To be frank about it, it seemed to me that only a scandalous act could make the white spectators question themselves and feel anxious in front of a concrete historical problem which normally poses little disturbance to their souls. (838)

The emphasis that Genet places on "wounding" the white spectator, and on providing access to a space of mutual comprehension beyond the vagaries of history, problematizes any attempt to appropriate him as a post-structuralist playwright.[11] The "Preface to *The Blacks*" demonstrates that Genet's theatre is too optimistic, too utopian, to insist on a simple deferral of meaning. For Genet, a theatre that "wounds" has the capacity to free the subject from the prison house of language and the fetters of discourse. The instantaneous gap that the Genetian wound opens in consciousness— although painful—is intended to produce a utopian space where authentic communication can potentially take place. Accordingly, if Genet's politics are to be fully understood, an alternative model of political and artistic engagement is required. In my view, this is best supplied by looking at a political and avant-garde movement that was in operation in Paris at the same time that Genet was writing his plays: Situationism.

According to Guy Debord, Situationism's main theorist, conventional forms of politicized art, such as Sartre's famous theory of a "theatre of situations," have little chance of transforming the world. This is because, Debord claims, they erroneously insist on separating aesthetics from everyday life. As a result of this separation, the committed artwork, continues Debord, contradicts its original purpose: instead of weakening alienation, it merely reinforces it. The spectator is positioned in a passive role, forced to consume an always already appropriated product, a spectacle. Debord's answer to the useless passivity of Sartre's theatre of situations is to offer a more dynamic and democratic form of spatio-temporal exchange: the actual situation. In "Report on the Construction of Situations," Debord defines a situation first, as "the concrete construction of temporary settings of life and their transformation into a higher passionate nature" (2002: 44), and second, as an event that "begins on the other side of the modern collapse of the idea of the theatre" (47). In other words, a situation is a performance, a singular event designed to generate emotion within an everyday environment. There is no aesthetic sublimation involved in the situation. On the contrary, it is conceived as an act that dissolves the false consciousness of the spectacle, thus allowing the subject to discover the joys of the non-alienated life.

Although *The Blacks* is intended to be staged in a theatre and not in an everyday environment (for the Situationists this should be the city itself), there is nevertheless much in common between Genet's play and the Debordian situation.[12] Like Debord, Genet is interested in a theatre that would affect the audience by collapsing rigid distinctions between art and life. In *The Blacks*, Genet achieves this by deliberately betraying the essence of western drama. Instead of relying on vicarious experience through the representation of an act, Genet, as Elinor Fuchs argues, develops a "calculated dramaturgy of the real" (2001: 343), that is, a play that "cultivates *dis-illusion*" (345; original italics). Genet's tactic for dissolving the theatricality of theatre is to write a play in which a group of onstage black actors massacre a "white" court (also played by black actors) in order to conceal what is occurring offstage: the execution of a traitor by a band of concealed black militants. As the play develops, this supposedly "authentic" act is revealed to be just as illusory as the pantomimic events depicted onstage.

The confusing metatheatricality of Genet's play means that it is impossible to tell if the black actors are merely miming their anger, or using the performance as a type of camouflage to express their "real" hatred towards western society. As a result, the white audience in *The Blacks*, as Una Chaudhuri (1985) demonstrates, is unable to consume the labour of the actors as an object of entertainment. On the contrary, the spectator is put on trial, forced to witness black suffering, and accused of perpetuating white racism. By betraying the rules of theatrical *divertissement*, the play becomes an event, an actual encounter. The spatio-temporal dimension of theatre, the fact that it takes place in the present, is crucial to the political impact of *The Blacks*. By placing black bodies on a white stage and insisting that a white spectator be in the audience at all times, Genet provides a concrete example of the spatial relationship, which, the philosopher

Georgio Agamben (1998) claims, embodies the very essence of politics: the agonistic tie of "inclusive-exclusivity".[13] In this way, Genet removes the alibi from theatrical and political experience in the West. The physical presence of black actors performing in front of a white audience—and yet being distanced from it—draws attention to the inclusive-exclusion of the former. Read in this way, Genet's play exploits the "thereness" of the performance event in order to transform vicarious experience into actual experience. The proximity of the actors, combined with their ambiguous status, disturbs the theatrical frame and induces a form of panic. In doing so, *The Blacks* betrays its own dramatic logic (the replacement of the thing by the sign) and becomes a situation, which, to adopt Debord's language, starts on the far side of theatre. Crucially, the epistemological and ontological disturbance produced by Genet's deliberate cultivation of doubt is where he believes the potential for authentic communication resides, since the effect of such a process of disorientation is intended to interrupt our habitual response to the world.

The "Preface to *The Blacks*" shows that Genet was deliberately attempting to develop an effective notion of political theatre that would avoid the weaknesses of both Sartrean and Brechtian models of commitment. For Genet, theatre is at its most political when it deconstructs itself and encroaches on the real. By drawing attention to the "theatricality [...] that power can never do without" (2004:131), Genet believes that theatre has the potential to overcome its vicariousness and exist as a form of actual, non-semiotic exchange. From this perspective, it is disingenuous to criticize Genet for de-realizing the "reality" of the theatrical event, and/or refusing to offer a positive message. On the contrary, this is where the strategic dimension of his sophisticated theory of political performance resides. For Genet, the betrayal of theatre is both a tactic of resistance and an act of hope, an attempt to transcend what I referred to earlier, in reference to Genet's own language, as the vagaries of history.

NOTES

[1] In an interview with the German journalist Hubert Fichte in 1975, Genet attacked Brechtian theatre on the grounds that the cigar-smoking spectator so desired by Brecht was not a revolutionary producer of meaning, but, on the contrary, a bourgeois capitalist:

In his choice of a gesture, smoking a cigar, there is a casualness with regard to the work of art that is in fact not permitted […] I don't know the Rothschilds but with [them], you can probably talk about art. You can't go the Louvre and look at the Marquise of Solana with the same movement as with the Rotschilds who talk about art while smoking a cigar. (2004: 122)

[2] All translations are mine unless otherwise indicated in References.

[3] In an interview with *Playboy Magazine* in 1964, for instance, Genet claimed that his plays were written "to crystallize a theatrical and dramatic emotion. If my plays are useful to blacks, it's not my concern. I don't think they are in any case" (2004: 13).

[4] See Stewart and McGregor (1993), Marty (2003) and Jablonka (2004).

[5] This return to Genet is not a conservative attempt to police meaning. Rather, it is an attempt to respect his heterogeneity. When critics read Genet, there is a tendency to interpret his work through an overarching discourse which, for all its claims to the contrary, has little real interest in accommodating the contradictions of his theatre.

[6] Corvin's short essay (2002) is the only existing commentary on "The Preface to *The Blacks*" in either French or English.

[7] An abridged version of the "The Preface to *The Blacks*" first appeared as "L'art est un refuge" in Moraly (1988). Corvin and Dichy refer to the text as "Préface Inédite des *Nègres*," which can be translated as "The Unpublished Preface to *The Blacks*". Given that the text has now been published, I prefer to call it the 1956 "Preface to *The Blacks*." There is no English translation of either text.

[8] For related readings see Bersani (1994) and Bougon (1998).

[9] See John Warrick (2006) for a full discussion of African-American attitudes towards *The Blacks* when it was performed at the St Marks Playhouse in New York in the early 1960s.

[10] For Genet, poetry is synonymous with art in general. In theatrical terms, the poetry of theatre refers to its essential qualities: namely, its "liveness," the fact that it takes place in the present and occurs between bodies.

[11] Mara de Gennaro makes a similar point. For her, Genet's interest in transcending history problematizes the readings of critics committed to conceptions of "identity as 'socially constructed' and 'performed' on an on-going basis" (2003: 205).

[12] While Situationism is often thought to be antagonistic to any official cultural form, Debord was certainly interested in the performance practices of Brecht, Artaud and Kaprow. For a good discussion of this see Puchner (2004).

[13] Inclusive-exclusivity is agonistic because the sovereign/white subject needs the sacred/black subject to exist. In other words, whiteness is unable to do without its enemy, blackness (and vice versa).

REFERENCES

Agamben, Georgio. (1998) *Homo Sacer: Sovereign Power and Bare Life*. Trans. Daniel Heller-Roazen. Stanford: Stanford University Press.

Bersani, Leo. (1994) "The Gay Outlaw." *Diacritics*, 24 (2), 5-18.

Bharucha, Rustom. (2003) "Genet in Manila: Reclaiming the Chaos of The Times." *Third Text: Critical Perspectives on Contemporary Art and Culture* 62, 15-28.

Bougon, Patrice. (1998) "Translation, Tradition and Betrayal: From Political Commitment to Literary Freedom in *Les Paravents*. (Preceded by a Reflection on What Remains of a Larousse Dictionary in Colonial Politics)." Susan Marson, trans. *Parallex* 4 (2), 129-44.

Chaudhuri, Una. (1985) "The Politics of Theater: Play, Deceit and Threat in Genet's *The Blacks*". *Modern Drama* 28 (3), 362-76.

Corvin, Michel. (2002) "Préface inédite des *Nègres*: Notice" in Michel Corvin and Albert Dichy, eds, *Jean Genet: Théâtre complet*. Paris: Gallimard, 1329-32.

Debord, Guy. "Report on the Construction of Situations and on the Terms of Organization and Action of the International Situationist Tendency" in Tom McDonough, ed. and trans. *Guy Debord and The Situationist International: Texts and Documents*. Cambridge: MIT Press, 29-50.

De Gennaro, Mara. (2003) "What Remains of Jean Genet?". *Yale Journal of Criticism* 16 (1), 190-209.

Fuchs, Elinor. (2003) "Clown Shows: Anti-Theatricalist Theatricalism in Four Twentieth-Century Plays." *Modern Drama* 44 (3), 337-54.

Genet, Jean. (2002) "Préface inédite des *Nègres*" in Michel Corvin and Albert Dichy, eds. *Jean Genet: Théâtre complet*. Paris: Gallimard, 835-43.

———. (2004) *Jean Genet: The Declared Enemy. Texts and Interviews*. Jeff Fort, trans. Stanford: Stanford University Press.

Jablonka, Ivan. (2004) *Les Vérités inavouables de Jean Genet*. Paris: Seuil.

Khélil, Hédi. (2001) *Figures de l'altérité dans le théâtre de Jean Genet. Lecture des Nègres et des Paravents*. Paris: L'Harmattan.

Marty, Eric. (2003) *Bref Séjour à Jérusalem*. Paris: Gallimard.

Moraly, Jean-Bernard. (1988) "Les Cinq vies de Jean Genet" in Jean-Bernard Moraly, ed. *Les Nègres au Port de la Lune: Genet et les différences*. Bordeaux: Editions de la Différance.

Oswald, Laura. (1989) *Jean Genet and the Semiotics of Performance*. Bloomington: Indiana University Press.

Puchner, Martin. (2004) "Society of the Counter-Spectacle: Debord and the Theatre of the Situationists". *Theatre Research International* 29 (1), 4-15.

Redonnet, Marie. (2000) *Jean Genet, le poète travesti : Portrait d'une œuvre*. Paris: Grasset.

Said, Edward. (1995) "On Genet's Late Work" in J. Ellen Gainor, ed. *Imperialism and Theatre: Essays on World Theatre, Drama and Performance*. London: Routledge, 230-42.

Stewart, Harry and Rob Roy McGregor. (1993) *Jean Genet: From Fascism to Nihilism*. New York: Peter Lang.

Warrick, John. (2006) "*The Blacks* and its Impact on African-American Theatre in the United States" in Clare Finburgh, Carl Lavery and Maria Shevtsova, eds. *Jean Genet, Performance and Politics*. Basingstoke: Palgrave MacMillan, 131-42.

BARBARIANS AND BABES:
A FEMINIST CRITIQUE OF A POSTCOLONIAL
PERSIANS

SYDNEY CHEEK O'DONNELL

Aeschylus's tragedy *The Persians*, written in the early days of Athenian democracy, tells the story of Xerxes, a tyrant whose hubris leads to the destruction of his empire. Classicist Edith Hall points out:

> [T]his moral lesson [...] informs the whole play, but is formulated [...] in terms so distinctively Greek [...] that it is easy for modern critics to forget that this play is the earliest fully fledged testimony to one of the most important of the Greeks' ideological inventions and one of the most influential in western thought, the culturally other, the anti-Greek, the *barbarian*. (1989: 70)

Recently, the play has been interpreted as anti-war polemic, in part because of the uncanny resemblance of its protagonist and his father to Presidents George W. and George H. W. Bush, respectively. Capitalizing on these similarities during the summer of 2005, Waterwell Productions, a small theatre company in New York City, mounted an irreverent neo-vaudevillian adaptation of Aeschylus' play: *The Persians... A Comedy about War with Five Songs*. One of this adaptation's most remarkable features was the frequent use of gender stereotypes and the objectification of women as integral parts of its critique of Western imperialism and the idea of the "culturally other" "barbarian." Brechtian acting, in particular, enabled the company to represent gender as a social construct rather than as the mark of a fixed ontology. Drawing on postcolonial, feminist, psychoanalytic, and semiotic theory, the project of this essay is to describe and explain Waterwell's production vis-à-vis the construction of Otherness, particularly as it pertains to gendered bodies.

RACIAL AND NATIONAL IDENTITIES

The earliest extant play in the Western tradition, *The Persians* tells the story of a king who leads his people into a war of aggression and is humiliatingly defeated. As Aeschylus tells it, King Xerxes is the son of the great King Darius, who built the Asian empire. Young Xerxes comes to power upon Darius's death, and feels he must live up to his father's glorious reputation. Thus, he rashly leads his vast army across the Hellespont and into Greece in an attempt to avenge his father's defeat at Marathon and to subdue the rebellious Hellenes once and for all. As Edith Hall puts it, "the defeat of the Persian imperial army is presented as a historical paradigm of the moral truth that gods cut down the great," following on the "fundamental Greek law of human existence, which prescribed that excessive prosperity and satiety lead first to hubris and then to destruction" (1989: 70). The play takes place in Sousa, Persia's capitol city, where those who did not go off to fight wait anxiously for word of the invasion. Among them are the Council of Elders and Queen Atossa, widow of the late Darius and mother of Xerxes. The play's action revolves around the anticipation of information, the receipt of the news that the Persian forces have been utterly defeated, and a lamentation for the dead. Pericles presented *The Persians* at the Great Dionysia in 472 BCE (Hall 1989: 67), just eight years after King Xerxes' army had destroyed Athens and then, in turn, been destroyed during a series of battles on land and sea, including the Battle of Salamis which is described at length in the play.[1]

As Hall argues in her book *Inventing the Barbarian*, the ancient Greek literary preoccupation with "barbarians" or "anti-Greeks" was an "exercise in self-definition, for the barbarian is often portrayed as the opposite of the ideal Greek" (1989: 1). In other words, "barbarian" characters served as the shadow-selves of the Greeks,[2] helping to define what it meant to be Greek by demonstrating what it meant *not* to be Greek. Certainly this was the case with *The Persians*, which features no Greeks and yet implicitly instructs the audience in Greek ideals through their inversion as represented by the play's barbarian characters: respect for hierarchicalism rather than egalitarianism, luxury rather than austerity, and emotionalism rather than self-discipline (1989: 80). Waterwell, on the other hand, uses the play as an allegory of American imperialism and explicitly equates the Persians with Americans, minimizing the sense of Persian Otherness with which Hall argues the original text is "suffused" (1989: 99).[3] In this production, Persia's imagined flaws are America's actual flaws, not an inversion of America's virtues.

Because *The Persians* centers on the representation of an "oriental" Other, it makes sense that reviewers who saw Waterwell's production focused their attentions on questions of race and nationality. Actor Arian Moayed's status as an Iranian-American is fully exploited for both comic and tragic effect. During one exchange, actor Rodney Gardiner (who at this moment plays himself), refers to Moayed first as "white" and then as "Mexican," while Moayed vainly attempts to position himself outside the sphere of white privilege. Gardiner, who is African-American, sarcastically humors Moayed and exhorts him to "tell 'em yo' dream. You tell 'em yo' hopes and aspirations! Tell them white people [i.e., the audience]!" Interestingly, it was Moayed's brief portrayal of the defeated Xerxes that was cited most frequently by reviewers as the highlight of the production.[4]

Moayed delivered Xerxes' final speech in both Farsi and English and sang the names of the Persian dead – peppered with a few Western names – in a dirge accompanied by the three other performers. The bilingual approach to the text here draws on a convention established earlier in the comic song "Takhseer" ("Blame"). The first verse of "Takhseer," sung in Farsi and accompanied by English subtitles, introduces the audience to Moayed's intercultural upbringing as a first generation Iranian-American in Evanston, Illinois; the second verse, sung in English with Farsi subtitles, satirizes the ways in which Americans essentialize and universalize non-Western peoples. Moayed's hybrid Iranian-American identity – his Middle Eastern appearance, his American accent, his fluency in English and Farsi – shows us that the supposedly clear distinctions between West and East are, in fact, part of an ideological construct designed to naturalize oppression. The familiarity of Moayed's American upbringing, combined with his disarming and frequent direct address of the audience, also position Moayed as an empathetic figure. When, in the final scene, he assumes the role of Xerxes, who has heretofore consistently been described as stupid, cruel, and rash, the audience has been primed to empathize with Xerxes' pathos because it is inscribed on Moayed's body. He is both American and Persian Other, both one of Them and one of Us. His suffering is ours.

What all the reviews of Waterwell's production fail to acknowledge, however, is the basic paradigm upon which the construction of the Other in the play is based: the assumption of a masculine (or supposedly neuter) Subject that seeks self-definition in the feminine Other. As Hall aptly points out in the introduction to her translation of *Persians*, "The patriarchal ancient Athenians used gender differentials and gender hierarchies to help them explain their relations with many groups other than women: male supremacy over the female was regarded as natural" (1996: 13). The Greeks naturalized their defeat of Persia by characterizing it as the masculine domination of a feminine (foreign) Other. Unfortunately, the fact that no reviewer acknowledged the critique of gender that suffused Waterwell's production suggests that reviewers either simply did not recognize it or deemed it of only minimal importance to the company's overall critique of Western imperialism. It is in this critical shadow where I take up my discussion of *The Persians... a Comedy about War with Five Songs*.

ORIENTALISM AND GENDER
While Waterwell's read of *The Persians* takes a clear a position against the wars led by George W. Bush in Iraq and Afghanistan, the primary target of this adaptation is the discursive practice of Othering, whereby the feminine, "oriental" Other functions as a foil for the concerns of the white-Western-heterosexual male.[5] I take my understanding of the Other from several sources, including Edward Said (1979), Gayatri Chakravorty Spivak (1988), Jacques Lacan (1982), and Judith Butler (1999). In *Orientalism*, Said wrote about the production of the "Orient-as-other" through a system of knowledge (the study of language, geography, anthropology, and religions of the Orient) that essentializes Asia (especially the Islamic cultures of the Near and Middle East) and justifies its domination by the West. Of central importance to the present study is the fact that Orientalist thought uses the "natural" gender hierarchy that permits men to dominate women as an explicit metaphor for the dominance by the West of the East. According to Said, Asia is "routinely described as feminine, its riches as fertile, its main symbols the sensual woman [...] and the despotic – but curiously attractive – ruler" (1985: 23). In her essay "Can the Subaltern Speak?" Spivak describes the colonizer's discursive process of constructing an Other ("Othering"), and laments

the "doubly effaced" position of sexual difference in the subaltern subject. Inserting feminist politics into postcolonial studies, Spivak argues, "Between patriarchy and imperialism, subject-constitution and object-formation, the figure of the woman disappears" (1988: 306). In other words, in postcolonial (and subaltern) studies, so-called feminist issues are often ignored in favor of supposedly more universal concerns that "transcend" gender difference.

One of Aeschylus's Orientalist strategies in *The Persians* was to construct the enemy to the east as effeminate. As Hall points out, Aeschylus emphasizes the Persian court's lack of a "firm, adult male hand on the rudder of government" (1993: 117). Indeed, the Queen has been left in charge. The empire is portrayed as having been emptied of men, and those men who do remain are effeminate – the Council are very old, Xerxes is very young and his behavior (such as the rending of his garments when he witnesses the loss at Salamis) is womanish. Even the great King Darius wears robes that are described in terms usually reserved for women's clothing (Hall 1993: 120). Waterwell picks up on Aeschylus's ideological project and parodies it in the production's second scene, "Meet the Ghazis," which is structured like a reality television show that confines a group of people to a house or an island and assigns the participants absurd tasks.

The Ghazis are a Persian family whose father and younger son "are off bravely fighting for [their] country." The family members on the show include Mother (Hanna Cheek), Grandpa (Tom Ridgely), the conscientious-objector Brother (Moayed), and the Wife of the son who is at war (Gardiner). Significantly, each of the characters is identified only in terms of patriarchal family relationships. Throughout this section of the play, the effeminacy of the Persians constructed by Aeschylus is both emphasized and satirized by Waterwell. Grandpa, who is the first to sit in the show's "confessional," patriotically praises the "largest war machine ever assembled" and claims that it is "Persia's destiny to level cities and collect tribute." Yet, Ridgely portrays Grandpa as a feeble – if loud and crotchety – old man who can barely walk. Grandpa's effeminate body renders comic his hyper-masculine, enthusiastic pro-war rhetoric. Following a competition,[6] Brother enters the confessional to complain about the fact that Grandpa teases him: "Grandpa thinks it's funny to tease me, he teases me as if I wore the same armor as my noble brother. But you see, my armor is made of very thin, almost butterfly-like tissue. It tears easily, just like all my hopes and dreams." Brother then breaks down in tears and ends the confessional session. His second confessional ends with a repetition of this tearful collapse. Throughout "Meet the Ghazis," Grandpa attacks Brother's manhood because he has refused to fight the Greeks, recalling Hall's assertion that "[t]he rhetoric of militarism may characterize as homosexuals, or 'womanish', men [...] who fail to show enough aggression" (1993: 111). But Aeschylus's strategy of feminization is at least partially undermined by Waterwell because Grandpa's attacks are so disproportionately ferocious and couched in absurd ethnic slurs against the Greeks (e.g., "Faggy Faggadopolis" and "olive-stuffing feta cheese monkeys").

DESIRE AND PERFORMATIVITY
Because the Other in *The Persians* is feminized, objectified, and exoticized, the question of desire in relation to the Other is also important to consider. Lacan, in his essay "The Meaning of the Phallus," discusses the idea of the Phallus as a signifier of the "desire of the Other" (1982: 83). John P. Muller and William J. Richardson explain that this Other is, among other things, the object of desire that the Subject believes "will fill out his own ineluctable finitude, restoring the illusion of plenitude" (1982: 282). Supplementing this reading with a feminist interpretation, Judith Butler adds, "In other words, [to "be" the Phallus] is to be the object, the Other of a (heterosexualized) masculine desire, but also to represent or reflect that desire. This is an Other that constitutes [...] the site of a masculine self-elaboration" (1999: 56). If Othering – in this play and in Western society in general – is based in large part on the naturalization of patriarchal gender roles, it is of paramount importance to analyze the ways in which gender is constructed and critiqued in theatrical production. For in failing to do so we risk, as Spivak puts it, "continu[ing] the imperialist project" (1988: 298) because we neglect interrogating one of the ideological pillars upon which imperialism itself rests: patriarchy.

Significantly, the performance began and ended with the same image – a woman's face illuminated by a spotlight center stage. During a blackout at the top of the play, a match is struck to reveal with its flickering light the alabaster face of Hanna Cheek, the lone female performer in *The Persians*. As if out of nowhere, a male hand appears with a silver cigarette case, pulls out a cigarette, places it between Cheek's lips, and lights it. Cheek takes a long drag as the unseen drummer sets the tempo on the high-hat for the opening number, "Welcome to the Persians." This image codes the actress as the embodiment of the feminine as defined in patriarchal terms. She is a disembodied head floating in the darkness with large, slightly downcast eyes, lined in black kohl, peeking out from beneath the brim of a Fedora, and seeming to beckon coyly to the spectators. The cigarette is lit for her – she does not hold the hand steady and cup the flame as she inhales. Instead her body remains immobile. The combination of the spotlight, the male hand detached from an identifiable individual, and Cheek's gaze directed at the audience is reminiscent of a cinematic point-of-view shot, where the spectator is positioned as aligned with the male protagonist or the *subject*. The acceptance of "a light" is a flirtation, signaling her sexual availability to the protagonist/subject. Cheek's complete immobility – she does not even put the cigarette into her own mouth – comments on her status as an *object* of desire, or in Jacques Lacan's (1982) words, she is the desire of the Other, she *is* the Phallus.

As Atossa, Cheek performs the construct of heterosexual "Woman" with a vengeance. She makes her transformation into Atossa on stage in full view of the audience. Striptease music plays as Ridgely and Moayed strip Cheek of her suit. Looking seductively at the audience, Ridgely, and Moayed, she lets her jacket drop to the floor. Cheek lifts her arms languidly over her head while Ridgely and Moayed roll her sleeves up to her elbows. As she leans back into Ridgely's supportive embrace, Moayed removes her tie. Ridgely wraps the tie around Cheek's waist, creating a belt that gives shape to her boxy, white shirt, while Moayed drapes a long string of pearls around her neck. They slip her hands into a pair of elbow-length, satin gloves, and Ridgely finally pulls her slacks down to reveal bare legs in black, leather go-go boots. Meanwhile, Gardiner describes Cheek as a "divine specimen" and adlibs lines like, "This is my favorite part of the show," and "Isn't she beautiful, ladies and gentlemen?" Thus, the male performers inscribe the role of Atossa onto Cheek's body, constructing her identity. During the process, Cheek's hands absently stroke Moayed and Ridgely's heads, shoulders, and torsos in a grotesque parody of a woman taking pleasure in her own objectification.

Cheek, Ridgely, and Moayed repeat this transformation a second time just prior to Darius's return from the dead. This time, Cheek is almost mechanical in her physicality. She no longer seems to be taking pleasure in the construction of Atossa; rather, she perfunctorily goes through the same choreography, blankly staring at the audience while Ridgely and Moayed efficiently, if somewhat roughly, remove her clothing and accessorize her as the Queen. In *Gender Trouble*, Judith Butler writes, "Consider gender [...] as *a corporeal style*, an 'act,' as it were, which is both intentional and performative, where *'performative'* suggests a dramatic and contingent construction of meaning" (1999: 177). The juxtaposition of the *quality* of these two moments – one deliberately sexy, the other perfunctory – reveals the contingency of Cheek's gender as an "identity tenuously constituted in time, instituted in an exterior space through a *stylized repetition of acts*" (Butler 1999: 179).During an exchange in "Meet the Ghazis" between Mother and Wife in which they discuss how much they miss their husbands, each woman turns privately to the audience and confesses that she feels liberated on her own. The differences between the women as they present themselves to their family – as obedient, patient, self-sacrificing women who need men to feel complete – and to the audience – as independent women who would prefer life without their husbands – emphasize the performativity of gender roles and the political isolation into which women are forced by patriarchal ideology. Mother has found sexual liberation in her husband's absence, and Wife, who now has time on her hands because she doesn't have to care for her husband, has become an inventor. Wife claims to have discovered electricity and subsequently to have invented the light bulb. Yet, the liberation these two women achieve must be kept secret, even from each other.

The scene ends when Mother and Wife are discovered in a "compromising sexual position" by Grandpa and Brother. While on one level, this can be read as a lesbian encounter between the Ghazi household's two female members, one of the sexual partners is actually being played by Gardiner, an African-American man wearing a ridiculous bleach blond wig. In addition, this is the actor who later plays Darius, Atossa's (Cheek's) husband. The lesbianness of the encounter, therefore, is, in a sense, erased by the heterosexual makeup of the actors engaged in the scene. At the same time, the play's opening number establishes an epic performance code as the dominant mode of character representation – that is, differences between actor and character are not disguised. This may frame the scene in such a way as to allow spectators to differentiate Gardiner from Wife and thus to recognize the relationship between Wife and Mother as lesbian. The signification of the stage image is further complicated by the fact that Cheek (as herself) has "outed" herself as a lesbian in the play's first scene. Yet Gardiner (as himself) has refused to recognize the validity of her homosexuality. As Butler points out, Lacan (among others) "takes lesbian sexuality to be a refusal of sexuality *per se* only because sexuality is presumed to be heterosexual" (1999: 63). The audience has the opportunity to see performed Cheek's previously-erased homosexuality performed by/on hetero-sexual bodies. She performs simultaneously gay *and* straight sexualities, confounding the polarity of the positions in which these two sexualities are usually located. Butler notes, "No longer believable as an interior 'truth' of dispositions and identity, sex will be shown to be a performatively enacted signification [...], one that [...] can occasion the parodic proliferation and subversive play of gendered meanings" (1999: 44).

BRECHTIAN ACTING
The Waterwellians, as they are called, are aided in their play of signification by their use of a fragmented, neo-vaudevillian structure with episodic scenes punctuated by song-and-dance numbers that disrupt and comment on the play's action. Its Brechtian dramaturgy employs, in Roland Barthes' words, a "semiological method" through which reality is not "expressed" but "signified" by distancing the signified from the signifier (1972: 74-5). But this production expressed the distanciation-through-signification most often through the acting. As spectators entered the theatre, they encountered a bare stage, save for a Persian rug covering the back wall, several simple wooden stools, a coat rack holding various costume pieces upstage left, and the three-piece band sitting stage left. The four-member cast of *The Persians* wandered on and off stage setting props and costume pieces, fixing their hair and costumes, and chatting with one another in a relaxed fashion. By framing the performance in this manner, the production team, led by actor-director Tom Ridgely, encouraged the spectators to view the performers *as actors* first and foremost. The

shared reality of the production was grounded in the theatre building itself, not Persia.

According to the Prague School semioticians, there are three formal aspects of realistic acting: (1) the *actor's personal characteristics*; (2) the *stage figure*, an image of the character created by the actor, designers and director; and (3) the *dramatic character*, an idea created in the minds of the spectators (Quinn 1990: 155-6). Whereas the so-called "dramatic theater" attempts to unify the these three elements, and, thus, encourage the spectator to think of the character as a "natural" and unified phenomenon, the epic theatre, as theorized by Bertolt Brecht, attempts to distance the signifier (the actor's personal characteristics and the stage figure) from the signified (the dramatic figure) (Brecht 1992: 124-6). The effect is to draw attention to the constructed nature of social relationships. Among these social relationships, one might argue, is identity itself.[7] This style of acting functions as a type of *Verfremdungseffket*, whereby the familiar is made strange in order to allow the audience to view supposedly natural social relationships as constructed. According to feminist performance scholar Elin Diamond, the *Verfremdungseffekt* "challenges [...] iconicity, or the conventional resemblance between the performer's body and the [...] character, to which it refers" (45). Thus, epic acting emphasizes and draws attention to the separation between actor, stage figure, and dramatic character. Feminist theatre practitioners and theorists have adopted the *Verfremdungseffekt* to reveal and critique what Teresa de Lauretis calls "technologies of gender," complex networks of power that effect "bodies, behaviors, and social relations" (1987: 3). During the course of *The Persians*, the actors challenge iconicity first by allowing the audience to see them *as* actors preparing for a performance and then by strategically revealing personal information about themselves, disrupting the tendency of American audiences to view the actor *as* the character, or to equate the actor's personal characteristics with both the stage figure and the dramatic character, thus ignoring the multiple layers of signification that exist in theatrical performance. "Welcome to the Persians," composed by Lauren Cregor, introduces the performers and the setting of the play to the audience. As Gardiner sings the bass-line, Ridgely exhorts the audience to imagine a time "when Persia was/ Where it's at when Persia was called the Persian Empire." Ridgely, an American actor of European descent, here plays the role of hip historian, instructing the audience about Persia's past greatness, now lost. Iranian-American Moayed repeatedly sings the line "I/ am from Iran/ and later on/ I'll sing a song/ All about how [...]," introducing the audience to a personal characteristic that seems to naturalize his presence in a play about Persia. By the same token, Moayed's ethnic "authenticity" emphasizes the apparent miscasting of two European-Americans and an African-American as the other Persians in the play. Cheek acknowledges the foreignness of her character and the place names in the play when she sings, "I play the queen, Queen Atossa/ Wife of the late, great king Darius-uh." The song frames the upcoming experience of the play by setting the tone, introducing the setting, and commenting on the cast's iconicity.

In the following scene, Gardiner, who functions intermittently as an insult-comic emcee, introduces the performers and comments on the roles that they will play in terms of the actors' personal characteristics. In other words, Gardiner points to the "authenticity" of the characterizations by drawing parallels between the characters and the actors. Thus, he suggests that each of the actors was typecast in an attempt to close the perceived distance between actor and dramatic character and thus to present more unified stage figures. But as he essentializes each of his co-stars' identities, they protest and correct him, introducing counter-discourses that violate notions of subjective and narrative unity. The most significant and far-reaching of the corrections occurs when Gardiner introduces Cheek, who is to play his wife, Queen Atossa. He claims she was cast in the role because she is "the classiest chick we know" and calls her "Hanna Gardiner," as though she were actually his wife. Clearly uneasy, but unwilling to let Gardiner co-opt her identity as signified by her own name, Cheek corrects his "Freudian slip." Gardiner ignores Cheek's correction and suggests lasciviously that she consider changing her name. Cheek again tries to rebuff him saying simply, "We're not getting married, Rodney." Mistaking her refusal of his advances as playing hard-to-get, Gardiner says that he, too, would prefer to avoid "all that attachment," at which point Cheek accidentally "outs" herself, shouting, "Rodney, I'm gay!" Instead of acknowledging this extremely personal revelation, Gardiner simply charges forward with an introduction of the play's given circumstances. Later in the performance, Moayed, too, makes a pass at Cheek, reiterating her status as an object of male desire. Gardiner reminds Moayed, "She gay, man," and Moayed responds with a somewhat dismissive, "Right, gay," as though her claim to lesbian sexuality is merely a way to avoid unwanted suitors. Her male co-stars' refusal to acknowledge or believe her sexual preference points to the socially constitutive nature of identity, particularly gender and sexual identity.

The introduction of specific personal characteristics of the actors in *The Persians* complicates the spectator's ability to fully identify the actors with the characters they play. It also establishes a secondary narrative, or counter-text, that is not about the defeat of the Persians but is instead about the actors, their pasts, and their present lives. Revealing Cheek's sexuality is part of a deliberate strategy to resist traditional female roles and patriarchal notions of femininity. In Aeschylus's *Persians,* Queen Atossa is defined almost exclusively in relation to men – her husband, Darius, her son, Xerxes, and the men who comprise the Council of Elders that is supposed to advise her while Xerxes is away. Gardiner's introduction of Cheek attempts to mask the separation between actor and dramatic character in an effort to naturalize patriarchal gender roles. By inserting Cheek's alleged lesbian sexuality into the performance text, however, Waterwell reveals the constructed nature of the stage figure Atossa, and disrupts the naturalization of Atossa's gender role as proscribed by a system of "compulsory heterosexuality" (Andermahr 2000: 42). By performing two conflicting identities – the "straight" Atossa and her own supposedly real queerness – Cheek deconstructs the sense of a stable gender identity and exposes the fact that, in Judith Butler's words, "gender is a performance that *produces the illusion* of an inner sex or essence or psychic gender core" (1991: 28).

As Cheek is stripped of the costume that visually equates her with her male colleagues, she is transformed into the exotic "Woman-as-other," object of (male) desire. She is a territory to be conquered and dominated through her "feminine" sexuality, physical weakness, and love of the sensual and luxurious, stereotypical qualities for which Persians were reviled by their Greek neighbors (Hall 1989; 1993). But the establishment of Cheek's professed identity as a lesbian challenges the iconicity of Cheek as Atossa and suggests that the highly sexualized role that Atossa plays in the world of *The Persians* is not natural, but constructed. In addition, the use of epic acting techniques serves as a strategy to illustrate the constructed and hybrid nature of human subjectivity. Epic acting shows the audience both the actor and the character in the stage figure, a hybrid moment in which "two or more historically separate realms come together in any degree that challenges their socially constructed autonomy" (Kapchan 1999: 242). The hybrid identity of Cheek-Atossa collapses the difference between Self and Other. As a wife-mother, Atossa represents the Other whose existence defines the Self of the white, heterosexual Western male. At the same time, Atossa's heterosexuality identifies her with the Self of a society that defines heterosexuality as the norm. But because Cheek herself claims to operate outside the sexual norm established by society, she is also coded as an Other. The audience must therefore either reconcile the signification of both Self and Other by the single dynamic stage figure of "Cheek-Atossa" or, better yet, question the limits of these terms.

THE ENEMY WITHIN

Ultimately, Waterwell effectively questions the construction of the Middle Eastern "enemy" as feminized Other by exposing gender as a construct tied to Western patriarchal and imperialist ideology founded upon a meaningless binary opposition. Waterwell's representational strategies illustrate the culturally constructed, fragmented, and contingent nature of identity itself. Thus, it offers a viable challenge to ideologies that capitalize on the notion of identity as a totalizing whole in order to pit Self against Other, Us against Them. This *Persians'* critique of gender is particularly apt given the now long-forgotten salve to the consciences of liberals who initially opposed the attack by the United States on Afghanistan: the notion that at least by overthrowing the Taliban the West would bring liberty to Afghan women. If ever there were evidence of the pervasiveness in Western culture of Orientalism as a phenomenon grounded in sexism, this is it. And it brings to mind Spivak's reflection on the nature of relations between the West and the "Third World:" "[W]hat interests me is that the protection of woman (today the 'third-world woman') becomes a signifier for the establishment of a *good* society" (1985: 298). The failure by reviewers to recognize that Waterwell was engaged in a critique of patriarchal gender construction as a founding principle of Western imperialism (and, by extension, U.S. foreign policy) merely underscores the need for feminist scholars to enter more vocally into both popular and academic discourse on subjects that do not at first glance seem to lend themselves to feminist analysis.

NOTES

[1] According to Edith Hall, *The Persians* is one of only three plays (the other two, by Phrynichis, are lost) that treat the Persian Wars, rather than the mythical past (Hall 1989, 63).

[2] In "Can the Subaltern Speak?" Gayatri Chakravorty Spivak writes of "the persistent constitution of Other as the Self's shadow" (1988: 280).

[3] Hall, in fact, argues that *The Persians* "represents the first unmistakable file in the archive of Orientalism, the discourse by which the European imagination has dominated Asia ever since by conceptualizing its inhabitants as defeated, luxurious, emotional, cruel, and always as dangerous" (99).

[4] See, for example, Miriam Horn's review for the *New York Times* 18 July 2005, and Marlon Hunt's review for *Off-Off Online* 14 July 2005 < http://offoffonline.com/archives.php?id=459> [Accessed 10 April 2009].

[5] Interestingly, at no time during the production is Tom Ridgely's identity as anything other than an actor explored. Ridgely is the only member of the cast who is also white and heterosexual. His Subjectivity is assumed, it seems, and needs no explanation or exploration.

[6] The activities the Ghazis participate in for the reality show are highly sexualized: sensual massages, a zip-line/pudding challenge. The show climaxes when Wife goes into labor. When the baby's head emerges, Mother shouts at Brother, "It looks like you!" implying that an illicit affair has taken place between Wife and Brother. Portraying Wife as the nexus of uncontrolled sexual appetite (Wife has an erotic encounter with Mother, too), follows along from the Aeschylean Orientalization of Persia, which also constructed the Persian brides and widows as longing for sex with their absent partners (Hall 1993: 126).

[7] For example, in Brecht's *A Man's a Man*, we witness the construction of Galy Gay as the "ultimate killing machine." To demonstrate the social nature of this construction, the actor playing Gay in Brecht's 1931 production, Peter Lorre, made an instantaneous and stylized transformation from the happy-go-lucky Gay to the killing machine Gay through the use of white face makeup (Brecht 1992: 55).

REFERENCES

Andermahr, Sonya, Terry Lovell, and Carol Wolkowitz. (2000) *A Glossary of Feminist Theory*. London: Arnold; New York: Oxford UP.

Barthes, Roland. (1972) "The Tasks of Brechtian Criticism." *Critical Essays*. Richard Howard, trans. Evanston, IL: Northwestern UP, 71-76.

Brecht, Bertolt. (1992) *Brecht on Theatre: The Development of an Aesthetic*. John Willett, trans. New York: Hill and Wang.

Butler, Judith. (1999) *Gender Trouble: Feminism and the Subversion of Identity*. New York and London: Routledge.

——. (1991) "Imitation and Gender Subordination," in Diana Fuss *Inside/Out: Lesbian Theories, Gay Theories*. London: Routledge, 13-31.

De Lauretis, Teresa. (1987) *Technologies of Gender*. Bloomington and Indianapolis, IN: Indiana UP.

Diamond, Elin. (1997) *Unmaking Mimesis: Essays on Feminism and Theater*. London; New York: Routledge.

Hall, Edith. (1989) *Inventing the Barbarian: Greek Self-Definition through Tragedy*. Oxford: Clarendon.

——. (1993) "Asia Unmanned: Images of Victory in Classical Athens," in John Rich and Graham Shipley *War and Society in the Greek World*. London: Routledge, 108-133.

——. (1996) "Introduction" in Aeschylus *Persians*. Warminster, England: Aris and Phillips.

Kapchan, Deborah A. and Pauline Turner Strong. (1999) "Theorizing the Hybrid." *The Journal of American Folklore* 112 (445), 239-253.

Lacan, Jacques. (1982) "The Meaning of the Phallus," in Juliet Mitchell, ed., and Jacqueline Rose, ed. trans. *Feminine Sexuality*. New York and London: W.W. Norton, 74-85.

Quinn, Michael. (1990) "Celebrity and the Semiotics of Acting." *New Theatre Quarterly* 4 (22), 154-161.

Said, Edward. (1979) *Orientalism*. London: Routledge.

Spivak, Gayatri Chakravorty. (1988) "Can the Subaltern Speak?" in Cary Nelson and Lawrence Grossberg, eds. *Marxism and the Interpretation of Culture*. Urbana and Chicago, IL: U of IL P, 271-313.

The Persians… A Comedy about War with Five Songs. (2005) By Hanna Cheek, Rodney Gardiner, Arian Moayed, and Tom Ridgely. Directed by Tom Ridgely. Waterwell Productions. Perry Street Theatre (13 July – 20 August), New York, NY.

PERFORMING STEREOTYPES
AT HOME AND ABROAD

TOM MAGUIRE

In reviewing Gary Mitchell's *Trust* (1999),[1] Nick Curtis stated that, "Gary Mitchell wants to redeem his fellow Belfast Protestants from the stereotype of angry, red-faced, bowler-hatted old men" (1999: 339). This raises a question regarding theatrical representation which is the principal focus of this article: whether the function of such stereotypes might be differentiated depending on the constitution of the audience. I will respond to it by examining works by two playwrights who have each sought to engage with stereotypes of paramilitaries within Northern Ireland: Gary Mitchell in *As the Beast Sleeps* (1998) and Martin McDonagh in his *The Lieutenant of Inishmore* (2001).

In making sense of the world, we impose categories on our experiences as a way of ordering them (Stangor 2000: 27-31). Where this instinctive process denies "any flexible thinking with categories [...] in the interests of the structures of power which it upholds" (Pickering 2001: 3), stereotypes arise. Pickering develops this further by suggesting that:

> Stereotypes are usually considered inaccurate because of the way they portray a social group or category as homogenous. Certain forms of behaviour, disposition or propensity are isolated, taken out of context and attributed to everyone associated with a particular group or category. (2001: 4)

Thus, dual processes of homogenisation and selective representation have political dimensions insofar as they relate to or enact structures of power. The demonstrable empirical basis (or otherwise) of a stereotype is less important than how that stereotype operates within historically defined power formations.[2] I will return to this point later.

Stangor identifies five possible negative actions that may result from stereotypes: "antilocution," "avoidance," "discrimination," "physical attack," and "extermination" (2000: 25-6).

Stangor notes that prejudice may also work to advantage a group to which unfounded characteristics are attributed. He develops this by introducing the concept of "in-groups," that is groups of which an individual is a member either by achievement or ascription and with whom the individual uses "the term *we* with the same essential significance" (2000: 32). Such in-groups may then become reference groups, that is sets to which a person "feels he belongs, wants to belong, relates himself, psychologically" (Sherif and Sherif 1964: 6).[3] Membership of an in-group will make demands on the individual in terms of normative values, beliefs and standards, determining the individual's sense of self (Cohen 1989). As Pickering notes, "National character was a form of positively stereotyping a collective 'we' through an imagined personification of this identity in its ideal essence" (2001: 95). Those who do not conform to these normative models become an "out-group," an Other, either merely different or, in extreme circumstances, enemies to a given social order. As Pickering writes, "emphasising normative values and established conventions via stereotyping always entails some form of judgement about differences, about what departs from the putative sameness endorsed by the process of stereotyping in the interests of configuration of order" (2001: 5).

In the context of The Troubles[4] in Northern Ireland, stereotypes have become the focus for much activity in processes of conflict resolution, on the assumption that if communities get to know each other properly then the conflict will cease.[5] Such activity has assumed that the conflict has been essentially between two mutually exclusive identities which have generated fixed stereotypes of themselves and each other and consequently become locked into a sectarian struggle. As Ruane and Todd state, according to such accounts:

> the roots of the conflict in Northern Ireland lie in a cluster of abnormal and problematic values, beliefs and attitudes. These include: an obsession with the past conceived in mythical terms, extreme nationalism, religious intolerance, an unwillingness to compromise and a willingness to use or condone political violence. Each side is said to be in a time warp, out of touch with present-day reality, entrapped in a mythical view of the past which leads to an endless repetition of old tribal conflicts. (1991: 29)

Such explanatory frameworks reduce the complexity of the political issues to a primitive tribal struggle in which each of two sides can be categorised by the same set of stereotypes. Here then is a territory into which theatre might make an intervention, exposing such stereotypes and the power structures which they support. Indeed, this very aspiration was expressed by the directors of Field Day Theatre Company: the company "could and should contribute to the solution of the present crisis by producing analyses of the established opinions, myths and stereotypes which had become both a symptom and a cause of the current situation" (Deane *et al* 1985: vii). However, this apparent clarion call has gone largely unheeded in relation to dramatic representations of participants in the violence. Fintan O'Toole's comments on Graham Reid's *Callers* (1985) capture the dominant trend in theatrical representation:

> Writing out of a Belfast experience, he has consistently tried to root violence in the community from which it springs, exploring the intersections between personal family relations, the daily intimate cruelties and the problems of endemic pathological aggression. Like almost everyone else, however, he has held back from exploring the mind and motivations of the killers. (1985b: 11)

In turning now to my specific examples, I have chosen plays which have been staged within and outside Ireland. The first is by Gary Mitchell. In the reception of his work, much is made of Mitchell's own background in the loyalist community of Northern Ireland. He grew up and until recently lived in Rathcoole, a large Protestant housing estate in North Belfast.[6] He refuses to be categorized as an Irish playwright since he is from and seeks to address the experiences of working class loyalists who are resolutely British (Arnold 2000: 64). He is one of the few playwrights from Northern Ireland who have been subjected to intimidation by paramilitaries, recently being forced into hiding under threat from local thugs. Nonetheless, he can be regarded as part of the community about which he writes, a member of that in-group. *As The Beast Sleeps* was premiered in June 1998 on the Peacock stage of the Abbey Theatre in Dublin.[7] He has had work produced in Belfast, Derry, Dublin and London where he was writer-in-residence at the Royal National Theatre.

Briefly, *As The Beast Sleeps* explores the difficulties faced by members of a former unit of the Ulster Defence Association (UDA), as it seeks to set aside its legacy of violence. In ten scenes, the play analyses the dilemma faced by Kyle, the former unit leader, who is trapped between loyalty to the organisation and its command structure and loyalty to his wife, Sandra, and to his best friend and fellow paramilitary, Freddie. Freddie and Sandra are disenchanted, feeling discarded now that the unit's violent role and the status they enjoyed because of it have gone. Whilst Freddie has a pathological hatred of Catholics, Kyle's position is made worse by his sensitivity to the nuances of all the pressures placed on him and his inability to resist them. Mitchell includes three figures from the higher strata of the loyalist hierarchy in addition to the central trio of foot soldiers: Jack who is responsible for a local loyalist club, and is ambitious to take on the role of the legitimate entrepreneur; Larry, the next up the chain of command, who has aspirations to a part in the new politics, but is too sullied by his connections with direct action to be included; and Alec, the public face of loyalist politics, a man who talks peace and negotiations while extorting money from Larry and issuing threats of violence which he will never have to implement personally.

Initially Martin McDonagh's *The Lieutenant of Inishmore* was refused a production by three companies who had previously produced his work: Druid in Galway, and both the Royal Court and Royal National Theatre in London.[8] It was eventually produced by The Royal Shakespeare Company at The Other Place in May 2001, winning an Olivier Award for Best Comedy and transferring to the West End.[9] McDonagh was brought up in London, within the expatriate Irish community, spending most of his childhood summers at the home of his grandparents in Connemara. From the production of his first play, *The Beauty Queen of Leenane* (1996), he has had unrivalled success. He is regarded as a satirist of Irish cultural representations, a position facilitated by his English vantage point (O'Toole 2006: 42). In writing *The Lieutenant of Inishmore*, nonetheless, he sought to make a specific intervention in Irish politics, rejecting his parents' sympathy to Northern Ireland's nationalists and articulating his continued suspicion of the 'sentimental cult surrounding the men who died for the cause' (O'Toole 2006: 42). The play was a deliberate provocation. McDonagh said in 2001, "The point of it was to be dangerous, so not to do it for those reasons smacked of crass stupidity and gutlessness" (Dening 2001: 12). In a later interview, he states, "I was trying to write a play that would get me killed […] I had no real fear that I would be, because the paramilitaries never bothered with playwrights anyway, but if they were going to start I wanted to write something that would put me top of the list" (O'Toole 2006: 45).

In *The Lieutenant of Inishmore*, McDonagh starts with the death of a cat, Wee Thomas, and the effects of this death on his owner, Padraic, a former member of the Irish National Liberation Army (INLA) who now leads his own splinter group. The action spirals farcically through the consequences of the cat's death for Padraic; his father, Donny; Davey a teenage neighbour; and Davey's sixteen-year-old sister, Mairead, who is eager to demonstrate her capacities as a terrorist (which exceed even Padraic's). Padraic is being lured back to Inishmore to be punished by three INLA members for his actions in tackling a drug dealer. Thus, the principal setting is not urban Belfast or the border countryside of south Armagh, the traditional heartland of the INLA; instead, the play is set in 1993 on the island of Inishmore in County Galway.[10] This isolated location is the setting for a series of violent encounters which culminate in the murder and dismemberment of the three INLA men, and indeed of Padraic himself, so that "in the final scene the almost parodically homely cottage had become a blood-bathed slaughterhouse strewn with sundered body parts which are methodically hacked into smaller pieces" (Billington 2001: 99).

Each play is configured in relation to pre-existing stereotypes. *Belfast Telegraph* columnist Lindy McDowell, commenting on Mitchell's *Marching On* (2000), provides a short taxonomy of stereotypical representations of Protestants against which Mitchell writes: "*A* The landed gentry Anglo Prod living in The Big House. *B* The Bible-thumping Prod short on Christian charity. And *C* The Prod half of the love across the barricades couple, deeply ashamed of his/her community's intransigence" (2000: 14). Moreover, the range of representations of loyalists onstage, in film, and in literature remains extremely narrow in contrast to the lived culture of loyalists in Northern Ireland. Sierz, in reviewing Mitchell's *Trust*, commented that "Our image of Belfast loyalism is dominated by pictures of Union Jacks, bowler-hatted fanatics and marching bands; the hard men of loyalist paramilitaries are seen as cold-blooded killers – even worse than the IRA. So the first victory scored by Gary Mitchell's *Trust* is to show how even the ethnic group you love to hate are human beings too" (1999: 338). This is hardly news to loyalists themselves. Dominic Cavendish's review of *As The Beast Sleeps* recommended it as "compulsory viewing for anyone wanting to understand the current situation" (2001: 575). So, in its extension of the representation of Ulster Protestants, *As The Beast Sleeps* resists the homogenisation and selective representation of previous stereotypes.

In *The Lieutenant of Inishmore,* the figuration of Padraic *and* Mairead does much to resist the positive stereotyping through which support has been garnered for republican violence. McDonagh carefully deploys traditional republican songs throughout the play which valorise dying for the cause.[11] Against these myths of noble sacrifice, he establishes Padraic's murderous confusion of values in which an animal's life is worth more than that of a human being. Such confusion is pathological, a form of madness in which ideology can be turned to justify any action that suits Padraic in a constant readjustment of loyalties. Padraic is constantly referred to as mad, indeed in the opening scene Davey asks, "Isn't it him the IRA wouldn't let in because he was *too* mad?" (p.7). Even his own former comrades refer to him as the "Madman of Aran" (p. 29).[12] Crucially, Mitchell's depiction of Freddie in *As The Beast Sleeps* echoes almost all the same characteristics: an inflexibility in the face of changing circumstances, a proclivity for violence as the first option in problem-solving, an irrational hatred.

In the figure of Mairead, too, McDonagh usurps existing stereotypes about the relationship between women and violence. It has been suggested that:

> terrorism is a man's game. The preferred qualities of violent activism, and willingness to make use of others all constitute terrorism as an extreme expression of militant machismo [...] Women, by contrast, can only ever be 'token terrorists', masochistic victims of this demon lover, who seduces them into an alien world (Greenhalgh 1990: 161).[13]

At every turn, Mairead out-Padraics Padraic in her capacity for the extremes and capriciousness of the violence in which each revels. In *As The Beast Sleeps*, Mitchell too allows Sandra a more active role as Freddie's accomplice to a robbery than that typically provided for women in reality or female characters on the stage.

However, there is an important question which begs to be addressed: for whom were these stereotypes and resistance to them active and in what ways? To the extent that the staging of these plays engaged with spectators for whom Northern Ireland's paramilitaries are members of out-groups, they risked conforming to (and confirming) the long-established dominant discourse which separated out those engaged in political violence in Ireland as barbarians acting outside the rule of law upheld by agents of the British state. In this discourse, the Northern Irish terrorist is Irish; Catholic or extreme Protestant; from a working class background; unemployed but dependent on the State he despises; violent; and drunken (Deane 1983). This is the dominant structure of power within which these plays might be received. Patrick Magee's survey of the representation of Republicans in prose fiction reveals that "the composite Irish republican to materialise was of a Mother-Ireland fixated psycho-killer, aka a Provo Godfather, readily discernible with recourse to an identikit indebted to Tenniel's 'Irish Frankenstein' and other images from *Punch* redolent of Victorian racism" (2001: 2). Padraic could have been composed as an embodiment of this composite figure, an embodiment even more evident in the relationship suggested between his sexuality and his appetite for violence. Koenig, in reviewing Mitchell's *Loyal Women* (2003) notes that "Other playwrights, notably Martin McDonagh, have suggested that the attraction of the IRA could be the feeling of masculinity it confers on men who make up, with violence and rhetoric, their sexual and emotional failings" (2003: 1534).[14] Padraic's ideological fanaticism prevents him from reacting appropriately to the advances of Mairead until he witnesses her prowess for violence, the cold-blooded execution of the three INLA men serving as sexual foreplay. Hill discusses the link between sexuality and republican violence in cinematic representations in which IRA commandants are "not simply cold and emotionless but positively pathological. In both cases, this pathology is closely connected to sexual abnormality" (1987: 166). This suggests that in Padraic, McDonagh has drawn on a long-established typification of the militant republican.

Magee explains why the persistence of these dominant representations requires to be challenged, "To read these works uncritically is to accept at face value many assumptions that continue to hinder a resolution of the divisions in Ireland. Gross negatives of the IRA gunman, like the Irish joke or the Cummings' cartoon, offer non-explanations that have befogged the issues central to the conflict and detract from the ongoing search for a just and lasting peace settlement" (2001: 2). This sense in which both plays are available to be recuperated by out-groups in terms of pre-existing stereotypes is evident in their critical reception. In reviewing *As The Beast Sleeps* at London's Tricycle Theatre in 2001, Brian Logan wrote, "The plays of Gary Mitchell are an indispensable means of understanding the *intransigence* of the Ulster Protestant community in the face of the Irish peace process" (2001: 1219-20); while Charles Spencer for *The Daily Telegraph* wrote "Mitchell comes from the North, and the Protestant North at that. He gets right to the heart of the *dour, stubborn* Protestant mindset " (2001: 1221) [my emphases]. Thus, instead of opening up the conception of what motivates loyalists *politically*, the play has merely expanded the typifications of loyalists to which the stereotypical epithets might be applied. Likewise, an American review of *The Lieutenant of Inishmore* concludes, "Only McDonagh has had the nerve to show up terrorism as the last resort of fools, a moronic solution to injustice that only breeds more atrocious behaviour. It would interesting to see how this comedy would play in, say, Tehran--- that is, if anyone would allow that to happen" (Barbour 2006 [online]).

In neither instance have the productions been able to challenge the 'in-groups' which support the paramilitaries. Rather, they implicate the spectator as a member of a community who regards the paramilitaries as other. Relatedly, neither play has had a production for the communities from which the paramilitaries are drawn. The theatre work of companies like Frontline in Derry and DubbelJoint in West Belfast did much to challenge the boundaries of republican communities in a series of expansive acts.[15] As Daniel Baron Cohen (2001) explains, Derry Frontline's work over four years from the late 1980s was informed by the work of Freire and Boal and sought to enable participants to analyse and critique their lives and experiment with alternatives. They produced three plays *Inside Out* (1988), *Time will Tell* (1989) and *Threshold* (1992) which challenged dominant conceptions of gender and sexuality; the role of the Catholic Church; and global capitalism. DubbelJoint was established in 1991 by playwright Marie Jones and director Pam Brighton, mounting premieres of a number of Jones's plays, including *A Night in November* (1994) and the original production of *Stones in his Pockets* (1996). However, over the course of its history the company's work engaged in crucial debates as Republicans sought to move beyond armed struggle. Bill McDonnell cites a press release for *A Cold House*

(2003) by former prisoners, Laurence McKeown and Brian Campbell, which situates the production within this dialogic process:

> *A Cold House* is about what happens when war ends and people are forced to drop the convenient stereotypes that conflict fosters and recognize a more complex humanity in each other. Whatever name one gives to the other, terrorist or state terrorist, each is compelled to recognize the human across the kitchen table and see themselves in the other's eyes (2008: 186).

Such a production might be regarded then as one of a series of expansive acts which "will aim to encourage and expand social meanings wherever they are strong. They will move beyond the determinist fallacy of seeing people solely as the products of a given, and pre-existing, culture, and take into account their roles as co-authors of that culture" (Kelly 1984: 51). Productions which engage in such expansive acts offer those communities the opportunity to regard themselves within a process of internal dialogue, posing questions with a resonance which requires real and local rather than aesthetic resolutions.

The argument here is not that there should be a greater balance in the depiction of paramilitaries: a more complete or less homogenised representation. Rather, it is to demonstrate that for spectators for whom Northern Irish paramilitaries are already an out-group, these plays conform to hegemonic stereotypes, reinforcing existing structures of power. They thereby limit the possibility of engaging with loyalism or republicanism as political forces within the peace processes which they attempt to address. It has been by recognising the possibility of negotiated change that participants in peace-building processes have been able to engage with each other in Northern Ireland. The deployment of stereotypes within dramatic representations, however, suggests that it is fixity rather than flexibility that characterises those involved in conflict. To this extent then when these productions are staged in theatres outside of the communities which they represent, they conform both to dominant conventions for the experience of theatre and globally-mediatised stereotypes of the paramilitaries and the conflict. For such audiences and in such contexts, spectators are able to engage in a theatrical voyeurism inflected with the distance of class and political identity, viewing the paramilitary heartlands as a foreign country where the mad people do things differently.

NOTES

[1] The production opened at London's Royal Court Upstairs in March. Date references are to the first productions of the plays. Parenthetical page references refer to the published editions cited in the bibliography.

[2] This resolves the difficulty in distinguishing stereotypes as conceptual categories from prejudice as actual behaviour (for example, O'Donnell 1977).

[3] This latter part may account for Fanon's ideas of inferiorism.

[4] This is the widely used term for the most recent period of political violence in Northern Ireland: its use, however, has occluded the lived reality of many people and their experiences of politics which have not been focused on either the constitutional status of Northern Ireland or the sectarian conflict which has fuelled the violence.

[5] For a critique of this see, for example, Bell (1998).

[6] The estate had been built in the 1950s as an area of integrated social housing. At the start of the Troubles, when working-class areas became segregated along sectarian lines (see Boal 1987) Catholics were forced to leave.

[7] The original production was directed by Conall Morrison and the play was subsequently produced in April 2001 at The Lyric Theatre in Belfast under the direction of John Sheehan and then at London's Tricycle Theatre in September 2001. In 2001, BBC Northern Ireland produced a film version which premiered at the Edinburgh Film Festival and was screened on BBC2 in February 2002.

[8] Lonergan (2005) demolishes the myth that this was because the play was "too dangerous to be done," despite McDonagh's self-promotion to the contrary.

[9] The original production (re-cast to tour) was subsequently presented at the Olympia Theatre, Dublin, opening on 29th September 2003, as part of the 2003 Dublin Theatre Festival. The play received its American premiere at the Atlantic Theatre Company in February 2006 and transferred to the Lyceum Theatre on Broadway. It was nominated for five Tony Awards, including best play.

[10] McDonagh asserts that the play was set on the Aran islands because for plot purposes he needed a place in Ireland that would take a long time to get to from Belfast (Dening 2001: 12).

[11] He borrows from the conventions of the musical so that Mairead and Padraic conduct a form of courtship through sharing the same song.

[12] There is a parallel between Padraic's activities and those of the actual INLA, one of whose members, Dessie O'Hare was, for example, responsible for the kidnap of a Dublin dentist whose fingers he hacked off with a hammer and chisel.

[13] It is ironic that feminist analyses which emphasize essential differences between men and women have coincided with the same kind of gender role fixing in Northern Ireland within which actual women activists have been marginalized within masculinist discourses. One of the Republican women interviewed by Dowler puts the point forcibly: "There are a couple of songs about women but most of them are about the men. It is absolutely desperate it is, the bold Fenian Men. What of the bold Fenian *Women?*" (1998: 170).

[14] Lonergan (2005) explores this as a positive facet of the play's political intervention.

[15] See Maguire 2006 and McDonnell 2008 for a further discussion of such work.

REFERENCES

Arnold, Bruce (2000). "The State of Irish Theatre" in Eamonn Jordan, ed. *Theatre Stuff: Critical Essays on Contemporary Irish Theatre*. Dublin: Carysfort Press, 59-66.

Barbour, David (2006). "Broadway: *The Lieutenant of Inishmore* (Lyceum Theatre)." *Lighting&Sound America Online,* Theatre in Review (15 May). <http://www.lightingandsoundamerica.com/news/story.asp?ID=VP45YO> [Accessed 17 July 2006].

Baron Cohen, Dan (2001). *Theatre of Self-Determination: The Plays of Derry Frontline, Culture and Education*. Derry: Guildhall Press.

Bell, Desmond (1998). "Modernising history: the real politik of heritage and cultural tradition in Northern Ireland" in David Miller, ed. *Rethinking Northern Ireland*. London: Longman, 228-252.

Billington, Michael (2001). *"The Lieutenant of Inishmore." Irish Theatre Magazine* 2 (9), 97-99.

Boal, Frederick W. (1987). "Segregation" in Michael Pacione, ed. *Social Geography: Progress and Prospect*. London: Croom Helm, 90-128.

Brantley, Ben (2006). "Terrorism Meets Absurdism in a Rural Village in Ireland." *New York Times*. (28 February) <http://theater2.nytimes.com/2006/02/28/theater/reviews/28inis.html> [Accessed 2 July 2006].

Cavendish, Dominic (2001). *"As The Beast Sleeps." Daily Telegraph* (3 May) in *Theatre Record* (23 April- 6 May), 575.

Cohen, Anthony P. (1989). *The Symbolic Construction of Community*. London: Routledge.

Cornell, Jennifer C. (1999). "Recontextualising the Conflict: Northern Ireland, Television Drama, and the Politics of Validation" in John P Harrington and Elizabeth J. Mitchell, eds. *Politics and Performance in Contemporary Northern Ireland*. Amherst: University of Massachusetts Press, 197-218.

Curtis, Nick, (1999). *"Trust." Evening Standard* (16 March) in *Theatre Record* (12-25 March 1999), 339.

Deane, Seamus (1983). *Civilians and Barbarians*. Derry: Field Day Theatre Company.

Deane, Seamus, et. al. (1985*). Ireland's Field Day: Field Day Theatre Company*. London: Hutchinson.

Dening, Penelope (2001). "The Scribe of Kilburn." *Irish Times* (23 April), 12.

Dowler, L. (1998) "'And They Think I'm just a Nice Old Lady' Women and War in Belfast, Northern Ireland." *Gender, Place and Culture* 5 (2), 159-76.

Greenhalgh, Susan (1990). "The Bomb in the Baby Carriage: Women and Terrorism in Contemporary Drama" in John Orr and Dragan Klaić, eds. *Terrorism and Modern Drama*. Edinburgh: Edinburgh University Press, 160-83.

Hill, John (1987). "Images of Violence" in Kevin Rockett, Luke Gibbons, and John Hill. *Cinema and Ireland*. London: Croom Helm, 147-93.

Kelly, Owen (1984). *Community, Art, and the State: Storming the Citadels*. London: Comedia.

Koenig, Rhoda (2003). *"Loyal Women." Independent* (13 November) in *Theatre Record* (5-18 November,) 1534.

Logan, Brian (2001). "*As The Beast Sleeps.*" *Time Out* (26 September) in *Theatre Record* (9-23 September), 1219-20.

Lonergan, Patrick (2005). "Too Dangerous to be Done? Martin McDonagh's *Lieutenant of Inishmore.*" *Irish Studies Review* 13 (1), 65-78.

Magee, Patrick (2001). *Gangsters or Guerrillas? Representations of Irish Republicans in 'Troubles' Fiction.* Belfast: Beyond the Pale Publications.

Maguire, Tom (2006). *Making Theatre in Northern Ireland: Through and Beyond the Troubles.* Exeter: University of Exeter Press.

McDonagh, Martin (2001). *The Lieutenant of Inishmore.* London: Methuen.

McDonnell, Bill (2008). *Theatres of the Troubles: Theatre, Resistance and Liberation in Ireland.* Exeter: University of Exeter Press.

McDowell, Lindy (2004). "Marching on to a new appreciation." *Belfast Telegraph* (23 June), 14.

Mitchell, Gary (2001). *As The Beast Sleeps.* London: Nick Hern Books.

O'Donnell, Edward E. (1977). *Northern Irish Stereotypes.* Dublin: College of Industrial Relations.

O'Toole, Fintan (2006). "A Mind in Connemara: The Savage World of Martin McDonagh." *The New Yorker* (6 March), 40-47.

Pickering, Michael (2001). *Stereotyping: The Politics of Representation.* Basingstoke: Palgrave.

Sherif, Muzafer and Sherif, Carolyn W. (1964). *Reference Groups. Exploration into Conformity and Deviation of Adolescents.* New York and London: Harper and Row.

Sierz, Aleks (1999). "*Trust.*" *Tribune* (26 March) in *Theatre Record* (12 –25 March), 338.

Spencer, Charles (2001). "*As The Beast Sleeps.*" *Daily Telegraph* (25 September) in *Theatre Record* (9-23 September), 1221.

Stangor, Charles (2000). *Stereotypes and Prejudice: Essential Readings.* Philadelphia, PA: Psychology Press.

THE COMEBACK OF POLITICAL DRAMA IN CROATIA: OR *HOW TO KILL A PRESIDENT* BY MIRO GAVRAN[1]

SANJA NIKČEVIĆ

Although Croatian drama was very subversive during the communist system, after the fall of communism so called political drama disappeared from Croatian theatre as well as from other theatres in the countries of former Yugoslavia. If 'political drama' is talking about the social and political forces that destroy the life of an individual, it looked like playwrights in the new political system could not define who the representatives of life-shaping forces were: bureaucracy, nationalist governments, mafia in rise, *nouveau riche*... At some point, war plays tried to fulfill that function but were marginalized in Croatian theatre. On the other side, plays about dysfunctional families were offered as the best political plays possible although in those plays society was so unrecognizable that no political representative could see the criticism. The comeback of political drama in Croatia happened with the play by Miro Gavran, *How to Kill a President* (2003). This defined globalization as a force that shapes and destroys our lives.

POLITICAL DRAMA IN THE SEVENTIES
Political drama describes political and social forces that shape the life of an individual; actually, not just shape but also destroy because political drama is always critical of or subversive toward society and its political representatives. He considers affirmative political plays as mere propaganda (Melchinger 1971: 10). Boris Senker defined Croatian plays that were especially critical toward society at the end of sixties and in the seventies as *a political wave* (Senker 2001: 24-32). In order to escape political repercussions, these plays were applying a kind of genre mimicry—the playwrights were running

away from the mainstream dramatic forms of high art (drama, tragedy) into the lower genres,[2] mostly comedies or absurd grotesques, later nominated as *political grotesques* (Mrkonjić 1985: 55). Nevertheless, representatives of political structures in power recognized themselves in the grotesque picture and struck back.

There were some very direct, very personal, and very dangerous attacks in the media or at festivals' round tables. A Cornerstone of this kind of political writing is Ivo Brešan, whose play, *Hamlet u selu Mrduša Donja/Performance of Hamlet in Small Town,* written in 1965 (published and staged 1971), (Milutinović 2004: 161-177) was severely criticized *as dangerous and anti-socialist* on prime-time TV news by an esteemed literary critic who was also a highly political figure. The play was about a rural attempt to stage Shakespeare's *Hamlet* and during that staging Hamlet's story is repeated in a contemporary version and with communistic vocabulary. The main communist is a crook who sacrificed the honest accountant and is now using his own daughter to destroy the accountant's son because the son seeks the truth and revenge. Skrabe-Mujčić-Senker's *Domagojada/Play about Domagoj* (1975), a play about historical misunderstandings of Croats, was openly and directly attacked at the round table of the Sarajevo international festival MESS with similar arguments.

Sometimes plays were silenced soon after opening nights. Nedeljko Fabrio's *Reformers* (1968) is a historical play about real historical figures who actually represent the highest contemporary political figures: Martin Luther, as an old charismatic leader who is now enjoying laurels and some worldly enjoyments was a picture of our president Tito, while a Croatian reformer, Matthias Flacius Illyricus, the only one who stayed pure in following revolutionary ideas because of which he was expelled and abandoned, was easily recognized as representing some of our contemporary communist dissidents.

The political pressure on theatres and directors became so high that after a while they were not willing to stage contemporary Croatian drama at all. For that reason, not just political, but Croatian drama in general, was silenced during the eighties. At the end of the sixties and in the seventies we had more than twenty very active new playwrights, mostly political (e.g. Brešan, Bakamaz, Bužimski, Bakarić, Fabrio, Kušan, Šoljan, Šnajder, Škrabe-Mujčić-Senker, and so on), but in the eighties most of these names were not staged, and we got just three new names (Miro Gavran, Lada Kaštelan, and Mate Matišić). Obviously, the sword of political drama was broken.

THE NINETIES OR THE SILENCED POLITICAL SUBVERSIVE VOICES

When we finally gained the longed for independence in 1991, everybody expected that freedom from the communistic regime and the proclaimed democracy would allow playwrights to write about all the "forbidden topics." But quite the opposite happened. Playwrights that used to be the most subversive in the seventies were either still silenced, or changed their genre and began to write prose (Ivan Kušan, Nedjeljko Fabrio, Dubravko Jelačić Bužimski) or poetry (Tahir Mujčić). Some others started to write other dramatic genres: Boris Senker writes intertextual postmodern literary cabarets (*Frietzspil* from 2002 gives several different funny versions of the Croatian classical play *Noble Glembay's/ Gospoda Glembajevi* by M. Krleža), Nino Skrabe writes religious plays and melodramas, and Ivan Bakmaz dramatizes biblical stories.

It looks as if, with the independence of Croatia, writers could not precisely define the political force that governs our lives. They could not recognize clear personifications of power that can then be shown in the play. That personification in the former system was an uneducated, primitive person of power who, in the name of big ideas about "equality, rights for small men" and "a bright future," destroys everybody who opposes, especially intellectuals who constantly criticize the reality.

WAR PLAYS IN THE POLITICAL FUNCTION

The nineties are important for Croatia not just because we gained political independence but because the price for that independence was a terrible war. The war shaped our lives for nearly ten years and maybe that is why war plays tried to take over the political function of the plays. War plays that were written in Croatia in the nineties can be roughly divided into the emotional and political. Emotional plays like Lydija Scheurman Hodak's *Maria's Pictures/Slike Marijine* (1992),[3] Hrvoje Barbir's *Telmah* (1996), and Renato Orlić's *Between Two Sky /Između dva neba* (1997) show victims without much debate about guilt. Political war plays are written from a very obvious political point of view (they talk about the guilt, the aim, the goals and reasons for the war, and about the role of politics in it) and you can easily define the political stand of the plays as "left" or "right." The so called "left" tried to find the explanation or reasons for this war in Croatian guilt or by explaining that guilt is equally shared (Slobodan Šnajder *Snake's Skin / Zmijin svlak*, 1994).[4] The so called "right" were very clear about Croatian innocence and tried to show that all the guilt rests with the Serbian aggressor or international forces that simply inhibited Croatian defenses and in that way helped the aggressor (Tomislav Bakarić *Whiskey for his excellence /Whiskey za njegovu ekscelenciju*, 1994).

Political war plays were written from a sense of duty to express the attitude toward war. For that reason, these plays very often turned into a cold, unemotional construction; whereas emotional versions were much better. But, as Croatian theatre avoided that topic in either political or emotional versions, war plays never had the same power of political plays from the seventies and stayed marginalized in Croatian theatre. Those kinds of plays were staged on off productions in Croatia and their reception was greater outside Croatia (Nikčević 2003: 49-67).

Croatian theatre in the nineties offered plays that described the worst sides of society (which used to be called *new pessimism*) as political drama. The work of Ivan Vidic and Asja Srnec-Todorović, P. Marinković, and M. Brumec[5] fitted into the contemporary fashionable trends of postmodernism (quoting, metatextuality, mixing the styles and genres, open form...) and deconstruction (abolishing the meaning of the character and the world around). The latter characteristic meant that flat, reduced characters lived in a sort of vacuum meaning that the political forces could not be defined or recognized. This fit into the European trend of the so-called *new European drama* that flourished in Europe during the nineties, as clones of British playwrights Sarah Kane and Mark Ravenhill. Although that trend was usually advertised as political and subversive, these plays offered only shocking pictures from the edge of society (drug addicts, prostitutes, and abusers) and were emotionally implosive and apolitical (Nikčević 2005: 255-272). The same situation was with British representatives, most known examples of new European drama (Marius von Mayenburg) or mentioned Croatian playwrights.

FIGHTING THE PAST

The third kind of plays that were considered political in the nineties in Croatia were the "fight with the past" plays. New plays about sins of the former system were written or old ones staged, and the audience was supposed to detect the parallels and understand the new world around them. But the attempts to write new plays about the old system were not very successful, even for the most successful former political playwrights like Ivo Brešan or Slobodan Šnajder.

More media attention was given to the theatrical "fight with the past," especially the newly started Theatre Ulysses by Rade Serbedžija, on the famous island of Brijuni (the island where former president Tito had his summer residence and was visited by famous guests from all over the world). Rade Serbedžija is an excellent Croatian actor who attained world fame through Hollywood movies. With performances at Theatre Ulysses (*King Lear* 2002, *Marat-Sade* 2003, *Play Becket,* 2004) he tried to depict the main sins of the former regime as reasons for its failure. These performances, however, were made from the point of view that the communistic system was good but just had some aberrations—the same position that Rade Serbedžija held before. He played in some of the most critical performances of the former system but was nevertheless devoted to the system and the idea of Yugoslavia, up to the point that he really lost his homeland with the rupture of Yugoslavia.

In spite of different theatrical successes, these plays could not find answers to today's problem. The critical performances used to be an exhaustive valve in the former system—the opponents of the system were glad to see the aberrations publicly exposed, the true followers of the system believed that the exposure of the bad sides would improve the system. After the fall of communism emotions stayed the same but the positions are different. The believers in the communist system do not want to see its faults today and the general affirmation of the communistic idea in these plays are not enough for them. The opponents do not like affirmation of the main communistic ideas on stage and revealing only some faults of the system is not enough for them.

In spite of media attention, these plays could not help today's audience understand much about their lives, because, in spite of the ghost from our past that periodically disturbs us, the modern world is moving forward and our lives are shaped by some other influences, forces other than former communism.

It is very interesting that a similar situation was found in other former republics of Yugoslavia. The most subversive, the most political playwrights from the former system are lost in the new one. Dušan Jovanović, from Slovenia, wrote a play with an English title (*Exhibitionist*), under the pseudonym O. J. Traven. Set in New York it talks about brokers, prostitutes, and drug dealers—a world that has nothing to do with the author. He publically admitted *that this play was like a safe and I didn't have a key for it* (Traven 2001: 6). For earlier plays like *Liberation of Skopje /Oslobodenje Skopja* (1979), one of his most famous plays, he had the key for sure. A similar thing happened to Dušan Kovačević, a Serbian playwright, one of the best and one of the most critical about the former system (*Balkanski špijun/Balkan Spy*, 1982, *Profesionalac/Professional* 1990). He still writes about Serbia but his plays have become a pastiche of topics and ideas (*Fife Star Dumpster/Kontejner sa pet zvezdica*, 1999) without the political subversiveness of former plays.[6]

POLITICS AROUND THE PRESIDENT

Obviously, all former political playwrights lost the enemies that symbolized the system, so they could not recognize new forces that shape us. Most of them still live in the old world (in the apartments they got from the state, doing the jobs that are paid by state, staging plays in governmentally subsided theaters, publishing books with financial support form Ministry of Culture…).

Although there were some attempts by younger playwrights to describe our contemporary society and detect the problems within it (in the work of Nina Mitrović, *Neighborhood Upside down /Komšiluk naglavačke*, 2002 or some plays of Ivan Vidić like *Octopussy* 2002, *The Big White Rabbit/ Veliki bijeli zec* 2004) the real comeback of political drama in Croatia is the play *How to Kill a President/Kako ubiti predsjednika* (2003) by Miro Gavran.

This play could answer the question of why the former political playwrights were silenced—maybe because they were searching for their enemies too closely, in some local bureaucrat or some political figure, or some new rich and powerful person (mafia). Miro Gavran went a little bit further and broadened the view. *How to Kill a President* is a political play because it defines globalization as a force that shapes (destroys) our personal lives and all small countries including Croatia. Globalization is a tendency that is explored in Gavran's play (and in a lot of sociological, philosophical, or political contemporary works), considered also as Americanization.

"The plot takes place in a transitional European country at the beginning of the 21st century,"[7] that recently gained independence and changed its political system, from communism into democracy. The four characters are in front of us.

Robert, a former dissident and a very ardent opponent of the communist system is now a director of the state Institute of Sociology and an esteemed professor. He is satisfied with his life, which includes his wife Stella (a director of a psychiatric hospital) and the twins. He is just preparing an affirmative paper for an upcoming conference on globalization.

After nine years of silence, Robert received an e-mail form his younger brother Igor who went to study for a Ph.D. in the USA years ago. Soon, Igor is arriving and we learn why he is in his homeland again. Igor became the head of an anti-globalization movement that consists of a lot of educated people who are terrified by the process of globalization and the results of it—destruction of any freedom in the name of profit, destruction of any diversity and quality and culture in the name of a unified lowest common denominator that is coming from one source. This movement has decided to act and that is why Igor has come back to his former country. He is supposed to kill the American president while he is visiting this country. Igor believes that this murder, and some other planned murders of influential people from the top of the globalization movement, would send a clear message. It would also make a centre of globalization power a tool for Igor and his friend to *make this world a better place.*

Igor chose his country to fulfill that task not just because he knows the country but also because he wanted to show his brother that he is still fighting for mutual ideals, *for a better world.* He believes that this is the best way to continue the fight that was fought by his father and his older brother. But things are not going as he planed. The conversation of the two brothers begins with emotions and memories of childhood, ideals about independence of the country, the wished-for fall of the communist regime… but very soon it becomes obvious that they now take different positions. The conversation soon becomes a debate on the topic of globalization. Whereas Robert thinks that globalization is the only chance for small countries to enter into the *society of the civilized world*, Igor has a completely different opinion; he considers it as a terrible defeat of the entire ideal for which they fought and sacrificed:

> This system is highly dangerous for small countries, I can even say destructive, they fall from debt to debt, and depend on international financial institutes, such as the World Bank and the International Monetary Fund. The result of this is that their free activities are drastically limited. A country in debt has to reduce the income of its own citizens, cut down on social services, and invest in the manner in which their creditors order, if they should be able to pay off their overdue credits which are greater and greater every year. This is pure usury, modern colonialism. And what is saddest is that such vassal colonized countries, and ours is one of them, must have such a government, which knows how to wrap up its vassalage in an acceptable package and sell it to its citizens, so that all this would proceed under the conditions of social peace and apparent national pride [...] for how can you tell a beggar that he is a beggar. Big corporations invest big money to discredit local, national movements, and for the very idea of national states to be destroyed as obsolete and fascist. What is most absurd is that capitalist corporations find today in this slave labor the best allies in the rows of former Communists, left-wingers and humanists, who reject every idea of national domiciliation. Some kind of united front is formed, between left-wing internationalism and globalized capitalism. And the perspective of mankind, the perspective of all of us, is so black that it couldn't be blacker: the empire of a big, inhumane multi-national corporation—the blackest dictatorship, like no single futurist could imagine. The small are left with desperation and false hopes [...]. They want individuals to disappear, and for only consumers and producers to remain. When they destroy all natural wealth and pollute every river, they know that the last source of drinkable water will be in their hands. Although, certainly, it will not be found in the territory of their state. (Scene 8)

Igor is ready to go on, fight, and sacrifice more, but Robert is tired of all fights and longs for a normal life:

> ROBERT: [...] I just ask you, don't now do something that could destroy you. Don't jeopardize yourself, and don't jeopardize my family, my wife and my children. I want at least a relatively normal life. My father destroyed my childhood, and I destroyed my youth myself, tilting exhaustingly at windmills. I lived so many years as an outcast, like a scabby cur. I no longer have the strength for this. Do not do this to yourself. I was a lone wolf. I thought that it was best for a man of my mould to go through life alone. Luckily, Stella appeared. Only in the last few years have I lived a normal life, accepted by the community. Please, don't take this away from me.

IGOR: You've become a slimy Philistine. (Scene 11)

This play is *a thesis*, but Miro Gavran is well known for his lively characters and emotional situations. So here we have not just the emotional conflict of two brothers, but women characters as well who bring real-life problems into the play. The first female character is Igor's girlfriend and collaborator until a private tragedy befalls her. Her parents were killed in a car accident and in the deepest grief she has found faith and cannot go on with Igor's terrorist ideas.

The second female character is Stella, "an ideal Robert's wife," as she said. Not just because she loves him, but because she has transformed Robert from an *unreal idealist* into a *real man of flesh and blood who can enjoy the family life*. She is even more terrified with Igor's idea. Robert and Stella are not just afraid for their family but also for the reputation of their country which can be expelled from the *circle of civilized countries* if it is host to such a terrible event. So Robert and Stella have to decide how to react to such a plan—should they just watch, should they report their own brother to the police, or…?

In the play we have four different attitudes toward globalization (from terrorism to a return to spiritual values) and sort of an open end because nobody persuaded other character in the play (force does not count). With a conflict of two brothers, Gavran gives a picture of the world around us very strongly, and the very clear cut at the end will leave nobody without a stand. In this play Gavran is following Brecht and the main position of political plays by asking the audience not just to think about it, but to act in the world. Gavran asks for participation of the audience, a continuation of the discussion, but also that we choose our own stand. Everybody in the audience has to decide who he/she is—a conformist who can go to the reception of the minister who was "yesterday publicly accusing you of being anti-socialist" or a real person who thinks that the biggest conformism is to "stay in the status of eternal rebellion." Are you the uncompromised idealist in a faith against "injustice of this world," or a radically blinded stubborn person who ends by committing the crime called terrorism? Are we ready to accept the changes of the society, are we aware who is making decisions about our lives and how to survive in new circumstances, or are we just candidates for Stella's new ward in the hospital—the one for new psychic diseases caused "by fear of new trends"—from globalization to GMO?

This comeback of the political play perfectly corresponds with European theatre trends (documentary plays, called *verbatim* in Great Britain). Tired of the socially unrecognizable worlds of the *new brutalism* or *in-yer-face* drama, Anglo-American theatre is turning toward real social problems presented in the real words of participants. Although I can understand the reasons for verbatim theatre, I consider it a braver move to make an artistic artifact with real social problems and solutions and not just hide yourself with exact words and a lot of questions.

Maybe that is why Gavran's play is so successful: it was published in Slovakia in 2003, a year before the first Croatian production (Zagreb, Teatar ITD, directed by Zoran Muzic, 2004), the same year it was staged in Wien (Teatar Brett); in 2005 in Sarajevo, BIH (Kamerni teatar/Chamber theatre); in 2006 in Germany (Theatre Sensemble from Augsburg) and published in France. As Robert would say: "You cannot deny that globalization has some good sides."

But the picture is not so simple. In one eastern European country, the TV show was not made because it was considered to be too dangerous. So obviously it is not just me who recognizes the play as strongly political.

NOTES

[1] The first version of this article was presented in 2005 at a symposium on "Playwriting today in Bosnia and Herzegovina, Croatia, Serbia and Montenegro," held in Zagreb and organized by the Slavic department from Sorbonne Paris and Department of Comparative literature from the Faculty of Philosophy at Zagreb. It was titled "Return of political drama." The article was subsequently published in a book (Disput, Zagreb, 2007). With the continuation of research I developed the article as part of the chapter "Croatian political drama" that has just recently been published in my new book *What is Croatian drama to us?* (Croatia, Zagreb, 2008). Both editions are in Croatian. I presented that topic in English at 2006 FIRT congress in Helsinki.

[2] Similar processes of dramatic mimicry happened in Russia where, a decade later, subversive plays and performances were staged in puppet theatres.

[3] Published in PAJ, 77/2004

[4] Published in PAJ 60/1998
[5] A good source about Croatian drama is the website of the Croatian Centre of ITI, http: //www.hciti.hr/
[6] http: //en.wikipedia.org/wiki/Du%C5%A1an_Kova%C4%8Devi%C4%87
[7] Quotes from a play from <http://www.mgavran2.htnet.hr/plays/complete/president.html> [Accessed 20 March 2009].

REFERENCES

Melchinger, Siegried. (1989) *Povijest političkog kazališta*. Vida Flaker, trans. Zagreb: GZH.

Senker, Boris. (2001) *Hrestomatija novije hrvatske drame* 2. *1941-1995*. Zagreb: Disput.

Mrkonjić, Zvonimir. (1985) *Ogledalo mahnitosti*. Zagreb: CKD.

Milutinović, Zoran. (2004) "The People are Hamlet's Friend: Meta-theatricality and Politics in Ivo Brešan's *Predstava Hamleta u selu Mrduša Donja*." *Central Europe* 2 (2), 161-177.

Nikčević, Sanja. (2003) "Croatian Theatre and War," *Slavic and Eastern European Performance* 23 (2), 49-67.

———. (2005) "British Brutalism, the 'New European Drama,' and the Role of the Director." *New Theatre Quarterly* 83, 255-272.

Traven, O. J. (2001). "Moj pseudonym," in O. J. Traven *Exhibitionist* [Slovenian national theater, Ljubljana] playbill, 4-10.

LOCAL KNOWLEDGES, MEMORIES, AND COMMUNITY: FROM ORAL HISTORY TO PERFORMANCE

DAVID WATT

Documentary theatre appears to have made a comeback since the 1990s, and is even more prominent as a performative form within what Baz Kershaw has referred to as the "theatre estate" (Kershaw 1999) than in its two earlier boom periods, the 1930s and 1960s. This comeback has given us, in Britain, the series of "Tribunal Plays" (from *Half the Picture*, based on the Scott Arms to Iraq Inquiry, in 1994 to *Guantanamo* in 2006, to a variant of "verbatim" in *Called to Account* in 2007), which have increasingly moved out of the tiny Tricycle Theatre and toured internationally; Max Stafford-Clark's recent work in the form with his company, Out Of Joint, including Robin Soans' *A State Affair* (2000) and *Talking to Terrorists* (2005) and David Hare's *The Permanent Way* (2005); and a number of one-offs such as Soans' *Arab-Israeli Cookbook* (at the Gate Theatre in London in 2004 and then on tour*)*, and *Blackwatch* at the National Theatre of Scotland in 2006 before an international tour. The USA has seen, since Emily Mann's work of the 1980s, the ongoing work of Anna Deavere Smith which has contributed to the development of a strand of solo-performer work based on oral history interviews such as Ron Vawter's *Roy Cohn/Jack Smith* (1992), and Marc Wolf's *Another American* (1999) and *The Road Home* (2005); Tectonic Theatre Project's *Gross Indecency: The Three Trials of Oscar Wilde* (1997) and *The Laramie Project* (1999); and a number of one-off "verbatim" plays, from Eve Ensler's *The Vagina Monologues* in 1996 to *The Exonerated* in 2002. In the last few years in Australia we have seen two verbatim pieces by Alana Valentine at Belvoir Street Theatre, *Run Rabbit Run* (2004) and *Parramatta Girls* (2007); *Embers* (2006), by Campion Decent, on the 2003 bushfires in eastern Australia at the

Sydney Theatre Company (via Hothouse in Albury/Wodonga, a community-based company), and a number of works on Australia's refugee crisis, like Ros Horin's *Through the Wire*, which toured nationally in 2005, and *Citizen X* (2002), by the Sidetrack Performance Group, and the emergence of a company, Version 1.0, which, since it's *CMI (A Certain Maritime Incident)* toured the country in 2004, has consistently utilised documentary material in ways which owe at least as much to the experimental work descendent from the Wooster Group and Forced Entertainment as to "conventional" documentary practices. And this is merely the high profile work: much more can be found on the fringes of the "theatre estate."

This surge in popularity, even seen as displacing "the 1990s vogue for 'in your face' plays" in Britain (Bottoms 2006: 56), has also been reflected in a new academic interest in documentary theatre, indicated by the publication of Atilio Favorini's anthology, *Voicings* (1995), the publication of Gary Fisher Dawson's *Documentary Theatre in the United States* (1999), the production of a special issue of *The Drama Review* devoted entirely to it in 2006, which indicates a similar re-emergence of the form in Germany, Israel and other places, and Della Pollock's recent collection of essays, *Remembering*, which indicates a somewhat different strain of performative work to which I will return.

The movement of plays which have piqued the interest of the "theatre estate" and moved from small alternative performance spaces to national or even international touring indicates their new-found status as highly saleable international commodities. Interestingly, it is what Derek Paget dubbed the "verbatim" play (Paget 1987) which has been, in the words of a recent newspaper reviewer, "deeply fashionable" (Higgins 2004): in a paradox of globalization, verbatim plays—often rendered "authentic" by their "localism"—have become "universal" in their appeal to cosmopolitan theatergoers, reducing "authenticity" to the status of yet another global commodity. The "fashionability"—indicated by the fact that Googling "verbatim theatre" produces 1,020,000 hits in 0.18 seconds—has not always extended to a particularly clear sense of what it is or, more to the point, where it came from. It also hides the fact that the documentary impulse has been there all along, if not in the mainstream, and in a fairly direct line from the origins of a more community-based and localised version of the form in the 1960s and 1970s. My concern here is to trace this other, buried tradition of verbatim theatre from its emergence in the 1960s through its development as a staple for what used to be called "community theatre" and is now more commonly referred to as "applied theatre" in Britain and Australia, or "community-based theatre" in North America. This, I believe, is the more interesting strand, in that its resistance of the commodity status of work within the "theatre estate" opens out a range of possibilities of a more fully socially engaged practice.

When "documentary theatre" *first* emerged, and Bertolt Brecht gave it the name in 1926—the same year as John Greirson coined the term in relation to documentary film (Favorini 1995: xviii)—it did so with a commitment to social engagement and some "world-historical" ambitions. Erwin Piscator's stated intention for the documentary theatre he is customarily credited with having invented indicates that ambition: "the essential point of my whole work," he said in 1929, was:

> the presentation of solid proof that our philosophy and all that can be deduced from it is the one and only valid approach for our time [...]. Conclusive proof can be based only on scientific analysis of the material. This I can only do, in the language of the stage, if I can get beyond scenes from life, beyond the purely individual aspect of the characters and the fortuitous nature of their fates. And the way to do this is to show the link between events on the stage and the great forces active in history. (Piscator 1978: 93)

The initial appeal of the documentary mode in the 1930s, for the leftwing theatre practitioners who greeted it with such enthusiasm in Germany, Russia, Britain, and the USA, was this sense of its explanatory power, exemplified as clearly in the Living Newspapers of the Federal Theatre Project and in Ewan MacColl and Joan Littlewood's experiments in Manchester, both of which made use of verbatim material, even if not gathered by tape recorder. For Peter Weiss almost 40 years later, the attraction was much the same: documentary theatre, he claimed, as a result of the form's "ability to shape a useful pattern from fragments of reality, to build a model of actual occurrences, [...] asserts [...] that reality, however opaque it may appear, can be explained in every detail" (Weiss 1971b: 42-3). There were many who shared his confidence, but it became increasingly difficult to sustain such a point of view, and Weiss's own

The Investigation fails to "explain" the Holocaust, although his *Discourse on Vietnam*, which was fresher in his mind at the time he wrote, certainly attempted to explain that conflict.

Piscator's "world-historical" documentary theatre and the "explanatory" model which followed it in the 1960s have now been replaced by a more circumspect and less confident model more reliant on the presentation of a multiplicity of voices derived via oral history techniques. At a superficial level, this indicates a shift in emphasis from paper document to the products of audiovisual technologies as source material—we need to remember that it's not so long ago that recording technologies got to be portable, and this actually made possible the form we now know as "verbatim theatre" back in the 1950s. And this has also made possible the movement from a theatre of "fact" to a theatre of "actuality" (John Grierson's 1920s term for documentary material gathered via film, picked up by the English originators of verbatim theatre to describe audiotaped source material), and from a globalising vision to a grainy localism, even if that localism is sometimes being converted into a commodity for "global" consumption, and despite the fact that localism does not preclude a global perspective (as in the case of some of the examples I will refer to).

The ditching of the explanatory possibilities of the form has not been complete, but in many cases of verbatim theatre they have been replaced by a return to the essentially naturalist impulse which documentary theatre was initially designed to circumvent. This is particularly reflected in an emergent "theatre of testimony" (a term particularly associated with the work of Emily Mann), in which disparate "authentic" voices speak apparently directly (but actually through the medium of the actor) to an audience able to vicariously experience "another world," on the assumption that such vicarious experience offers access to real knowledge. This sort of work is reflected by Robin Soans' *A State Affair* for Out of Joint in 2000, described by one reviewer as a "powerful collage of direct-to-audience testimonies" (Taylor 2000) based on interviews (actually not recorded and transcribed but reconstructed from notes and memory) conducted with people living on a Bradford housing estate. Another reviewer has described the experience of the play as "like falling down a deep, dark well" (Gardner 2000), but presumably tempered by the awareness that you can go home to a much more comfortable environment before you hit the bottom.

There are several issues worth considering here. Firstly, the "authenticity" of what one is presented with is in question: as Angela O'Brien has pointed out, the "dangerous stories" offering "audiences an opportunity to transgress the borders of safe bourgeois art and experience" have often been generated through interviewees succumbing to the "seductive appeal to fame, even if modest," and in circumstances which reward them for "performing" a role.[1] Secondly, as she also points out, there is an immediate ethical concern about whether this "telling and retelling might have the effect of re-enforcing rather than liberating their victim-hood" (O'Brien 2003: 8). This point is picked up by Julie Salverson, in a discussion of a number of Canadian popular theatre pieces concerned with the "testimony" of survivors of violence, who also questions whether the vicarious experiencing, through "the performing of testimony," of the pain of others as "an unexamined spectacle" does anything other than pander to an "erotics of suffering" of a theatre audience comfortable in the knowledge that "we" are not "them" (Salverson 2001).

And thirdly, there is some doubt that the "experience" we are being offered constitutes useful knowledge. Much of the new verbatim theatre remains in thrall to the naturalist habit. This is clearly the case in the "tribunal plays" at the Tricycle Theatre in London, which played edited versions of transcripts in a set representing a court room and with actors cast for their resemblance to the real figures they portrayed. But more surprisingly, verbatim theatre practitioners, concerned to offer spectators the experience of the "authentic" voices of ordinary people, have taken to re-staging the interview itself, often inscribing the spectator as interviewer (a situation made particularly acute for me while watching David Hare's *The Permanent Way*, during which actors kept actually addressing me by name...). As someone once said, the worst possible perspective from which to understand a tennis match is that of the ball...

Anna Deavere Smith's work has no doubt been influential in a propensity for restaging the interview, particularly as it has been built on solo performance, and thus on a sequence of monologues as its most obvious formal device. This has distinguished her work from the more self-consciously Brechtian "quoting" and narrating techniques reflected in Moises Kaufman's introduction to *The Laramie Project*, for example (Kaufman 2001: vii), but she has nonetheless not succumbed entirely to the naturalist impulse, despite the use of a notion of acting which sounds suspiciously like "channelling:"

> If we were to inhabit the speech pattern of another, and walk in the speech of another, we could find the individuality of the other and experience that individuality viscerally. (Smith 1993: xxvii)

Her propensity to play across race and gender renders naturalism an unavailable option anyway, and she thus stands between her audiences and her interviewees in a manner which continually reminds us of the mediated nature of what we are watching, while the constant movement from one voice to the next maintains the sense of the montage which gives her pieces their often rich complexity. More significantly, she has seen the limitations of the experiential knowledge this form of verbatim generates and has attempted to reach beyond the "local" and into the realm of something approaching the "world historical," or at least the "national historical" via combining with her interviews with "ordinary people" some slightly less "ordinary" voices able to broaden our understanding of particular situations, for example in the addition of the voices of Cornell West and Homi Bhabha to those of the people caught up in the LA riots which are the subject of *Twilight Los Angeles*.

Nonetheless, the "local" has been a prime concern of verbatim theatre ever since its emergence in the 1970s, and particularly so in Australia in recent years.[2] It's the "local" which creates the sense of "authenticity," which can then be taken to the centres of cultural power, rendered a commodity, and then magically have the quality of "universality" conferred upon it. My own experience of that came with my involvement in *Aftershocks*, a "local" show which has taken on a national life, and which offered a clear indication of what can happen.

Aftershocks was a project initiated by a grassroots organisation of which I was a member, the Workers' Cultural Action Committee of Newcastle Trades Hall Council, about the Newcastle earthquake in 1989—a small earthquake in the grand scheme of things, but twelve people died, mostly in the wreckage of the Newcastle Workers' Club, which housed Trades Hall, and many of us were still living with the consequences in one way or another, so a big event locally. It was very strictly verbatim, consisting entirely of edited transcriptions of interviews with staff and members of the Workers' Club, and was first performed with a local cast in 1991 and revived for a small tour of the region in 1992. We tried to interest a Sydney-based publisher in the script, but were told that there really wasn't a market for parochial stuff like this. However, in 1992 a Sydney director picked the show up and staged it at Belvoir Street Theatre. The script was published (by the same publisher) to coincide with the production, the show was a commercial and critical success, and it suddenly became "universal" which, as far as I could see, basically meant it was enjoyed by a group of middle-class people from inner suburban Sydney. The play has been reasonably successful: it went onto school and university curricula in various places, has had several amateur and professional productions round the country, has been through two published editions, and is generally seen, a bit to our surprise, as an innovative show which pioneered verbatim theatre in Australia. Belvoir Street Theatre prides itself in having since done more verbatim pieces described as "in the tradition of *Aftershocks.*"

This "success" came at a cost. The Belvoir opening night was a bizarre event for some of us. The setting of the play had been "naturalised:" our original performance had been on a bare stage with six chairs in front of a blackboard on which were listed the titles of the scenes. Now the play was set in a Sydney theatre designer's version of a workers' club:[3] ugly garish carpet, audiotaped noises of poker machines etc. In our production, actors were "costumed" as themselves, and clearly "quoting" the interviewees, not "being" them. Actors were now costumed—people one had got to know during the process of researching and making the show were suddenly being portrayed onstage in caricatures of working-class garb they wouldn't have been seen dead in, and actors were "being" them, in relatively unrecognisable caricatured accents. It was as if we spectators were being briefly invited in to "another world" to hear their stories, in the clear knowledge we would be able to escape later. At the end of the performance on opening night, as a final marker of "authenticity," a number of the interviewees, who had been bussed down the freeway from Newcastle, were brought onstage to stand like bemused anthropological exhibits, or rabbits in the spotlight, for an audience some members of which I heard afterwards in the foyer expressing amazement at how well the piece had captured "the nuances of working-class speech"—I resisted asking how they would know. The universalising impulse which, as original cast member Paul Makeham has pointed out, was in this case an act of "appropriation" (Makeham 1998: 180), had entailed a caricaturing of the people and their club so that it could conform to a Sydney understanding of what they thought we were rather than what we *actually* were: our "local" had been stolen and caricatured to become their dose of "authenticity," rendered "universal" by their approval.

There has been, though, and *Aftershocks* started life as, a different version of verbatim theatre than this "deeply fashionable" one, which is centrally engaged with the grainy specificities of the "local," but for larger reasons than just an appeal to "authenticity." Community-based work utilizing the "authenticity" of "local voices" has been a vital feature of our cultural ecology at least since Paget coined the term "verbatim" to describe some of it. It has gone unremarked largely because it has not impinged on the "theatre estate" in metropolitan capitals until quite recently. While not always strictly "verbatim," it has habitually used stories collected via the developing techniques of the oral historian, transmuting them into "local acts," to use Jan Cohen-Cruz's term (Cohen-Cruz 2005), through varying processes of collaboration with their sources. It is marked by a substantially more enlightened, and ethically sound, understanding of the roles and techniques of the oral historian than that indicated by the quarrying of communities for "source material" implicit in some of the examples of verbatim theatre which have become fashionable, and has also found other ways of being "political" than in the manner of Piscator or Weiss.

To a large extent, oral history and documentary performance have shared a history, particularly as the performative nature and possibilities of the interview itself have been more clearly understood. Mary Marshall Clark has recently written on the oral history interview as performance, and on the use of this fact in the work of Elders Share the Arts in New York, and in the "reminiscence workers movement" more broadly (Clark 2002). Pam Schweitzer's *Reminiscence Theatre* details her own work with oral history and verbatim theatre with the elderly from the early 1980s (Schweitzer 2007). Della Pollock's recently-published collection of essays has explored oral history performance projects from a wide range of community contexts, and the function and role of oral history in community development with groups ranging from the elderly to young people, prisoners and union activists (Pollock 2005). A less strict embrace of the techniques associated with verbatim theatre has also seen oral history occupy a central role in an unbroken and vital tradition of community-based theatre work in the English-speaking world for at least 30 years. While verbatim theatre is now a form of use to a voracious "theatre estate," perhaps more importantly it has been an implement which legitimates and dignifies "local knowledge" and assists in the building and sustaining of the sorts of community identities which globalization threatens to erode, and thus bulwarks of participatory democracy in an otherwise disempowering environment.

In the article which coined the term, Paget described verbatim theatre as:

> [...] a form of theatre firmly predicated upon the taping and subsequent transcription of interviews with "ordinary" people, done in the context of research into a particular region, subject area, issue, event, or combination of these things.

He also remarked upon the fact that "[a]s often as not, such plays are then *fed back* into the communities (which have, in a real sense, created them), via performance in those communities" (Paget 1987: 317). He sketched a lineage of the form which paid credit to several progenitors, two of the most important of whom were Charles Parker and Peter Cheeseman, who developed the form through a series of experiments with documentary material beginning in the late 1950s. Paget expressed a concern that:

> [...] work such as Charles Parker's and even Cheeseman's is now often being received by younger practitioners through the *tradition* it established, rather than from direct experience of the work itself. (Paget 1987: 319)

The "tradition" has become somewhat attenuated by now, as indicated by recent claims about where it all came from –, for example, on the website of Recorded Delivery, the company founded by Alecky Blythe following the success of her verbatim play, *Come Out Eli*, in 2003, one finds the claim that it was "Anna Deavere Smith who first combined the journalistic technique of interviewing subjects from all walks of life with the art of recreating their exact words in performance" ("Recorded Delivery"), and this is a not uncommon view in the USA in particular. Nicholas Kent, interviewed about the

Tricycle "Tribunal Plays" which he directed, refers to "[…] a tradition of verbatim theatre which had actually been done in the 60s and 70s by John McGrath, the 7:84 theatre company, and even by David Hare with *Fanshen*" (not exactly true in either case), and claims to have got "absolutely false credit" for having invented the form himself (Stoller 2005). Canadian reviewer Alec Scott, somewhat parochially, and no doubt inspired by Alan Filewod's account of a strong tradition of Canadian documentary theatre, *Collective Encounters*, has claimed that "Canadians actually pioneered the documentary theatre form in the early 1970s" (Scott 2006). In Australia there is an assumption abroad that the form was invented for *Aftershocks*.

This confusion, and the sense that verbatim theatre is something new, is basically the result of its having maintained its grip on the consciousness of theatre makers outside Kershaw's "theatre estate." The verbatim theatre which has re-entered that arena in recent years has largely been produced in ignorance of its antecedents. Robin Soans has attempted to clear the fog a little in the resource material that accompanies the published edition of *Talking to Terrorists*, his 2005 verbatim piece for Out of Joint, by including Peter Cheeseman in the group of four practitioners who supply brief accounts of their work in the tradition (with Blythe, Hare and Elyse Dodgson from the Royal Court). What a knowledge of Parker and Cheeseman and their development of verbatim theatre in the 1950s and 60s indicates, and Dodgson's account of her introduction of verbatim techniques to groups in Africa, South America and Russia (Dodgson) attests to, is another direction entirely in which oral history-based documentary performance could (and in fact did) go, and one which gives the form a political bite of a different kind.

Cheeseman was one of the pioneer Artistic Directors of the professional regional repertory theatre scene which emerged after the war in Britain and ran the Victoria Theatre in Stoke-on-Trent. Inspired by *Oh What a Lovely War!* (as were many others), he got into the documentary as a form because the Victoria Theatre's writer-in-residence (Alan Ayckbourne) went to London to get famous, a route which it was assumed one would logically take from a regional rep at the time. He decided they should make a documentary to fill the gap in the programme Ayckbourne's departure left. But he did so out of what turned out to be an unusual commitment to the region he had chosen to work in, and an insistence that his company should become "as useful and as necessary [to the local community] as the doctor and the shop on the corner" (Cheeseman 1967: 55). "For me," he said, "there's only one kind of theatre worth working in: one permanently running within a coherent community." (Cheeseman 1968: 64) "This is no time for vagabonds" he said and, true to his word, spent the next 37 years working there, and still lives within spitting distance of the New Victoria Theatre, which he devoted much of his life to getting built. This meant that what have since come to be called the Stoke documentaries were always determinedly local.

This offered Cheeseman a sense of what they were doing in Stoke:

> The only human situations we can truly comprehend are the ones small enough for us to feel a significant or effective part of. Otherwise our actual sense of existing at all is depressingly diminished. (Cheeseman 1971: xix)

In such circumstances the artist has a:

> [...] key role in society, to give us back our own identities in a huge, lonely and amorphous world; to make sense of a universe that has become a nightmare; to stand up the man, the family, the town, against the world community, to reassert human values, to make sense of the abstract. (Cheeseman 1968: 65)

His commitment to staging in the round rested on this sense of mission:

> Forms of theatre differ in their techniques of performance, but also philosophically and even politically in the relationships implied in the human structure of the events they create. People form the partial or total background to the action presented in a thrust or round stage, each spectator can see almost the entire audience, the drama is played out in a space cleared in the middle of a community. (Cheeseman 1969: 40)

It is this attempt to clear a space "in the middle of a community" which gives Cheeseman a chapter in Baz Kershaw's Doctoral thesis on the development of community theatre in Britain (though sadly this hit the cutting room floor on the way to his book, *The Politics of Performance*). It also places the work in close proximity to the British community arts movement which emerged in the decade that followed. In the 1980s, community arts advocate and theorist Owen Kelly drew a distinction between the experiential, even visceral, "knowledge" we have of our "place," and "information," centrally constructed via mass media and increasingly globally distributed. The former, he pointed out, is built out of the ongoing process of negotiating movement through it, and thus out of individual and collective processes of making sense of it, making it cohere, which offers people a "cumulative, and comprehensible, view of how their world operates...which is a necessary condition of democratic participation" (Kelly 1984: 84). "Information," on the other hand, prepackaged and presented as individuated items of "news," decentres us by suggesting that everything important happens elsewhere. It is:

> [...] a window to a world for which there is no door. We ignore what is going on around us, and stand with our noses pressed up against the window trying to peer into this other world to find out what is *really* going on. (Kelly 1984: 79).

The first two of the Stoke documentaries, *The Jolly Potters* (about the rise of Chartism in the Potteries) and *The Staffordshire Rebels* (about the Civil War), were documentaries in the conventional sense of the time, based entirely on written sources. But Cheeseman quickly fell under the influence of two powerful personalities from the BBC, the film and TV documentary maker Phillip Donellan, and Charles Parker who in the late 1950s developed a documentary form on BBC radio, with Ewan MacColl and Peggy Seeger, which they called the Radio Ballad, a combination of audiotaped interviews, mostly with workers in particular industries (fishing, coal mining etc.), and folk songs, mostly written by MacColl and Seeger in the idiom, which framed, shaped and contextualised the "actuality" collected by MacColl and Parker (See Cox 2008). Parker then went on to conduct a series of experiments in documentary performance based on the format of the Radio Ballads with amateur groups in Birmingham (see Watt 2003). The Radio Ballads offered Cheeseman the bones of the form of a documentary theatre in which the "interplay of songs, in which the words are more important than the music, and people's ordinary speech, reproduced in a simple and direct fashion" (Nevitt 1986: 24) became the core elements. The commitment to and respect for "actuality" he drew from the work of Donellan and Parker grounded his work in the local and in oral history. It was with the third documentary, *The Knotty*, in 1966, about the North Staffordshire Railway (and you don't get much more local than that), that

Cheeseman and his collaborators moved into the realm of the verbatim, and even then accidentally.

Researching the show had involved taping interviews with some retired employees. The two published texts of the Stoke Documentaries (Cheeseman: 1970 and 1977)[4] come with elaborate and useful notes from Cheeseman on the development of the shows, and a note to *The Knotty* offers a description of what was apparently a familiar crisis in the devising of the documentaries, undertaken on the floor by the whole company:

> On the last Saturday morning before our first night on the following Tuesday the show as usual was just being completed. As a stopgap I decided to get the actors simply to speak the transcribed speeches of the old men who had remembered their feelings "when Amalgamation came about" and include some of the emotional speech by the new General Manager, Barnwell. It was the first time we had used any of our oral material at any length, seriously. They were to be plain statements by actors standing still, talking to the audience as they took off coat and cap with the Knotty badge for the last time. The great fear was that it would sound both corny and, much worse, patronising. It didn't. Providing the actors didn't characterize and let the speeches speak for themselves it made one of the most eloquent scenes in the documentary. (Cheeseman 1971: 95-6.)

And there beginneth verbatim theatre.

The play which made the full break to verbatim, which Paget (Paget 1987: 323) lists as the first verbatim play in Britain, was *Hands Up—For You the War Is Ended* (1971), based on interviews with local ex POWs. As Cheeseman has pointed out, the work quickly moved beyond the simple one-on-one oral history interview characteristic of the Radio Ballads, for example, and into some highly creative uses of both the tape recorder and the interview process:

> One of the men, Frank Bailey, runs a newstand twenty paces from the Victoria Theatre. He and his compatriots were gathered together for several evenings of beer and recording in the theatre. Portions of the conversations were used during the performance, in the form of dialogue for the actors and as narration using the actual voices of Frank Bailey and his friends. (Cited in Elvgren 1974: 94)

They also interviewed a number of wives and girlfriends of the POWs, and found their memories were crystal clear, which led to engaging them in the process, not just of supplying dialogue, but actually making scenes:

> We'd interview the woman first, write down exactly what she said, then we would get her into rehearsal and say "let's do it." We'd have somebody playing the Italian prisoner, other people on the bus, and so on—re-enact the whole scene so that it stimulated her memory. (Cheeseman, "Talk at the Vic," 15 Nov. 1993, cited in Woodruff: 113-4)

This begins to bring interviewees into the process as collaborators rather than as merely "sources," but the real breakthrough in the relationship between theatre makers and interviewees comes with the next documentary, and probably the most famous, *Fight For Shelton Bar* (1974). This project was not a proposal from Cheeseman or the company, but came in response to a request from the Action Committee set up to fight the proposed closure of the Shelton Bar steelworks, and marks, for the time and the context (a regional repertory company), an extraordinary relationship between artists and a community. For the first time, the research was conducted as events took place, with the researchers on the spot, and it remains a remarkable model of the theatrical use of verbatim material, detailed in Cheeseman's notes to the published text. Perhaps most revealing about the real originality of the piece is this note on one scene:

> The reflective discussion which is interleaved with it took place in the theatre on the Saturday morning at the end of the first week of the documentary in its original form. About forty members of the Action Committee attended and we asked them "What have we left out? Have we misrepresented anything?"
> Their main response was to discuss the way in which nationalisation seemed to be represented as the cause of their problem. As Socialists this bothered them, and they tried to disentangle this issue from what seemed to them to be the true causes, and to define the ways in which they felt nationalisation could be made to work better. The discussion (which involved Philip Donellan [who was filming proceedings for a documentary on the process] too) seemed to me to be important enough to be included in a new ending, and this replaced a rather garbled [earlier scene] [...]. (Cheeseman 1977: 62)

This is not verbatim theatre concerned to give a middle class audience a brief glimpse into "another world," but theatre artists collaborating with community activists on a political task and, particularly significantly, the making of theatre as a means by which a community may consolidate itself and clarify its own understandings of the world.

Cheeseman probably, in this case and in several other attempts over the next decade, took such a method about as far as was possible within the context of a regional repertory company.

Baz Kershaw, in possibly the best piece of writing on the Stoke documentaries (unfortunately hidden away in his PhD thesis), refers to the threatened closure of the steelworks as:

> an ironic kind of luck, [...] for it happened at just the historical point when the Stoke documentaries had reached a kind of sophisticated maturity, able to handle complex socio-political situations with more than a modicum of theatrical clarity.

He points out that "the micro-problem of Shelton Bar's future was intimately bound up with the macro-issues affecting the whole of the Western world" at the time, by virtue of

> [...] the national struggle to save the British heavy industries [...] heightened, of course, by the international oil crisis and by the subsequent domestic power crisis which eventually forced the Heath Government to declare a state of emergency. (Kershaw 1991: 250)[5]

The potentiality of verbatim theatre grounded in the local is revealed in the fact that the show "raised questions of national, even international, importance even as it reinforced local community allegiances" (Kershaw 1991: 251). Cheeseman's "space cleared in the middle of a community" reached beyond the merely parochial to a global level, all the better understood for being "known" locally. While "the aim to let the community speak for itself through the documentary presentation reduced the company's latitude in entering into a critical dialogue, so to speak, with its community" (Kershaw 1991: 260), it did assist a community in forging "a local ideological identity through unity" (Kershaw 1991: 253).

The beginnings of verbatim theatre thus reveal the possibility of four important elements absent from most of the later versions of the form circulating in the "theatre estate:"

1. the play is made with interviewees as active collaborators rather than merely sources of information and markers of "authenticity"
2. the generation of the play facilitates and encourages the process of community formation and "knowledge production" via dialogue within that community

3. the local/global nexus becomes central so that the play is at least
   potentially about a broader international issue as it is lived at the local level
   (the global is always local somewhere)
4. the play, including the process of generating it, is viewed as political
   activism—as Peter Weiss's 1968 manifesto on documentary theatre
   pointed out, "documentary theatre takes sides" (Weiss 1971b: 42)

That version of documentary was picked up all over the place in
Britain, and appears to have emerged in other places either
independently (in the USA, for example), or directly or indirectly
influenced by Cheeseman's pioneering work (in Canada and Australia
for example). There is plenty of evidence to suggest that something
like this is fairly widespread in community-based theatre, from the
popular theatre models Alan Filewod wrote about in Canada in the
1970s and 80s, to use of the story circle as a central mode of
generating material described by Jan Cohen-Cruz in her book on the
"grassroots" or "community-based" theatre movement in the USA,
Local Acts, to some of the community theatre Kershaw described in
The Politics of Performance, and the proliferation of interview-based
work in the Australian community theatre scene. In all these
circumstances the form has developed hand in hand with dialogic
modes of generating performance which have produced a different,
and more productive, relationship between the subjects of the drama
and its makers.

Returning briefly to my story about *Aftershocks*, I should point
out that it took the form it did as a result of a conversation about
Paget's article on verbatim theatre. Paul Brown, the writer on the
project, had spent some years as a community theatre worker in an
ethos where consultation and collaboration with a "community" was
natural, even mandatory. The way into "community" was normally a
process of oral history interviewing, either formally or informally, and
plays were usually loosely based on the material thus derived. For
him, *Aftershocks* was not so much a new approach but just an
interesting experiment in accepting the ramifications of Cheeseman's
hard rule that a verbatim play should not present anything onstage for
which there isn't a documentary referent. (see Cheeseman 1970: xiv)

Brown has recently reflected on one of the projects which
preceded *Aftershocks*. This produced a play in the 1980s for one of
Australia's pioneering community theatre companies, the Murray
River Performing Group, based in the twin cities of Albury and

Wodonga which sit either side of the river which marks the border between Victoria and NSW. The play, *The Murray River Story*, was a large-scale participatory piece generated via methods, popular at the time in Australia, drawn from Ann Jellicoe's handbook, *Community Plays*, although with a stronger inbuilt element of community consultation than she advocates. The performance took place outdoors at a popular picnic spot on the banks of the river the degradation of which formed the play's major thematic thread. The consultative process by which it was generated was not untypical of community theatre practice at the time:

> By the time rehearsals began, a great deal of oral history material had been collected, within which emphasis was given to recording what people had seen and heard along the river. Actors workshopped potential scenes for the play under guidance from the director and a group of facilitators, with only raw research material as a starting point. The writer travelled a feedback loop between the workshops and a word processor then back to the workshops with scripted scenes that both reflected what the actors had devised and fed in new ideas from the research. This is how participants in the project developed their collective wisdom about the river and its problems. (Brown and Crittenden 2007: 106)

Community theatre in Australia has always been informed by a Community Cultural Development (CCD) perspective, to some extent because that has been the perspective of the major source of public sector subsidy through the 1980s and 90s, the Community Cultural Development Board of the Australia Council, although the policy which embodied it was always a work in progress being constructed in a dialogue between the funding body and its clients. Central to CCD practice has been the assumption that "community," in the words of one of the formative theorizations within the movement, is "a goal, a target" of a CCD process and is characterised by "a set of shared social meanings which are constantly created and mutated through the actions and interactions of its members" (Kelly 1984: 50-1), who are members through an act of choice rather than an external process of categorisation. CCD practice is based on three principles:

1. ordinary people are "makers" of their own "culture" rather than merely consumers of somebody else's
2. CCD "artsworkers" are facilitators of the cultural expression of others and thus "agents of transformation" (Adams and Goldbard 2001: 14)

3. "making culture" through collaborative and dialogic processes can build and/or consolidate diverse, multivocal "communities," and thus enhance individual and social wellbeing through creating a sense of social participation

CCD is now internationally acknowledged as a tool in the promotion of public health and wellbeing (see Mayo 2000, for example), particularly in Australia (see Mills and Brown 2004 for a brief survey), which is internationally recognized as having "the best-developed public apparatus for support of community cultural development of any nation on earth" (Adams and Goldbard 2002: 189). What this meant in the community theatre movement was that a community was not "another world," a quarry for information which could be transmuted into performances for the pleasure of theatregoers, but a group of artistic collaborators, engaged in making performances out of their own material with the assistance of some skilled artisans.

For Brown, the work was thus predicated on the assumption that the CCD perspectives which underpinned it could offer "a space for integrated and democratised knowledge making" (Brown and Crittenden 2007: 100), particularly given that "[t]he diversity of contributors made the project a forum for contesting attitudes and values" (Brown and Crittenden 2007: 107). Therefore, the process of collaborative dialogue upon which the making of performance depended:

> [...] might be capable of providing the knowledge making space in which the community, in a state of suspended doubt, can process its own understanding of critical life decisions and the knowledge needed to make them. (Brown and Crittenden 2007: 110)

The process of making performance thus becomes, explicitly, an implement in the making of community and in the generation and negotiation of knowledge which will serve that community's ends, as had been implicit in Cheeseman's work on *Fight For Shelton Bar*. Brown has continued that work into *Maralinga*, made as an act of advocacy for and with the Australian Nuclear Veterans' Association, another strictly verbatim piece but one which has not made it to the "theatre estate" (See Arvanitakis 2008; Brown 2006).

Experiments conducted with my students at the University of Newcastle have been fed by research into the working methods of

Australian community theatre workers like Brown, and have indicated the usefulness of verbatim techniques in community formation. A particularly revealing example for me was a project conducted over a three-year period with a group of teenage mothers, clients of the Child and Youth Health Network, whose Youth Health Resource Team met them weekly at the Family Care Cottage at a local hospital, and offered them support, counselling and assistance. This group of young women had been through hard times which had seriously eroded their sense of self-esteem, and one-on-one interviews by students they had not grown to trust were clearly not going to generate much information. The painstakingly accurate transcriptions we made of these interviews, including every nuance of pronunciation, every verbal infelicity and hesitation, only served to increase their understandable suspicion of us and our motives. But when we suggested that they interview each other, with a brief list of agreed topics, we found ourselves inundated with information, expressed with extraordinary candour and passion, and enormous humour. This gave us material it was easy to edit and splice into performable bits which could be read back to them for comment.

In the first year, the students ran a visual arts project with the young women to produce a mural on a portable screen, which we presented to the local Hospital in a ceremonial in which the first of our little scripts was read to an audience of hospital staff and family and friends. The script, consisting of several people's stories spliced together so that they became a collective story rather than anybody's individuated narrative, was read by the students and just two of the young mothers, and it was well enough received for the others to think that they wanted to carry on with the work. In the second year the students and I developed and refined the script, and succeeded in getting a number of the young women involved in a small performance of it for the Christmas party at the Family Care Cottage. They enjoyed the rehearsals, began to take a more active role in the process, and managed a performance which was so well received that a core group of them moved towards the development of a full play, which involved them in further developing the material through oral history techniques.

We kept producing draft scripts with obvious holes in them (a strategy picked up from Brown) and when they pointed them out to us we suggested that they might write something to fill them.

Occasionally they did, but more often they went off into a corner with a tape recorder and talked out new material which we plugged into the gaps. Now they were not only performers, embracing some skills of physical theatre and mime in rehearsal, but writers as well, crafting material out of their own experiences, and splicing it into a collectivised tale of the rigours of childbirth and the struggle with parenting in some particularly adverse circumstances. By this point, a group which had consisted of shy, defensive, isolated teenagers struggling to cope had become a self-assertive, exuberant "community," more than happy to perform their work-in-progress for a gathering of health workers at a conference on post-natal depression, where they reduced some of the delegates to tears and elicited requests for repeat performances. None took place—it appeared that the opportunity to speak back to the health system which many felt had abused them was enough—and the project went no further, but it had indicated to us the strength of verbatim as an implement in a CCD process.

Since then, particularly with my erstwhile colleague Kerrie Schaefer but also with colleagues in Aboriginal Studies and Cultural Geography, I have been involved in attempts to extend the process into projects in partnership with public sector organisations and experienced CCD workers in Newcastle and environs. We have documented one of these experiments, a project to facilitate a processional performance to mark the closure of the Royal Newcastle Hospital (Schaefer and Watt 2007), and others are in train. In all cases, dialogue with a particular community is the basis of the work, and the oral history techniques associated with verbatim theatre are being used to generate performable material for the "feedback loop" which sets that dialogue in motion. The generation of these dialogues is a slow process, because we have chosen to work with groups who are usually not heard (indigenous groups, public housing tenants, ex-inmates of a local prison etc.), and consequently need some coaxing into speech—verbatim theatre is for us a valuable tool in a CCD process rather than a speedy means of generating "authentic" material for the "theatre estate." In this we feel we are being true to at least some of the most valuable possibilities of verbatim theatre. We haven't become "as useful and as necessary as the doctor and the shop on the corner" (Cheeseman 1967: 55), but we see this work as a direct legacy of the aspiration of Cheeseman and his co-workers to clear spaces for dialogue "in the middle of a community" via live performance. And we are confident that for communities to become consolidated, self-directive entities serves the political purpose of engaging people in the democratic process.

NOTES

[1] It is also worth pointing out that "verbatim" can be faked—Nicholas Kent has pointed out, for example, that *"The Permanent Way* was not verbatim theatre in that David [Hare] made twenty-five percent of that up, and I think it was very difficult to distinguish what were David's words and what were the actual words spoken." (Stoller 2005)

[2] See for example Alana Valentine's two verbatim plays for the Belvoir Street Theatre, *Run Rabbit Run*, based on the fight to save the South Sydney Rugby League Football Club, the Rabbitoh's, from being thrown out of the National Rugby League as economically unviable, and *Parramatta Girls* on a group of Aboriginal women who survived the Parramatta Girls' Training School in Sydney. Campion Decent's *Embers*, on the 2003 Victorian bushfires, emerged from a community context, toured in the area from which it was generated and then moved to a successful season at the Sydney Theatre Company.

[3] New South Wales has a system of licensing premises as "clubs," which allows them to sell liquor and food, run poker machines, operate venues for live performance etc. Licenses have mostly been given to sporting clubs, an organisations of war veterans (the Returned Servicemen's League) and, in this case, trade union bodies. They have usually become very wealthy organisations which offer a range of services and activities and a social focal point for their members, who pay a small annual fee.

[4] While these have both been long out of print, Favorini includes *Fight for Shelton Bar*, complete with Cheeseman's original notes, in his anthology, *Voicings*.

[5] It is worth noting that the Heath government actually fell, following the 1973 miners' strike, during the run of the play.

REFERENCES

Adams, Don and Arlene Goldbard. (2001) *Creative Community: The Art of Cultural Development*. New York: Rockefeller Foundation.

——, eds. (2002) *Community, Culture, and Globalisation*. New York: Rockefeller Foundation.

Arvanitakis, James. (2008) "Staging *Maralinga* and desiring community: (Or why there is no such thing as a 'natural' community)." *Community Development Journal*. <http://cdj.oxfordjournals.org/cgi/content/full/bsn021> [Accessed 4 December 2008].

Blank, Jessica and Erik Jensen. (2003) *The Exonerated: A Play*. London: Faber & Faber.

Bottoms, Stephen. (2006) "Putting the Document into Documentary: An Unwelcome Corrective?" *The Drama Review* 50 (3), 56-68.

Brittain, Victoria and Gillian Slovo. (2004) *Guantanamo: Honour Bound to Defend Freedom*. London: Oberon Books.

Brown, Paul and Workers' Cultural Action Committee. (2001) *Aftershocks*. Sydney: Currency Press.

Brown, Paul and Xanthe-Rose Crittenden. (2007) "Nature Moves Centre Stage: Eco-centrism in Community Theatre," in Gay McAuley, ed. *Local Acts: Site-Based Performance Practice. About Performance* 7. Sydney: Department of Performance Studies, University of Sydney, 99-116.

Brown, Paul. (2006) "Maralinga: Theatre From a Place of War," in Gay McAuley, ed. *Unstable Ground: Performance and the Politics of Place*. Brussels: Peter Lang, 205-226.

Cheeseman, Peter. (1967) "'Not a Job for Vagabonds': Peter Cheeseman talks to Peter Roberts about regional theatre." *Plays and Players* 14 (6), 54-55.

——. (1968) "The Director in Rep.—No. 6." *Plays and Players* 15 (6), 64-65.

——. (1969) "To Thrust or Not To Thrust." *Plays and Players* 17 (3), 40-42.

——. (1970) *The Knotty*. London: Methuen.

——. (1971) "A Community Theatre-in-the-Round." *Theatre Quarterly* 1 (1), 71-82.

——. (1977) *Fight for Shelton Bar*. London: Methuen.

——. (2005) "On Documentary Theatre," in Robin Soans. *Talking to Terrorists*. London: Oberon Books: 104-7.

Cheeseman, Peter and Jim Lagden. (1971) "Place and Performance No. 1: Stoke-on-Trent." *Theatre Quarterly* 1(1), 66-69.

Clark, Mary Marshall. (2002) "Oral History: Art and Praxis," in Don Adams and Arlene Goldbard, eds. *Community, Culture and Globalisation*. New York: Rockefeller Foundation, 87-106.

Cohen-Cruz, Jan. (2005) *Local acts: community-based performance in the United States*. New Brunswick, N.J: Rutgers University Press.

Cox, Peter. (2008) Set Into Song: Ewan McColl, Charles Parker, Peggy Seeger and the Radio Ballads. London: Labatie Books.

Dawson, Gary Fisher. (1999) Documentary Theatre in The United States: an Historical Survey and Analysis of Its Content, Form, and Stagecraft. Westport, Conn: Greenwood Press.

Dodgson, Elise. (2005) "On Personal Testimony," in Robin Soans. *Talking to Terrorists*. London: Oberon Books, 108-110.

Dunbar, Andrea and Robin Soans. (2000) *Rita, Sue and Bob Too/A State Affair*. London: Methuen.

Elvgren, Gillette A. (1974) "Documentary Theatre at Stoke-on-Trent." *Educational Theatre Journal* 26 (4), 86-98.

Ensler, Eve. (2002) *The Vagina Monologues*. London: Virago Press.

Favorini, Attillio, ed. (1995) *Voicings: Ten Plays From the Documentary Theater*. Hopewell, New Jersey: The Ecco Press.

Filewod, Alan. (1987) Collective Encounters: Documentary Theatre in English Canada. Toronto: University of Toronto Press.

Gardner, Lyn. (2000) "Rita, Sue . . . /A State Affair [review]." *The Guardian*. (26 October) <http://www.guardian.co.uk/stage/2000/oct/26/theatre.artsfeatures1> [Accessed 3 March 2009].

Higgins, Charlotte. (2004) "National rediscovers politics." *The Guardian*. (7 October) <http://www.guardian.co.uk/stage/2004/oct/07/politicaltheatre.theatre> [Accessed 26 February 2009].

Itzen, Catherine, ed. (1971) "Production Casebook: No. 1 *The Staffordshire Rebels*." *Theatre Quarterly* 1 (1), 86-102.

Jellicoe, Anne. (1987) *Community Plays: How to Put Them On*. London: Methuen.

Kaufman, Moises and Stephen Wangh. (1999) *Gross Indecency: The Three Trials of Oscar Wilde*. Dramatists Play Service, Inc.

Kaufman, Moises. (2001) *The Laramie Project*. New York: Vintage Books.

Kelly, Owen. (1984) Community, Art, and the State: Storming the Citadels. London: Commedia.

Kershaw, Baz. (1991) Theatre and Community: Alternative and Community Theatre in Britain, 1960-1985; An Investigation into Cultural History and Performance Efficacy. Thesis (PhD), University of Exeter.

——. (1992) The Politics of Performance: Radical Theatre as Cultural Intervention. London: Routledge.

——. (1999) The Radical in Performance: Between Brecht and Baudrillard. London: Routledge.

Makeham, Paul(1998) "Community Stories: *Aftershocks* and Verbatim Theatre," in Veronica Kelly, ed. *Our Australian Theatre in the 1990s*. Amsterdam: Rodopi, 168-181.

Mayo, Marjorie. (2000) *Cultures, Communities, Identities*. Houndsmill: Palgrave Macmillan.

Mills, Deborah and Paul Brown. (2004) *Art and Wellbeing*. Sydney: Australia Council.

Nevitt, Roy. (1986) "Documentary Theatre—A Professional Repertory Theatre Perspective: Interview with Peter Cheeseman." *Documentary Arts Report* No. 2, The Living Archive Project, Milton Keynes Documentary Arts Trust, 22-25.

O'Brien, Angela. (2003) "Art Through Pain—The Panacea." *Double Dialogues* 4 (Winter), 8. <http://www.doubledialogues.com/archives/issuefour/> [Accessed 4 December 2008].

Paget, Derek. (1987) "'Verbatim Theatre:' Oral History and Documentary Techniques." *New Theatre Quarterly*, 12: 317-336.

Piscator, Erwin. (1978) *The Political Theatre*. Hugh Rorrison, trans and ed. New York: Avon.

Pollock, Della, ed. (2005) *Remembering: Oral History Performance*. New York: Palgrave Macmillan.

Recorded Delivery. (n. d.) "Technique." <http://www.recordeddelivery.net/> [Accessed 4 December 2008)

Salverson, Julie. (2001) "Change on Whose Terms? Testimony and an Erotics of Injury." *Theater* 31 (3), 119-125.

Schaefer, Kerrie and David Watt. (2007) "Not Going Quietly: The Royal on the Move Procession," in Gay McAuley, ed. *Local Acts: Site-Based Performance Practice. About Performance* 7. Sydney: Department of Performance Studies, University of Sydney: 117- 131.

Schweitzer, Pam. (2007) *Reminiscence Theatre: Making Theatre From Memories*. London: Jessica Kingsley Publishers.

Scott, Alec. (2006) "Reality Bites: Documentary Theatre Fails to Illuminate the Truth." Canadian Broadcasting Commission (16 March), <www.cbc.ca/arts/theatre/reality.html> [Accessed 4 December 2008].

Sidetrack Performance Group. (2003) *Citizen X*, in *Australasian Drama Studies* 42, 31-56.

Smith, Anna Deavere. (1993) *Fires in the Mirror*. New York: Anchor Books.

——. (1994) Twilight — Los Angeles, 1992 on the Road: A Search for American Character. New York: Anchor Books.

Soans, Robin. (2004) *The Arab-Israeli Cookbook*, Eastbourne: Aurora Metro Press.

——. (2005) *Talking to Terrorists*. London: Oberon Books.

Stoller, Terry. (2005) "Tribunals at the Tricycle: In Conversation with Nicolas Kent." <http://www.hotreview.org/articles/tribunalsatthet.htm> [Accessed 4th December 2008].

Taylor, Paul. (2000) "Rita, Sue and Bob (again) too." *The Independent* (6 December). <http://www.independent.co.uk/arts-entertainment/theatre-dance/features/rita-sue-and-bob-again-too-629781.html> [Accessed 26 February 2009].

Valentine, Alana. (2004) *Run Rabbit Run*. Sydney: Currency Press.

——. (2007) *Parramatta Girls*. Sydney: Currency Press.

Watt, David. (2003) "*The Maker and the* Tool: Charles Parker, Documentary Performance, and the Search for a Popular Culture," *New Theatre Quarterly* 19 (1), 41-66.

Weiss, Peter. (1966) *The Investigation*. Alexander Gross, trans. London: Marion Boyars.

——. (1971a) *Discourse on Vietnam*. Geoffrey Skelton, trans. London: Marion Boyars.

——. (1971b) "The Material and the Models: Notes Towards a Definition of Documentary Theatre." Heinz Bernard, trans. *Theatre Quarterly* 1 (1), 40-42.

Woodruff, Graham. (1995), "*Nice Girls*: The Vic Gives a Voice to Women of the Working Class." *New Theatre Quarterly* 11 (3), 109-127.

Wright, David. (1966) "Documentary Theatre." *Plays and Players* 14 (3), 60-61.

PART THREE: CONTEXTS

MODALITIES OF ISRAELI POLITICAL THEATRE: *PLONTER*, *ARNA'S CHILDREN*, AND THE RUTH KANNER GROUP

SHIMON LEVY

Israel enjoys an exceptionally high and still growing *per capita* theatre attendance. In the last years, however, the nine better subsidized theatres, playing to an overwhelming majority of about 85% (Pilat Report 2004), have learned to avoid the constantly burning socio-political issues, many of which are related to the ongoing occupation of Palestinians, and have been supplying a socially and politically lukewarm repertoire. Some fringe theatres, on the other hand, are still too often stuck with overly blatant, simplistic message-oriented shows, addressed to the already convinced but dwindling left-wing minority. Moreover, since (only) Jewish Israelis live in a moderately democratic regime, it should be noted that there is no censorship on Israeli theatre productions, except theatre managers who cut "dangerous" lines and situations, not out of fear of the authorities but of losing audiences. Israelis, quite clearly, don't want to repeat on stage the horrors they see presented on TV.

In a survey/research conducted in the year 2000, about 100 interviewed leading Israeli theatre makers, actors, designers, and musicians expressed a high degree of dissatisfaction with their art. An overwhelming majority believes most Israeli theatre performances are "much too commercial and simplistic," that they are "sweetish" and lack taste, "art," and sophistication (Levy 2007). Despite such devastating opinions, strongly supported by theatre and cultural critics, the nine bigger and relatively better-subsidized theatres in Israel enjoy a still growing number of audiences, and the main houses are often full to the brim. A recent follow-up survey to that of 2000 clearly indicates that the "satisfaction" factor has dropped yet further, as shown in the scathing reviews, among others, by Marmari (2008) and Hatab (2008). Facing not only the Israeli-Palestinian conflict, but the weakening of social benefit systems (for the sick, the elderly, the poor), as well as public scandals regarding the corruption of political and economic leaders, Israeli mainstream theatres keep offering slick "low message-oriented" melodramas, often quite well acted, sometimes even well designed. To Vladimir's question "Was I sleeping (*alias*: enjoying a fun show) while the others suffered?" (Beckett 1986: 83), most (frustrated) Israeli theatre makers and goers will have to respond "not really asleep, just nodding, and the cries I heard were in Arabic, far away, couldn't figure them out […]."

This article focuses on three socio-artistic positive examples of Israeli theatre, and proposes to deal with re/presentations of the immoral reality of the Israeli occupation of the Palestinians, primarily from the oppressor's point of view. I contend that the socio-artistic and often ideological discrepancy between the theatre makers described here and their audiences is dealt with through various modalities of "psycho-political" self-referential stratagems. Instead of a head-on attack on the (assumed) moral complacency of the audience, *Plonter* (April 2005) employs humour relying on existing models used by Israeli stand-up TV comedians. By mocking the medium the show often ridicules both the message and its recipients. The Ruth Kanner Group performances resort to pseudo-self-referential modes, e.g., to exposing onstage a number of financial and public-relations aspects, as in *At Sea* (May 2006). They use "soft" aesthetic techniques of meta-theatricality. Juliano Mer-Khamis's documentary film *Arna's Children* (Released 2003) plays with the medium-oriented discrepancy between theatre and film and harnesses the gap to its political-moral message. In this sense, the onstage fictitious dialogue both reflects and necessitates the yearned for real offstage dialogue.

The Ruth Kanner theatre Group was established in 1998 in Tel Aviv and has since developed a unique theatre language that ensues from an indigenous contemporary Israeli "feeling." Kanner has succeeded in theatrically reflecting some of the crucial identity quests in contemporary Israel, thus being socially relevant and often quite political, as well as the Israeli geo-cultural landscapes, expressed in the acting, gestures, colours and sounds, cries, whispers, speech and silences. Kanner studied acting and directing at Tel Aviv University's theatre Department and at NYU and has been teaching at TAU almost since her graduation. Following Max Reinhardt, she believes that the purpose of acting is to expose lies and rid people of senseless conventions. "To do this, you don't need only talent, perseverance and a certain measure of letting-go of the actor's private self, but a lot of courage too," says Kanner (2006). Creativity, in Kanner's group, is indeed a liberating activity through which the members shake off stage artistic and social-political conventions. Some of Kanner's latest productions, moreover, offer a unique political theatre model to Israeli audiences, Arab and Jewish alike.

More intensively than most Israeli theatre directors, Ruth Kanner has been exploring the unique encounter between the Hebrew language and the real as well as dramatic Israeli spaces, on- and off-stage. Since theatre, as such, requires language/place interaction, Israeli theatre too had to forge such an interaction, both a "language" to play with and a space to play in. Modern Israeli theatre "returned" to the Promised Land after hundreds of years of Jewish exile with the first immigration waves of Zionism in the early 1900s and needed to reinvent Hebrew and use it for non-religious purposes, like theatre. Space, on the other hand, also needed "reappropriation." In a sense, the socialist Zionists in those early days transposed European notions of theatrical space to their new-old country. They superimposed their previous exile yearnings over the now very real and harsh "Land of Our Fathers." Moreover, the actual "offstage," stretching not only into the auditorium but right beyond the walls of any theatre building in Palestine in those days, meant that Hebrew theatre then was indeed a celebration of "acting ourselves in our country and language." This culturally and historically particular combination of language and space is in itself politically explosive. Since 1998, Kanner and her group have been thoroughly engaged in long-term workshop explorations and relatively short-lived production runs—often an obvious give-away for non-commercial "quality theatre"—that have managed to convincingly re/present some of the main Israeli identity *qua* political issues on stage.

Kanner's theatrical language is suggestive, imagistic, and often profoundly metaphorical. She orchestrates texts, costumes, music, lights, and movement usually in deliberately small, intimate spaces where interaction between stage and audience is understandably intensified, often highly self-referential. Though politically explicit, her productions are never blatantly aggressive. With exquisite tactfulness, nevertheless, she succeeds in bridging the oversimplification of Israel's poor, political fringe theatres and the escapist, overly "poetic" and relatively rich in production-value tendency of the main stages. The delicate balance between aesthetics and "politicalness" is particularly noticeable in Kanner's productions *Amos* (1999), *Discovering Elijah's* (2005) and *Dionysus at the Dizengoff Centre* (2004).

Amos examines the fate of a field rodent stuck in an irrigation pipe in a field below the Carmel ridge minutes before the water is turned on. If Aristotle was right, the only dramatic space in this presentation is narrow, besieged and totally closed; the time is equally condensed, hence the plot inevitably becomes a theatrical metaphor, suggesting, obviously, inescapability. The self-conscious little personified animal soon turns into a truly stunning "other" in this allegory, which indeed leaves the extrication of the metaphor to the spectators' imagination. Structurally, Kanner organized a cycle within a cycle: "the rodent in the pipe, above it Man, above Man the narrator, who can be perceived as a divine voice" (Burstein 1999). Actress Tali Kark does not pretend to be a rodent in her role, but delivers this creature's existential plight with virtuoso conviction, thus linking between the necessarily first-person, trapped situation of the condemned on the one hand, and the potential pity it may receive from the on-lookers, on the other. Cheap catharsis is certainly not tried here. Stage metaphors are usually an invitation to a double dialogue: between their own "signifier" and "signified," as well as between the theatrical event and its audience. Rather than placating audiences with ready-made images, as many main stage productions do, Kanner appeals to her audience's creative and intelligent imagination, implicitly encouraging people to be active spectators.

To indulge in a brief comparison, the main-stage production of *Hebron* by Tamir Greenberg (2007) portrays the universal meta-narrative of the Palestinian-Israeli conflict through a mytho-poetic universal language, but uses some of the most clichéd stage semiotics and a richly decorated set for portraying Arabs with kaffias and religious Jews who kill each other's babies, without dealing with the actual horrors of the Israeli occupation in the West Bank. Kanner offers the opposite: in *Amos* "only a rodent" is about to die in a besieged space (not unlike the streets of the real Hebron and lately Gaza), economically designed with a few real irrigation pipes on an empty stage, exposing both its staginess and emptiness. This design indeed proved to serve as a gap, a discrepancy that both critics and audiences could fill with their own interpretations. In yet another comparison with fringe theatre productions, at the other extreme of the Israeli "Rep versus Fringe" axis, *Ziona's Trip* by Omri Yavin (2007) is a snide but loosely structured pseudo-quest play that takes its audience on a little stroll in Old Jaffa's streets, deliberately ignoring some 1,000 years of Arab history that have shaped the place just as Hebrew history in the past 100 years has, or Napoleon's short-lived attack—in fact an apt ironic remark. Despite a few delightful images (mock interpretation of a sculpture depicting the Binding of Isaac and Jacob's Dream, for one), interesting movement patterns and a lively, direct stage-audience interaction, the show does not succeed in combining the personal story with Jaffa the city. Jaffa was a blooming Palestinian cultural **centre** around the turn of the 20th century, but the implied, yet still too obvious national-moral-political undercurrent narrative did not really pay homage to its past, or alternatively— satirize the present Israeli regime.

The most typical dramatic space in pre-State Israeli drama is a cultivated field, indeed a perfect meeting place between the returning sons and their Promised Land. "We've come to build and be rebuilt," as the Zionist slogan promised. A passing rodent stuck in the irrigation pipes is of little consequence. This image alone, to be thus interpreted, already places Kanner as a conscious (though she has explicitly admitted it only lately, alas, in a private conversation) political director who, nevertheless, does not impose her message on the audience but demands a profound re-examination of both old and contemporary pioneering myths. In *Amos*, the rodent is not necessarily Palestinian. He can just as well represent environmental issues or Thai foreign workers who have lately been tilling our land. Still, the rodent's "other" consciousness is portrayed as inescapable as his sure death. *Amos* received the first prize at the Acco Fringe Festival in 1999: "A masterfully constructed theatrical work of art, which integrates story-telling theatre and Movement theatre [...] Directed with flair and beautifully acted. The director, the musician and the two actresses created a total event, combining text, movement, music and visual elements into a stirring, spellbound show" (The Award Document 28 September 1999). Critics joined with equally rave reviews. "While chasing 'the other' [...] *Amos* presents the most unexpected 'other,' and, moreover, surprisingly, the most exciting 'other' in a fascinating theatre piece which is also pure poetry" (Bar Yaacov, 29 October 1999). On their tour in Japan—to mention just one review, the Kanner Group received more excellent press, such as "*Amos* from Israel presented a fresh taste of direction with live music performance... this movement will stimulate the Japanese theatre industry" (Imamura, 5 April 2001). Michael Handelsaltz (28 September 1999) wrote: "A show with unique qualities on a totally different level, a clear theatrical language, a moving world against all odds, a unique aesthetics, a little beautiful pearl." Amir Yefeth (30 September 1999) wrote: "An engaging, painful struggle for survival, flashes of brilliancy and original theatrical messages that make for a rare, special, different theatrical experience. It is the world of all those who have found themselves in impossible situations and tried to find a way out."

Discovering Elijah evokes the event of the 1973 war with Egypt through the searing text by S. Yizhar (one of Israel's highly appreciated writers), which, in and from a perspective of time, tries to penetrate the surface down to the individual tremor and ask the moral questions that seep through the story of that war. A narrator in a participant-observer role, alternately appearing and disappearing, investigates the events, perhaps as an outsider who becomes an insider. Five actors create the events. The show consists of thirteen separated images of various action zones, lightly marked and then erased, like drawings on (the desert's) sand. After each scene the actors leave the central acting area and sit on the verge of "offstage," half "there," half resting and waiting. From the end of scene nine onwards, however, the action plays continuously, as if the separation into scenes is no longer necessary, or possible, or relevant. The progression of the show reflects the standpoint of the observer in the internal structure of the show. At first the narrator is documenting, examining the events. Gradually and gently he indeed becomes an insider, an active participant, drawn more and more into the depth of horror, into his own vulnerability, into the fragile boundary between life and death: the semi-fictitious onstage situation reflects a desired same response from the audience.

The production presents a disintegrated reality made of fragments bereft of their normal contexts. It re-examines the elements constituting war: words, images, violent impulses, fear and its concealment, running in the desert, searching for consolation. Elijah is not only the person looked for. In Jewish tradition, it should be noted, the prophet Elijah is the forerunner of the Messiah, He who brings peace. At the same time, this is an investigation of the modes of representation of the local war narrative, a typical motif in Israeli drama.

The desert, where the war was fought, is beautifully portrayed through sand dripping from an army shoe. Live music is performed with unconventional instruments, specially made for the production. String, wind, and percussion instruments are played by currents of hot air heated by fire. If sound can be a space, Ori Drommer's music created it. His sound establishes order, determines fates, envelopes the show and carries it to nonverbal places, turning into an inseparable part of the actors' bodies.

Critical response to the show was exceptionally positive: "It affected me like a stroke of lightning. An original, highly imaginative theatrical orchestration [...] this is a tremendous undermining of the myth of war," wrote Elyakim Yaron (3 March 2001). Michael Handelsaltz (3 October 2001) said: "The text, in astonishing Yizharic Hebrew, describes the despair and chaos of the Yom Kippur War. [...] The power and uniqueness of *Discovering Elijah* is such that it puts one off viewing anything else after it." Shai Bar Yaakov (October 22 2001) wrote about " [a] highly imaginative, hair-raising performance that turns into a hallucinatory, heartrending voyage into the past. A slippery truth lurks among the dead bodies and the still living people in the battlefield. An agonizing, fascinating, and, regretfully, highly relevant performance." Eitan Bar Yossef (11 October 2001) talked of "a stirring theatrical experience, which attempts to dismantle and reassemble the war experience, the fear, stupidity, violence, horror, glory and death. Apparently the nightmare of 1973, it is, actually, an apocalypse that takes place now [...] in front of our eyes [...] What happens here is that one-time miracle, which cannot be described in words; one cannot help but fall under its spell. Rumor has it that even S. Yizhar himself, who sat in the audience with that legendary Elijah by his side, was sobbing [...] This is an extraordinary work in the full and deepest sense of the word."

In the final scene, performed by actors alone the narrator is driving the blue Volkswagen van—no props, no design - through the scorched battlefields. Soldiers are trapped in black holes, swirling round as if in perpetual motion. The Volkswagen character is asking:

"Did it have to be this way, really?" The narrator is entering Suez City:

> [A]nd suddenly there's a big house with big balconies covered in red
> bougainvillea [...] and underneath, below the balconies [...] luxurious sofas
> **are** scattered [...] and on one of them someone **is** sitting, feasting on white
> grapes. "Hey, visitors," he says, motionless. And then something happens,
> because someone raises his head and sees something, and then he jumps up
> from his place like fire flaring up, jumps up and stands, stands and jumps,
> jumps and runs, ahh, he screams, ahhh, and comes and takes his large arms
> and spreads them [...] and throws himself hugging, and hugging and hugging
> [...] and in fact it's him, it's really him, look at him, it's him, it's Elijah, here
> he is, and it's him, our Elijah, smiling at us [...] Shalom, Elijah [...]. (Yizhar
> 1999: 198)

Conventional "good theatre" often plays on a functional, aesthetically well-designed stage. This exceptional ("good") theatre designs its own dramatic spaces through words and movements and as few as possible props, as the story develops. Especially if it is a quest play, trying to reveal or discover (the Hebrew word *gilui* means both) a character called Elijah, a prophet and a regular guy at the same time. A touch of tentative optimism hovers over the very end of this apocalypse provided we make fewer wars.

Based on Tamar Berger's book and adapted by Avner Ben Amos and Ruth Kanner, *Dionysus at the Dizengoff Centre* was produced by the Tel Aviv University theatre and the Acco Theatre Festival. The piece deals with a central Tel Aviv shopping centre known country-wide, built on top of a poor Jewish neighborhood located, in turn, on top of a Palestinian vineyard. Here Kanner again presents "others," this time explicitly Palestinians, some rich, some poor, some honest, some not. When "we" (predominantly Jewish audiences), however, look into this stage mirror, we do not know whether the reflected image is truly ours, because it may be "theirs." The piece does not accuse its mixed Arab and Jewish audiences. Rather, it seems to demand a profound understanding of the victim's position, in which one feels forever bereft of any possible moral and emotional reparation/redress.

In *Dionysus at the Dizengoff Centre* Kanner digs downward and manages to theatrically merge archaeology with psychoanalysis. The result is a unique estrangement, like coincidentally meeting a close relative in a bus station. We know every wrinkle on his forehead, but feel unsettled: how will strangers look at him? Thus we become the others. *Dionysus at the Dizengoff Centre* certainly suggests it is not only the actual name of the shopping mall. He is also the god of theatre. It is a study in comparative suffering, an archaeological-theatrical dig into the multilayered past, ours and theirs. Like other archaeological digs, this one, too, is intensely political: how deep do we want to dig? As deep as we believe our roots are hidden? Or those of the people who were there before us? After us? With us? Does the layer we reach really reflect who we are? Want to be?

Kanner's story-theatre works teach the slick, commercial stages as well as the simplistic, highly committed fringe theatre a lesson in therapeutic art, not because they are meant to be didactic, but because they do not compromise their art and manage to be political as a result of their quality. Kanner's political theatre avoids measures taken by real politicians. It excels in fine brinkmanship between the aesthetic and the social-political mainly because she lets her audiences draw the conclusions by themselves.

THE ISRAELI *PLONTER*—POLITICAL THEATRE ON THE ISRAELI MAIN STAGE

Plonter (a complicated "knot" or "tangle" in Israeli slang) is a 2006 Israeli production, staged by the Cameri Theatre in Tel Aviv, one of the biggest and best-subsidized theatres in Israel. The aim behind the *Plonter* project was to create a dramatic dialogue involving four Arab-Israeli and five Jewish-Israeli actors in the explosive thematic of the century-long Palestinian-Israeli conflict in order "to identify with the Other" (as quoted in the programme). *Plonter* presents a unique blend of daring and consensus; or, more blatantly, as the Arab saying goes, " [it] throw [s] stones after the caravan has passed." I thought of presenting this play as a test case of the Israeli theatre's artistic-political daring some time ago, when the Lebanon war was still lurking in the back drawer of the Israeli Defense Ministry. Now that it had actually been fought, as had another terrible one in Gaza (winter 2008-9), reality seems to have changed completely, and the ongoing Israeli-Palestinian conflict is overshadowed by much larger world forces, such as extreme Shiite movements (Hezbollah), Iranian nuclear policies and US interests. Whereas "our" own direct problem as Israelis is that of the Occupation, Israel, at the same time, serves as a powerful force in a much larger context. The feet of reality are faster than the wings of imagination—especially in Israeli theatrical fiction, *Plonter* included.

Plonter is, in fact, the collaborative work of nine Israeli and Palestinian (from the occupied territories) actors who were invited to participate in the project soon left, because their people at home did not tolerate their collaborating with the Jewish Israeli actors. Israeli Arab actors were hence invited to replace them, and prepared for their roles with field research and history lessons, and visited Palestinian towns, Jewish settlements and checkpoints over a period of seven months. The work constitutes part of a growing body of political fiction in Israel, generated mostly by young Jewish writers, reflecting a broader intellectual movement known as post-Zionism, which questions the validity of Israel as a Jewish state. In the English programme Yael Ronen, initiator and director of this group, says: "This is a new generation's quest to define our own identity as Israelis." Ronen also co-wrote and directed *The Guide to a Good Life*, a scathing critique on the moral deterioration of 12 young Israelis as a result of the occupation and its detrimental influence on inter-personal relationships.

On the small stage of the 165-seat Cameri auditorium *Plonter* has run several times a week for more than three months. A German friend, theatre director Alex Stillmark, who had worked at the Berliner Ensemble, had seen *Plonter* before I did, and recommended it to me: "I did not know Israeli theatre was so daring, so self-critical." At the time I begged to differ, because of the many more daring Israeli productions I had seen. Now I think he was right, at least in this particular context of a blatantly political show mounted on an Israeli main repertory theatre stage. Hence, the question to be addressed is whether *Plonter* has achieved its intended goals—aesthetic as well as message-oriented—in the particular setting of a commercial theatre that has otherwise been defined as "extremely moderate"...

The set, illuminated at times by actual television footage of Jewish and Palestinian funerals, terror acts, Arab towns, Jewish settlements, demonstrations, smoke and fire background, brings the already very close offstage on to the stage as an inescapable mixture of reality and virtuality, not without the added ironic touch of the audience being forced to experience in the theatre what they all know from watching TV at home or seeing on the street. The main stage set is a wall, representing the very one that is being built to separate Israel and the West Bank, cutting through Palestinian houses. One actor plays the "role" of the constantly active TV and radio, and is often slapped across the face to shut him up, signifying both the Israeli's understandable addiction to the media and their equally understandable disgust with it.

Plonter is the result of a work in progress of the entire cast, who all play both Arab and Jewish roles. It can roughly be described as neo-Brechtian, a loosely linked series of 17 scenes of interspersed comparative suffering, filtered mostly through the individual gaze of individually, often emotionally characterized occupied and occupiers, of mutual terror, humiliation, bereavement, rage and revenge. The play also deals semi-humorously with the relatively minor incidents of Israeli prejudice and ignorance regarding Palestinians. In one of the more touching scenes, a Palestinian is asked to show his ID card on an Israeli bus, and finally bares his bottom. In another scene Israeli soldiers catch an Arab boy who has thrown stones at them, beat him up and act out his mock execution in front of a firing squad. They then bring him to his father who beats him up again, by which time even the soldiers find the beating too harsh and try to stop the father. He finally responds with rage: "No, no! This is as far as it goes! You won't tell me what to do. Excuse me! This is my child! This is my house!" In another scene Palestinian children play a game in which they all want to be a *shaheed* (suicide bomber, martyr), and the little girl gets the role, because she can pretend to be pregnant by hiding the explosives on her belly.

The narrative is loosely structured around the killing of the 11-year-old Khalil Barhoum by an Israeli soldier. For the sake of both dramatic and actual balance, a Jewish baby is killed too, by a Palestinian terrorist. Mourning and revenge on both sides are presented as practically identical. The play mocks Israeli moderate left-wing attitudes and ends with an almost overt call to refuse to serve in the army. Mother Zippi asks her soldier son: "Shall I give you a lift to your army base?" And the final answer, closing the show is "No." In the final scene both Palestinians and Israelis come and go, enter and exit, indeed sharing the actual stage that has developed in the show into one country. It is a pessimistic ending, proving that violence cannot be restricted to inflicting it only on "Others." The end of *Plonter* presents parents separating, beating up children, an external situation that becomes profoundly personal, internal and inescapable.

The audience is almost forced to draw the conclusion: stop the occupation.

Ronen did not want to preach to the converted, namely, to the Israeli radical left. Rather, "I want this play to reach as wide an audience as possible." She has probably succeeded, at least according to the overall analysis by most Israeli theatre critics and some foreign ones as well: "Even though lightened by flashes of comedy, the impact on audiences is profoundly disturbing" (Doudai 16 June 2005). Michael Handelsaltz (29 May 2005) observed that *Plonter* is played by actors whose involvement is personal, human, banal—rather than explicitly political. Noting that one woman in the audience had commented that "it's too long," Handelsaltz added: "Correct. The occupation too." He concludes:

> The show is not without flaws, and it polarizes and simplifies reality. But this is also its strength. The great danger, of course, is that the Israeli audience will see the play, check it off on the square marked "conscience," and go home full-bellied and pleased. Theatre cannot do much more than that. Usually it does a lot less. If viewers go home with one image that bothers them, it's already something.

Elyakim Yaron (6 June 2005) regarded the show as a brave and honest attempt to bring the painful conflict onstage, indeed a dialogue "under fire," that gives the show its fuel—"theatre returns here to its therapeutic roots"; and he repeated his complimentary review on the radio. Sarit Fuchs (3 June 2005) saw *Plonter* as a heart winner. High-school students would be taken to see it, she (rightly) prophesied, because the show is replete with directorial inventions, humorous moments and a lot of dynamic zest. However, Fuchs was unsure as to whether it is, in the end, an optimistic production implying that we are all simply being carried away with momentary craze and fury; or else profoundly pessimistic because the actual message is that reality cannot be changed, therefore let's laugh at it. Eli Weisbert (n.d.) praised the artistic integrity of *Plonter* in bringing normal characters onstage, in avoiding sentimentality, and in inserting many moments of true compassion for both sides. He also noted the voice given to the Arab characters and their players—the sound of Arabic is rare on Israeli stages--and the fact that there is no "Other" in this presentation. Ben Ami Feingold (n.d.) used his review to give director Ronen a history lesson and encouraged her to write a more balanced play, in which not "the occupation" is the culprit but pan-Islamic myths and the Arab countries' refusal, for example, to accept the partition plan in 1937. Matan Vilnai, ex-Minister of Culture and ex-army general, called Yael Ronen on the phone, too, to correct her knowledge of history (Haaretz, 20 October 2005).

Besides enjoying a much larger than usual critical coverage, the *Plonter* creators were frequently interviewed on TV and radio. In one such interview, Ronen said that left-wing Israelis are sometimes worse than the right-wing extremists; they are the "full-bellied Tel Aviv bourgeoisie that goes to a demonstration once a month but insists that its sons join a specialized top combat unit [...] " The cast held numerous after-show discussions with the audience, adults and youngsters alike. The Cameri Theatre produced a rich programme booklet in the show's two languages, Arabic and Hebrew, and— assuming foreign visitors would come to see it—an English one too. In the larger Hebrew booklet all the actors were interviewed, and wisely so, about their personal connections to this particular project. The Cameri also published a Hebrew collection of quotes from seminal articles on the Palestinian-Israeli conflict and added a number of anti-war, anti-Israeli government poems by laureate poets Dalia Rabikowitz, Mahmoud Darwish and others.

To be a victim means to "own" something you once lost and cannot retrieve. Only the victim can decide upon the proper reparation (Ophir 2001: 263). Both Israelis and Palestinians argue that they are victims—of the Holocaust, of the Naqba, of the occupation—and *Plonter* indeed insists that this exclusivity is the main issue of its unsolvable theatrical conflict. Using a soft-core version of post-Zionism, directorial ingenuity and an inventive mixture of post-modern techniques, *Plonter* often goes deeper than meets the eye. True, the production suffers from various flaws, such as oversimplification, superficial texts, lack of good argumentation and a TV-oriented sequence structure. On the other hand, it is self-consciously aware of its flaws, flaunts its own artifice in ridiculing the typical TV approach (its own and its audience's) and presents a moderate version of an Israeli docudrama.

Rather than conclude, I may ask whether an established commercial theatre like the Cameri, in the particular context of the entire Israeli theatre scene, should have avoided producing this inconclusive, sometimes repetitive and perhaps politically not clear enough production, or else should have offered it to its audience (as it did) in the hope that some of them might take action? Brecht, as we know, failed. Whereas the Cameri itself produced Hanoch Levin's (the most scathing satirist and playwright in Israel until his death in 1999) *Murder* and other plays, theatres such as The Arab-Hebrew theatre and productions like *Dual Solitude* were more explicit by far in condemning the occupation. One may, then, truly wonder about the degree of "daring" expressed in the theatrical techniques of humour, relative understatement and political explicitness that the Cameri employed. *Plonter* is as daring as the Cameri's expectations of its middle-class audience. Based on the financial and critical success, the Cameri was right to produce the play.

"BRING THE SUN TO THE CASTLE"—
ON THEATRE IN *ARNA'S CHILDREN*
Arna's Children (2003) is a personal documentary about children in Jenin who participated in a theatre established and run by Arna Mer-Khamis, written and directed by her son, Juliano, an actor and director, and primarily a theatre maker. A decade later these children become Palestinian freedom fighters in the battle of the Jenin refugee camp, and suicide bombers in the Jewish town of Hadera. The film is replete with profoundly humanistic, social and political issues; it is shot and edited with unsentimental matter-of-factness, yet another reason why it is convincing and exciting; many professional film critics as well as deeply moved spectators have responded to it. Rather than dealing with the overall qualities of the film, the following discussion proposes to focus on "theatre." Theatre functions as "a place to see," it is also a main component and central motivating image in the film and serves as its built-in interpretation. Moreover, it reveals a dramatic layer that illuminates both the filmmakers and its participants-protagonists.

The film opens with a mass demonstration against the curfew imposed by the IDF on the refugee camp in Jenin, focusing on Arna organizing the event, shouting to the Palestinian drivers to honk their horns, asking them to ignore the demand to stop at the improvised barriers for identity control and weapon checks. Arna wears a kaffia, the most easily identifiable piece of Arab clothing, and speaks Arabic with a strong Israeli accent. She had already worn the kaffia when she was in the "Palmach," the pre-1948 War Jewish commando unit to which she belonged. Now she wears it also in order to hide her head, bald because of radiation against cancer, of which she will soon die. Arna behaves as an actress in complete accord with the role she took upon herself. As a woman who established children's homes, support and learning centres, as well as a Children and Youth Theatre in Jenin, Arna's "costume" is a complex theatrical-cinematographic metaphor, happening in "reality," since the film is a documentary . . . Wearing the same headdress, she identifies with her explicitly anti-Arab army pals of long ago who liked to wear kaffias and, much more so, with her Palestinian friends now. The kaffia indeed covers Arna's bald head; it is a "theatrical prop" and an image which, in this context, represents friends and foes then and now.

In the next sequence Arna's five years of work with the children is celebrated in a Jenin auditorium. Arna, in a simple white dress, with brusque cordiality asks one child whether he is willing to "accept responsibility"—"to do what?" we, the spectators, ask, already prepared for some kind of a political message. The child nods, and Arna commands: "Don't let anyone get on the stage!" The subtext of this request for keeping order, in the social, national, and clearly political sense of the film, really suggests: "the stage is ours." The following sequences support this impression. First, a child choir sings with Arna: "Why are all the children of the world free and I am not?" Then Arna holds a brief speech in front of a largely young, chirpy, and noisy audience: "The *Intifada* [uprising, "awakening"] for us means fighting for freedom, liberty and knowledge—these are basic values!" She yells, perspires and her theatrical body language is utterly convincing, because she obviously believes in these things.

Throughout the film Juliano's voice-over intervenes, explains, but does not interpret the events. Arna received the alternative Nobel Prize, and used the US$ 50,000 to build a little theatre on top of Zachary Zbeide's parents' home. At the time one of the children in the theatre, he will later be the commander of the El-Akza regiment in Jenin, known also for his intimate relationships with the Israeli peace activist Tali Fahima (Shohat 31 December 2004).

The next scene is a theatre class where the children shout, roar, and perform animal exercises, fully convincing as children who enjoy an exciting teacher. Juliano reveals what will happen to them, and will later return in a flashback to this sequence of rehearsals, indeed the very reason why he returned to Jenin: Nidal will be killed, Yussuf will be killed, little Ashraf, Yussuf's friend, will be killed in a battle into which he flung himself after watching an Israeli shell kill a girl who died in his hands. Ala'a will be killed. He is being filmed a number of times, sitting on the ruins of his home, introverted, wringing his hands. In another psycho-dramatic exercise Arna attempts to help the children cope with their wrath about the demolition of their homes. Ashraf, following Arna's explicit demand, shows what he would do to those who destroyed his house. He begins to beat her up, and she encourages: "Good, good, that's how it is when you're angry." She gives all the children some brown paper sheets to tear. They do, with bemused yet full awareness that this is at once serious and a game. "When we're angry, we must express our anger," she says and sends the kids to paint and draw. Ala'a paints a ruined house with a flag on top. In eight years he will lead a Palestinian unit to war. Did Arna's theatre "educate" him to do so? Most Palestinian towns and villages never had a children's (or any other) theatre, and still raised a generation of fighters against the occupation.

Arna's theatre, as seen in her son's film, is the theatre of the oppressed, often close in its techniques to Augusto Boal's (1985: 124 ff.), with reference to how the actor relates to him/herself and to the audience. However, Juliano does not employ active audience participation, including suggestions to alternative developments in the plot. Rather, he believes in the magic of stage lighting, sets, and music, namely, in the illusory nature of theatre. The lively audience, as the one sequence shows, clearly enjoyed an intensive theatre experience, understood the story, and gratefully applauded at the "right" moments in a play by Gassan Kanafani, author, playwright and PLO activist, killed when his car was booby-trapped and blown up by the Israeli Defense Forces.

In the next sequence Juliano asks one child to copycat his English teacher, a person who does not appear in the film but is obviously presented as a physically abusive educator. Though physical punishment is known to be common in many Arab schools, and, therefore, beating up pupils tends not to be taken too seriously, Juliano implies that oppression from the outside corrupts, in the sense that it encourages violence within the oppressed community just as badly. Juliano stops the child, noticing he was truly getting carried away in the game and had lost the necessary distance required in theatre. The child does not manage to be both "in" and "out of" the played role.

The rehearsal in a scene called "I Shall Bring the Sun" takes place on a ladder. "Watch the ladder, the floor is slippery too," warns Juliano (who manages with great elegance to be both "in" the film as well as direct it), but one must not stop at the literal meaning of the rehearsal safety measures. In the filmed reality it might well have been that alone, but in the finally edited and screened product this is a subtly ambiguous premonition about dangerous climbing and a highly slippery non-theatrical reality of the children-to-become-fighters.

An Israeli TV team comes to interview the children. The children speak of their initial distrust toward Juliano and Arna, suspecting them of spying for the Israelis. Soon they changed their minds: "Arna's like my mother." Juliano encourages the child to speak directly to the camera and say (to him): "I thought YOU were a spy" instead of "I thought Juliano was a spy." This too is an important lesson for a young actor: address your partner on- and off-stage directly, Juliano tells him, directly referring to both politics and theatre. The child continues: "Then we saw you favor us, you're for us, not against us. No Arab has ever done with us such things." Juliano, son to a Jewish mother and an Arab Palestinian father, did not teach only theatre to the children of Jenin, who had never seen a theatre performance in their lives. He obviously taught them *through* theatre.

Then come the scenes when the young actors receive their newly prepared costumes for the show. The film, indeed a documentary about the company, shows them trying them on with the deeply meditative excitement of Kathakali actors, who wear their makeup, masks, and costumes while "entering" their roles in a similar process. The costumes shaped the children's behavior, helped them internalize a glory and royalty quite different from the destruction, filth and poverty in the refugee camp. Then the performance itself: "My dear daughter, I hereby command you to bring the sun into the castle. If not—thou shalt not be Queen!" The little princess cries, claiming this is not possible, and runs away, for the time being. Later she will perform her mission superbly. The children's acting style is lucid, precise, and charming, though when needed, also gross, and even violent when they exchange smacks. Reality is not far off stage, despite the required stage propriety. Whoever has worked in

community theatre or with children is well aware of the empowerment
process the participants and staff often undergo during the process and
of the underlying psycho-social messages.

In a TV interview inserted in Juliano's documentary as a play-
within-a-play, one child says, seemingly fully conscious of the triple
medium (film, theatre, television): "I want to use my power [...] " The
interviewer asks whether he'd be willing to imitate an Israeli soldier,
and immediately the child assaults one of his buddies, beats him up,
draws an imaginary pistol, pretending to be an interrogator. In Jenin
not only Mer-Khamis is the director, reality is too. Yussuf the child
wears a typically Israeli army "dubbon" (thick wind-proof jacket),
indeed the complementary opposite to Arna's kaffia. Asked if he
wants to be a soldier, Ashraf says boldly, with slight scorn and
pseudo-friendliness to the Israeli TV interviewer: "Yes, a Syrian
soldier:"

> Q. Theatre expresses anger, protest [...] you protest through the theatre [...]
> A. Yes, identity, love of life [...]
> Q. Does theatre have the power to influence, to show "the situation" to the
> audience?
> A. I forget the audience, concentrate on my feelings, I give myself from
> within, so that the audience will be with us.
> Q. Do you feel it is like throwing stones?
> A. Like a Molotov cocktail, power, happiness, pride [...]
> Q. What's your dream?
> A. (After Juliano whispered to him on camera) I want to be the Palestinian
> Romeo, Julia will be from the family, from Jenin [...] "

Ashraf may or may not have known about the Shakespearean
Romeo's end. Was Julia's character an image of his homeland? Or the
girl who will die in his arms in just a few years? Could Arna herself
be a kind of Julia from "another" family? Ashraf will be killed, his
shrouded body carried on a tractor platform brought to be buried. The
thematic links created here between Julia, Arna, homeland and Jenin
mothers interviewed in the film before and after their sons were killed
is, again, extremely suggestive in its subtlety.

Juliano drives to the hospital to bring his dying mother for a last
visit to Jenin. On the way he asks her about the Palmach. In
unmistakable Palmach-like slang she says that those were splendid
times, "age, age, from 17 till 19." "Has she done bad things?" he asks,
focusing on her then politics towards Palestinians. She replies: "It was

a time of bragging, beauty, hubris. I drove a jeep, took hitchhikers, let them off, drove on the sidewalks, and drove everybody off, down to the road." Arna, we learn, was also Gandi's chauffeur and as such chased Bedouins. Gandi, nickname for Rehavam Zeevi, later became an extreme right-wing politician, killed by Palestinian fighters. Since those days Arna has worn the kaffia, but the head underneath it has been significantly transformed. Here and now, through making theatre in Jenin, she seems to correct the wrongs of her youth. There are hugs, kisses and tears when she is filmed in the Jenin street, her friends happy to see her, knowing also that she is going to die.

Juliano receives his mother's body for the necessary ritual identification "of the deceased" and the Julia motif hovers again in the film, yet in a different context. Arna is wrapped in blue shrouds; Jenin's dead fighters in white. After her death the theatre closes. Thirteen days after the Jenin siege, Juliano visits the town again, and all the "future" flash-forward sequences in the first part become the recent past in the second, almost "a present."

Contrary to a film that works as a continuum, and because of the time gap between filming and screening, live theatre is necessarily bound to the present, always re/presenting whatever is "presentified" onstage. In this sense, too, Juliano's documentary is surprisingly theatrical. The "presentness" of theatre *qua* back and forwards flashes, as a theme and motivating force in *Arna's Children*, as well as an image of tension between "the real human being" and its artificial-fictive representation, is exquisitely combined in the film. Even the ritual reading of the "farewell" letter, shortly before Yussuf and Nidal perform their suicide bombing mission in Hadera, fully clad in their combat costumes, is deeply moving in its artificial, almost kitschy theatricality. In an improvised memorial session Juliano holds for the fallen children of the theatre, he mentions that his "anger broke out again," a sequence referring to the beginning of the documentary and the psychodrama exercised years back. Ritual is a long tested mode of coping with a killed son, great injustice, or a demolished home. Traditional modes of behaviour, sometimes blatantly extroverted and deliberately rigid, not unlike certain theatre traditions, attempt to keep together what otherwise might be emotionally torn to pieces.

Among all the ruined houses in Jenin, the little theatre built on top of one of them is a home for the children who played there themselves, some of them practicing as play what will later be their real role: "When I play I feel power, happiness, pride [...]." They will not rise to take their bows at the end of the real show. Unlike Muhammad Bakri, who underlined the slaughter in his film *Jenin*, or Nizar Hasan, who emphasized the military encounter between the Israelis and the (he suggests winning) Palestinians, Juliano Mer-Khamis deals with the humanness of his children-fighters and their personal and social background (Schnitzer, 9 March 2004). He does not judge his characters and is able, therefore, to portray convincing biographies. In the theatre, to remind again of that sequence, Juliano asks Ashraf to say "you" instead of "he." The same is asked of the film's spectator. In theatre the "you" cannot be ignored because all share the same stage. As film critic Uri Klein put it, "Beyond 'us' and 'they' there's a common destiny, a common tragedy, common wrath and despair, and, perhaps beyond all that, the common necessity to put an end to the cycle of blood [...]." (Klein 16 April 2004).

Juliano Mer-Khamis's film is, I believe, an attempt to bridge reality and theatre and expose on screen what is common to "them" and "us." He claims that *Arna's Children* is not a political film. Nevertheless, in its profound humanism it is highly political. He portrays the lives and deaths of those who try to "bring the sun to their castle" through their artistic activity and take theatre fully seriously. In a way, the youngsters are invited to take their roles to the extreme, perhaps even commit suicide, not only onstage. Answering the question whether he would have felt the same towards the miserable lives lived in refugee camps had he not been the son of an Arab father and a Jewish mother, he said: "Every person with a dollop of humanness would have reached this very same conclusion" (Namer, 2 March 2004).

NOTE
All translations are by the author.

REFERENCES
Amos. (1999) By Moshe Yizraeli, adapted and directed by Ruth Kanner. The Ruth Kanner Group (October). Tel Aviv and Acco Festival.
Arna's Children. (2003) Written, directed, and produced by Juliano Mer-Khamis. Tel Aviv: [film: 35 mm]. <http://www.arna.info/arna/index.php> [Accessed 11 July 2008].

At Sea. (2005) By S. Yizhar. Adapted and directed by Ruth Kanner. The Ruth Kanner Group. Bat Sheva Dance Ensemble, Susanne Delal Centre: Tel Aviv.

Bar Yaacov, Shai. (1999) "On *Amos.*" *Yediot Aharonot* (29 October).

——. (2001) *Yediot Aharonot* (22 October).

Bar Yossef, Eitan. (2001) *Ha'ir* (11 October), 64.

Beckett, Samuel. (1986) *Waiting for Godot.* London, Boston: Faber & Faber.

Boal, Augusto. (1985) *The Theatre of the Oppressed.* New York: Theatre Communications Group.

Discovering Elijah. (1999) By S. Yizhar, adapted and directed by Ruth Kanner. The Ruth Kanner Group (October). Tel Aviv and Acco Festival.

Dionysus at the Dizengoff Centre. (2004). By Tamar Berger, adapted and directed by Ruth Kanner. The Ruth Kanner Group (October).Tel Aviv University Theatre Department, Acco Festival and Susanne Delal Centre: Tel Aviv.

Doudai, Naomi. (2005) "On *Plonter.*" *Jerusalem Post* (16 June).

Elyakim, Yaron. (2001) *Ma'ariv* (3 October).

——. (2005) "On *Plonter.*" *Maariv* (6 June).

Fuchs, Sarit. (2005) "On *Plonter.*" *Maariv* (3 June).

Handelsaltz, Michael. (1999) *Haaretz* (28 September).

——. (2001) *Haaretz,* 3 October.

——. (2005) "On *Plonter.*" *Haaretz,* 29 May.

Hebron. (2007). By Tamir Greenberg, Directed by Oded Kotler. Habima & Cameri Theatres (August). Tel Aviv.

Hatab, Yoram. (2008) *Time Out, Tel Aviv (*April/May), 62.

Imamura, Osamu. (2001) "On *Amos.*" *Asahi Shimbun* (5 April).

Yizhar, S. *Discovering Elijah.* (1990) Tel Aviv: Zmora-Bitan Publishers.

Kanner, Ruth. (2006) Program sheet of *At Sea.* Tel Aviv: Bat Sheva Dance Ensemble, Susanne Delal Centre.

Klein, Uri. (2004) "On *Bring the Sun to the Castle.*" *Haaretz* (16 April).

Levy, Shimon. (2007) "Mekatrim Babamot." *Mifne: Journal for Social Issues* 54, 12-21.

Marmari, Hanoch. (2008) *On Arna's Children, Time Out, Tel Aviv* (April/May), 44.

Namer, Shmulik. (2004) "Interview with Juliano Mer-Khamis." *Publication* (2 March), 54.

Ophir, Adi. (2001) *Working for the Present: Essays on Contemporary Israeli Culture.* Tel Aviv: Hakibbutz Hameuchad.

PILAT Report. (2004) Centre for Information and Culture Studies, Ministry of Culture, Science and Sport, State of Israel, Tel Aviv. See also <http://www.pilat.co.il/tarbut-report> [Accessed 12 April 2008].

Plonter. (2006) Directed by Yael Ronen. Tel Aviv: Cameri Theatre.

Schnitzer, Meir. (2004) "On *Bring the Sun to the Castle.*" *Maariv* (9 March).

Shohat, Orit. (2004) "On *Bring the Sun to the Castle.*" *Haaretz* (31 December).

Vilnai, Matan. (2005) "On *Plonter.*" *Yediot Ahronot* (20 October).

Yefeth, Amir. (1999) "*On* Arna's Children." *HaKibbutz Weekly Magazine* (30 September), 15.

Ziona's Trip. (2007) Directed by Omri Yavin. Jaffa: Hassimta.

DOCUMENTING THE INVISIBLE: DRAMATIZING THE ALGERIAN CIVIL WAR OF THE 1990S

SUSAN C. HAEDICKE

> Yacine: I am the prodigal son who is returning home after a long, long, a very long exile. A child born of the dawn […].
> Wisdom: What dawn are you talking about?
> Yacine: The dawn of the first day of our country's independence! Perhaps you've forgotten it!
> Wisdom: Listen, my boy, that dawn you keep talking about was drawn and quartered by predatory men only a few days after independence, it was lynched!
> Yacine: Your bilious words repel me.
> Wisdom: To tell the truth, I despair of this night that has fallen over the land. I am afraid it will be split asunder by a thousand and one bolts of deadly lightening! […] Your dawn was lynched!
> Yacine: I don't believe you. You're lying, or you've lost your mind […]. It was on the first day of independence. A dawn unlike any other dawning since the beginning of time. We had been waiting a hundred years for that dawn, for that arc of light reaching up into the sky […].
> Wisdom: Thirty years after independence nothing has changed. There is still contempt, there is still poverty (Aba 1997: 268-79).[1]

Yacine and Wisdom, two characters in Algerian playwright Noureddine Aba's polemical play, *Une Si Grande Espérance, Ou le Chant Retrouvé au Pays Perdu* (*Such a Great Hope, or the New Song of a Lost Country*[2]), challenge each other with opposing versions of the aftermath of Algeria's independence from France, especially in light of the violence and social chaos during what Benjamin Stora has called the "invisible war" (*La Guerre Invisible* 2001) of the 1990s. The play's porous boundaries between historical events and dramatic creation and its testing of the authenticity of contradictory memories and interpretations of the past offer a possible way to document the events of this invisible war. Aba, by embodying the contrasting histories in his characters, struggles to construct an historical narrative, not just a fictional account, that explains the descent into the violence of the 1990s, but that also suggests a way to reclaim and redirect the hope and the promise of Algerian independence.

One version of post-1962 Algeria is offered by Yacine, a freedom fighter during the revolution who has finally returned to his homeland after a self-imposed exile of thirty years. He claims that Algeria achieved victory over oppression, poverty, and injustice at the moment that France relinquished its colonial authority. With Algeria in what he assumed were the capable hands of the leaders of the victorious revolutionary party, Yacine felt that he had completed his job in his homeland and that his new task was to proclaim the success of the revolution abroad, to become the self-appointed "poet and the intermediary of my people [...] The poet go-between" (1997: 275). He emigrated to France "bearing in my arms the dawn, to show it to the world, to tell everyone everywhere that we had fought, not to force our truth on others but only to make it known where it had not been known before" (1997: 282). In contrast, the blind old man called Wisdom (as well as the other characters in the play) remained in Algeria after 1962 to implement the aspirations of independence. Presenting the opposing position, Wisdom claims that the goals of freedom and an end to poverty were sabotaged at every turn both by the new leaders who placed personal gain over success of the new nation and by a population of "sleep-walkers" (1997: 297) willing to turn a blind eye either out of ignorance of what was happening or as a protection of the gains they had achieved. As the play opens, Yacine, still reveling in the promise of independence, has finally returned to his homeland just as the civil war of the 1990s begins to turn Algeria into a bloodbath, and what he imagines will be a glorious homecoming turns out to be his funeral.

Algeria won its independence from France in July 1962, after eight long years of bloody revolution and stood at the dawn of a new age of freedom and self-determination. Other nations still subjugated by colonial oppression looked to Algeria as a beacon of an independent future; however the thirty-year long dictatorial rule of the revolutionary party, the FLN (National Liberation Front), and its misguided, often destructive policies plunged the nation into political, cultural, and economic chaos. Its corruption and secularization encouraged the disaffected population, especially the young, to turn to the only viable ideology, Islam, as represented by the opposition movement of the Islamic Salvation Front (FIS). Wisdom, in Aba's play, explains the appeal of the FIS: "When the people supported them in the past, the Islamists hadn't yet killed anyone. They supported them because they were denouncing the depravity and corruption of the State Party and promising to punish all FLN leaders who were responsible" (338). In mid-1991, the military cancelled the elections that the Islamist party would have won. It did not take long for Islamic militants, who claimed that they represented the cheated and disempowered Algerian people, to resort to violence to bring down the regime. The country descended into a brutal civil war claiming over 120,000 lives by 1999 and maiming countless more.[3] The Algerian civil war is so poorly documented, so shrouded in obscurity, that historian Benjamin Stora names this deadly conflict the "invisible war." During this period, the Algerian government denied access to foreign journalists and photographers, and intimidation silenced others. Those who spoke out took great personal risks as thousands of Algerian intellectuals, especially French-speaking ones, were targeted for assassination.[4] In spite of the personal risk, Stora calls on the playwrights, novelists, and poets—the storytellers—to help construct an historical record that offers a creative interpretation into past and present events.

Aba and so many other Algerian artists, especially those living outside Algeria, do feel compelled to make sense of the culture of violence that swept over their homeland with such ferocity in the 1990s and to unravel the intertwined allegiances and opposing goals.[5] *Such a Great Hope*, one of the first works to look at the civil war, was published in 1994, only two years after the extreme violence had started and well before it began to abate at the end of the century. Thus Aba attempts to understand the events as they are unfolding. He clearly seeks to explore the disintegration of independence into violence, but he does not want to investigate the events, the "facts" alone. Rather he attempts to construct an historical record of this culture of violence by relying on a fictional narrative to fill in the gaps, highlight the repetitions, and understand the contradictions. This interpretation offers a viable historical analysis of the events, a fiction only in the sense that it is "something made, something fashioned," not in the sense that it is "false, unfactual" (Geertz 1973: 15).

The historical narrative that Aba constructs in *Such a Great Hope* unambiguously portrays this brutal second Algerian war as an inevitable consequence of the leaders' betrayal of the ideals of the revolution. Aba not only forcefully rejects Yacine's idealistic view of history: "You're nothing but a poet!" accuses one of the characters, "A poor poet taken in by the magic of his own words! You've made that deceptive and false independence into some kind of phosphorescent flood that will burst the dam of heaven with the weight of a million stars! You deceived yourself, Yacine!" (282). He also implies that interpretations like Yacine's contributed to the world's blindness toward the escalating violence. On his arrival in Algeria, without even stopping in the city, Yacine has rushed to the Eagle's Nest, a rocky shelf high on a mountain where he lived during the war and where he now wants to relive the thrill of the "new dawn," the day Algeria achieved independence. He repeatedly paints the picture of the rapture he felt to the Old Man Wisdom whom he meets at the Eagle's Nest. "I experienced that exalted moment when nature and mankind breathe through the same mouth, when light, mankind, and nature seem to understand each other—no, more than that: seem to communicate with each other. It was as though, before, the people had been victims of some mass amnesia and then, all at once, they had regained their memory [...] all their memory of all their age-old past! [...] The streets were filled with history, it took us by the hand" (276). Yacine hopes to celebrate what he thinks are the triumphs of independent Algeria. "I returned to this country to tell its ragged veterans that in the eyes of the world they were a life-giving example of noble courage [...]. Abroad, Algeria's image was excellent. Our leaders were regarded as statesmen, with a sense of history" (287-8, 307).

But the Algeria he seeks is an aestheticized one, cosmetically created in his poetic storytelling from his memories of the promise of independence, and the other characters who organize themselves into a Tribunal led by Wisdom, reject Yacine's interpretation of the events and demand that he "recant the false dawn" (289). They absolutely refuse to allow him to continue to spread his "lies about that so-called glowing dawn" (293), and so force him to renounce the "myth" which seduced Wisdom—and the audience—with its beauty and hope.

> Wisdom: Recant the false dawn, the deceptive dawn [...]
> Yacine: (*breaking in*) A while ago, old man, you believed in it as well!
> Wisdom: Yes, I believed you! That's why we want you to recant. Because

you will use any kind of sorcery. We do not want others to fall victim to the
same witchcraft. Recant your error! (289)

The Tribunal composed of Wisdom, Yacine's former fiancée Sahira
who was severely scarred when extremists threw acid in her face for
walking on the streets unveiled, and three other emblematic
characters, Justice, Charity, and Tolerance, expose how the leaders of
the new nation allowed ambition and greed to overtake the
revolutionary ideals so that all that happened after independence was
"a transfer of power from the long time European settlers, who were
on their way out, to the smart new men, the brand-new men" (297).[6]
Aba clearly places the blame for the rise of Islamist extremism on the
government, but there is no doubt that he also condemns the actions of
the fanatics. The audience experiences the horrors of their senseless
violence in a scene in the park where the extremists, the "Bearded
Men," threaten Yacine and gun down the Old Woman who tries to
warn him and Sahira of imminent danger. The audience easily
sympathizes with the characters who suffer at the hands of the
extremists: Yacine, who is assassinated, the maimed Sahira, and the
murdered Old Woman. In addition, the fanatics are depicted as
buffoons, slapstick comics, who bicker over religious fervor and trip
over their own tongues. They are cowards who attack only defenseless
targets.

    But Aba also asks questions about moral responsibility and
denies amnesty for ignorance and inaction. We are responsible not just
for the things we cause, he says, but also for the things we allow to
happen, and thus he accuses those who choose not to act or pretend
not to see as among those who contribute to the atrocities. His play
dramatizes the devastating results of what Diane Taylor calls
"percepticide," a cultivated blindness that allows people "to deny
what they saw and, by turning away, collude with the violence around
them" (1997: 123). Yacine's poetic encomiums on Algeria during his
years of exile have allowed the corruption to fester and strengthen
unfettered by outside scrutiny. Yet at the same time, *Such a Great
Hope* clearly exposes the great risk incurred in choosing to be a
witness. During the play, Yacine shifts from being an unwitting
collaborator to being an outspoken critic who finds hope for the
country only in a willingness to "see" what is happening and to stand
up to the perpetrators, even though it costs him his life. "It is our
country, Sahira!" cries Yacine. "Its history is entrusted to us, we are

responsible even for the lives of those who lived here centuries ago, and for those who live here today. Whatever we say, whatever we do, we are an extension of them, we do not have the right to be indifferent!" (339).

Yacine's initial ignorance of the "lynched dawn" provides no shelter against those who find his words dangerous, and his inevitable fate is clear from the beginning of the play. Scenes in a hospital where the dying poet, a victim of an assassination attempt by the extremists, lies comatose, frame the play. In fact, Aba's stage directions insist that these hospital scenes also punctuate the play and so they provide an almost constant presence: "The scene switches suddenly back to the hospital room [...]. This reminder of the real world can be repeated as required" (283). The "dream sequences" in the Eagle's Nest and the park act like flashbacks leading up to the hospital scenes, but the metaphoric quality of the open exterior spaces, particularly the Eagle's Nest, hints that they could also be imagined. In fact, trying to decipher the *real* from the *memory* from the *hallucination* results in several possible interpretations: all events in the play actually took place and were presented in present time or in flashbacks; the hospital and the park scenes took place, but the Eagle's Nest was imagined; or none of the scenes took place, except Yacine's murder (although in France, not Algeria) and the hallucinations were the dying man's struggle to understand the plight of his country and his own meaningless death. The two voice-overs, spoken by Yacine, support this last possibility since one mentions violence against him in France and the other places him back in France.

This blurring of the real and the imagined within the world of the play acts as a porthole to a more far-reaching blurring between history and fiction that extends beyond the play itself. Linda Hutcheon, in *A Poetics of Postmodernism*, interprets this strategy: "both history and fiction are discourses, [...] both constitute systems of signification by which we make sense of the past [...]. In other words, the meaning and shape are not *in the events*, but *in the systems* which make those past 'events' into present 'facts.' This is not a 'dishonest refuge from the truth' [as argued by Gerald Graff] but an acknowledgement of the meaning-making function of human constructs [...]. This mixing of the historical and the fictive and this tampering with the 'facts' [...] is the major means of making the reader aware of the particular nature of the historical referent" (1988:

89). Rather than negating historical knowledge, the narrative with its gaps, contradictions, and speculations in these plays and novels marks "a shift from validation to signification, to the way systems of discourse make sense of the past, [...] one that implies a pluralist (and perhaps troubling) view of historiography as consisting of different but equally meaningful constructions of past reality—or rather, of the textualized remains (documents, archival evidence, witnesses' testimony) of that past" (96). Aba, in *Such a Great Hope*, attempts to construct just such a "system of signification." One method he uses creates close parallels between what occurs in the fictional narrative and "facts" gleaned from other sources of information. One such example contextualizes Yacine's decision to leave his homeland right after independence. He exclaims, "I wanted to tell our former enemies that we had fought without hatred, that amid all the madness and horror we had not lost either the warmth of our souls or the plain words to express it" (Aba 1997: 277-8). Writers were among the many Algerians[7] who immigrated to the land of the former colonizer soon after independence was won. In fact, in 1962, just about every European professional (and family) left Algeria. Stone writes, "The flight of the *pieds noirs* to France in 1962 was one of the largest single movements of refugees in the twentieth century" (1997: 236). Stora confirms, "The *pieds noirs* left Algeria en masse and the emigration of Algerian workers in the same direction increased. Seven and a half years of war, marked by destruction and the displacement of populations, the OAS's relentless efforts to destroy the country's infrastructures, the rapid mass exodus of the Europeans, the profound disorganization in Algeria that resulted, the sudden arrival on the labor markets of tens of thousands of freed Algerian prisoners or demobilized soldiers, and the "civil war" for power were all factors that explain the resumption of emigration to France in the summer 1962. From September 1, 1962, up to and including November 11, 1962, the entry of 91,744 Algerians into France was recorded" (2001: 128).

Sahira's experience in post-independence Algeria offers another fiction/history parallel. Like so many women who fought in the revolution, Sahira found herself being denied recognition as a *mujahideen*: "no one wanted to be reminded that she had shared in the hunger, the thirst, the fear, the sound of gunfire" (294). The complex relationship between the new nation and Islam contributed to the post-war erasure of the role of women during the war for independence, and as Islamist parties gained political strength, the social policies they advocated became common practice. By the late 1960s, Islamists called on the government to impose *sharia* and by 1984, the Family Code restricting the rights of women became law.[8] The characters in *Such a Great Hope* express the excesses of the Islamists: "There was a call for a jihad against the infidels, the renegades: death to bad Muslims, to the drinkers of wine, the eaters of impure flesh. Down with emancipated women! Throw acid on brazen women who dare to show their face in public, who dare to laugh, to sing, to dance, to tan themselves in the sun!" (296)—exactly Sahira's fate, and the fate of many Algerian women who opposed the restrictions.

In these and many other ways, Aba, tentatively and yet provocatively, plays with rewriting the construct for documentary theatre by filling in the gaps in the historical narrative with unverifiable, yet so possibly real, moments and events. He offers the possibility of a documentary theatre that constructs and imagines Algeria's invisible history, and his play stands as a model for the only possible archival document when others have been deliberately erased. Within this world of the "documentary" play, the moving back and forth between the "real world" moments and the "dream sequences" constructs a multileveled historical narrative with spatial and temporal ambiguities from which Aba embarks on an historical interpretation that functions like what Clifford Geertz calls a "thick description" of the events. Like the ethnographer, he is faced with "a multiplicity of complex conceptual structures, many of them superimposed upon or knotted into one another, which are at once strange, irregular, and inexplicit, and which he must contrive somehow first to grasp and then to render" (1973: 10). Aba's resulting analysis sorts through "the structures of signification [...] and [determines] their social ground and import" (1973: 9) to create "a form of knowledge" (1973: 6). The Tribunal's pessimistic analysis of the causes of the civil war are tested against Yacine's idealistic optimism, but once he is convinced of the failure of the revolution, the enormity of the loss seems overwhelming. "Do you realize, Yacine, that you, that I, have just cursed our own land? Do you realize that we are the ones who have given voice to our hatred? My God, what are we to do?" asks Sahira. "My tongue tastes of salt and bile. I do not know!" responds Yacine (305). The "facts" are not enough, Aba implies. They just lead to paralysis. The "aborted revolution" must be merged with the hope of a "new dawn"—not Yacine's former naïve hope, but a hope informed with knowledge. The people must be reawakened. But the "great hope" for Algeria if people speak out is put into perspective as the hospital scenes keep reminding the audience of the fate of Yacine (and others who question). Yet the hospital moments do not have the last word as Yacine's disembodied voice commenting on the violence and the hope ends the first and last scenes in the hospital: the "recovered song for a lost country."

Whether Yacine is an actual writer who was killed by extremists (as so many were) or whether he represents the many individuals murdered for who they were or what they represented is less important than the questions of moral responsibility that the play raises and the reality of the senseless violence that it reveals. Even though Aba rejects Yacine's idealism, the play seems to support the position that it is only Yacine's faith in the Algerian people and in the promise of the revolution in spite of the "facts" that he has learned that offers any hope for the nation, that can provide an antidote for intolerance. That is why his voice must be silenced by the opposition, but again Aba's position is ambiguous. Yacine, unconscious and dying, has no hope of survival, yet his disembodied voice speaks eloquently as a plea to his people, but, within the world of the play in Yacine's hospital room, the doctor can only hear mumbling. The audience, however, does hear the words and so they are clearly implicated in the moral ambiguities of the play. They are the witnesses who must make sense of the events and who must choose to act or to commit "percepticide."

Aba also complicates the interpretation with ambiguities of identity in the doubling of roles. He uses only six actors to perform thirteen characters, "not out of economy but because of the symbolism inherent in the dream sequences" (264). The actors playing Yacine and Sahira do not double roles, but all the others shift between the medical team trying to save Yacine's life and the fanatics who kill him, between the Tribunal who forces Yacine to recant, the Old Woman who tries to protect him, and two actors rehearsing a play about what is happening in Algeria in the park where Yacine and Sahira first met and pledged to fight for freedom. Is there any real difference in the harm these various people have done to Algeria, he asks.

The clarification—"making the reader aware" (to use Hutcheon's phrase)—of the big picture is exactly what was feared by those holding on to power by intimidation, those who accused writers of being traitors and corrupting influences from within and so legitimate targets for elimination. *The Last Summer of Reason*, Tahar Djaout's final novel (found among his papers soon after his assassination on May 26, 1993 and published posthumously), bears witness to the assaults against the power of words waged by religious fanatics. The novel's main character Boulem Yekker, the bookstore owner, conducts a solitary protest against the extremists who charge art and literature with heresy. He explains, "they understand the danger in words, all the words they cannot manage to domesticate and anesthetize. For words, put end to end, bring doubt and change. Words above all must not conceive of the utopia of another form of truth, of unsuspected paths, of another place of thought. You do not easily part with utopia; it is an acid that cuts holes in the opacity of dogma" (143-4). It is exactly that "acid" that the poet Yacine (and author Aba himself) begins to articulate as he comes to realize that those being killed are not members of the FLN, but ordinary citizens, that "the Islamists are children of the FLN. A child doesn't kill its father, even if he secretly hates him" (338). No wonder the fanatics must silence Yacine as he starts to find the words to express "such a great hope" for the nation as long as the people can break the cycle:

> beware that your innocence and trust do not again fall into the trap that the father is already setting to ensure his son will come into his inheritance. The father and son are one and the same. They are both sensation mongers, smooth talkers avid for power. With the father, you had a vain, contemptuous, corrupt nomenklatura. With the son, you will have the pitiless theocracy of the Ayatollahs, equally vain, equally depraved. The father brought you ruin. The son will bring you calamity. The father severed you from the world. The son will cut you off from mankind. The father lynched the dawn, the son will consume your future in fire, along with any chance of your becoming a part of the world at large. (347)

This position (of Yacine and Aba) was startling and dangerous to hold in 1994 when the civil war seemed to be a struggle between the government's security forces and the Islamist extremists, but many scholars now support it. French-Algerian historian Luis Martinez (writing under a pseudonym for safety) argues the same position in

The Algerian Civil War: 1990-1998 as he looks at how the leaders of Algeria appropriated the independence. According to Martinez, these men laid aside social progress for personal gain, but more importantly they saw social advancement as achieved most efficiently through violence and heralded the "political bandit" as the most effective leader. Civil war was less a "breakdown of the political system [than] an economic and political resource" (4-5). This "war-oriented *imaginaire*" (or world view) as Martinez calls this political strategy, posits violence as the best "method for accumulating wealth and prestige," and it is thus self-perpetuating.

This complicated and multilayered play with its spatial and temporal ambiguities, its blurred boundaries between actual verifiable events in Algerian history and fictional events in the world of the play, and its arguments over the authenticity and purpose of opposing interpretations of the past actually functions as a way to explore the process of construction of historical narrative. Aba contrasts the strident voice of the fact-finder—the "historian;" the poetic narrative voice of the "storyteller;" and the satiric voice as represented by the complicated scene in the park where two actors rehearse a play about contemporary Algeria. The actual relationship between the actors parallels the abusive relationship between the rich and the poor in the play, and the play itself presents a ridiculous portrait of a power-hungry politician humiliating the poor, but the actor who wrote the play insists: "I'm denouncing the poor! They've become a plague, they multiply by leaps and bounds! And what's worse, they're the majority of the fundamentalist faction!" (320). Throughout the play, the characters experiment with the most efficacious form in which to present "history": as an objective summary of "facts" like those presented by the Tribunal, as a poetic epic harking back to the indigenous oral tradition—the "recovered song"—a form used not only by Yacine, but also by Sahira and Wisdom, or as a parody of the events as presented both in the rehearsal and Yacine's angry exchange with the actors. Aba's play argues for the importance of all forms if one hopes to understand the tangled and erased past. What pass for facts, he demonstrates, are only meaningful in the context of a story, but a story that is not grounded in a specific cultural and historical context is meaningless.

As he struggles to construct Algeria's history, Aba does not shy away from depicting assassinations and maiming, the "verifiable facts" of this brutal decade, but he does not present the violence done to these bodies as an end in itself. Instead it becomes a powerful image of the more horrifying massacre of the promise of Algeria. As Aba writes in his Author's Note to *Such a Great Hope*, "When a poet chooses French or Arab to express his fraternal vision of the world and when fanatics who, hostile to his choice, assassinate him, at the same time as they kill him they are also killing the humanism produced by great and age-old cultures. It is as a witness to this dual murder that I cry out here. It is my hope that intermediaries in either of the two languages will not let this cry be lost in the wilderness" (262). The fate of the artist and the nation are inextricably tied. Yacine is independent Algeria; Yacine, like Algeria, is betrayed, lynched, massacred. But Aba demonstrates that extreme violence cannot really be comprehended in statistics, but only in lives. As Wole Soyinka wrote in the foreword to Djaout's *The Last Summer of Reason*, "It is not a universal principle that gets stabbed, shot, or even mutilated. It is a very specific voice, one that has made a conscious choice and died in defense of that choice. And it is only by recognizing that individuality that we are enabled to recollect, and respond to the fate of individuals" (xiv). *Such a Great Hope* places a face on the statistic of another writer assassinated, a face that could be based on an actual person or just inspired by the events, and Aba asks whether the "reality" of the events really matter since they could be real. What is most important is that, like his homeland, Yacine cannot be silenced. While his physical body has been destroyed his words live on, and his hope and his newly-found need to write the truth of Algeria ring in his final prayer for his homeland's survival:

> You must take control of your fate, you must assume responsibility for your country. Act with brotherhood toward each other, but drive away both father and son [FLN and FIS], send them back to the devil, for from there they came! If you don't, and if you don't do it now, then Algeria will sink into the darkness, like a ship sinking on the high seas, deep under the waters. And your uprising will have been for nothing! You will go back to what you were before, the pariah of nations, and—know this my people—if that should happen, then you will have no excuse in the eyes of history. (347)

Yacine's cry is to the people, not the ruling elite, to end the conflict of the civil war. Aba uses the construction of history not just to understand the past, but to structure the future.

NOTES

[1] All references to Aba's text are to the English translation unless otherwise noted.

[2] This is Richard Miller's 1997 translation of the title, but the translation of "le chant retrouvé au pays perdu" that more accurately reflects the spirit of the play is "the recovered song for a lost country." Aba is playing with the contrast of "lost and found" (*trouvé et perdu*) which offers the possibility of the hope (*espérance*) of regaining what is lost. His title also seems to resonate with Proust's *Le Temps Retrouvé*, translated as *The Past Recaptured*, which explores the interplay of physical details and memory.

[3] See the histories of Algeria written by Martin Stone, Benjamin Stora, and James D. Le Sueur.

[4] The years 1993 and 1994 alone, saw the murders of novelist Tahar Djaout; poet Youssef Sebti; psychologist and author Mahfoud Beucebci; sociologist M'Hamed Boukhobza; playwright Abdelkader Alloula (murdered in Paris); the former Minister of Higher Education, Djilali Liabès; a member of the National Advisory Council, Ladi Flici; the director of the Advanced School of Fine Arts, Ahmed Asselah; the president of the Algerian League of Human Rights, Youcef Fathallah; and rai singer Cheb Hasni were just a few among the many killed. Between 1993 and 1996, fifty-seven journalists were murdered and five disappeared. See Assia Djebar's *Le Blanc de l'Algérie* in which she creates an homage to the many intellectuals killed by the assassin's bullet.

[5] Playwrights such as Sophie Amrouche, Slimane Benaïssa, Aziz Chouaki, and Achour Ouamara and novelists such as Tahar Djaout, Assia Djebar, and Khalida Messaoudi are just a few who have looked at the trauma of the 1990s in their works.

[6] The French text reads: "Une passation de pouvoir entre les pieds-noirs qui commençaient à s'user et des pieds rois flambant neuf!" (50) which linguistically connects the *pieds noirs* (the term used for the French colonists, many of whom had lived in Algeria for generations) and the *pieds rois* (referring to the new leaders whose one-party rule established them as the new nobility in spite of the claim that Algeria was a socialist state).

[7] At the time of Algerian independence, "Algerians" included the two ethno-linguistic groups of Arabs and Berbers as well as those who were called *pieds noirs*, the name given to Algerians of French descent. *Pieds Noirs* families had often lived in Algeria for generations. The notion of Algerian identity pre-1962 is complicated further by the fact that Algeria was an integral part of France, not a colony.

[8] See Stone and Stora for more details.

REFERENCES

Aba, Noureddine. (1997) *Such a Great Hope, or the New Song of a Lost Country.* Trans. Richard Miller. *Playwrights of Exile: An International Anthology.* New York: Ubu Repertory Theatre Publications, 259-348.

———. (1994) *Une Si Grande Espérance, ou Le Chant Retrouvé au Pays Perdu.* Paris: Editions l' Harmattan.

Baudrillard, Jean. (1994) *Simulacra and Simulation.* Trans. Sheila Faria Glaser. Ann Arbor: University of Michigan Press.

Djaout, Tahar. (2001) *The Last Summer of Reason*. Trans. Marjolijn de Jager. St. Paul, MN: Ruminator Books.

Geertz, Clifford. (1973) *Interpretation of Culture*. New York: Basic Books.

Graff, Gerald. (1973) "The Myth of the Postmodernist Breakthrough." *TriQuarterly* 26, 383-417.

Hutcheon, Linda. (1988) *A Poetics of Postmodernism: History, Theory, Fiction*. New York and London: Routledge.

Pierre, Andrew J. and William B. Quandt. (1996) *Algerian Crisis: Policy Options for the West*. New York: Carnegie Endowment for International Peace.

Le Sueur, James D. (2001) *Uncivil War: Intellectuals and Identity Politics During the Decolonization of Algeria*. Philadelphia: University of Pennsylvania Press.

Martinez, Luis. (2000) *The Algerian Civil War: 1990-1998*. Trans. Jonathan Derrick. New York: Columbia University Press.

Naylor, Phillip C.. (2000) *France and Algeria: A History of Decolonization and Transformation*. Gainesville: University Press of Florida.

Stone, Martin. (1997) *The Agony of Algeria*. New York: Columbia UP.

Stora, Benjamin. (2001) *Algeria, 1830-2000: A Short History*. Trans. William B. Quandt. Ithaca: Cornell University Press.

——. (2001) *La Guerre Invisible: Algérie, années 90*. Paris: Presses de Sciences Po.

Taylor, Diana. (1997) *Disappearing Acts: Spectacles of Gender and Nationalism in Argentina's Dirty War*. Durham, North Carolina: Duke University Press.

THE EROTIC POLITICS OF *CRITICAL TITS*: EXHIBITIONISM OR FEMINIST STATEMENT?

WENDY CLUPPER

It is Friday at 1:00 p.m. at Burning Man, the week-long fire and arts festival that takes place every summer in the Nevada desert, and women are lining up to get their breasts painted. Volunteer artists, men and women, are working from a pair of card tables filled with palates, brushes, and jars of paint. This "breast painting workshop" is hosted by a camp of participants in preparation for the staging of an enormous all-woman topless bike ride. Participatory breast painting workshops are just one aspect of the phenomenon of *Critical Tits*: a popular parade and performance that has inspired debates over feminism and sexism for years. First staged in 1996 by five female festival attendees and planned to coincide at the same time as the Critical Mass bike ride in San Francisco, *Critical Tits* has grown into one of the largest participatory performances of nude women in the world.

      Significant amongst festival performances for its popularity, the *Critical Tits* bike ride or the *Ride,* has in the intervening years, gained a status as one of the singularly women-only performances at Burning Man that brings attention to both the diversity of the female form and the desire for empowerment demonstrated by the hundreds of women who have participated in it over the years. Participatory performance with its blurring of actor and spectator, the freedom associated with outdoor performance, and the anonymity of a large-scale festival site, together provide a unique platform for staging eroticism and the feminist politics that have produced *Critical Tits*. Within this essay, I will consider how *Critical Tits* is a feminist statement of solidarity and acceptance of one's body and an opportunity for exhibitionism in the face of exploitation, weaving critical theory, ethnography based on participant accounts, as well as my own participant-experience.

THE PERFORMANCE OF CRITICAL TITS

A deeper consideration of the 'breast painting workshop' held in preparation for the Critical Tits bike ride, reveals a particular place for me to start as a participant observer, as well as something unique to outdoor performance, where *random festival participants* and *transient crowds* may transform into make-up artists helping performers prepare for the show, and/or cheering, exuberant audiences. Not all participants however attend the *Ride* and not all women who attend, ride.

Critical Tits invites all women and girls who attend Burning Man to join in the mass topless bike ride at 4:00 Pacific Standard Time across the festival space of dusty and bumpy road. No restrictions are made nor are they enforced regarding whether or not any given woman is actually topless, and participation totals vary from year to year but are not recorded. The *Ride* is actually one of hundreds of participatory performances and activities that include parades, staged throughout the week. However, *Critical Tits* has evolved into a performance that is *now* overtly political and has spawned debates over feminism and exploitation. According to participant Bethany Wells:

> What I had heard about *Critical Tits* prior to participating in it was that it was a parade and party of women and for women, exclusively. I expected to have an empowering pro-woman experience, full of camaraderie and girlish bliss. I was sad to realize that the parade of half-naked women was not honored but completely objectified by rows upon rows of half naked men on the sidelines, making lewd comments and gestures to the hundreds of ladies passing by. (personal communication, 26 January 2009)

For this reason, many women Burners or Burning Man enthusiasts refuse to participate in the *Critical Tits Ride;* however, the truth is that for many women, this voluntary parade as performance involving nudity is an important part of their participation at Burning Man as women, and as feminists. These participants enjoy the public spectacle and the sisterhood of riding with hundreds of other women around the playa.[1] Indeed, the primary reason this participatory performance is so large is because many women participants who attend Burning Man desire to experience that mode of theatrical liberation. Likewise, *Critical Tits* also draws many male spectators who enjoy the spectacle of this very public and personal display by many women. According to Howard Gutknecht, *Critical Tits* spectator and breast painting volunteer:

> As I recall, before I'd ever been to Burning Man, this event was described as one of the hallmarks of what makes Burning Man different. At my first Burning Man I took time to bicycle out to find a good position from which to observe. I noticed people referred to this event as something unusual, even for Burning Man, and yet I can't remember, over the years, many people saying why. I have heard women tell stories about how they felt anxiety as they contemplated whether to participate and feelings of exhilaration and confidence and liberation as they participated. I actually saw this in one of the women in our group. She was positively transformed in the days afterward. (personal communication, 2 January 2009)

Burning Man is, to its devotees, known as a space for transformation, for shedding one's usual social roles, and for making bold moves publicly, such as going nude or voluntarily performing on a stage. The festival itself is as well, an event supporting various liberating modes of radical self-expression by its participants, including art-making, general nudity, and revelry. At the event, attendees live communally, and are encouraged to celebrate and present themselves wildly in or out of costumes. These behaviours are rewarded with attention. And this outdoor event also stands at the crossroads of what performance theorist Karl Toepfer would suggest is "Orgy culture," a place which, like Carnival, is theatrical and architectural in its luxurious visual pleasures and where too, the naked performer speaks (1991: 9-13). The landscape at Burning Man, six miles of elaborately built theme camps, stages, and artifices, is populated throughout by provocatively dressed, masked and semi-nude or completely nude participants. Throughout the event, these performers utilize the theatrical space of the festival by participating in parades, performances, and activities that encourage or present nudity. According to Ray Allen, Government Relations and Legal Affairs Manager for the Burning Man Project:

> Laws governing nudity are usually enacted and enforced on the state and local level. Burning Man is on federal land that resides within the remote parts of Pershing County, Nevada. Bureau of Land Management Rangers are part of the federal government so their jurisdiction is to simply enforce the federal laws. Since there are no federal nudity laws affecting the Black Rock Desert, they have no reason to cite or arrest for nudity. Pershing County also has jurisdiction over the Black Rock Desert, but they have made an informal

policy decision not to enforce state nudity laws presumably because of the
remoteness of the event, and because Black Rock City has different standards
of what is acceptable than other places within the County [...] nudity is
separate from other laws such as lewd behavior, exposing oneself to a minor,
etc. [...]. Those laws have been enforced within Black Rock City. (personal
communication, 3 December 2009)

The legal concept the Burning Man Project here suggests is that
nudity at the festival falls under the sovereignty of the First
Amendment of the Constitution of the United States, that guarantees
freedom of speech, and that authorities there do not punish nudity as
lewd because the dictates of prurient interest in community standards
authorize such behaviours. What is implicit in this is the notion that
Burners are granted freedom and power of self-expression, and so
show themselves political when they exercise that right in the
theatrical space. Participants therefore choose each year, given the
opportunity to cross the line socially or break the law, to express
themselves openly via nudity *sans censor*.

Exhibitionism as a human phenomenon defined in psychiatry is
the compulsive need to display one's genitals to others, and it is also
as a metaphor wrapped-up in theatre. Actors and performers have
historically been accused of behaving in vulgar ways to attract
attention from paying audiences, just as strippers and erotic dancers
have been accused of being licentious and revealing too much of their
bodies in order to attract clients for more compensation. But between
the gaze and wallet, there lies a simpler truth about desire and distaste.
Karl Toepfer in "Nudity and Textuality in Postmodern Performance,"
suggests: "Nudity isn't obscene unless it transgresses some threshold
of shock, but shock is possible only when performance uncovers the
power of desire to violate bodies and expose the spectator's capacity
for pleasure in bodily disgust" (1996: 86).

How then does one explain a participant's own desire to disrobe
at a theatrical event? We may start by acknowledging that to many
people, theatrical events are *other worlds*. Michel Foucault referred to
them as heterotopias (1986: 22-27). They are worlds where special
rules apply. Those rules extend to and include voyeurism and
exhibitionism. Nudity and the demonstration of ones' lowered
inhibitions to sexualized visual imagery and heightened sexual
behaviours may be normal and welcomed in these special other
worlds. However, seen in its larger context, the heterotopia of the

Figure 1. *The Critical Tits Ride* in 2006. An all-woman bike parade, participants go topless in a demonstration of solidarity to other women at Burning Man. This is the most widely participated inclusive woman-only activity on the playa. The Critical Tits Ride began in 1996 to coincide with the Critical Mass bike ride in San Francisco which happens in the summer on Friday afternoons. Photograph by Wendy Clupper.

outdoor performance space becomes a microcosm for the larger societies' political debates that efface individual identity.

Festivals and theatres that have moved outdoors in the United States have often done so in an effort to strategically protect their artists against censorship and arrest –to which urban indoor theatres as venues for performance would make them more vulnerable, subject to strict local laws and public scrutiny. Interestingly, just as North American festivals as theatrical events have located themselves outdoors in the liberated space that nature and the street as environments provide, the barriers between spectators and performers break down, as participants become a part of the performance. Aesthetically, being outside, also frees artists from the tight, controlled, and intimate confines of the playhouse. The physical place and symbolic space of the outdoors changes the medium of the theatre and it makes the vision of the performance space taller, bigger, and wider. It helps expand the audience's notion of the world that is being created by the performance and to an extent, their own place in that world.

In his writing on sex and nudity in theatre historically, Toepfer lays out several definitions and delineations about the ways nudity may be presented on and off the stage in a theatrical manner (1996: 76-91). Several kinds of theatrical nudity pervade at Burning Man, according to Karl Toepfer's definitions of the theatrical classification. These categories of theatrical nudity, include: Ritual Nudity, as with the voluntary participant fire operas premiered at Burning Man by the artist Pepe Ozan; Mythic Nudity, when festival participants spontaneously go nude anonymously; Model Nudity, when Burning Man participants, pose during theatrical moments during the event for aesthetic purposes (read: to have their picture taken); Pornographic Nudity, wherein the nude participant speaks and demonstrates their excitement; and Balletic Nudity, or nude physical virtuosity.

Performance theory does offer an important metaphor for this theatrical event that is subculture, and social *orgy* in one. It may be understood that in an attempt to subvert social order, Burning Man allows participants to celebrate in common their temporary liberation without class distinctions through an economy which discourages commodification in favour of gift-giving. Theoretically, the liberated nude bodies of all participants become apart of a new culture based on the values of the festival community, where "radical self-expression" is a respected tenet. Women at Burning Man are encouraged and praised when they exhibit their breasts and genitals. Despite this fact, women participants who perform in the nude do remain subject to the same sexist scrutiny as outside of the community. For Toepfer, this implies that: "Theatrical nudity thus awakens complicated 'problems' concerning the 'reality' of the performing body" (1996: 76).

At Burning Man, there exists as well, a variety of performances, art installations, and exhibitions that portray or allow for the display of the naked human body. Nudity in theatrical events confronts issues of taste, privacy, and censorship, as much as it tests an audience's aesthetic sensibilities to what theatre can do for society off the stage. Staged eroticism is a theatrical equation that involves the performer's body, the sexualized interaction with the spectator and the spectator's performing body. The staged erotic performance occurs as well in specific public areas of exhibitionism in the sites for performing at a theatrical event –in the case of Burning Man, this is the parade route for the female riders. Further consideration of staged eroticism reveals that there exists within the art form of staged eroticism: informal public nudity, sexualized behaviours made public, and formal performances by artists in the nude.

Burning Man's carnivalesque or *orgiastic* culture includes necessarily, open and ambiguous adult sexuality and nudity, sex-oriented performances and demonstrations, and the wider acceptance of exhibitionism. According to Burning Man artist, Harrod Blank, "Certainly many people are attracted to the nudity and the fire and the overall spectacle of the event, and granted, I too revel in it all […]. Burning Man to me is like a giant adult rated show n" tell, a smorgasbord of art, identity, and passion" (*Art Cars and Burning Man*, n.d.) An exciting example of avant-garde carnival with a postmodern sensibility, Burning Man provides a play place to theoretically examine how nudity, ritual, sexuality, tastes, and eroticism meld.

As for *Critical Tits*, often the female participant's choice to go topless or to ride in it becomes the central message as to how much one supports the *Ride* overall, given the many complicated potential circumstances which may result, including a participant feeling either uncomfortable or, even, unsafe. Further, just as for any activity that takes place at Burning Man, a participant's willingness for engagement depends almost entirely on the weather, as well as one's own general health and well-being, which usually guides their social prerogative.

Riders are instructed, if they like, to paint their chests and meet at the Man, at a particular time to join the *Ride*. The *Ride* was in the beginning, and continues to be, a women-only space at the event, and while the group's original intent was empowerment for women, this idea has increasingly come under debate by women owing to the eager audiences of men who watch the *Ride*. This sentiment is supported by performer/ artist Jessica Hobbs, a long-time Burning Man participant and one-time *Critical Tits* supporter. According to Hobbs:

> Many personal experiences and stories have kept me away from the *Ride*. In 2006 […] I cheered and yelled encouragement towards my topless sisters, but as the *Ride* moved off into the distance I saw the strange parade within a parade that the *Ride* had become. The central parade, the women painted and beautified, the other sandwiching it […] I had already made a decision not to

participate in this spectacle, and this visual only solidified my decision. (personal communication, 27 January 2009)

One version of the parade is the women who are riding half-nude on bicycles; the other, encompasses the parade of spectators who walk along side. In spite of the vision Jessica Hobbs presents, many event participants do feel strongly that *Critical Tits* has always been an opportunity for women to demonstrate solidarity, as well as publicly illustrate a show of mass force against men at Burning Man who would gawk and flank the riders in a kind of "gauntlet." This gauntlet or sandwiching of the procession of women along the *Ride* route, to a performer within the *Ride*, appears to be made up almost entirely of men. And so, this fact reveals one of the major criticisms of *Critical Tits* in the past several years, namely, that while the *Ride* is supposed to be an opportunity for women to unite in camaraderie and demonstrate pride in their bodies, as well as to gain strength in being partially nude en masse, men at Burning Man use the *Ride* as a opportunity to gaze at women and capture their images for exploitative purposes. Continues Hobbs:

> As a twelve year veteran of the playa, I have never participated as a rider in *Critical Tits*. I have seen and appreciated the parade, but I have chosen not to participate in the spectacle. My mode of free expression usually does not include taking off my clothes at Burning Man, as it does for so many others. I do not derive a great deal of meaning from the *Ride*. I don't feel empowered when my picture is being taken hundreds of times by gawking onlookers. (personal communication, 27 January 2009)

Issues of sexism and exploitation are now primarily those related to the debates over *Critical Tits*. Sexism remains an issue because the nature of the *Ride* calls for women to come together before a primarily male audience where immediate feedback can be perceived as chauvinistic or misogynistic. While the women who participate in the *Ride* do demonstrate bodily pride, impositions brought on by a voyeuristic masculine public gaze can cause offense to the women themselves. The issue from both sides of the "the gaze versus objectification" debate is that on one hand, women want to be seen by men and acknowledged but risk a reception by those men which is demeaning. Conversely, these same women may know that risk exists and yet still choose to perform because either they do not care how they are received by the audience or feel the experience outweighs that potential outcome. It is a very subjective, political quandary that reveals how women participants tread the line that constantly risks exploitation in choosing the experience of exhibitionism.

Exploitation as an important element of the political debates over the event enters the framework of *Critical Tits* as a public performance of female empowerment, when some men utilize the opportunity of the *Ride* to demoralize or objectify women because they are baring their breasts. However, the debate is confused when male audiences seem to glorify the partially nude women with supportive comments or *gifting* women during the *Ride* by spraying them with water to cool them down or offering women drinks, because male audiences still take pictures without permission or simply gawk. These issues are troubling because their existence undermines the purpose of the *Ride* in a political sense, and as a demonstration by female participants to celebrate power and beauty.

Here then, is an important juncture to consider what distinguishes "sex" as a cultural category as it determines who are predetermined to be the performers in *Critical Tits* and who are the spectators. According to theorist James Loxley:

> So what we call "sex", and distinguish as the pre-cultural component of identity, can perhaps instead be understood as only culturally designated as such. The binary division of a bodily sex, that is to say, is not a given but a cultural category; if it is dissimulated as "nature" in accounts of identity, then feminism ought to challenge this dissimulation, not participate in it. Perhaps then a future beyond the duality of sex would become a political possibility. (2007: 116)

Thus, if the performance of femininity and personal politics during participation at *Critical Tits* is signalled by one's presence in the *Ride*, it then requires only that one have *breasts* and a *bicycle*. To be clear, sometimes one does see women participating in the *Ride* who are not exposing their breasts. This represents the portion of women riders who support the concept of the *Ride* by their participation but decline to go nude, thereby refusing to contribute to the sexual exhibitionist *versus* male voyeur debate. Many other women are simply not comfortable with the performance and also, other women feel that resulting sunburned nipples are just *not* worth the effort. Some women, despite having attended Burning Man for many years, still maintain their distance from the *Ride*, in conversation and proximity. For many years, that percentage of participants included me.

As a new participant to Burning Man in 2000, I heard right away about the topless all-woman bike ride and my first reaction was to laugh. The thought of it, to me, seemed comical. However, as I learned how excited my female friends were to join the *Ride* that Friday, I began to consider how they saw the event. To them, the *Ride* was about unity and solidarity, a communication of sisterhood. For them, it was about personal politics and unashamed self-presentation. For me, there was an uneasy feeling that as a performer, I would be under a kind of scrutiny that I did not want. Having attended Burning Man seven times, I refused to participate for years, primarily because I had these strong political misgivings. However, in 2006, I decided for ethnographic research to ride in *Critical Tits*. The analysis as follows is based on a performance studies evaluation of the *Ride*.

A PERFORMANCE ANALYSIS OF *CRITICAL TITS*
The pre-performance time of *Critical Tits* is marked by many of the women preparing for the *Ride*, by painting or adorning their bare breasts and bodies. Breast painting and body painting by one's self or others is both a ritual and a performance. As with many popular performances at Burning Man, activities are born and thrive to coincide with those events within a theatrical event, the festival site. With *Critical Tits*, it is breast painting parties and the after-*Ride* parties. For several years, a few theme camps have hosted breast painting workshops or parties. These include, for example, Black Rock University, where I camped in 2006. According to Bethany Wells, who also participated in the *Ride* that year:

> I did [...] enjoy the painting party at our camp immensely! That was where some real connections were made. The feeling of cold paint on your hot skin, especially those areas that aren't often exposed is exhilarating! And so special to share the moments of giving and receiving art and physical sensations with people I hardly knew. (personal communication, 26 January 2009)

As with many female participants, Wells' comments to the connectivity and immediacy of the shared erotic moment pre-performance, gives strength to the notion that it is the *privately* shared rituals associated with the *Ride* that may offer a better opportunity for feminist political activity, despite that these are enacted in *public* space with strangers, men and women, helping the performers prepare. This reinforces the theory which Sue-Ellen Case puts forth regarding the creation of a new poetics for theatrical activity, as the feminist performer adopts new modes of form and practice in order to influence an audience's response and change, through performance, the culture (1988: 143). These women and performers need a new outlet for personal growth, and they have come to Burning Man to find it. Therefore they will use this performance as the opportunity to gather that strength, with the friends they have in tow.

Gathering together in smaller groups or riding up as individuals to the first stage of the *Ride*, women riders join a massive collective parade that indeed resembles a Broadway spectacular: very colourful naked breasts and a palpable excitement amongst the women participants about to perform, many of whom are chatting and laughing with the women surrounding them. During the *Ride* or performance itself, the process and movement of the performers is marked by an audience on either side. This audience is alternately watching, cheering, taking pictures, or attempting to sprinkle the women with water, owing to the fierce heat.

The *Ride* itself, which last about an hour, snakes through the most prominent open areas within the space of the theatrical event site. As an individual performer, my initial feelings of excitement about participation tended to be focused on the show of force created by having joined a massive collective of women proudly displaying their nude bodies and vocalizing their excitement. Toepfer refers to this theatrical state as Therapeutic Nudity, when artists' proud and casual self-displays serve to circumvent the seer's desire to treat the nude as an object (1996: 80). However, within some short period of time, the possibly respectful yet solid gaze of the gauntlet of men seemed to revert to blatant gawking after many bare breasted women had passed. Men began calling out specifically to those women whose bodies might be considered most erotic by sexist standards.

As a performer, I became acutely aware that while we women *may have* seen ourselves as players in a political performance, a parade of solidarity and a show of collective force that would overpower the critical, objectifying male gaze, the audience *may not have*. The audience in fact may have been seeing a scene of what Toepfer would classify, Balletic Nudity, involving hundreds of pairs of breasts of all kinds, colourfully painted, and bouncing along a rocky terrain (1996: 83). What resulted during the performance for this performer was a *performance anxiety* somewhere between feeling pride and shame, integrity and obscenity, fearlessness and subjugation. Sometimes as performers we responded to the men, sometimes we ignored them. But as the *Ride* ended and the audience dissipated, this performer experienced the post-performance period with mixed emotions, much like a participant finishing a political rally. Having been a participant in both, I can confirm to the pride one feels for having participated and also, a deep sense of ultimately not being fulfilled. That is, the uneasiness of the experience left its final imprint on me, knowing that maybe *nothing* had changed.

Finally, the post-performance, after *Critical Tits*, is historically marked by all women riders being invited to a party in their "honour" by a hosting theme camp, often with men serving the women drinks or offering the riders foot-rubs. Here, women may reunite, congregate, discuss, decompress, and celebrate. Here, they can create their own finale to the performance they were not solely responsible for constructing. Thus, considering once again Sue-Ellen Case's notions of a critical dialogue about feminist theatre, *Critical Tits* is both a successful attempt at and ultimate failure of the desire to achieve liberation of body and the forging of sisterhood (2002: 193). Women coming together in the hopes of solidarity in a political performance, together, as individuals, and as performers, will always suffer the threat of being disillusioned, distracted and disappointed, if men as spectators to that moment cannot, or will not, freely give up domination.

In truth, the real presence of men seeking to exploit the *Ride*, whether actual or perceived, serves to undermine the feminist purpose of *Critical Tits*. However, the *Ride* is successful as a political performance for a variety of reasons. As an example of staged eroticism, the *Ride* gives permission to women to stage their own bodies by *choice*. Further, the mass show of female force *communicates* solidarity regardless of whether or not an individual performer feels actual female camaraderie. And finally, it is a successful performance because it is a popular one that keeps alive the very critical feminist debates over equality in our society.

FEMINISTS STAGING EROTICISM AND POLITICS

While *Critical Tits* is one example of nudity staged for political purposes at an outdoor theatrical event in the United States, it is by no means the ideal model. Neither is it the only example of nudity and exhibitionism at Burning Man itself. Throughout the week of the event, there are numerous strip tease shows and nude fire displays, as well as art installations which depict the nude human body. One example of performance conceived at Burning Man by feminist artists in an effort to draw attention to issues of gender, in contrast to *Critical Tits*, is the Pink Pleasure Palace's Glitter Oil Wrestling Shows, which were participatory performances staged for five years at Burning Man. They offer one critical example of feminist art-making in action. According to artist Jessica Hobbs:

> Performing as *The Bunny Girls*, we created a wrestling spectacle of oily glittery girly pinkness. A decidedly "over the top tongue in cheek girly" performance, with all the aspects of real arena wrestling, announcers, judges, and referees. The first performance was done topless but we quickly rethought that aspect, realizing we wanted to get away from eroticism that can be assumed with nudity. Our intentions were to keep the performance within the arena of interactive play. We, I and Brandi Hugo, would give the opening wrestling exhibition and then invite others from the audience to participate in the wrestling ring. (personal communication, 26 January 2009)

Strategically, the choice for these performers was to attempt nude staging. They altered that approach when confronted by their own politics. Ultimately, women and their choice to go nude at Burning Man is one that is highly political because it locates them between a desire to demonstrate self-pride and connectivity with self and other women, while revealing the sexually exploitative nature of hetero-male spectatorship as theorized by Sue-Ellen Case (1990: 10-25). Hobbs' performance strategies suggest, as well, her own intentions for melding aspects of political performance, that it is participatory, entertaining, and even thought-provoking. Hobbs also indicates a desire for performance as social experiment:

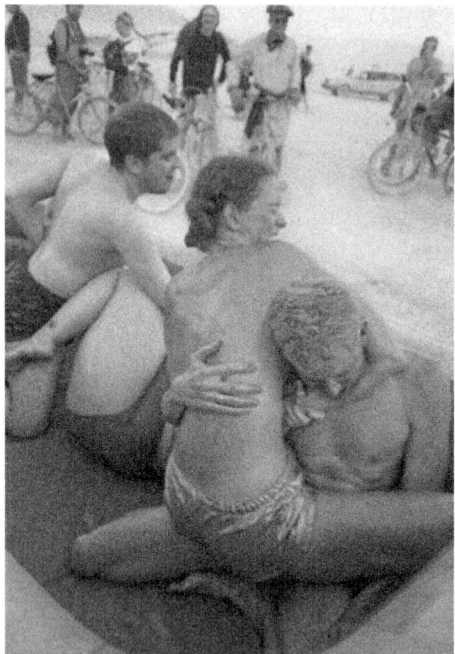

Figure 2. *Bunny Oil Wrestling.*
This image was taken at Burning
Man in 2001 at the Pink Pleasure
Palace within a collection of
theme   camps   known   as
Illumination Village. The picture
shows   performance   activity
called Bunny Oil Wrestling. The
women who 'ran' the wrestling
pit are known as the 'Bunnies.'
In the picture, half naked men
and women wrestle before a
transient crowd. Photograph by
Jess Hobbs.

The performance was a way for us to visually explore the stereotypes of being
female by embracing these definitions as a process of subversion. We realized
that battling sexism in the normal way sometimes alienates our intended
viewer. By bringing a subtle sense of humor to our performances we catch
participants unaware. We create a world where you must step in the wrestling
ring with your pink sparkly outfit and show the world it is okay to be both
happy and strong. (personal communication, 26 January 2009)

As with the Pink Bunny Glitter Oil Wrestling Shows, performance
and nudity at Burning Man is playful, in that it involves room for both
reflective and comedic readings: consequently performance and
nudity at Burning Man is *also* political.

CONCLUSION
Theatrical events in the United States, such as large-scale outdoor
festivals, have, in the past forty years, provided a space for artists and
audiences to explore taboo topics and to advance political discussions
over censorship, constitutional rights, and free speech. Further,

questions about the nature of art and eroticism, as well as the advancement of certain genres within the theatre have been a result. Just as theatre fought the restrictive confines of indoor venues, so too did the nature of public theatrical presentations move beyond the boundaries of puritanical approaches to making and presenting performance.

Festivals and outdoor theatres, in particular, help the more contemporary theatrical notion of the audience member as *no mere spectator* but as participant. In the vast expanse of the festival as a theatrical space, particularly at Burning Man in the immense desert space it occupies, the participant experience takes them through a transient journey where one can move between roles as witness to performance and, also, as contributor. The outdoors does not, though, change the nature of performance and theatre as an *industry*. Audiences are still needed to pay, just as festival-goers must pay for their experience. The economic element to the equation serves here to complicate the issue of nudity at theatrical events even more. The politics of capital and sex are necessarily bound up in a historical landscape where the performing naked human body and the naked female body in particular, are always seen as a commodity.

Another important issue related to the growth and controversy over *Critical Tits* has to do with the inclusivity of *all women* in the *Ride*. Few women who participate in *Critical Tits* are women of colour.[2] However, this fact can be stated for Burning Man as a whole, where a very small percentage of people of colour attend as compared to their white counterparts. Women riders in *Critical Tits* who are of colour are, like Burning Man participants of colour, arguably subject to more scrutiny because they are cultural anomalies. Problems further arise when one begins to consider the social and political implications at Burning Man for women and people of colour when they are not only some of the few representing a particularly designated social category, but that their naked bodies may draw to them even more unwanted attention. Social problems rise to the surface theoretically in this visual exchange when one recognizes the "Other."

When all bodies are present within the orgiastic theatrical scene, this reveals social tribulations over racism and sexism. Bodies of colour performing in *Critical Tits* extends both the critical importance of a feminist understanding of the *Ride*, and its implications as a site for asserting women's *personal* power. Implicit in the ongoing debates about women of colour and sexism is though a decidedly hopeful assertion, one that suggests women who hold a critical feminist stance about *Critical Tits* do so in what Jill Dolan would suggest is positively political: "By exposing the ways in which dominant ideology is naturalized by the performance's address to the ideal spectator, feminist performance criticism works as a political intervention in an effort toward cultural change" (1988: 288).

The women who debate *Critical Tits* are a part of that same effort as feminist performance critics, discussing the positive and negative political ramifications of the performance. For those women who do ride in *Critical Tits*, likewise, the nude body of the participant is political because of her *choice* to perform. In conclusion, I wish to argue that the nude body presented publicly in the outdoor theatrical space of Burning Man during *Critical Tits* takes on the political power afforded it as long as possible, and offers dis/comfort and excitement to others who witness this exhibitionism as performance as, implicitly, even *those* spectators are reminded of their own human condition and sexuality.

NOTES

[1] Playa is the term for the prehistoric dry lakebed on which Burning Man takes place in the Black Rock Desert, Nevada, which 50,000 people attend.
[2] Since the site of the performance is the US, I am using the term commonly used in the US for non-white people, "people of color." In the UK, the equivalent term is "black" or "minority ethnic."

REFERENCES

Allen, Ray. (2009) Personal communication. 3 December.
Blank, Harrod. (n.d.) *Art Cars and Burning Man*. The Burning Man Project. <http://www.burningman.com/art_of_burningman/art_cars_on_the_playa.htm l> [Accessed on 5 February 2009].
Brill, Louis M. (2007) "At the Opera." *Thoughts of Burning Man: A Beacon to 21st-Century Culture, Art, and Ritual*. Unpublished manuscript.
Bruder, Jesscia. (2207) *Burning Book: A Visual History of Burning Man*. New York: Simon and Schuster.
Case, Sue-Ellen. (2002) "The Emperor's New Clothes: The Naked Body and Theories of Performance." SubStance. Issue 98/99. Vol. 31, No. 2 and 3. p. 193.
Case, Sue-Ellen. (1990) "Introduction," in Sue-Ellen Case, ed. *Performing Feminisms: Feminist Critical Theory and Theatre*. Baltimore: Johns Hopkins University Press, 1-15.

Case, Sue-Ellen. (1988) "Towards a New Poetics," in Lizbeth Goodman, ed. (1998) *The Routledge Reader in Gender and Performance.* New York: Routledge. 143.

Cover, Rob. (2003) "The Naked Subject: Nudity, Context and Sexualization in Contemporary Culture." *Body and Society* 9 (3), 53-72.

Dolan, Jill. (1988) "The Discourse of Feminisms: The Spectator and Representation," in Lizbeth Goodman, ed. *The Routledge Reader in Gender and Performance.* New York: Routledge, 288.

Foucault, Michel. (1986) "Of Other Spaces." *Diacritics* 16 (Spring), 22-27.

Goodman, Lizbeth with Jane de Gay, eds. (1998) *The Routledge Reader in Gender and Performance.* New York: Routledge.

Gutknecht, Howard. (2009) Personal communication (26 January). Email to the author.

Hobbs, Jessica. (2009) Personal communication (27 January). Email to the author.

Houchin, John H. (2003) *Censorship of the American Theatre in the Twentieth Century.* Cambridge: Cambridge University Press.

Kershaw, Baz. (2003) "Curiosity or Contempt: On Spectacle, the Human, and Activism." *Theatre Journal* 55 (4), 591 - 611.

Liepe-Levinson, Katherine. (2002) *Strip Show: Performances of Gender and Desire.* London: Routledge.

Loxley, James. (2007) *Performativity: The New Critical Idiom.* New York: Routledge, 112-138.

Martin, Randy. (1990) *Performance as a Political Act: The Embodied Self.* New York: Bergin & Garvey Publishers.

Nash, A. Leo and Daniel Pinchbeck. (2007) *Burning Man: Art in the Desert.* New York: Abrams.

Schneider, Rebecca. (1997) *The Explicit Body in Performance.* London: Routledge.

Toepfer, Karl. (1996) "Nudity and Textuality in Postmodern Performance." *Performing Arts Journal* (3), 76-91.

Toepfer, Karl. (1991) *Theatre, Aristocracy, and Pornocracy: The Orgy Calculus.* New York: PAJ Publications.

Wells, Bethany. (2009) Personal communication (26 January). Email to the author.

Wilson, Glenn D., ed. (1991) *Psychology and Performing Arts.* Amsterdam: Swets & Zeitlinger.

THE GÜEGÜENCE[1] EFFECT: THE NATIONAL CHARACTER AND THE NICARAGUAN POLITICAL PROCESS

E.J. WESTLAKE

In July of 2000, *The Economist*, in a story recounting Vicente Fox's surprising victory in Mexico, referred to something they called the "Nicaragua Effect." According to the story:

> With almost all ballots counted, Mr. Fox had won 42.7% to 35.8% for the PRI's Francisco Labastida. That baffled the many pollsters who had predicted a narrow PRI win. In the 1990 election [in Nicaragua] which ejected the Sandinistas, [...] many voters told pollsters they were undecided right up until the end, then apparently plumped for the opposition. ("Happy birthday, Señor Fox," 2004)

The Nicaraguans have named this the "Güegüence Effect," reflecting a close identification with the title character from *El Güegüence*, a hybrid indigenous and Spanish dance-drama, and what appears to be the oldest recorded dramatic text in Nicaragua. The analogy also appeared during the 2000 mayoral elections in Managua. Pollsters projected that the FSLN (Sandinista) candidate, Herty Lewites, would be the clear winner. One political analyst agreed, but urged caution. As he noted: "Glory cannot be sung. *El Güegüence* can never be discounted" (García Castillo 2000).

The title character from the national dance-drama, an old man who is a thief and a trickster, has come to symbolize the Nicaraguan habit of dissembling to pollsters before the election, a signification that has grown out of the popular idea that the liar represents every Nicaraguan. The multilayered and multivalent uses of Güegüence as a political symbol can be traced through the spoken text of the dance-drama, its deployment as a national sign by twentieth-century intellectuals, and the recent drive by the Ministry of Culture to have the performance classified as Intangible Heritage by UNESCO. The old man has entered into Nicaraguan politics in other ways as well, as politicians on the left and right have been given the name of "El Güegüence." That candidates and incumbents from every party have used this label, either to describe themselves or the opposition, reveals an ambivalence about the character and a reluctance by some to completely embrace him as a national figure. With the recent reelection of Daniel Ortega, the use of the figure and the dance-drama as allegory reveals a dynamic in Nicaraguan national politics, a dynamic of resistance that is often accompanied by a dynamic of exploitation.

THE PLAY
In the colonial play, performed in a hybrid of Spanish and Nahuatl, Old Man Güegüence goes to see the governor. Initially the governor, thinking Güegüence is rich, means to get the old man's money, but Güegüence tricks the governor into marrying his daughter to Güegüence's son instead. According to several philologists who have studied *El Güegüence,* the drama has decisively indigenous roots. No purely indigenous dramatic text has survived in Nicaragua. Presently, The U.S. Library of Congress estimates Nicaragua's population as 76% mestizo, 10% white, 11% black, and only 3% indigenous (Merrill 1993), reflecting a nation that has obliterated or absorbed much of its indigenous culture. *El Güegüence* is presented in Diriamba every year in January for the Festival of St. Sebastian by descendents of the Mangue (or Chorotega) people. It is likely that the drama was originally performed in Mangue and then later in Nahuatl as a Nahua band from Mexico displaced the Mangue people. The two copies of *El Güegüence* that are extant are in a blended language of Nahuatl and Spanish.

The performance of *El Güegüence* shares some elements with indigenous ritual dance-drama, like the Mayan *Rabinal Achí*, such as the use of music, dancing, and masks. However, authorities are divided on the subject of the performance of *El Güegüence* before the twentieth century. There are no tangible records that note when the drama may have been performed. In the preface to the translation published by nineteenth-century anthropologist Daniel G. Brinton, he writes that Nicaraguans had performed *El Güegüence* in conjunction with St. Jerome's Day, and that the dance-drama took on the importance of a religious ritual (xli). He states, however, that his sources informed him that the practice of staging the drama had ceased, in part due to the expense for the person assuming responsibility for the festivities.

Currently, the annual performance in Diriamba involves only a few of the dance steps as scholars surmise that much of the actual dance has been lost. Masked dancers perform the steps as they move in procession toward the main square. The performance I observed in January of 2008 involved several groups throughout the square performing in overlapping versions of the piece alongside groups performing other traditional dances, such as the Toro Huaco, the dance of Moors and Christians, and the local *indita*. A sound crew moved from group to group, providing microphones to each group for an episode of the play. At various breaks in the action, the performers would break into dance, the main characters moving back and forth in a line dance in the center, with a group of men masked as mules moving in a circle on the outside. The performers used an indigenous

Figure 1. The lead dancer of the mules, carrying the chischil and the chest of Güegüence's wares. Photograph by E.J. Westlake.

rattle, known as the chischíl, to punctuate the music, played by an accompanying band of a guitar, a drum, and a fiddle. When I attended in 2009, the performers had abandoned the idea of attempting to perform the text and stuck to the dance alone.

The performances form part of a festival dedicated to the patron saint of Diriamba, Saint Sebastian. The beginning of the festival involves a procession with the saint to a meeting known as "El Tope," where the saint encounters the saints of the two neighboring towns. The saints are housed in the cathedral until Saint Sebastian's Day. While dancers perform in the square, the priests offer a dedicated mass. Afterwards, men bring the saints out of the cathedral and a procession moves down the street into a local neighborhood. Promesantes, aided by supporters, approach Saint Sebastian on their knees in fulfillment of a promise made earlier that year. Throughout the rest of the festival, the organizers offer entertainment, mostly in the evening. In 2009, the director of the Ballet Folklórico Nicaragüense and Diriamba native, Ronald Abud Vivas, presented his troupe's staging of the dance the evening of Saint Sebastian's Day.

The most well-known version of the text of *El Güegüence* was discovered, or rediscovered, in the late nineteenth century by German philologist Karl Hermann Berendt who obtained it from the papers of a deceased Nicaraguan scholar, Juan Eligio de Rocha. Berendt sold his handwritten copy to U.S. ethnologist Daniel Brinton who published the text, along with his "loose paraphrase" (iii) in his *Library of Aboriginal American Literature* in 1883. In modern performances in Diriamba, performers use Berendt's text as it appears in Brinton's edition, in the blended Nahuatl-Spanish dialect.

The text of the drama also shares features with indigenous drama, most notably the frequent repetition of dialogue. For example, the play begins while Gobernador Tastuanes, a name that literally means in Spanish and Nahuatl respectively "Governor Governor," laments the fact that he doesn't have enough luxuries in his office. He and his sheriff, Alguacil (a name that simply means bailiff or sheriff) repeat extensive greetings to each other followed by a repetition of elaborate lamentations over the state of the furnishings.

What sets *El Güegüence* apart from the indigenous dance-dramas is the use of the hybrid language in a combination that creates clever double meanings. The entire play hinges on what is misheard or misunderstood. When the Governor hears that Güegüence has money and is moving through the province, he sends Alguacil, the sheriff, to fetch him. As the sheriff approaches him, right away Güegüence feigns poor eyesight so that he can insult him. He asks if it is a servant girl or washerwoman who is calling for him. The sheriff tells Güegüence that he is to "run and fly," or to come as quickly as possible, to see the Governor, an expression Güegüence pretends to take literally, all the while protesting and complaining of his pains and aches: "Run and fly (as quickly as possible)? How does he expect a poor old man, full of pains and aches, to run and fly?" (Mántica 2001: 38)[2]

Güegüence proceeds to solicit a lesson in etiquette for his appearance before the Governor. Alguacil will comply, but for a price. Güegüence becomes conveniently deaf. He cannot hear the word "salario" or "salary," saying that he certainly could pay him in "salados," or "salted fish" (16). Alguacil says he does not want "salted fish," but silver coins, or "reales de plata." Güegüence agrees to give him his "redes de platos," or bags of plates. Frustrated, the sheriff stresses that he wants hard currency, or "pesos duros," to which Güegüence responds that he will give him "quesos duros," or hard cheeses. Alguacil attempts to be as specific as he possibly can and requests "doblones de oro y de plata," or gold and silver doubloons. Güegüence hears "dobles" instead of "doblones" and asks his sons to "doblar" or "toll for the dead." The dead, in this case, he laments is "my friend the Captain Chief Alguacil, with whom we were wheeling and dealing just a moment ago, and the Devil already took him" (48). The conclusion of this long passage of wordplay results in the absolute exasperation and rage by the sheriff, who exclaims: "¡Para tu cuerpo!" an archaic version of "Cut it out!" (52). By coolly feigning feebleness, Güegüence gets the upper hand.

In this way, Güegüence proves himself to be quite capable and wily. When Güegüence does finally count out payment to the sheriff, he does so in an intentionally confusing way: the half of this half of a *real* makes two *cuartillos*, a *cuartillo* is two *octavos*, an *octavo* is two *quartos*, and so on, until Alguacil, still reeling from the confusion of the scene, winds up receiving much less than it seems. Güegüence also complains about the lesson in etiquette he receives from Alguacil. Alguacil teaches him to bow before the governor with the complicated greeting:

Figure 2. Güegüence flanked by his two sons, Don Forcico and Don Ambrosio. The Governor Tastuanes and his daughter stand behind them. Children often dance the roles during the festival. Photograph by E.J. Westlake.

> I pray for Our Lord God to protect the Governor Tastuanes, and his father and his wife, the appointed mayors of the Holy Brotherhood, the registrars, notaries, and archivists, and all who reside at the Royal Court of Governor Tastuanes. (58)

Güegüence acts as if he can't begin to memorize such a long and complex greeting. He protests and attempts to get his money back: "I only need a book of verses and I could just recite it before Tastuanes," he protests (58). However, he has no difficulty repeating the greeting when the Governor suddenly appears.

In addition to feigned feebleness, Güegüence has the ability to use the weaknesses of the colonial authority as a way to circumvent that authority. The clever old man uses the governor's own greed to lure him into doing business with him. The entire piece opens with an examination of the governor's lust for fine furnishings. He and Aguacil list the many things they lack: "In the first place, because it is shameful to be without gilded tables, without embroidered portfolios, without golden inkwells, without golden pens, without a golden blotter, and we don't even have paper with the government seal for acts of the Royal Court" (28). The colonial governor needs to collect money from the merchants to support the extravagant lifestyle he would like to have. Güegüence already understands the base motivations of his adversary.

Tastuanes attempts to accuse Güegüence of entering the district without a permit. Güegüence proceeds to dazzle the Governor with stories of the wealth of goods and contraband he and his sons carry. Güegüence performs the colonial subject he knows the Governor imagines him to be, a hard-working, wealthy merchant ripe for exploitation, and plays out the imperialist fantasy. He boasts of his inventory: "[…] [C]hests of gold, chests of silver, Castillian cloth, smuggled cloth, vests, feathered blouses, silk stockings, golden shoes, hats of real beaver, stirrup straps of gold and silver lace, to satisfy and please the delighted Governor Tastuanes" (62). Güegüence induces his sons to corroborate his account of their wealth, each account further whetting the appetite of the Governor as Güegüence insinuates that a deal could be struck: Don Forcico should marry the Governor's daughter Suche-Malinche (not to be confused with the infamous Malinche of the Cortés story) in an exchange of property.

A dance with their tent of merchandise follows. A presentation of their goods ends with Güegüence's presentation of Don Forcico. Güegüence suggests that Forcico has his "hand in many trades," in a way that suggests Forcico demonstrated great talent in stealing the goods. He lists Forcico's virtues and his professions: sculptor, metalworker, grinder, and pilot. But all of these words, in the indigenous language, sound like words for "scoundrel," "thief," "sloth," and "garbage collector" (74). Even the celebratory wine that Güegüence produces for the Governor at the end comes from Forcico's exploits. When Güegüence asks him where he got the wine, Forcico replies: "In the house of a friend" (104), suggesting that he secured the wine from the Governor's own cellar.

Both of Güegüence's sons, Don Forcico and Don Ambrosio, accompany him in his travels. They provide representations of those who follow and those who resist the trickster's example. Don Forcico is a trickster in training and works with his father in out-witting their hosts. He corroborates his father's lies, engages in the play of double meanings, and makes his father proud when he steals the celebratory wine from the Governor, especially when the wine is produced before Güegüence can even ask him to find it. When Forcico says the wine is from the house of "a friend," Güegüence asks him who taught him how to make "a friend." This prompts another angry comment from Don Ambrosio about how Güegüence teaches Don Forcico his evil ways.

Don Ambrosio, on the other hand, only reluctantly obeys his father. He refuses to back up his father's account of their wealth and calls his father an "embustero," a con artist. He explains that their wares are only ratty, old objects that bear no resemblance to Güegüence's description. Güegüence silences him as Don Forcico blames Don Ambrosio's apparent bad behavior on his mother's infidelity:

> Don't be shocked, Governor, at what you hear from this babbler; for when I went with my father on the road to Mexico, and when we came back, already my mother was pregnant by another man, and that is why this one turned out to be such a bad breed, Governor Tastuanes. (70)

Following Güegüence's lead after he hints in his speech about traveling without a permit, that he was also "permitted" to "enter" by a young woman (62), the sons create openings in the text for the bawdier humour that punctuates the drama.

Güegüence mistakes Alguacil for a servant girl with a sexual gesture, both belittling the sheriff, but also expressing his desire for a sexual object. He punctuates his lists of treasures with lewd suggestions, one being that he use a "golden syringe" to "medicate the royal court" (72). In the 2008 Diriamba performance, the actor thrust his hips to illustrate.

As the favored son, Don Forcico, gets ready to marry the Governor's daughter, the governor brings several women before the guests, none of whom are to Forcico's liking. He complains that his bad brother has already impregnated two of the women. Güegüence asks how it is that Don Ambrosio learned to do such things (94). "De dormir con vos, Güegüence," he replies, "From sleeping with you." Carlos Mántica translates this as "going to bed with you" or "lying down with you" and suggests that Ambrosio learned about sex from being molested by Güegüence. (95)

They bring up the mules or "machos" for a dance-procession to celebrate. The men examine them. Güegüence again feigns deafness when Forcico says that they have been corralled, or "cogidos." Güegüence misunderstands the word to be "encogidos," or "shriveled," and asks if it is from the cold. Don Forcico repeats that they are cogidos, which Güegüence hears as "cojudos" or castrated (106). The rest of them are examined: the old one, the rowdy one, the quarrelsome one, and the thin one. Güegüence begins to wonder about their health:

> Güegüence:How can [this one] be well if it has such a stick in the front of it? Where did this mule get this stick run into himself, boy? (110)

Don Forcico replies that it is in the colt yard, or the "potrero," but Güegüence replies that that's what he gets for running from potrero to putrero, suggesting a double meaning of colt yard for "putero" or whorehouse. Güegüence moves on to the next mule and Forcico insists that it is healthy:

> Güegüence: How can it be well, boy, if the inflammation has passed down beneath the legs, and there's a great swelling there. Burst it, boy.
> Don Forcico: You burst it yourself, little papa.
> Güegüence: Well, it will burst on its own, boy. (111-112)

After a few more jokes about coming in front or coming from behind, the procession begins. The Governor and Güegüence pass the wine as they ride the machos down the street. The dance-drama ends as the audience follows the procession through the streets of Diriamba.

THE BATTLE OVER SIGNIFICATION
According to Les Field in his 1991 study of southwest Nicaraguan artisans, Brinton's English copy of his "loose paraphrase" of *El Güegüence* came to the attention of the Nicaraguan literary intelligencia through the writing of national poet Rubén Darío and also through comments made by the Cuban José Martí, who was also familiar with Brinton's text. Both conservative writer Pablo Antonio Cuadra and Marxist theatre director Alan Bolt were drawn to the street theatre format of *El Güegüence*, and sought to use similar forms in their own work. Bolt, in the introduction to his drama *Banana republic,* states:

> With *Banana republic* we hope to begin anew a process of recuperation of the forms that our people have used in the traditional performances, from *El Güegüence* and the Indians to the circus of Firuliche. [...]. In the struggle against every form of oppression, for the development of a revolutionary culture, our duty is to recover the forms created by our people and engage with the future that we have all created. (1982: 11)

The dance-drama as street theatre gave them a popular model they believed was inherently Nicaraguan.

However, Cuadra claimed that the true subversive potential lay in the mixing of language to create purposeful misunderstanding and double meaning. Güegüence can stand in front of the governor and tell him to his face that Don Forcico is a thief as he recounts the boy's resume because the Nahuatl words he uses have double meanings. As Cuadra notes, Güegüence's power lies in:

> [S]ubtle games with not only the possible double meaning of a word but with the quid pro quo of translation from one language to another, what is revealed to us is a spirit of mischievous, playful, and satirical weaving of a new language with great creative freedom. So what we see under the language is laughter, fun and a vital ingredient that the x-ray of Güegüence shows us as early as the seventeenth century, in our mestizo formation, that will never leave us, as a small angel of creative joy, in our Nicaraguan dramatic history. (1998: 23)

The mestizo wins in *El Güegüence* because he upsets the terms of the balance of power, and sets new terms where he swims in the waters of the new hybrid language, leaving the colonial authority staring at the surface.

Nicaraguans hold up the figure of Güegüence as the mestizo spirit who resists colonial rule, imperialism from the United States, and corrupt government. Güegüence represents the Nicaraguan, who in resistance to oppression *is* a trickster by birthright. As Pablo Antonio Cuadra notes, Güegüence is a:

> satirist, a rogue, an equalizer, suspicious, acting deaf and speaking the first sentence of double meaning at his first entrance [...] [he] mocks authority, satirizes sharply the constant tariffs and taxes that empty the piggy bank, is deaf when it's convenient, plays with words and with his false deafness. (18)

Cuadra goes on to contend that: "The old rogue—illuminating our unstable Nicaraguan family, [is the] fruit of our mestizaje" (19).

While Cuadra was the first to suggest that Güegüence represented the typical Nicaraguan in his Vanguardia 1969 publication of *El Nicaragüense*, other intellectuals and analysts have pondered the possibilities of such a comparison. Polanco echoes Cuadra when he states that: "*El Güegüence* represents the prototype of the Nica, through his adventures, ruses, through social conditions and socio-political relations, [he] is an x-ray of the personality of the Nicaraguan being" (2004).

The idea of Güegüence as Nicaraguan plays out in popular discourse in many ways and formed part of the reasoning behind the drive to have the dance-drama classified by UNESCO as Intangible Heritage. The most pervasive analogy of Güegüence as the Nicaraguan national character seems to surface during election time. Going back to Castillo's predictions for the 2000 mayoral election, he noted what would turn out to be true:

> With less than 15 days before the municipal elections it is possible to consider that the surveys already project as a winner the candidate of the FSLN, Herty Lewites. But glory cannot be sung. *El Güegüence* can never be discounted. When we speak of *El Güegüence*—the oldest play of Nicaragua, [...] we speak of the capacity of the Nicaraguan [...] to dissemble, to mask, to disguise his or her true intentions. In Mexico, in the last elections in which Fox was elected, they spoke of the "Nicaragua effect," that is to say, the Güegüence effect. [...]. In my view, and of other political analysts, the Güegüence effect isn't likely. The conditions are very different from the previous elections in 1990, but you never know. ("La Recta Final Electoral" 2000)

Ironically, it *was* likely, the Güegüence effect recurred, and the character's prominence as the Nicaraguan Everyman was cemented.

Political analysts now refer to the Güegüence Effect with regularity, in much the same way "October Surprise," the idea that a party will reveal something damning about the opposing candidate or orchestrate favorable circumstances for their own candidate in the short weeks just before the general election, or more recently the "Bradley Effect," the phenomenon where people profess to support an African American candidate when they do not, have made their way into the electoral discourse in the United States. Political commentators will often qualify their electoral analysis with a warning that there could be a Güegüence Effect, and suggest that their findings could be off. It is not uncommon to hear commentators discuss possible upsets in terms of the mythological being. In a 2006 radio interview, Edgar Tijerino interrupted William Grigsby's analysis of the Sandinista's chances: "William, we always have to speak here of the apparition of Güegüence" ("Los yankis le tienen miedo a la democracia"). The commentators acknowledge that there can be no discussion of electoral politics without invoking the popular figure and the tricky ways of the electorate. The Güegüence Effect suggests that Nicaraguans "hide their true identity and intentions to those in power" (Cortés 2006)). They are somehow naturally reluctant to reveal their vote to anyone, particularly to anyone who may be connected with the government. It suggests that Nicaraguans will always wear a mask as a form of popular resistance when faced with authority.

Nicaraguan candidates will routinely dismiss or invoke Güegüence depending on their standing in the latest polls. In a 2000 interview, William Báez Sacasa, a Conservative Party candidate for mayor of Managua asserted: "the Nicaraguan Güegüense is the one that assures me that I am going to win" ("El Güegüense me va a dar el triunfo, asegura Báez"). Sandinista presidential candidate Víctor Hugo Tinoco also "put his trust in Güegüense" for the elections in 2001 (Briones). The party that the candidate represents seems not to matter. Nicaraguans hide their voting intentions regardless of party, a trend that suggests a mistrust of anyone in power.

In the last couple of election cycles, political posters have featured an image of the voter as Güegüence. In the town of San Juan del Oriente, I encountered a small political mural urging voters to act as if they are supporting one party while planning to secretly vote for another. Specifically, the Sandinistas were giving out food and toys to curry favor with voters at their rallies. The mural was created by a liberal political alliance, and told voters to go ahead and take the gifts, even if they were going to vote for the PLC candidate in the local mayoral election (Fernandez and Reyes 2009).

But the characterization of Güegüence as the typical Nicaraguan is far from straightforward. On one hand, Güegüence does subvert oppressive and arbitrary government. The Governor and all of his staff act out of greed and seek to exploit the merchant traveling through their province. While many celebrate Güegüence's artful defiance of their authority, others question his own means and motives. Although the trend of referring to the propensity of Nicaraguan voters to keep their intentions private as the Güegüence Effect began after the surprise upset of the Sandinista president by UNO coalition leader Violeta Chamorro in 1990, the following presidency of Arnoldo Alemán (president from 1997 to 2002) gave Nicaraguans even more reasons to be suspicious of the government. While president, Alemán embezzled millions from the country and his administration was riddled with unbridled corruption. Interestingly, while Alemán was occasionally associated with Governor Tastuanes, he was often viewed as Güegüence himself. Güegüence becomes a figure not of trickery in service of resistance, but of trickery in the

Figure 3. A Liberal Alliance political mural urges voters to "Take what they give you. Your vote is secret [...]. Then, vote without fear." Photograph by E.J. Westlake.

service of himself. Blandón notes the shift in signification: "the rogue no longer represented opposing the abuse of authority but as exerting authority from abusive power" (211). For Blandón, Alemán is the ultimate example of this new idea of the trickster because he, "in every way behaved in accordance with the characteristics of a swashbuckling character, smooth-talking, unscrupulous, greedy, lying and corrupt" (210). Alemán came to stand for all that is despicable about the figure of Güegüence.

For Blandón, however, this has a cynical purpose and disastrous results in that the likeable attributes of the character (his quick wit and cleverness) help to legitimize corruption. As he observes, the new discourse on the character, "has dangerously served as an epistemological basis of a perverse exercise of public office, which legitimates the looting of the treasury by inversion of ethical values, to proclaim that the cunning and clever is he who steals, who is corrupt" (210). Icaza laments: "the Güegüense is also a symbol of human duplicity. Hypocrisy is our favorite form of defense or attack [...]. What was a system of a defensive front against arbitrary and unjust institutions has become a cynical interest that runs from top to bottom in our culture" (2001: 145). Güegüence as the clever, but corrupt politician, undermined a sense of outrage toward Alemán's embezzlement and helped forge within the public a deep apathy toward a political culture driven by self interest.

If Nicaraguans come to see themselves and their leaders as liars and thieves, who would feel empowered to enact change? During Alemán's tenure, a sense of helplessness was high among voters. Nicaraguan arts critic Mercedes Gordillo noted the popular feeling:

> "The thief who robs a thief has 100 years of forgiveness," which means that it is not really stealing or it does not matter much to steal from those who are themselves evil. Values, this wonderful family heritage of honest people, who in days past did not need to sign contracts or promissory notes in order to uphold one's end of the bargain, before we had enshrined in our society the lying fink Güegüense, with due respect to the actual dance-drama. ("El buen ejemplo de una herencia familiar," 2002)

In other words, Nicaraguans could ignore the corruption of the Alemán government because he embezzled money from the government, from those in power, a narrative of transgression that runs parallel with an image of a resistant Güegüence, arriving at the Governor's court and helping himself to the spoils of imperialism.

Author and editorialist Rui Manuel Grácio das Neves explains the political apathy as a logical outcome of colonialism. In an editorial in *Acción Cultural Cristiana*:

> It would be necessary to consider a history of 500 years of marginalization [...] it has caused an "ethics" of hidden resistance ("philosophy of the güegüense"), based on dissimulation, saying one thing and thinking and doing another, "keeping quiet," and "leaving it alone." They are comprehensible attitudes from a history of unending strong oppression. ("Notas para una corrupción generalizada," 2000)

Grácio cites a political system and cultural attitudes inherited from a long history of colonial rule by Spain and then economic and military imperialism from the United States. Such a history, Grácio believes, has left Nicaragua with a legacy of "caudillismo," factions led by warlords vying for political control. During colonial rule and in the period immediately following independence, this was literally true. With an entrenched system of feudal patrones with vertical political relationships and syndicate allies, powerful political families emerged, which held tight control often by inviting foreign intervention. This drive for power invites corruption, Grácio claims, because of the desperate circumstances created for many and the view that stealing shows cleverness or strength, while honesty shows weakness. This was never so apparent as it was in 1999 with the power-sharing agreement between the Sandinistas and Alemán's Liberal Party, known popularly as "The Pact."

THE MARRIAGE AGREEMENT

I have mentioned before that the Güegüence Effect did not seem to work in favor of any particular party, that Nicaraguan voters often hid their intentions from anyone in power, regardless of ideological leaning or political platform. This may be a symptom of the fact that "caudillismo"-style power struggle seems to cause each party to adopt similar means to gain power. In other words, the real differences between viable political parties is negligible. As Kampwirth notes in her article on Alemán's economic policy: "In the era of neoliberal pressures to exclude citizens economically (by eliminating formal sector jobs and public services) at the same time that they are to be included politically (by mobilizing them electorally), politicians of various sorts find themselves promoting (or at least acquiescing to) neoliberal policies that contribute to the impoverishment of the very citizens whose votes they seek" (2003: 134). In other words, even parties that claim populist policies will work to exclude competitors and exercise control in other ways.

Both the use of foreign pressure (the Liberal and Conservative Parties have invited the U.S. to invade Nicaragua several times throughout the last two centuries) and the mechanisms of power sharing have helped to secure power for one party or another while neutralizing opponents. In the case of the famous 1999 Pact, the Sandinistas and the Liberal Party worked together to limit the power of the Supreme Court, add Supreme Court seats filled with people loyal to either party, and curtail the power of the Comptroller, the office that would investigate corruption (Kampwirth 2003: 135). This agreement between the revolutionary party of Daniel Ortega and the corrupt government of Alemán came as a shock to many citizens who viewed themselves as Sandinistas. But read within the history of Nicaraguan politics, the Pact is hardly surprising.

Michael Kryzanek notes in his essay on political parties in Latin America that, "the practice of opposition party politics in Latin America is generally characterized by government-initiated harassment, incarceration, and repression, as authoritarian regimes have consistently shown an unwillingness to recognize the democratic institution of the loyal opposition" (1980: 127), or opposition parties that together agree to uphold constitutional and electoral law whether they are in power or not. While opposition parties continuously face the real danger of being declared illegal or of constitutional law being suspended by those in power, party leaders may elect certain strategies to survive. One such strategy might be to agree to be "superficial party opposition" (131), engaging in certain compromises in order to remain viable.

While Enrique Bolaños, the Liberal Party candidate who won the presidency following Alemán's term in 2002, successfully prosecuted Alemán in 2003 and sent him to prison for 20 years, he did so at his own peril, ostensibly ending his own political career. At the same time, the Pact had changed electoral law, making a run-off election unnecessary if a candidate gained 35% of the vote in the presidential election, in turn making it possible for the Sandinistas, and Daniel Ortega, to win in 2006. In exchange for the political gains, Ortega initially agreed to an extremely loose house arrest for Alemán instead of prison, and there had been talk for shortening the sentence. However, the present state of the Pact is unclear as Ortega gains increasing power, and Ortega may have secured the better end of the deal.

If anyone wears the mask of Güegüence, it is Ortega, the original leader of the Nicaraguan Revolution of 1979, a Revolution that overthrew one of the most brutal dictators in Nicaragua's history. While Ortega and the original Sandinistas stood up to U.S. imperialism throughout the 1980s, Ortega's recent concessions to corrupt power resemble the tricky deals of the Güegüence, who subverts authority, but only for his own gain. In his current term as President, Ortega continues to promote popular participation. He advocates the establishment of citizen's councils, whose resolutions he promises he will include in his presidential deliberations (McKinley 2008). He also continues to speak out against imperial power as he continually voices opposition to U.S. foreign policy. But his actions, using the councils to reward supporters and using the Supreme Court to remove political challengers, show a cynical plan to consolidate his own power. He knows how to use the effective double-speak of the trickster.

If we cast Alemán in the role of the Governor once again, Ortega as Güegüence effectively caught him in his own web of greed, by playing the part of the feeble superficial opposition. Güegüence managed to marry himself into the Governor's household through the Pact, and now comfortably situates himself in the Governor's chair. On one hand, Ortega's wife Rosario Murillo, who he recently remarried to obtain the blessing of the Catholic Church, does not resemble the women of *El Güegüence*, such as the silent and unmasked Suche-Malinche, who the Mayor marries to Don Forscico. Instead, this accomplished poet from a prominent family joins him in the role of double-talking trickster, mirroring his position as a powerful co-president. And in a tragic twist of an already perverse national tale, Murillo's oldest daughter Zoilamerica Narvaez made her accusations of sexual abuse against Ortega public in 1998, allowing the last piece of the puzzle, Güegüence as sexual predator, to fall into place.

The last few years have been extremely disheartening for those who stood up to Somoza and struggled through the trying times following the Revolution. Party faithful, like Don Forcico, are set to inherit the estate under the tutelage of Güegüence. But some hold out hope that Daniel Ortega continues to be the resistant Güegüence, the Güegüence who successfully subverted the imperialist domination of the United States by deposing the U.S.-supported dictator. Others remain loyal to the ideals of the Sandinista Party, but reject Ortega as a representative of those ideals. Like Don Ambrosio, they aren't afraid to refer to Güegüence as an "embustero" to his face. As many Nicaraguans have said to me: "Yo soy Sandinista, pero no soy Danielista."[3] To that end, a new "Sandinista" party (the Sandinista Renovation Movement) has emerged. Although some question its viability now that Ortega has used the courts to remove their candidates from the ballot during this last round of elections, Güegüence-style wiliness and persistence may keep the party afloat.

When I traveled to Nicaragua in 2008, I attended a workshop sponsored by Grupo Relajo outside of the northern city of Estelí. One of the group's leaders, Mercedes Gonzalez, questioned Güegüence's appropriateness as a national symbol, given its specificity to the Carazo region of the country and that the character as a national figure flattens rather than articulates Nicaraguan identities (personal communication, 24 February 2008). The group sought to explore the myriad identities and personal stories of the participants, using Güegüence as a jumping off place, but not an end in itself. The workshop asked people to consider ways they gave up personal power, took sides in the political landscape, and related to each other. Güegüence became a symbol of liberation, but only in the moment participants were unmasked. The facilitators asked:

> Who is the Güegüense? Is it the mask or what is behind the mask? Are they the feudal lords that make pacts and seek to dominate everyone for their own benefit? Or is Güegüence he who has at one time used the mask in order to avoid being persecuted and destroyed and now desires and demands freedom in order to, without the mask, denounce the situation without fear, and open the way to the sharing of the construction of a more just, equal, and integrated society? We "the Güegüenses" decide. Do we remove the mask? or do we continue to allow "false Güegüenses" who use us while hiding behind the mask of The Pact, power, religion, and politics? ("Workshop handout," 2008)

The workshop facilitators suggest that stripping away the masks to reveal the relationships of power may be the way toward political change.

While Ortega continues to consolidate power, international observers have declared that fraud was rampant in the 2008 municipal elections. But as Ortega alienates political allies and loses international support, observers wonder if the Sandinistas will survive the term. Güegüence, the trickster, creates unstable political openings, positions of resistance as well as opportunities for exploitation. He may defeat the Governor, but he cannot be trusted since he thinks only of his own gain. Ultimately, what is most admirable about him is also what is most dangerous. The challenge for those who want to implement change is to follow him through the openings he creates without being taken in by him in the process.

NOTES

[1] I am using the spelling used by several scholars, including Karl Berendt and Daniel Brinton. It has various spellings, including "Güegüense" or, in Mántica's book, "Cuecuence."

[2] I am relying mostly on the translation from the hybrid language into Spanish by Carlos Mántica (2001). The translation from his Spanish text to English is my own.

[3] "I am a Sandinista, but I'm not a Danielista."

REFERENCES

Blandón Guevara, Erick. (2003) *Barroco descalzo*. Managua: URACCAN.

Bolt, Alan. (1982) *Banana republic* in *Cuadernos universitarios* 28, 9-40.

Brinton, Daniel G., ed. and trans. (1883) *The Güegüence; a Comedy Ballet in The Nahuatl-Spanish Dialect of Nicaragua*. Library of Aboriginal American Literature 3. Philadelphia: D.G. Brinton. Reprint (1969), New York: AMS Press.

Briones Loáisiga, William. (2001) "Tinoco confía en el 'Güegüense.'" *La Prensa: el Diario del Nicaragüenses, Digital*, 18 January <http://www.laprensa.com.ni/archivo/2001/enero/18/politica/politica-20010118-06.html> [Accessed 17 December 2008].

Castillo, Carlos García. (2000) "La Recta Final Electoral," *Boletín Informativo de Nicaragua*, Fundación Popol Na 40 (21 October).

Cortés Ramos, Alberto. (2006) "El espíritu del güegüense ronda la elección presidencial." *America Latina en movimiento*, 2 November <http://alainet.org/active/14300&lang=es> [Accessed 4 December 2008].

Cuadra, Pablo Antonio. (1998) *"El Güegüence y El Macho Ratón."* in *Baile de El Güegüence, o Macho Ratón,* ed. Carlos Mántica Abaunza. Managua: Editorial Hispamer, Costado Este de la UCA.

Fernández, Montserrat and Rubén Reyes. (2009) Personal communication (21 January). Conversation with the author.

Field, Les W. (1999) *The Grimace of Macho Ratón: Artisans, Identity, and Nation in Late-Twentieth-Century Western Nicaragua.* Durham: Duke University Press.

González, Mercedes. (2008) Personal communication (2 February). Email to the author.

Gordillo, Mercedes. (2002) "El buen ejemplo de una herencia familiar." *La Prensa: el Diario del Nicaragüenses, Digital,* 5 October <http://www.laprensa.com.ni/archivo/2002/octubre/05/opinion/opinion-20021005-02.html> [Accessed 17 December 2008].

Grácio das Neves, Rui Manuel. (2000) "Notas para una corrupción generalizada." *Cultura para la esperanza.* Accion Cultural Cristiana (Madrid), 39 (spring) <http://www.eurosur.org/acc/html/revista/r39/39ruym.htm> [Accessed 17 October 2007].

"El Güegüense me va a dar el triunfo, asegura Báez." (2000) *Bolsa de Noticias. Opinión,* 27 October <http://www.grupoese.com.ni/2000/bn/10/27/op1MM1027.htm> [Accessed 4 December 2008].

"Happy birthday, Señor Fox." (2004) *The Economist,* 7 February <http://www.economist.com/displaystory.cfm?story_id=4557> [Accessed 17 October 2007].

Icaza Gallard, Julio. (2001) "Constitution y proyecto de nación," in *La Democracia y sus Desafíos en Nicaragua.* Alejandro Serrano Caldera, ed. Managua: Fundación Friedrich Ebert, 127-166.

Kampwirth, Karen. (2003) "Arnoldo Alemán Takes on the NGOs: Antifeminism and the New Populism in Nicaragua." *Latin American Politics and Society* 45 (2), 133-158.

Kryzanek, Michael J. (1980) "Political Parties, Opposition Parties, and Democracy," in Howard J. Wiarda, ed. *The Continuing Struggle for Democracy in Latin America.* Boulder: Westview Press.

Mántica Abaunza, Carlos. *El Cüecüence o El gran sinvergüeza: obra maestra de la picaresca indoamerica.* Managua: Academia Nicaragüence de la Lengua, 2001.

McKinley Jr., James C. (2008) " Nicaraguan Councils Stir Fear of Dictatorship." *New York Times. Online Edition,* 4 May <http://www.nytimes.com/2008/05/04/world/americas/04nicaragua.html?ref=world> [Accessed 17 December 2008].

Merrill, Tim, ed. *Nicaragua: A Country Study.* Washington: GPO for the Library of Congress, 1993. <http://countrystudies.us/nicaragua/23.htm> [Accessed 17 October 2007].

Polanco, Ulises Juárez. (2004) "¿Cuál es el Güegüense que corre en nuestra sangre?" *El Nuevo Diario,* 1 February <http://www-ni.elnuevodiario.com.ni/archivo/2004/febrero/01-febrero-2004/opinion/opinion2.html> [Accessed 5 October 2007].

"Workshop handout." (2008) "Taller: ¡GüEGgüENSE, JUEgüénSE, JUEGUENse: sacate la máscara y soná tu "chischil!" Grupo Relajo (26 January), Estelí, Nicaragua.

"Los yankis le tienen miedo a la democracia. Entrevista con William Grigsby." (2006) *Radio La Primerísima*, 23 October
<http://www.radiolaprimerisima.com/noticias/5358> [Accessed 17 December 2008].

PART FOUR: PRACTICE

DO THE ENDS JUSTIFY THE MEANS?
CONSIDERING HOMELESS LIVES AS
PROPAGANDA AND PRODUCT

BEVERLY REDMAN

In the years 1999 and 2000, I worked with current and former residents of a homeless shelter in Pasadena, California, on two different series of workshops, which included practices in oral history documentation and modified Playback and Forum Theatre techniques employed to generate performances and accompanying texts. Although I held the title of Director, in each case I was not the initiating agent. In 1999, as an artist under temporary contract, I served two producers, the Cornerstone Theatre Company of Los Angeles and the Union Station Foundation of Pasadena, California, an operator of a homeless shelter and long-term recovery program. In 2000, the Union Station Foundation alone contracted me, since the success of the first collaboration prompted plans for a second one with the Foundation's administration, which alone served as producer. When referring to those with whom I worked, I would be remiss not to include the performers, or formerly homeless citizen artists. Throughout this article, I use the term "citizen artists," recognizing that all people, including those who do not retain a stable residence, do not contribute consistently to the wage-earning workforce and do not participate consistently as purchasers of merchandise, hold, nevertheless, the capacity to exercise citizenship by contributing art to their communities.[1] Furthermore, when exercising that capacity, they may come to see community as something they have the ability to form in collaboration with others rather than as something received passively.

Refection upon these two collaborations is not wholly celebratory. While the first year's workshops ran smoothly and came to fruition in the form of a successful public performance, the second year's collaboration ended in breach after a power struggle between all parties involved. Although I answered questions regarding representation of homelessness for myself in the form of a mission statement the second year, which served as part of my contract, concerns over who controls the representation of homelessness and why homelessness should be represented to the non-homeless public were never really addressed by all parties until late in the process. In retrospect, I see that failure to address distinctions between our agendas and the potential for them to conflict during the early, conceptual phases of the work resulted in a break up that could, perhaps, have been avoided with better early communication.

For the Foundation, the production itself was of greatest concern the second year; in particular, the image of homelessness, especially as it relates to racial composition, became increasingly important as the project came to be recognized for its potential as a fund raising tool. For me and for the citizen artists involved in the second year, the process rather than the product engaged us. Under my leadership, we deferred consideration of the end result, a public performance. Inside our artistic process, we held a kind of faith that the material generated would lead eventually to a strong, truthful final product. After all, it had done so the first year with little to no interaction from the Foundation and with great public success.

During the first year of work together, when the Cornerstone Theatre Company also sponsored the work, both the Foundation and Theatre Company's varying degrees of absence from the creative activities of the workshops left me in the position of speaking on behalf of the formerly homeless citizen artists in production meetings, interpreting and then relaying both my own and their agendas regarding play making and performance activities as best I could. Because I acted as a fellow artistic collaborator yet also as a member of the production team, I found myself in the position of mediator, much like any director does when meeting with the designers and producer separately from the actors. I enjoyed the artistic freedom that comes from such a position. Unlike a typical process grounded by use of a common, pre-determined script, this process included generation of a text that both parties, the Foundation administrators and the citizen artists, felt they had the authority to compose, since both parties were experts in the experience of homelessness. As the go between and person who ultimately put the text together, I succeeded that first year in creating a text that pleased both parties.

Furthermore, it served my own interests in community-based work. When entering the negotiations in 1999, I must admit that I brought my own beliefs about why and how collaborations between professional artists and citizen artists should occur, since I carried a history of doing such work. During my undergraduate days at St. Mary's College of Maryland, for instance, I served for two years as the student assistant to an on-going oral history project, The St. Mary's County Documentation Project, originally founded by Andrea Hammer in 1985 and now in existence under the direction of Julia King as The Slackwater Center, an organization which collects stories, music, and images from inhabitants of the Tidewater Region of Maryland. Subjects covered in the early days of the project included regional Gospel music practices, the history and practices of segregation in the various farming communities, the government takeover of choice farming land for the construction of the Patuxent Naval Air Station in 1942, women's work in the region, and the long traditions of fishing, crabbing, oystering, and bootlegging. Between the ages of nineteen and twenty-one, I learned to conduct field interviews, transcribe recordings, and transform transcripts into oral history monologues in close consultation with the field subjects.

Although a complete novice in regards to any sense of history at that age, this work left me with a sense of the past as something generated to further entirely present objectives. I became aware that the representations I constructed of people's lives were themselves interpretations of interpretations, or semblances upon semblances, and that the actions involved in reading and making versions of the world in text carried with them both personal and broader political agendas, as well. From their complex personal histories and complex socio-economic perspectives, the men and women I interviewed presented versions of their lives, I must assume, tempered by their interpretations of me. In turn, I performed a close reading of their lives, based on what they gave me, as much born out of my own complex personal and socio-economic positions.

The experience in my twenties introduced me for the first time to the gulf between the thing and the word. Not only does one represent place and people of that place with these distinct entities called words, the actions of representing others also represents one's self. Despite indeterminacy between that which we represent and that which we use to do the representing, we somehow persist in the faith that the capture—of a place, a people, or even just a self—is possible. Otherwise, we would surely cease to persist in our activities. Therefore, while working on the Oral History project in college, for the first time education stopped being about the acquisition of contained blocks of information, information paraded as if it has object status, and instead became about a creative negotiation between self, subjects, world and words. Furthermore, questions of authority, who owned and profited from the stories and how were they to be used in the long term, were central to subjects' concerns. When community members continued to negotiate with us after transforming their stories into printed matter, they wanted assurance that we would not seek economic gain without including them. They also wanted to know that they would be brought in on negotiation should the text undergo further transformation and production in years to come. In short, they wanted the same kinds of controls that authors fought to obtain via intellectual property laws. We gave them these controls in the form of standard release documents, which, as mutual protection, detailed the nature and duration of their donations to us.

I mention the St. Mary's County Documentation Project because it informed my subsequent years, in particular, both years I facilitated the citizen artists from the Union Station Foundation program, who were brought together because they shared a history of surviving homelessness. It prepared me to make narratives with the citizen artists and to contract them for their work in a way that allowed them some control over their own words and images; however, it did not prepare me to anticipate fully the degree to which stories and images could be employed and shaped to fit into an on-going campaign of propaganda and fund raising regarding race and life on the streets.

As preparation for our coming together for the first time in the spring of 1999, I met with representatives of the Cornerstone Theatre Company, the Union Station Foundation, and One Colorado Mall of Pasadena, California. At this meeting I learned how the collaboration between Cornerstone, Union Station, and the mall came about. Cornerstone was just completing a residency at One Colorado, which representatives from the Foundation witnessed. This Cornerstone residency functioned as part of a series of community collaborations in various locations in the Los Angeles area, which Cornerstone referred to as their mall plays. As Sonja Kuftinec notes in her book, *Staging America: Cornerstone and Community-Based Theatre*, in the mid to late nineties the company became drawn to what members felt the American mall exemplified, "the archetypal American community, the national agora of modern times" and "the site that provides social congregation and cultural reproduction" (2003: 54). Subsequent to seeing the One Colorado mall plays, the Union Station Foundation contacted Cornerstone, in the hopes of extending the theatre company's work in Pasadena to include a show based on the lives of homelessness survivors. The Union Station Foundation was about to enter a collaboration with the mall, as well, which would function as part of the mall's on-going community-service programs. The Foundation proposed that a show, celebrating both its own accomplishments and its residents' and former residents' accomplishments, was in order, and they wanted Cornerstone to help.

Cornerstone's schedule was full, not allowing for the possibility of releasing a company member to facilitate a production with the Union Station Foundation. Therefore, a representative from the company invited me to an interview, where I pitched to both parties the idea of creating a performance born out of Playback and Forum workshops and based on the oral and self-written histories of the participants themselves. The representatives accepted the pitch, even though it stood as a departure from the typical structure of Cornerstone's mall plays.

Once hired by Cornerstone, the party that paid my fee the first year, I received no other guidance from their representatives and only met with them again at the closing night of the performances in late October 1999. I received administrative guidance from a Union Station Foundation representative who attended most of the workshops as an observer. This minimal guidance I enjoyed, perceiving my artistic freedom to be intact. Although I perceived few strictures, in retrospect I realize that many conceptual decisions had been pre-determined prior to my arrival, among them the selection of a racially diverse group of workshop participants. The representative that acted as a liaison between the Foundation and me referred to the group members as "volunteers;" however, citizen artists returning a second year informed me that the Foundation hand selected the first group, so as to obtain a racially diverse visual representation of homelessness. Furthermore, according to many group members, the single representative of white America during the first year never participated in the Foundation's programs but served as a temporary agency employee at the Foundation offices. She happened to have issues with addiction and mental health, which she shared willingly and publicly.

We rehearsed the first year in a few donated spaces, including a church, a community centre, and a vacant store at the mall itself. Our very presence in the mall during both the rehearsal period and the performance period, at which time many current members of the homeless population came to stand side-by-side shopper-spectators, could be interpreted as a subversive act. After all, far from being, as Kuftinec represents Cornerstone's interpretation of malls, "the archetypal American community, the national agora of modern times" or "the site that provides social congregation and cultural reproduction," for the formerly homeless citizen artists of the project, this shopping district, whose list of stores includes Armani Exchange, Patagonia, and Saks Fifth Avenue, hardly exemplified their version or even my economically challenged graduate student version of community. The homeless population of Pasadena, often roused from such public centres of commerce, primarily exists outside and around the perimeters of the mall. A park just a few blocks away from One Colorado holds the unofficial name of "Relapse Park" by many members of the homeless and formerly homeless population in the area, so named for its identity as another kind of American community marketplace, that of the illegal drug trade.

When rehearsing at the mall or other centres provided us, I drew on the work of proponents of community-based practice, such as Paolo Freire, Henry Giroux, Augusto Boal, and Jo Salas. Our work began with a series of workshops, alternating between storytelling, improvisation, and journal writing exercises. We also began breakout sessions, in which group members conducted short tape-recorded interviews with each other, after which I completed verbatim transcriptions. These first sessions, entirely open in regards to subjects for narration and performance, allowed the citizen artists to determine the telling events of their lives in a variety of forms. Even though all of the participants appeared to have shared the experiences of life on the streets, drug addiction and life-long recovery processes, all did not share the same interpretation of how those events and conditions came about. Therefore, the early weeks entailed generation of material that would allow for negotiation on the subject of the causes of homelessness.

While some members of the group expressed discomfort regarding the writing exercises, two of the participants relished writing activities. Another had considerable gifts with language and music, holding the ability to improvise on narratives in rap style. All the citizen artists cited their experiences in Narcotics Anonymous, Alcoholics Anonymous, or both, as training in storytelling practices, since narration of life stories via oration functions as an integral part of the recovery process. During sessions, we practiced hybridized versions of Playback and Forum Theatre. Typically, a group member told a story somehow recognized as formative from his or her life, and, after narrating the story, she or he casts members of the group to improvise the narration. The storyteller directed the improvisation, retold the story, re-cast and replayed the story or transformed the story into his or her vision of the ideal. Depending upon the storyteller's wishes, the whole group shared the transformation and performance direction as a large collaboration, or the storyteller conducted the changes him- or herself. Sometimes the stories returned session after session, and sometimes the efforts underwent duplication in interviewing sessions or journaling sessions. Through experimentation and negotiation, in other words, the group discovered the stories that begged to be included in the final script. I cannot deny that my authoritative presence as the leader of the group influenced decisions about stories' worth. I can only say that I encouraged the citizen artists to consider me as a collaborator as much as a facilitator. In all honesty, however, surely we all carried and carried out our versions of teaching and learning. My authority came not merely from my own agency but from our collective histories of every version of teacher we had encountered, which we toted about as we worked.

Furthermore, I acted not only as a classroom teacher and head facilitating playwright, but as a theatre director, as well, when, upon generating a script, I found myself in the odd position of coaching group members to perform their own stories. The script consisted mainly of monologues cut up into small text cells, allowing three or four people at a time to tell thematically-linked stories. I helped to shape these not only by bundling them together and cutting them into pieces, but also by directing the performance levels, the diction, the physicality, and the pacing. I also taught the group the basic concept of choosing and playing strong objectives. One would not have thought that the performers would have needed such coaching, but they did. It was as if, once the stories separated from them, went home with me, and existed as part of a text I constructed in its final form, an alienation set in that could only be mediated by the study and incorporation of acting techniques. I may have taught the acting techniques, but I believe they functioned to return a sense of authority to the citizen artists.

At the end of three months of workshops, we had a show in the form of reader's theatre, *Face to Face: Stories from the Street and Back*, which ran three nights, six shows per week for a little over the month of October 1999 in the open courtyard of One Colorado Mall. Via release forms, the existence of which I shared with the Foundation through the in-rehearsal Administrator, the citizen artists donated their stories to this and only this project with its limited run. Were the project to have continued, additional written negotiation would have been required. The show received tremendous coverage considering its moderate size and minimal production values. A total of eight local papers, including *The Pasadena Weekly* and *The Pasadena Star News,* covered the show, which was expected. However, news of the project attracted major papers and even local television stations. The *Los Angeles Times* ran a full-page article on the cover of the "Metro" section, and *Backstage West* reviewed *Face to Face*, prompting writer, Madeleine Shaner, to dub it, "gentle guerrilla theatre" and "a paean to hope and the reincarnation of the human spirit" (1999: 4).

Although I celebrated these performances as such a "paean," in retrospect, I am not sure the work could be described as "guerrilla" theatre, "gentle" or otherwise. As it has been defined in the United States in the twentieth and twenty-first centuries, guerrilla theatre opposes the concept of American capitalism as an immutable way of life. This theatre project celebrated the citizen artists' survival of homelessness and the return to a state of improved physical health, which is undoubtedly worthy of celebration, but in so doing it also celebrated a return to unquestioned participation in and acceptance of the class system. For the members of this project, that meant a return to the life of a tax paying, bill paying wage earner. Viewed in this way, the mall was, I suppose, the quintessential place to hold such a theatrical celebration. It represented a welcome return to such centres of commerce. In admitting the project's limitations, I am in no way advocating for homelessness and addiction. Rather, I am simply pointing out that life on the streets quite literally embodied a radical alternative to American capitalism. This celebration, held in honour of a return from a radical existence, may have failed to see beyond a capitalist model because there are no viable alternatives.

While the performance location, a mall, and the show's title, *Stories from the Street and Back*, functioned collectively to uphold a return to a version of American life marked by getting and spending, the stories told during the performance often functioned as a counter force, revealing, for example, a childhood love for a mother's Sunday morning breakfast or a friend's trip to an amusement park that somehow resulted in life-long loyalties. Like survivors of a great flood, the citizen artists defined what was most important to them—all manner of love between human beings, physical and mental health, and the role that conscience played in their return to society. These narratives held a worth that stood as an alternative to the merchandise inside the stores surrounding the performance, and it is this alternative definition of value that may have prompted Shaner to use the words, "guerrilla," and "paean."

Perhaps it was the media attention that impelled the Union Station Foundation's administration to consider a second project the following year, or perhaps they, too, recognized this alternative value. Before the end of the first run, I received verbal notification of a forthcoming employment offer with the Foundation the following summer and fall of the year 2000. Proud of my work with the group, despite the lingering questions regarding the lifestyle it advocated, I awaited the following summer with anticipation.

Although returning to the Foundation in the year 2000, I re-initiated the connection with the work rather than the Foundation. I would learn in October of 2000 that Union Station had launched a Capital Campaign, which appeared to have been taking all available administrative resources for some time prior. The website of the current organization, Union Station Homeless Services, describes this campaign and sets its start date at September 2000, which explains why Union Station may have found it challenging to devote resources to the performance workshops a season before the campaign's inauguration (Union Station Homeless Services, "History") When contact resumed in late spring and early summer, the Foundation requested I write my own contract, mission statement and budget, which it accepted without revisions. In my mission statement I described the purpose of the project for the public as aiming "to dispel myths about homelessness by educating the public on why and how people become homeless." I also indicated the intended audience to be high school students, taking as my model a series of educational plays created by a health care provider.

In my contract and verbally, I indicated that neither the Foundation nor I owned the participants' donations of personal stories outright, stipulating the existence of release forms. These gave the Foundation ownership of the group members' images and words for this project and this project only. Furthermore, I indicated that I would be willing to take part in recruitment of citizen artists, in consultation with the Foundation administration. The new Foundation Administrator assigned to the 2000 show worked with me to assemble a cast. She did not express to me any requirements regarding the racial backgrounds of the group we were to assemble. Later in the process, she also claimed never to have been instructed to obtain a racially diverse cast before proceeding.

In fact, upon reading an early draft of this essay, this same Administrator, formally employed at Union Station, agreed to share her own memories, provided I paraphrase them and refrain from using her name for fear of reprisal (personal communication, 20 September 2007). In some of her interview commentaries, she recalled the racial composition of the group and her casting instructions, or lack thereof, saying that she was never told of racial/ethnic requirements in casting. However, in year one, prior to her work on the project, she noted that there did seem to be a mix of ethnicities, including African American, Asian, Latino and Caucasian, and she also confirmed that in the first year of the project a Caucasian woman, employed at Union Station under temporary contract, performed in the cast but had not accessed services at the Foundation. In fact, she explained, during the first year project initiators encouraged other staff members to perform but they declined. She also provided me with some background on clients at Union Station in 1999 and 2000, emphasizing that African Americans made up the vast majority of Foundation clients. Gradually, she said, with the advent of assistance programs designed to aid women and families, an increased number of Latinos accessed services, despite fears amongst the undocumented of being exposed.

In our interview recollecting events, she reminded me that she served for a limited time as a cast member (personal communication, 20 September 2007). Representing herself not as homeless or formerly homeless, she presented herself honestly as a staff member at Union Station, whose own reflections on lived experience included figurative rather than literal journeys to the streets and back. The citizen artists and I did not see her joining the cast as a problem because we were not misrepresenting her identity. In fact, because she is Caucasian, we viewed her membership as aiding to the diversity of the group. Although the Foundation Director allowed a member of his staff to perform in the show at One Colorado Mall the first year, falsely representing herself as a formerly homeless Caucasian woman with a history of accessing the Foundation's services, upon learning that the Foundation representative participated in performance activities the second year, the Director ordered an immediate return to administrative-only duties for reasons never made clear.

In regards to the goals and objectives for the project's participants, in my contract I outlined two distinct phases of work, which retained similarities to the first year: "The project will begin with a series workshops, utilizing theatre games, story-telling exercises and journal-writing techniques, as a way of both generating the raw material for the production and acquiring advanced performance skills" and "the construction of a script, resulting in a one-hour performance that will address the audience goals described above." Both the mission statement and contract listed the "development of self-empowerment and self-awareness, as well as the strengthening of literacy skills," as its objectives. I carefully listed goals that addressed community outreach and utilitarianism, or ways that the experience could serve basic-survival needs, with emphasis on the education in the theatre for its own sake. As artist and teacher, Stephani Etheridge Woodson, notes in her essay, "Creating an Educational Theatre Program for the Twenty-First Century," theatre educators have "inherited an educational organization heavily based in Progressive Education ideals," which envision theatre work with citizens as a "service" employed to "domesticate." Addressing theatre as it exists for young people in public schools, she articulates how youth are often defined as a "set of social problems to be managed." Theatre at the primary and secondary levels of education is often forced to justify itself within the perimeters of this model, emphasizing how it can help can "fix" people. Rather than define people as a set of problems to be fixed, she calls for a theatre-for-theatre's-sake pedagogy that explores deeply the "lived experience of being young" (2004: 26). Clearly, as the operator of a theatre project for people in recovery and recently off the streets, I, too, felt required to justify our work by citing its contribution to fixing "a set of problems." However, by listing "advanced performance skills" and "self-empowerment and self-awareness" in my contract, I gave credence to theatre making for its own sake, with its non-utilitarian but nevertheless invaluable practices of reflection upon life.

The complete artistic freedom I enjoyed the first year, when I was able to work with citizen artists at length with little to no external directives, ended mid way into rehearsals the second year. Without Cornerstone on board and with a Union Station Foundation capital campaign looming, the project's sense of purpose appeared to shift away from that of self-reflection, education and community outreach to that of fund-raising. The administration interrupted the workshop phase to take an increasingly more active role in deciding upon and shaping the show's content, ultimately resulting in a break up of all parties involved.

The major dispute arose one evening in September 2000 over the issue of racial representation. Shortly after the first visit of Foundation Senior administrators to rehearsal, I was informed of fears that the wider community would read the all-African-American cast as a racist representation of homelessness. This visit occurred late in the process; over two months into the rehearsals. The citizen artists had already generated the material for their show and were about to begin the shaping process, which would result in a script. When the administrators understood that weeks of cast recruitment early on yielded only African American graduates of their shelter and recovery programs, they called for a suspension of rehearsals and a return to the recruitment phase of operations. Furthermore, in response to citizen artists' rebuttals that administrative staff sought out Caucasians unsuccessfully the previous year, the administrators suggested that, if no Caucasian participants could be found, they might hire professional actors who could use some of the material generated from the personal lives of the African American participants and perform it as their own.

While the citizen artists and I unanimously agreed with the administration on the idea that homelessness not be represented as a problem of the African American community alone, we did not agree with the administration on the ideas of how to alter the situation. We suggested that the show itself address the absence of Caucasians on-stage, by providing current statistical data on cultural groups that experience homelessness and by narrating stories of how Caucasian members of the Union Station Community refused to participate for fear of discrimination in the mainstream communities to which they had returned. By addressing the audience directly, the artists and I believed we could challenge spectators to question their assumptions about who becomes homeless.

In regards to the insertion of new participants into the group, the citizen artists and I objected for a number of reasons. The bond created by the participants in rehearsal developed in part out of their shared history on the streets and in the rooms of recovery and in part out of the two months they had taken to develop artistic relationships in the workshops. Indeed, for those coming back a second year, the bonding period was considerably longer and deeper. While they considered deeply and ultimately agreed with the Foundation's reasoning behind presenting the face of homelessness with a show of diversity, they also felt that no one in the Foundation administration would listen to their proposed strategies for addressing the problem. The citizen artists did not understand why these issues had been so long overlooked by the Foundation administrators, and they also wished to have an equal voice in the decision making process once visual representation became of concern.

Furthermore, the citizen artists objected to the possible insertion of people with other backgrounds who might not have experienced homelessness, especially once the Foundation suggested that some of the participants' own stories be shared as material for the new actors to perform as their own. Although everyone in the group may have come to see theatricalization of personal stories as a few steps removed from actuality, they set limits on the degree to which these stories could be removed from their own bodies and voices. By opposing the idea that their material be shared with actors, they also asserted a belief in the truth of their performances and the boundaries by which they must remain truthful.

Initially, we all saw the very reason for the show to be about a celebration of the participants' identities as formerly homeless people now in recovery. The insertion of others purely on the grounds of racial background appeared not only to be racist itself but also a profound betrayal performed by the very people who had taken part in the participants' recovery processes. For up until this point, the citizen artists lauded the Union Station Foundation as a place where people received healing and salvation. These events did not appear to change the past, but they did appear to make the past more complex in light of the present.

Furthermore, on that same evening, when the Foundation administrators visited and recognized the racial composition as problematic, they also informed us of their intention to make a documentary film about our work, asking us to prepare to receive the filmmaker into our future rehearsals. This additional project would serve as a fund-raising tool, since the Foundation wished to have something it could send out to donors quickly and easily, as part of their capital campaign initiatives. The former Foundation Administrator I interviewed also confirmed that the documentary film was intended to function as support for the capital campaign, saying that there could be no better advertising for the shelter and the capital campaign than a film (personal communication, 20 September 2007).

I objected to the imposed film idea immediately, informing the administration that performances occurring in the closed, private situation of the rehearsal space allowed for a kind of risk taking that could be destroyed by the presence of another artist with her own, or the Foundation's, agenda. Furthermore, when beginning the process with the group, I invited them to sign release forms, which gave me and the Foundation the right to use their stories for the purpose of that year's show and only that year's show. Beyond that, they retained control over their life narratives and their images. The Foundation had been informed of my intention to use this standard release form each year I worked with the groups both verbally and in writing, but appeared to have taken no notice of it until reminded at this juncture. We were willing to allow a documentary filmmaker to enter our process if, and only if, the participants signed new release forms that included mention of the film, and if, and only if, I signed a new contract that gave me formal control over the manner in which my image and my work were presented in the film.

While reflection upon these events are in no way meant to degrade the Foundation, for clearly my work with it over two years demonstrated to me that its employees, the social workers and the development officers alike, are a dedicated lot that have helped numerous people to get off the streets and stay in recovery, it is to consider the differences of opinion that arose over that which constitutes politically correct behaviour when making policy decisions about race, representation and artistic control. While the administrators' actions could not only be justified as a necessary evil in keeping such a beneficial organization running but also as an acute sensitivity to avoiding any accusations of racism, the African American participants in the project ironically saw these very acts as racist, due to the fact that the Foundation's entirely Caucasian leadership was making decisions based on skin colour alone, without listening seriously to the opinions of the citizen artists themselves. One might say that the Foundation administrators acted as parents, assuming that their children were not ready to make decisions for themselves. It is completely understandable that the Foundation would approach the situation in this manner, considering that its very existence depends upon speaking for people that do not have the strength to speak for themselves. Viewed in this way, the injustice is to be identified in their refusal to collaborate with their former clients in any kind of serious manner just at the point when the former clients demonstrated a keen ability to self-direct. While such paternalism is, perhaps, understandable, it could also, nevertheless, be interpreted as akin to a long history of white co-option of African American cultural products. As Clovis Semmes points out in his essay, "The Dialectics of Cultural Survival and the Community Artist," African American "cultural products," especially "music, language, dance, and stylistic norms," have long been "absorbed into the broader White-controlled commodity system, redefined and used to advance the economic dominance of mainstream institutions" (1994: 447).

The situation between me, the Foundation and the citizen artists concluded in the fall of 2000 with a break up. In a closed session away from the formally arranged rehearsal space, the participants and I voted unanimously to reject the Foundation's imposed modifications to our work and to disband. When, in preparation for writing this essay, I asked the Foundation liaison to recall her own memories of the break up, she cited another meeting, one of which I had no knowledge and in which the Foundation director confronted the citizen artists, attempting to get them on-board for his future plans. She said that the Director started off by claiming I had abandoned the cast, which she recalled made the group angry. He presented the re-casting and ethnic diversity issues and said that he could not have an all African American cast because the African American Community would reject it as a racist portrayal. She explained that the group expressed the pain of having to deal with racism in one form or another all their lives, but they told him that they never dreamed they would have to deal with it coming from Union Station (personal communication, 20 September 2007).

Although I possessed no knowledge of this particular meeting, I was aware that the Foundation hoped to continue its plans for a show and that it represented me to the citizen artists as having abandoned them and the project. I knew this because I was continuing to meet with many of the artists informally in coffee shops or at my home, where we would journal together and talk. Without funding sources, we eventually disbanded altogether in the spring of the following year, 2001, and it is true that at that point, months after the breakup with the Foundation, I felt that I had abandoned the group.

The former member of Union Station's administration also took part in these extended writing workshops. In preparing her recollections for inclusion in this essay, she also shared her own break up with the Foundation over the *Face to Face* project, citing her support of the citizen artists as the reason she ultimately left, or had to leave, her position. She recalled the evening of the confrontation between the cast and the Foundation Director as the point at which her treatment at work changed drastically (personal communication, 20 September 2007).

Shortly after disbanding, the administration asked me to hand over all of the material generated out of the workshops, saying that they would create their own show with or without people who had actually been homeless. In their opinion, I suppose, the ends justified the means. At that point, however, even though I was still meeting with some of the citizen artists, I had already relinquished all materials to them. Although I fully supported and do still fully support the tremendously beneficial work of the Union Station Foundation, in respect for the citizen artists with whom I collaborated, I could not be a part of the Foundation's claim to assume ownership of the participants' personal narratives and images outright. I had already come dangerously close to such an act as a director of their own stories, exerting my own influence in the narratives' developments, which included subsequent editing and performance coaching that my eyes, not the subjects' eyes, controlled. Not for these reasons alone, support of the citizen artists also functioned for me personally as a form of self-definition. As Suzanne Lacy says in her essay, "Seeking An American Identity (Working Inward From the Margins)," which is based on her experience at the Chicago Learning Exchange, being a community-based artist means that one joins the ranks of people who have made it their business to "testify to the specific histories of excluded people," "to name and give presence" to such people "in a society that preferred the silence of well-behaved ghosts" (2001: 2). While I had spoken throughout the process and here continue to speak for the citizen artists of the group, I also saw my job to be about making sure they had the opportunity to speak for themselves in performance. This is the very nature of theatre direction, since the director must ultimately step away from the performance and allow the actors to assume authority on their own. Here, working as a community-based director, I sought control of the performance only in as much as it allowed the citizen artists to speak for themselves, to tell their stories in their own voices without concern about the degree to which either their stories or their collective image equalled a version of homelessness in agreement with politically correct notions.

After disbanding, the Foundation refused to pay me on the grounds that I had broken my contract by not finishing the job. I countered with a letter suggesting that, in fact, my contract did not indicate I would be required to release my methods of working and my image to a documentary filmmaker and that their demand of the material generated in the workshops had broken the agreement on participants' release forms that had, in fact, been noted in my own contractual agreement. Therefore, I claimed that they were in actuality responsible for the breach. I also threatened to take the Foundation to court on these grounds. I will probably never know if they agreed with me or not, but within a few weeks I received my payment for services in full.

In retrospect I see that the dispute arose over a crisis of representation within a context of paternalism, economics and multi-culturist dogma. It appears that the Foundation's very existence is derived from its combined practices of speaking for its clients and representing homelessness to the broader community in a manner considered most politically correct, which will allow it to obtain ongoing funding much needed for survival. These practices hold, indisputably, the best intentions. However, if discussions about this break up could have continued between all parties involved, we might have come to see that the clients no longer needed anyone to speak *for* them but to speak *with* them By voicing not only their personal narratives but also their opinions about how to frame and present their narratives to the public, they were exercising their own agency, *self* determining how their lives might serve as fund-raising tools, as propaganda, and as products. We might have also addressed both the benefits and, in this discreet case, the limitations of homelessness representation as multi-cultural, considering the idea that specific instances of representation require honest and true consideration of the situation at hand. That said, if I had the ability to go back and fix the past, I would from the earliest phases of production insist on deeper collaboration. While I much prefer a process that finds its way to a product without pre-set versions of outcome, in future I will surely address the sponsoring agency's vision of eventual outcome and insist that all are in agreement regarding that outcome before the casting process even begins.

NOTES

[1] I presented this story publicly for the first time at the International Federation of Theatre Research Conference of 2005. "Citizen Artist" was that year's theme.

REFERENCES

Anonymous [Union Station Foundation administrator, name withheld]. (2007) Personal Communication (20 September). Email to the author.

King, Julia A. (2005) "The SlackWater Center." <www.smcm.edu/slackwater/> [accessed 20 January 2009].

Kuftinec, Sonja. (2003) *Staging America: Cornerstone and Community-Based Theatre.* Carbondale: Southern Illinois University Press.

Lacy, Suzanne. (2001) "Seeking An American Identity (Working Inward From The Margins)." The Animating Democracy Project, Reading Room. <http://www.americansforthearts.org/AnimatingDemocracy/pdf/reading_roo m/seeking_an_american_idenity_lacy.pdf> [accessed 20 January 2009].

Semmes, Clovis E. (1994) "The Dialectics of Cultural Survival and the Community Artist." *Journal of Black Studies* 24 (4), 447-461.

Shaner, Madeleine. (1999) "Face to Face." *Back stage West* 6 (43), 18-19.

Woodson, Stephani Etheridge. (2004) "Creating an educational theatre program for the twenty-first century." *Arts Education Policy Review* 105 (4), 25-30.

THE BIRABAHN/THRELKELD PROJECT: PLACE, HISTORY, MEMORY, PERFORMANCE, AND COEXISTENCE

KERRIE SCHAEFER

The Birabahn/Threlkeld project is a collaborative research project that seeks to investigate the efficacy of community cultural development (CCD)[1] techniques in building coexistence between Indigenous and non-Indigenous Australians in Lake Macquarie. The project takes its name from the Reverend Lancelot Edward Threlkeld, missionary to Aboriginal peoples in Lake Macquarie between 1826 and 1841, and Birabahn (Johnny M'Gill), a tribal leader from the Lake Macquarie area described as "the greatest English language scholar of the 19th century" (Maynard in Roberts, Carey, and Grieves 2002). Working together, Threlkeld and Birabahn produced the first written documentation of an Indigenous language in Australia (see Threlkeld 1827, 1834, 1836, 1850, 1891, 1892). As Jan Cohen-Cruz has noted, "community-based performance has become less about homogenous communities and more about different participants exploring a common concern together" (2005: 3). The Birabahn/Threlkeld project aims to involve Indigenous and non-Indigenous Australians in Lake Macquarie in the exploration of a shared (contact) history, a unique story of cross-cultural collaboration that is also recognised to be "complex or multidimensional; cross-cutting [...]; and contested by various stakeholders, eliciting multiple and often conflicting perspectives [...]." (Animating Democracy Initiative n.d., quoted in Cohen-Cruz 2005: 3-4). At the centre of the collaborative research project is the making of a documentary (see Watt in this collection) and site-based performance via a CCD and participatory action research (PAR) process. The performance aims to tell the story of contact and cooperation between Threlkeld and Birabahn, and to explore the cultural significance and value of that relationship then and now, drawing on the historical archive and the local knowledge and living memory of Indigenous communities in Lake Macquarie.

The collaborative research project involves a number of partner relationships. The first is between academic co-researchers from the disciplines of Drama (Schaefer and David Watt) and Aboriginal Studies (Deirdre Heitmeyer and Professor John Maynard) at the University of Newcastle. The second is between the University (Drama and Aboriginal Studies) and the director of Awarbukarl Cultural Resource Association (ACRA), an organization working towards the reclamation and revival of Awabakal culture and language (http://www.acra.org.au/). The third is between the University and Lake Macquarie City Council (LMCC). LMCC has a Statement of Commitment to Aboriginal people in Lake Macquarie (2001, renewed in 2008), employs an Aboriginal Community Worker and has strong links with local Indigenous communities via an Aboriginal Consultative Committee (ACC), a general representative body consulted for permission to conduct the project. The fourth relationship is between the University, LMCC, and ArtsNSW (the state arts funding body) via the position of the Lower Hunter Arts and Cultural Broker who provided a special grant under the Hunter Arts Strategy Grant Scheme to LMCC to support the project. Council provided matching funding and the research team then successfully applied for a University of Newcastle Collaborative Research Grant (a pilot research grant scheme meant to lead to further applications for external grant funding).

This paper is about the conceptual and practical underpinnings of the community-based performance at the centre of the ongoing collaborative research project. Here I want to unpack the question: why this particular performance, and why here (in Lake Macquarie) and now? In dealing with this question I will examine the current political context in Australia, one in which the process of Reconciliation has stalled;[2] the place that is Lake Macquarie now and then, when contact was made between the first white settler to the lake area and the traditional owners of the land; and, the place of the Rev. Threlkeld, a particularly controversial figure in Australian history then as now. Finally, I want to (briefly) examine the performance that emerged from the CCD/PAR process and how it raised questions, provoked dialogue, and explored performance in relation to place, history, and memory.

PART 1: COEXISTENCE. FRAMING THE
POST-RECONCILIATION DECADE
The research project was conceived in the early 2000s, at the end of a
period known in Australia as "the reconciliation decade." In 1991 an
act of Australian parliament established the Council for Aboriginal
Reconciliation (CAR) to oversee a formal ten-year long process to
"educate the wider Australian community about reconciliation and
Indigenous issues, foster a national commitment to address Indigenous
socio-economic disadvantage and investigate the desirability of
developing a document of reconciliation" (Gunstone 2005: 2). The
aim was to have concluded the process in time for the centenary of the
Commonwealth of Australia in 2001. However, the election of a
conservative (Liberal/National coalition) government in 1996 saw a
radical change in policy. The incoming Prime Minister (PM), John
Howard, initiated a public policy debate on the reconciliation process.
He argued that the previous Hawke/Keating Labour governments had
placed too great an emphasis on "symbolic" reconciliation—for
example, a national system of land rights, Indigenous self-
determination, an apology to the Stolen Generations—at the expense
of more "practical" outcomes, namely "socio-economic improvement"
(Altman and Hunter 2003: 1). The Howard government intended to
redress this imbalance by placing greater emphasis on "practical"
reconciliation, focusing on the key areas of health, housing, education
and employment (Altman and Hunter 2003:1). In fact, what the
Howard government instituted was an ideological wedge to contain
debate about Indigenous rights and the broad social justice agenda of
Indigenous policy makers, reflected in CAR.[3]

   In 2000, as Howard disbanded the Council for Aboriginal
Reconciliation (CAR), hundreds of thousands of people in Australian
cities and towns marched to protest the winding down of the
Reconciliation process. Sydney's Walk for Reconciliation travelled
over the Sydney Harbour Bridge attracting approximately a quarter of
a million people. It was made even more memorable by a plane, hired
by a group of citizens, writing in the sky the word the PM refused to
say: "sorry" (three times).[4] This was followed a month later by a
media stunt broadcast on *The Games*, a national TV program
parodying official preparations for the 2000 Sydney Olympics, in
which John Howard, an actor with the same name as the PM, offered
an apology[5] to Indigenous Australians. The statement began with the

caveat: "Any other John Howard who wishes to make this announcement should apply for copyright permission here, which will be granted immediately" (Howard 2000). Abandoned as a formal, national process of social change, local acts of DiY reconciliation flourished. This situation supports Angela Pratt's insight into reconciliation in Australia:

> the amorphous nature of the term "reconciliation" allows a broad range of political players to attach their own different, at times contradictory, meanings to the term. It can be argued that this is one of reconciliation's greatest strengths, in that it allows for a diverse range of views to co- exist. But at the same time, the lack of any coherent, shared understanding of reconciliation arguably means that while "reconciliation" is now a ubiquitous term in Australian political discourse, it is not an especially influential one (2005: vii –viii).

Conceptualising the project in the early 2000s, Heitmeyer said (in a meeting in her office in Wollotuka) that she preferred the term coexistence to that of "reconciliation," which had promised much and delivered little. There was also a question about whether atonement or reparation was even possible, a debate that hadn't been had with the shift from "symbolic" to "practical" reconciliation. The notion of coexistence admits that Indigenous and non-Indigenous Australians share a common place and a (post-contact) history. It also admits that place and history are contested categories and aims to negotiate (though not necessarily resolve) differences through dialogue. An Aboriginal historian, Heitmeyer's participation in the research project was premised on her interest in how to communicate her research/knowledge to the broader community. She was already experimenting with performative modes by running a cultural awareness bus tour through Newcastle and Lake Macquarie for education students. This tour explored the unique contact history of Newcastle, drawing on the landscape paintings of convict artist Joseph Lycett, and Lake Macquarie, drawing on the writings of Threlkeld (see Schaefer and Watt 2006). For Heitmeyer the challenge was in how to tell about these historical firsts of contact, encounter and exchange through which Aboriginal history was in the process of being reconstructed and re-imagined. She suggested that "rather than writing a paper, we can act it out" (Schaefer 2005). In other words, Heitmeyer supposed that performance might provide a more culturally appropriate way of sharing or transmitting knowledge. Heitmeyer also saw that a performance-based CCD project could, in the long term, involve Aboriginal youth "learning about local places and the stories attached to them, creating performances and leading cultural tours" (in Schaefer 2005).

PART 2: PLACE, HISTORY, AND MEMORY

The place known as Lake Macquarie refers both to one of the largest coastal salt water lakes in Australia with a body of water four times the size of Sydney Harbour, and a city which is the fourth largest local government area in New South Wales (NSW).[6] A ship's captain, William Reid, accidentally "discovered" the opening to Lake Macquarie in 1800 sailing from Sydney to the Coal River, some 23 kilometres north, to collect coals. In 1804 a penal settlement was made at the mouth of the Coal River, later re-named the Hunter River (after Governor Hunter). Newcastle, the settlement on the Hunter River, was a place of secondary punishment where recidivist convicts were put to hard labour mining coal, felling timber, and collecting and burning oyster shells to produce lime. The colonial government prohibited free settlement in the vicinity of "Reid's Mistake" due to its proximity to the penal settlement. It was important to isolate the open gaol that was Newcastle from the settled districts of the colony (Sydney and surrounds). During the time of the penal settlement, government officials based at Newcastle enjoyed local expeditions led by Aboriginal guides to the lake, known by Indigenous Australians as "Awaba" (the word refers to the *flat surface* of the lake). One participant's account of a touring party that set out from Newcastle to the lake in 1821 is cited in Windross and Ralston (1897):

> Our parson, the Rev. F.A. Middleton [...], started with myself with the whole tribe of upwards of 100 on a walking trip to Lake Macquarie. [...] On arrival, I was enchanted with its beautiful scenery, and can never forget it. The whole surrounding country and lake were serene and still; solitude reigned; no tree disturbed; and no trace of white man's civilisation, but all in its natural wild state. We enjoyed all the wild sports of Australian bush life in its primitive state as the aborigines of that day (before they were contaminated with our vices) were accustomed to enjoy them, shooting, fishing, kangarooing, and hunting, our game was ample for us all. They supplied us also (by diving) with the finest mud oysters for which the waters of the lake are noted. These we scalloped on our bush fires, and we spent five or six days of as much enjoyment as I ever had in any part of the world. (Walsh 1997: 21)

While Newcastle was a place of human misery and suffering for most of its early non-Indigenous inhabitants (convicts), Lake Macquarie was, in stark contrast, a pristine and plentiful wilderness. It acted as a natural buffer zone between Sydney and Newcastle, known as "Sydney's Siberia" (Turner 1980), as a tourist/leisure destination for military officers and as Awabakal land.

The lake area was settled by Europeans in 1825/6, three years after the closure of the penal settlement at Newcastle and its relocation some several hundred kilometres north to Port Macquarie. In 1825 Governor Brisbane granted the London Missionary Society (LMS) 10,000 acres of land on the south side of the lake "in trust for the aboriginal natives [...] with a view to instructing the natives, and preaching to them in their own language" (Clouten 1967: 23). In 1826 the Rev. Lancelot E. Threlkeld (1788-1859), a LMS missionary who had been stationed in Polynesia (1817-24), moved into a house he had built on the lake and began work ministering to the Awabakal, the peoples of the lake. Threlkeld's Lake Macquarie mission, the only LMS mission in Australia in the nineteenth century, was "one of the least successful and most publicly embarrassing of [the LMS's] many colonial ventures" (Johnston 2006: 73). Anna Johnston puts the "dramatic failure" (2006: 73) of the Lake Macquarie mission down to two factors. First, the mission was established contrary to mainstream colonial practices: "humanitarian interests were directly opposed to the explicitly genocidal alternatives to cross-cultural conflict endorsed by many Australian settlers" (Johnston 2006: 73). Second, the appointment of Threlkeld guaranteed that the mission would be controversial. He was a demonstrably "difficult personality, characterised by a high self-regard and a pompous and self-righteous sense of moral and intellectual superiority" (Johnston 2006: 62). At the same time, Threlkeld "identified strongly with the marginalised and dispossessed, and [...] invested fully in the complex colonial politics of each location he inhabited" (Johnston 2006: 62). This meant that he played a very active and public role witnessing, recording and circulating accounts of cross-cultural violence on the colonial frontier, which brought him into conflict with the colonial order and other European "settlers," most of whom preferred the more celebratory or heroic narrative of settlement to Threlkeld's counter-narrative of violent conflict and chaos. As Johnston notes, Threlkeld was a liminal figure in early Australian colonial culture situated as he was:

> on the borders of state governmentalities and evangelical concerns, both a
> "man of god" and a man who frequented the colonial law courts, newspapers
> and public forums. [...] [H]e constantly challenged the colonial order in
> Australia. His voluminous correspondence and strategic publications
> displayed this challenge repeatedly, as did his commitment to translating for
> Aboriginal witnesses in court. Threlkeld deliberately and strategically used
> private and public correspondence to publicise his opinions and causes. [...]
> In textual debates [...] the highly provisional nature of humanitarian ideas in
> the colonies was played out explicitly. (2006: 75)

Threlkeld's "activism" antagonised one man in particular, the Reverend Samuel Marsden, director of the LMS in the southern-hemisphere, and an extremely conservative (and cruel) man (Marsden was known as the "flogging parson" for the severe corporeal punishment he meted out to convicts in his pastoral care). When Threlkeld fell into dispute with the LMS over the inadequate level of financial support given to the fledgling Lake Macquarie mission, the LMS handed over financial control to Marsden. The relationship between Threlkeld and Marsden deteriorated further and in May 1828 the LMS notified Threlkeld that they had decided to abandon the mission and dismissed him from their employment. Threlkeld rallied and, together with a group of supporters, petitioned Governor Darling for a grant of 1280 acres of land for a second mission at what is now known as Toronto/Coal Point on the west side of the lake. The colonial government further supported Threlkeld's mission by granting him an annual salary and allowance for the maintenance of convict servants, requiring that Threlkeld present an annual report to the Governor on the progress of the venture. Threlkeld and family moved to Ebenezer mission at the end of 1830. This second mission was not as spectacular a failure as the first. It was, however, unsuccessful. For many and varied reasons Threlkeld couldn't convince local Aboriginal people to settle at Ebenezer and the mission eventually folded in 1841, after approximately eleven years.

Of all the curious contradictions that envelop the life and work of Lancelot Threlkeld, most notable is the central role his writings play in the dynamic process of forgetting and remembering that constitutes Australian history. Anna Johnston states that any reading of Threlkeld's missionary writings is carried out "in the context of contemporary cultural debates about the morality of colonisation in Australia, or more specifically the lack of it" (2006: 80). These debates revolve around the writings of revisionist Australian historians (published in the 1980s/90s) who took issue with earlier histories that "effectively elided [European] colonial violence and indigenous resistance to colonial invasion" (Johnston 2006: 81). Historian Henry Reynolds has been at the forefront of progressive re-imaginings of Australia's past and has made use of Threlkeld's writings as evidence that cross-cultural violence did take place on the colonial frontier. According to Reynolds, Threlkeld is one of a number of "outsiders, eccentrics and obsessives" who took a special interest in attempting to curb "the indiscriminate and disproportionate violence" against Indigenous people in the early days of the colonial settlement (1998: xiv). These revisionist histories have, in turn, incited a conservative backlash aimed at discrediting the notion that cross-cultural violence characterised the colonial settlement of Australia. Former media studies academic turned polemicist, Keith Windshuttle, has been one of the leading proponents of the counter-revisionist movement and he, too, has paid close attention to Threlkeld's writings in an attempt to call into question the veracity of his testimony and, thereby, disprove Reynold's thesis. According to Windshuttle, Threlkeld is, at best, a "fabricator" and, at worst, a "liar" (2000:12) who had a vested interest in "portraying colonial society as a cruel and hostile place that sought to destroy the Aborigines [...]. [T]he missionary could [then] create a heady vision of himself as their physical protector, their secular saviour and their spiritual redeemer" (2000: 10). The "History Wars" (Macintyre and Clark 2003), as these debates have been termed, reduce the field of Australian history to the "black arm-band" view (a term coined by historian Geoffrey Blainey and adopted by Prime Minister Howard) versus the "whitewash" (Manne 2003). According to Johnston "the history wars" mirror the "paper war" (2006: 80) Threlkeld was embroiled in the early nineteenth century: "the nature of these debates is uncannily similar: they focus on the dubious morality of colonisation, on the reliability or otherwise of testimony and on the dangerously unstable nature of strategic textuality" (2006: 82).

I have drawn considerably on the work of Anna Johnston, a literary studies scholar whose work analyses Threlkeld's writings as produced in the course of an imperial and evangelical career carried out in a fluid and improvisatory colonial context. Johnston problematises the exaltation of the archive as a site of ultimate authority on the past, posited in some of the more polemical positions on Australian history. Drawing on contemporary historiography and literary and cultural theory (including Derrida's work on "archive fever"), Johnston shifts primary focus from "the historical figure of Lancelot Threlkeld" (2006: 84) to an examination of the historical and discursive practices of textual production and reception. Johnston observes that Threlkeld is writing for both local *and* international readerships. On the international level, his utterances are situated, she claims, "within the context of abolitionist narratives, and as part of a broader international network of humanitarian activism" (2006: 86). Threlkeld's writings from the Lake Macquarie locality, thus, "serve to connect Australian colonial politics with an international debate about the ethics of colonisation" and they "resonated at this time with similar stories emanating from Britain's other colonial projects, connecting Australia, to Polynesia to the Caribbean" (Johnston 2006: 86). This awareness of Threlkeld performing an expanded role on a larger stage suggests that instrumental uses or critiques of Threlkeld's writings are limited (some more than others) as his witnessing "operate[s] only in a limited sense as local" (Johnston 2006: 86). Significantly, project participants were concerned to bring to public attention this more expansive understanding of Threlkeld's life and work. One member of the project steering committee, a descendent of the Awabakal peoples, commented that Threlkeld wasn't reporting massacre stories simply to secure his missionary post, but was engaged in a larger, humanitarian project:

> In 1928 Marsden said the LMS was going to cut all monies to Threlkeld. Threlkeld then explains what he needs the money for. He's paying people to build the mission. He recognises that peoples' way of life is changing, perhaps irrevocably, and is skilling them up. But that's why Marsden cut off his money. Threlkeld was helping people to set up farms. Yes he was anglicising them too, but if people did a fair day's work he felt he should pay them. That's not a man who's not in touch but a man who's a visionary. He was giving people whose lives he thought were going to change massively, giving them an opportunity to be educated, to earn a living. As far as the LMS was concerned Threlkeld was a total failure. But what he did here was amazing work. He was a missionary and humanitarian. I might not be here if not for Threlkeld. (Schaefer 2006a)

The interdisciplinary intervention of a literary theorist into the debate over Australian history acts as a reminder that, as historiographer Keith Jenkins states:

> history is basically a contested discourse, an embattled terrain wherein people(s), classes and groups autobiographically construct interpretations of the past literally to please themselves. There is no definitive history outside these pressures, any (temporary) consensus only being reached when dominant voices can silence others either by overt power or covert incorporation. (1991: 19)

This awareness of the "epistemological fragility" (Jenkins 1991: 11) and ideological and methodological limitations of history presents a major challenge to the Birabahn/Threlkeld project. One of its most interesting areas of problematic is the nature of "Aboriginal history" and of "History" itself: what it is or, more pertinently, whom it is for (Jenkins 1991: 18). The notion of "Aboriginal history" forces a re-examination of performance and other embodied practices (storytelling, dance, spoken language, song, bodily inscription, and so on) as systems of "learning, storing and transmitting knowledge" (Taylor 2003: 16). This expanded understanding of what constitutes knowledge places more importance on history as continuity into the present and as "memory," rather than as a body of recorded "facts" about the distant past. Performance Studies scholar Diana Taylor has recently argued that "archival memory"—"texts, documents, buildings, bones"—operates alongside and in dynamic interaction with "the repertoire [...] of embodied practice/knowledge (i.e., spoken language, dance, sports, ritual)" (2003: 19). Both the archive and the repertoire are mediated forms of knowledge: "the process of selection, memorization or internalization, and transmission takes place within (and in turn helps constitute) specific systems of re-presentation" (2003: 21), and both are subject to change or disappearance (thought the kind as well as degree differ). According to Taylor, what the discipline of performance studies permits is an expansion of the traditional archive via analysis of "the repertoire of embodied practices as an important system of knowing and transmitting knowledge" (2003: 26). Most importantly, given the aims of the Birabahn/Threlkeld project, analysis of the repertoire is linked, in Taylor's account, to the production of "an alternative perspective on historical processes of transnational contact" and invites a re-imagining of settler societies (the Americas, Australia, etc.) "by following traditions of embodied [and, I would add, emplaced] practice" (Taylor 2003: 20).

As the project title suggests Birabahn is a significant, if hitherto overlooked, historical figure. He is mentioned in the colonial archive and recent work by Historians (Indigenous scholars amongst them) at the University of Newcastle has created a more coherent narrative of his life and work. Birabahn (meaning "eagle hawk") was born circa 1800 in the Lake Macquarie area. He was taken to Sydney and grew up there as Johnny M'Gill, a servant of an officer at the military barracks (Roberts, Carey, and Grieves 2002). He returned to his birthplace as a young man and was designated chief of the Awabakal tribes by Governor Macquarie, a designation not recognised within Aboriginal culture but demonstrating that he was a well-known, well-respected person. In Newcastle/Lake Macquarie, Birabahn was variously employed by the colonial government - he re-captured convict escapees and was included in the expedition that set out to establish the penal settlement at Port Macquarie (Roberts, Carey, and Grieves 2002)—and came into contact with Threlkeld and his mission. From 1825 Birabahn was Threlkeld's "almost daily companion" (Clouten 1967: 35). Threlkeld acknowledges Birabahn as his instructor in the local language and describes him as "an intelligent, honourable and sensitive man who was feared and respected by his countryman" (Roberts, Carey, and Grieves 2002). His proficiency in several languages, including English, enabled Threlkeld's written recording of the local language and his advocacy role as he translated for Aboriginal defendants in colonial criminal courts. In 1830, Governor Darling honoured Birabahn with a brass plate, "Barabahn Chief of the Tribe at Bartabah," as reward for his "assistance in reducing his Native Tongue to a written language" (in Roberts, Carey, and Grieves 2002). Contemporary historians regard Birabahn as an outstanding scholar[7] (Maynard in Roberts, Carey, and Grieves 2002) and his and Threlkeld's studies are proving invaluable today as attempts are made to reclaim and revive language and culture.[8]

Birabahn, like Threlkeld, is a complex and intriguing figure. He lived between two cultures, Aboriginal and British colonial, both of which were in flux and improvisatory. Growing up in Sydney, Birabahn witnessed the impact of colonialism, its effects and affects,

on local Aboriginal peoples. Returning to Lake Macquarie he knew
the changes that were likely to follow and the kinds of challenges they
would present to his people. Perhaps he, more than anyone,
understood and appreciated what it was Threlkeld was trying to do. In
creating a performance to tell the story of contact and cooperation
between Birabahn and Threlkeld, the aim was to draw on archival
materials and to involve local Aboriginal people in a CCD/PAR
process of performance making wherein embodied and emplaced
practices/knowledge informed the re-imagination of post-contact
history and cross-cultural relations.

PART 3: *NGARRAMA*, PROCESS AND PERFORMANCE
After collaborative research partnerships were established (2002-
2005) a steering committee was formed to guide the CCD/PAR
process. The first meeting was held at LMCC in late 2005. It
comprised the research team (Schaefer, Watt, Heitmeyer, and an
ACRA representative), the Council's Aboriginal Community Worker,
members drawn from the Council's Aboriginal Consultative
Committee (including a descendent of the Traditional Owners of
Awabakal land), and the Lake Macquarie City Art Gallery's
Indigenous Reference Group. It met over the year to November 2006
when a public performance was presented in Lake Macquarie. In the
first two steering committee meetings group members sought to
establish the geographic boundaries of the project, which would
determine the tribal/clan groups and individuals the researchers would
consult; intellectual property matters; project protocols; and ethical
considerations relevant to collecting oral history from Indigenous
peoples. In February 2006, the steering committee moved on to
talking about the kind of performance that might emerge from the
project:

> Descendant of the Traditional Owners (DTO): where do you want to start?
>   With the meeting between Threlkeld and Birabahn?
> David Watt (DW): it would be interesting to play with the documentary
>   record, what's written down as one mode of access to history and then to
>   mix that with the oral history, what's not written down that we intend to
>   collect. How do we get into the contact story of Threlkeld and Birabahn?
> DW: we want to work with two kinds of historical sources: popular memory
>   and documents. Throw those things against each other. What are the really
>   quotable quotes, the bits that lend themselves to be read or said in

performance? What can we generate from oral history that we can use against that?

Aboriginal Community Worker (ACW): I'm trying to picture the show.

DW: we will pull bits and pieces together—say a journal reading against a reminiscence and then a song which might hold several of these pieces in some sort of a pattern.

ACW: what's the story and message behind it? […] I'd want a good story and a message […] the community loves a good yarn. There can be lots of political messages and historical stuff but it has to be a good yarn.

DW: I don't know your yarning tradition.

ACW: I don't know much about Threlkeld/Birabahn but I do know about my people. He's coming into an environment that's family. When white people come into the family group there's a lot of jesting. After a time that person understands your family then you don't have to explain everything to them—they just know. Threlkeld would have to have come into a family unit. He would have to have been accepted on some sort of level. They would have questioned him - sat him down and asked him a whole lot of questions.

DTO: So that meeting…they would have been having a piece of him all the time until things started to get serious and he is accepted so that Threlkeld can say about Birabahn "this is my trusted friend" […].

DW: It would be nice if an actor read that direct address—the performer can't pretend they're being Threlkeld on stage. All the performer can be is a guy who is quoting him all the time. The actor is there and has a relationship to the audience. It is a circular arrangement—like handing around a yarn. Inevitably it's a really complicated yarn because we haven't got all the information—the audience will go away with questions. We can go from this is the history way back then (we don't have the full record) and this is customarily how we do things (so this is how it may have been then) […] a nice sort of performance—simple - not spectacular - but engaging. (Schaefer 2006a)

Clearly at this stage there was some tension between the desire to create a piece of documentary theatre based on a combination of archival documents and oral history materials, and the desire to create a "good yarn." This was a productive tension and exciting possibilities emerged in relation to exploring documentary/verbatim theatre alongside an Indigenous storytelling or yarning tradition. At this meeting the group mentioned artists who might be employed to compose the script. It was hoped that artists and interviewees would become co-researchers and work together with the steering committee (as members of it) to co-create a performance script. However, shortly after hearing that the project had attained the necessary University research ethics clearance (June 2006), the researchers were contacted by ArtsNSW and informed that the deadline for the presentation of the performance was October 2006 (this was an arbitrary decision made by ArtsNSW alone). An extension to mid-November was negotiated. The short lead up time to performance meant that it wasn't possible to collect or collate oral history material. It also made it abundantly clear that the project required experienced community-based performance artists working on it. In July the researchers commissioned Ray Kelly and Brian Joyce to write and direct a performance.[9]

A steering committee meeting was held in August 2006. The group, including Kelly and Joyce and Professor John Maynard, the newly appointed head of the University of Newcastle's Wollotuka Aboriginal Studies, re-assessed the project aims given the new deadline and decided to engage in an intensive process of community consultation focused on the development of an emerging performance script, a "good yarn." As Kelly noted, "The problem will be being all things to all people. We want to make the performance as entertaining as we possibly can and try to stick to common ground…what we're hoping to do is at least get people together to communicate about the common issues" (Schaefer 2006b). LMCC encouraged this move not least because it had in its council area three Land Councils (Awabakal, Batabah, and Kompartoo) and four or five established groups of interest, an unusually large number of land councils and interest groups to serve in one local government area. LMCC noted that a large Indigenous population lived in the west lake area, an area managed by Kompartoo Land Council. The west side of the lake was also where the Lake Macquarie City Art Gallery (LMCAG) with its very active Indigenous Reference Group (IRG) was located and the place of Ebenezer, Threlkeld's second mission. Thus the more intensive phase of community consultation was conducted in the main with communities on the west side of the lake. In late October the script was read to the IRG of the LMCAG. The IRG approved the script for public performance and, at the end of the reading, gave their permission to hold the event at "the meeting place" dedicated to an Aboriginal elder in the grounds of the Lake Macquarie Art Gallery. A member of the group also allowed us to use a screen-printed image of an eagle hawk entitled "Biraban—Eaglehawk" for the performance poster and publicity. Finally the researchers attended a meeting of the LMCC ACC and informed the group of the progress that had been made and explained the script and performance concepts. Once the

ACC gave its approval the project moved into its final stage: casting, rehearsal, and public performance.

Ngarrama. Lakeside dialogue between Birabahn, Threlkeld and ... was performed in the gardens of the LMCAG on the western shore of Lake Macquarie on November 12 2006 between 2 and 5pm. The three-hour long event, held at a natural amphitheatre and meeting place dedicated to an Aboriginal elder, included an acknowledgement of country (by Ray Kelly) followed by the performance, structured audience interaction, a barbeque and informal discussion or "yarn time." The entire event was free (including the refreshments). Approximately 200 people, project participants and members of the public, attended the event. The programme notes explained the aim of the event and issued an invitation to people to participate in future events:

> Written and directed by Ray Kelly and Brian Joyce, *Ngarrama* examines the contact history of Lake Macquarie through the encounter between Birabahn and the Rev. Lancelot E. Threlkeld, missionary to the Aboriginal Peoples in Lake Macquarie, 1825-1841. An Awabakal word meaning "to listen and to make known," *Ngarrama* is about the encounter and contact relationship between two people and two cultures in Lake Macquarie, then and now.

> This performance of *Ngarrama* is the first phase of a research project which aims to tell the story of the relationship between Birabahn and Threlkeld. In telling this story we aim to initiate a dialogue between Indigenous and non-Indigenous Australians in Lake Macquarie about our shared history, as a basis for living and working together in the present.

> We hope that the Birabahn/Threlkeld Project will extend into a long-term engagement in cross-cultural dialogue between Indigenous and non-Indigenous Australians in Lake Macquarie. To this end we invite you to participate in the process of developing this work-in-progress performance. (Schaefer 2006c)

As the programme notes indicate the performance consisted of a series of scenes that told the story of Birabahn and Threlkeld and raised a number of questions arising from the research and performance making process. The prologue had Birabahn (played by Rodney Smith) returning to the lake after a long time away in Eora country (Sydney). In the first scene, set on Threlkeld's mission, Birabahn addressed his people (the audience) telling them what he had witnessed in Eora country and explaining what Threlkeld's mission offered. At the heart of the piece were dialogues between Birabahn and Threlkeld (played by Brian Joyce) in which the two men discussed topics ranging from everyday life on the mission to the names and meaning of places (part of the language instruction Threlkeld received from Birabahn) and spiritual principles. While the performance suggested an historical narrative, it unsettled the narrative flow through the insertion of scenes that disrupted the distinction between past and present, pointed to significant gaps in knowledge, and highlighted the dynamic interaction between the archive and the repertoire. For instance, an Aboriginal film/video crew (Ray Kelly Jr., Sarah and Kamara Kelly) arrived in the middle of one of Birabahn and Threlkeld's scenes. After introducing themselves to the bewildered main characters the crew sat on the edge of the amphitheatre between the audience and the performers, a constant reminder of the act of recording, in an attempt to remember after the event, the plenitudinous live performance. Similarly, a scene between two contemporary female characters, one Indigenous, Fay (played by Ursula Yovich), and the other a non-Indigenous researcher, Kathy (played by Leanne Guilhot), reflected the lead role Aboriginal women play and played in community/clan matters (her story) and in determining contemporary research agendas. This strong female presence was carried forward in the performance piece and back in time in terms of the "story." The historical figures of Birabahn and Threlkeld were placed in broader socio-cultural contexts in scenes with female characters: Birabahn with his wife "Patty" and Threlkeld with the researcher, Kathy. This examination of Birabahn and Threlkeld unsettled the men's positions as spokesmen for their respective peoples/cultures. It reinforced what became the project's main problematic: who speaks and for whom?

It is difficult to draw a project that is ongoing (in the form of grant application submissions, further script development and community consultation) to any kind of conclusion. The project did fulfil some of its aims, namely to tell the story of Birabahn and Threlkeld and to explore the possibilities of site-based performance and CCD techniques for developing co-existence between Indigenous and non-Indigenous Australians in Lake Macquarie (although that is another paper). In its first phase the project presented a performance that was well received by project partners, co-researchers (the core team as well as those consulted through the process) and the performance going public. The performance provided the opportunity for "a good yarn," and also succeeded in raising questions of method and problems worthy of further investigation. There is still much to be done, not least the collection of oral histories and the shaping of stories by those who own them into a performance that juxtaposes archival memory and embodied knowledge. As often happens in these kinds of projects, time constraints prevented that work which the project was poised to do. Any subsequent phase of the project would be well placed to undertake that next step and, hopefully, the ground has been laid for the ongoing expansion of the archive and a more nuanced understanding of a place, its peoples, and their relationships over time.

NOTES

[1] I use the term community cultural development because it is an established field of practice in Australia. It has much in common with community-based performance practice in the USA and I use these terms interchangeably.

[2] The formal apology to Indigenous Australians by the Australian Government on February 13 2008 is outside the timeline of this project and discussion.

[3] Altman and Hunter, in a longitudinal study undertaken in the Centre for Aboriginal Economic Policy Research at the Australian National University in Canberra, argue that "there is no statistical evidence that [the Howard government's] policies and programs are delivering better outcomes for Indigenous Australians, at the national level, than those of their political predecessors" (2003: 16). They argue that, in fact, the division of 'practical' and 'symbolic' reconciliation is only worsening deeply entrenched socio-economic inequalities.

[4] *Bringing Them Home*, the Human Rights and Equal Opportunity Commission's report into the separation of Indigenous children from their families, the so-called Stolen Generations, recommended that an apology be made by all Australian parliaments (and police forces and churches) for the laws, policies and practices that led to forced removal. The Howard government resolutely refused to make this apology.

[5] For the full text go to: http://www.abc.net.au/tv/thegames/howard.htm

[6] The three largest local government areas are all within metropolitan Sydney.

[7] In recognition of Birabahn's scholarship, The Wollotuka School of Aboriginal Studies on the Callaghan campus of the University of Newcastle is housed in an architectural and environmental award winning building named after him and designed in the shape of an eagle hawk.

[8] see the work of Arwarbukarl Cultural Resource Association (http://www.acra.org.au/) and Amanda Lissarrague's *A Salvage Grammar and Word List of the Language from the Hunter River and Lake Macquarie* (2006) produced for and published by Muurrbay Aboriginal Language and Culture Co-operative (http://www.muurrbay.org.au/).

⁹ Kelly's people are Dhangatti and Nganiawan from the Mid North Coast of NSW. He currently directs the performance company, *Burrgati [Culture] [Exchange]*. He founded the Awabakal Aboriginal Dance Group in 1980 and is an award-winning playwright: *Get Up and Dance, Somewhere in the Darkness* (the first Aboriginal play to be produced at the Sydney Theatre Company), and *Beyond the Gate*. In 2003 he was Director of the Aboriginal Torres Strait Islander Arts Board of the Australia Council for the Arts. He has been a leading member of various Aboriginal organisations including Awabakal Land Council and Awabakal Aboriginal Co-operative Ltd.

Joyce is Director of Hunter Writer's Centre in Newcastle, NSW. He has extensive experience in theatre, writing and community arts over a period of 30 years. He was a founding member of Pipi Storm in the 1970s, a community and children's theatre group specializing in theatre-in-education in schools, prisons, child welfare institutions, work places, isolated Aboriginal communities and remote communities generally. He was Artistic Director for Freewheels Theatre in Education for 14 years and responsible for the premier production of *Get Up and Dance* by Ray Kelly. He has a long-term involvement with a range of Indigenous theatre projects most notably a committed partnership with Ray Kelly and founding members Ngoroe-kah Indigenous Performance Group. Through the HWC he is exploring his long-standing commitment to new writers and new avenues for developing writing.

REFERENCES

Altman, John and Hunter, Boyd. (2003) "Monitoring Practical reconciliation: Evidence from the Reconciliation Decade, 1991-2001." Discussion paper No.254. *Centre for Aboriginal Economic Policy Research, Australian National University*. <http://www.anu.edu.au/caepr/Publications/DP/2003_DP254.pdf> [Accessed 8 August 2007].

Americans for the Arts. (n.d.) Animating Democracy Initiative. <http://www.AmericansForTheArts.org> [no accession date]. Quoted in Cohen-Cruz, Jan. (2005) *Local Acts: Community-based Performance in The United States*. New Jersey: Rutgers University Press.

Clouten, Keith. (1967) *Reid's Mistake: The Story of Lake Macquarie from its Discovery until 1890*. Lake Macquarie Shire Council.

Cohen-Cruz, Jan. (2005) *Local Acts: Community-based Performance in The United States*. New Jersey: Rutgers University Press.

Gunson, Neil, ed. (1974) "Australian Reminiscences and Papers of L.E. Threlkeld, Missionary to the Aborigines, 1824-1859." (Volumes 1 and 2) *Australian Aboriginal Studies* 40. Ethnohistory Series No. 2. Canberra, A.C.T.: Australian Institute of Aboriginal Studies.

Gunstone, Andrew. (2005) "The Formal Australian Reconciliation Process: 1991-2000." <http://www.reconciliation.org.au/downloads/94/AndrewGunstonePaper.pdf> [Accessed 23 September 2006].

Howard, John. (2000) "Apology Made by John Howard on the 3rd of July on National TV." *The Games.* Australian Broadcasting Corporation. <http://www.abc.net.au/tv/thegames/howard.htm> [Accessed 10 August 2000].

Jenkins, Keith. (2001) *Re-thinking History.* London: Routledge.

Johnston, Anna. (2006) "A blister on the imperial antipodes: Lancelot Edward Threlkeld in Polynesia and Australia" in David Lambert and Alan Lester, eds. *Colonial Lives Across the British Empire: Imperial Careering in the Long Nineteenth Century.* Cambridge: Cambridge University Press.

Kelly, Ray and Joyce, Brian. (2006) *Ngarrama. Lakeside Dialogue between Threlkeld, Birabahn and [...].* Lake Macquarie City Art Gallery (12 November). Lake Macquarie, New South Wales.

Macintyre, Stuart and Clark, Anna. (2003) *The History Wars.* Carlton, Victoria: Melbourne University Press.

Manne, Robert, ed.. (2003) *Whitewash: On Keith Windschuttle's Fabrication of Aboriginal History.* Melbourne: Black Inc.

Pratt, Angela. (2005) "Practicing Reconciliation? The Politics of Reconciliation in the Australian Parliament, 1991-2000." Parliament of Australia: Australian Parliamentary Fellow Monographs. <http://www.aph.gov.au/library/pubs/monographs/pratt/PractisingReconciliation.pdf> [Accessed 1 October 2006]

Reynolds, Henry. (1998) *This Whispering In Our Hearts.* St Leonards, NSW: Allen and Unwin.

Roberts, David, Carey, Hilary and Grieves, Vicki. (2002) "Awaba: A Database of Historical Materials Relating to the Aborigines of the Newcastle-Lake Macquarie Region." University of Newcastle. <http://www.newcastle.edu.au/group/amrhd/awaba/> [Accessed 23 June 2004].

Schaefer, Kerrie. (2005) "Steering Committee meeting notes." Lake Macquarie City Council, 19 December.

——. (2006a) "Steering Committee meeting notes." Lake Macquarie City Council, 16 February.

——. (2006b) "Steering Committee meeting notes." Lake Macquarie City Council, 18 August.

——. (2006c) "Programme Notes." *Ngarrama. Lakeside Dialogue between Threlkeld, Birabahn and [...].* Lake Macquarie City Art Gallery (12 November). Lake Macquarie, New South Wales.

Taylor, Diana. (2003) *The Archive and the Repertoire. Performing Cultural Memory in the Americas.* Durham and London: Duke University Press.

Threlkeld, L.E. (1827) *Specimens of a Dialect of the Aborigines of New South Wales: Being a First Attempt to Form Their Speech Into a Written Language.* Sydney: printed at the "Monitor office" by Arthur Hill.

——. (1834) *An Australian Grammar: Comprehending the Principles and Natural Rules of the Language, as Spoken by the Aborigines, in The Vicinity of Hunter's River, Lake MacQuarie, &c., New South Wales.* Sydney: Stephens and Stokes.

——. (1836) *An Australian Spelling Book, in the Language as Spoken by the Aborigines, in the Vicinity of Hunter's River, Lake Macquarrie, New South Wales*. Sydney: Stephens and Stokes.

——. (1850) *A Key to the Structure of the Aboriginal Language: Being an Analysis of the Particles Used as Affixes, to Form the Various Modifications of the Verbs, Shewing the Essential Powers, Abstract Roots, and Other Peculiarities of the Language Spoken by the Aborigines in the Vicinity of Hunter River, Lake Macquarie, etc., New South Wales, Together with Comparisons of Polynesian and Other Dialects*. Sydney: Kemp and Fairfax.

——., trans. (1891) *The Gospel by St Luke*. Sydney: Charles Potter, Government Printer.

——. (1892) *An Australian Language as Spoken by the Awabakal, the People of Awaba of Lake Macquarie. (near Newcastle, New South Wales): Being an Account of Their Language, Traditions, and Customs*. John Fraser, ed. Sydney: Charles Potter, Government Printer.

Turner, John. (1980) *When Newcastle Was Sydney's Siberia*. Stockton, NSW: Hunter History Publications.

Walsh, Paul, ed. (1997) *Novocastrian Tales*. Newcastle: Elephant Press.

Windschuttle, Keith. (2000) "The Myths of Frontier Massacres in Australian History: Part 3, Massacre Stories and the Policy of Separatism." *Quadrant* 44: 6-20.

NON-NATURALISTIC PERFORMANCE IN POLITICAL NARRATIVE DRAMA: METHODOLOGIES AND LANGUAGES FOR POLITICAL PERFORMANCE WITH REFERENCE TO THE REHEARSAL AND PRODUCTION OF *E TO THE POWER 3—EDUCATION, EDUCATION, EDUCATION*

LLOYD PETERS AND SUE BECKER

The production of *E to the Power 3—Education, Education, Education* (*E3*) was based on six months pre-production research and three months improvisation and rehearsal by a company of six gifted student actors at Salford University and four professional actors. The characterisations were depicted utilising distinctive non-naturalistic performance styles that combined melodrama and *gestus* with slapstick and song. The production premiered at The Robert Powell Theatre, Salford, UK from 25th-27th April 2002 to a wide audience profile of schoolchildren, schoolteachers, students, academics, and other members of the general public.

The narrative concerns the arrival of government inspectors from the Office for Standards in Education (OFSTED) at a failing, urban school. Panic grips the teachers knowing that another poor report could result in the school's closure. We see the preparation for and execution of the visit through the inspectors', the schoolteachers' and the pupils' eyes. One manipulative pupil uses the inspection to bribe a vulnerable teacher to give her a pass mark in maths in return for the promise of good behaviour during the visit. The teacher struggles to resolve the dilemma but in the end decides to reject the bribe resulting in a symbolic act of destruction of the school by the rebellious pupils.

BACKGROUND TO RESEARCH

The Conservative government in 1988, whose preconceptions were that standards of education were generally failing at that time, introduced the policy of statutory school inspection by OFSTED as a political muscle-flexing exercise to placate the marginal constituencies in "Middle England." The policy became refined and extended by the New Labour government in Tony Blair's first administration in 1997. Under the stewardship of hard-line ideologist and Chief Inspector of Schools Chris Woodhead, OFSTED was presented as more rigorous but the inspections were seen as intimidating by teachers and pupils alike.

What became apparent was that OFSTED inspection regimes were components of a political agenda to satisfy party manifesto commitments. The focus on raising standards of literacy and numeracy had produced a flurry of target setting, with key skills testing for all children being introduced from the age of seven onwards. As school and teacher performance became measurable and comparable through the publication of these national test results, pressure to account for why children performed differentially grew. Parental choice in school placement added pressure for schools to account for their performance. OFSTED was seen by many as part of this accounting process, enabling individual practices and regimes to be measured against arbitrary standards.

The rhetoric of inspection located the problems of differential literacy and numeracy rates as an issue of individual schools and teachers rather than as a product of political and socio-economic context. In the same way, New Labour's rhetoric of inclusion located the provision of special needs education as a product of individual difficulties rather than the barriers and boundaries constructed by a disabling society therefore avoiding the need to focus on changing values and ideologies (Armstrong 2005). The net effect of these rhetorical shifts has been to depoliticise education as a social and community issue and strip away the socio-economic context in which schools, teachers and pupils are located and to which they are inextricably linked. Although inspections deliver some important outcomes, specifically, by exposing poor teaching and/or administrative practice, they are also effective in concealing key areas of government and council policy failure, for example the lack of adequate resourcing and the detrimental effect this makes on the learning environment – whether it is staffing, building and/or equipment provision.

These deficiencies have a proportionally greater effect on schools in poorer or disadvantaged areas. Therefore, the outcome for a "failing school" could result in a double handicap - inadequate resourcing *and* public criticism by OFSTED and the media. The resultant decline in staff and student morale exacerbates quality decline and the school enters a spiral of disadvantage and condemnation.

A 1996 BBC "Panorama" television documentary on a "failing school," "The Ridings," in the author's hometown of Halifax – fuelled the debate. This acted as motor for the research of the author who was eager to dramatise the key issues thrown up by the controversies.

Especially relevant to establishing solid, believable characters in the play were the personal views of the pupils, for example, Michelle Foster (Ridings pupil) quoted by the Children's Express in 1998, "It wasn't our story. They had no evidence whether it was the worst school in Britain or not. They just kept using the same headlines over and over again [...]. The press portrayed it like a war zone, like it was really, really bad [...]. 'You won't learn anything'. And it gets to you. At first you're like 'no I'm not [...] but it gets to you'" (Headliners 1998). Dubbed by some sections of the press as Britain's worst school, The Ridings eventually closed in August 2009.

E to the Power 3 - Education, Education, Education (*E3*), devised by Lloyd Peters (in 2002) as a reaction to what he saw as the "moral panic" concerning educational standards in the late nineties, had three key aims: Firstly, the play aimed to examine the political, cultural, and psychological influences that determine definitions of education. The narrative examines current British education policy and, specifically, the arrangements for regulation when an inspection team (OFSTED) descends on an inner-city "failing" school.

The central narrative strand focuses on the moral dilemma faced by an over-stressed teacher who is offered a bribe by a desperate pupil anxious for a pass mark in Mathematics. It was in part inspired by a news story of a senior teacher dismissed for providing exam answers to his pupils. In 2000, other press stories began to emerge of teachers and Head Teachers engaging in illegal acts of massaging figures to either protect their own position OR protect the pupils they saw as being stigmatised.

The fictional pupil of *E3* threatens to disrupt the class during the OFSTED visit if the teacher does not agree to give the student a pass mark, thus endangering the teacher's own ethical position as well as the school's reputation if the bribe is discovered. The teacher's dilemma is at the heart of the drama as she tries anxiously to "do the right thing" by, on the one hand, her disadvantaged students and on the other, her own moral conscience and professional standing. This type of "binary projection of opposite alternatives" (Jameson 2000: 60) is most obviously demonstrated in Brecht's often over-looked, highly abstract, experimental early *Lehrstucke* plays ("Learning Play") such as, for example, *"Der Ja-sager" und "Der Nein-sager."* Brecht assigned these plays as central to his theatre work. *"Der Ja-sager" und "Der Nein-sager"* was first performed as a play for the radio, and broadcast by Radio Berlin in June 1930. The drama presents an injured boy who agrees to his own death in order to follow ritual custom and avoid the failure of the expedition; in the second "version," the boy refuses to be sacrificed and the expedition turns back. These "mirror-plays" present the binary-conflict "for" and "against" and compel the spectator to arrive at their own conclusion.

The second principle aim of the *E3* production was to investigate ways young people engage with political issues through the process of creating political theatre. This is valuable in the context of British general elections where research by Market & Opinion Research International (MORI Social Research Institute) at the time of the 2001 general election suggested that low turnout was particularly pronounced among young people, with an estimated 39% of 18-24 year olds casting a vote. That equates to under five million of eligible young people (18-24 year olds) turning out to vote (21%). By comparison the final of the Channel 4 Reality TV show "Big Brother" regularly attracts over six million young people voters.

The exploration of performer engagement developed to include an investigation of the efficacy of methodologies employed in practice-as-research models. Baz Kershaw's essay on The Iron Ship Project (2002) was instrumental in defining the parameters and ambition of the project. Kershaw states that the practice-as-research was used "as an investigation of spectacle in the performative society" and enabled contributors and spectators to "develop new insights or knowledge about the forms, genres, uses of performance itself, for example with regard to their relevance to broader social and/or cultural processes." (Kershaw 2002: 138). This was invaluable in helping define the "motives of intent" of the project.

Indeed, one of the intended outcomes of the *E3* project was specifically designed to politicise the performers as well as the spectators. In other words, the project aimed to engage and excite young performers in the business of political performance. Existing definitions of political theatre were considered, utilised and developed in the course of *E3*. The authors subscribe to the baseline definition of epic political theatre that is both engaged and engaging, combining "pleasure and instruction [...] that would activate its audiences, stage the movements of history as well as the agents who make it and envision justice as a necessary, not an impossible, task" (Colleran and Spencer 2001: 2). This definition was developed and refined as the production progressed (see Outcomes and Conclusions).

The third aim of the *E3* project was the attempt to develop an appropriate performance style that, firstly, conveyed the central conflict-dilemma clearly but, secondly conveyed excitement, challenge and even shock to the spectator. It was evident that *Verfremdungseffekt* epic performance techniques would serve to compel the audience to examine the evidence – the objects of enquiry – dispassionately and objectively. But in keeping with previous productions Lloyd Peters had devised, (most notably the practice-as-research expressionist dance-video "Now You See Her" (2000-04), physical theatre, ballet, tap dancing, expressionist gesture, slapstick, farce, multi-media, polemical address, stand-up comedy, political commentary and symbolism were also employed in an attempt to create an original, striking non-naturalistic performance style aimed at as wide a target audience as possible.

REHEARSAL PROCESS AND IMPACT ON THE PERFORMER
Experience with large-scale community film projects, (as detailed in Dixon and Peters' 2003 e-article "Big is Beautiful: emphasizing scale in community arts") helped to formulate a rehearsal and performance strategy for devising *E3*. Student and professional actors were auditioned and selected to form a company that contained a vibrant mix of complementary yet varied theatre skills, including singing, dance, movement and physical performance techniques.

Also, techniques that Lloyd Peters had experienced from his work with film and theatre director Mike Leigh (as actor in the BBC film "Home Sweet Home" (1981), and techniques that he employed devising the Community Film Projects, were also adapted for the rehearsals of *E3*. The most useful Leigh technique was to encourage the performers to develop a "running condition" for each character—a series of traits, mannerisms, and gestures linked to psychological preoccupations and obsessions.

Given these eclectic stylistic techniques, there was one important principle that needed to be enshrined before rehearsals commenced on the *E3* Project. The cast and crew were made aware that we were embarking on a political project, where content—specifically the government's education policy—was to be the central focus and that style shall not dictate content. In other words, we wanted to attack the very essence of what we saw as the prevalence of much contemporary "post-modernist" theatre that concerned itself more with aesthetic elegance than the presentation of radical ideas. To this end, we were guided by Terry Eagleton's statement—that: "it would be a good deal worse than dishonest" than "to relinquish the vision of a just society and so to acquiesce in the appalling mess which is the contemporary world" (Eagleton 2005: ix).

We asserted to the *E3* participants that political theatre can have no engagement with a "State of Being" that obfuscates, and blurs the bounds between justice and injustice, morality and immorality, that celebrates style over content. Political theatre needs to be clear, outspoken, and principled. Not old post-modern—but newly radical. As Alan Sokal and Jean Bricmont state in the introduction to their ground-breaking demolition of post-modern philosophers (Lacan, Latour, Baudrillard, and others) in their book "Intellectual Imposters": that if French philosophers' texts "seem incomprehensible, it is for the excellent reason that they mean precisely nothing" (Sokal and Bricmont 1998: 5).

Lloyd Peters reinforced the notion proposed by Colleran and Spencer (2001) that *E3* should present "a cultural practice that self-consciously operates at the level of interrogation, critique, and intervention, unable to stand outside the very institutions and attitudes it seeks to change" (Colleran and Spencer 2001: 1).

It was agreed before rehearsals began that experimentation with a range of non-naturalistic performance techniques would be explored. Brecht and Piscator's epic theatre ideas and methodologies were developed and modified, merging practice Lloyd Peters had developed from his research into German Expressionist film, most notably: "The Cabinet of Dr. Caligari" (1919), "Nosferatu" (1922), "Metropolis" (1926), "Pandora's Box" (1928), and "M" (1931). The distortion of the everyday, frenzied gestures, gargantuan laughter, grotesque body posture, even the "slight hesitation between cues to avoid naturalistic dialogue" (Eisner 1973: 141) informed the techniques employed in the directing of the company.

Brechtian influences that crucially informed performance style was the use of the third person when a character referred to him/herself. This was a deliberate "alienation effect" designed to estrange the actions and remarks of the characters being portrayed. The other "borrowed" technique was the extreme heightened use of *gestus*. Much debate exists on precise definitions of the term but, in rehearsal, we employed Brecht's favourite: "He (a Chinese player) developed a manner of speaking and using language which was stylised and natural all at once. He achieved the combination by paying attention to the stances that underlay the sentences: only turning stances into sentences, only writing those sentences through which stances could show through. He called this a *gestisch* or gestural language, as it was simply an expression of human gestures. You can read these sentences best by completing those specific physical movements that correspond to them" (Brecht quoted in Jameson 2000: 100).

However, it must be stressed that although the *E3* project utilised many Brechtian rehearsal and performance techniques, the production was not a Brechtian purist's charter. Indeed Augusto Boal's "Games for Actors and Non-Actors" (1992) was more of an inspiration for developing ritualistic gesture and physicalisation. In rehearsal, Lloyd Peters scored performances according to a 1 to 10 scale where 1 was overtly naturalistic and 10 was over-heightened stylisation. The most common direction he was heard to shout was "That's a 5, Give me a 10."

It is an essential requirement of the devised theatre process that the performers are compelled to immerse themselves in all aspects of the subject matter, so choices selected in improvisations and rehearsals are informed and contextualised. Consequently, each night, the *E3* performers were given general subject "homework" (for example, investigating science curricula requirements) and specific role study exercises (for example, writing biographies of their character). The performers were required to bring all this large quantity of appropriate research material to the workshops and improvisations that shaped the draft script. The *E3* project demanded awareness of not only British education policy, but the national and school curriculum and the individual subjects they were assigned to teach in the play. Most of the cast visited inner-city schools and actually taught classes shaping their relationship to the character's psychological "running condition" in quite profound ways – their experience of coping with a classroom of thirty disaffected schoolchildren was not only sobering, but as a scene, became the basis of the play's climax.

More than any other media form, it is argued that theatre by the nature of the audience experience has the potential to both to challenge, inform, and transform. Uniquely the theatrical experience is a holistic experience for the devising performer (as well as the audience), where the vicarious experience works on a number of cognitive levels.

As Arnold argues "theatre is to be construed neither as a pre-eminently visual, nor auditory, nor literary phenomenon, but as a perceptually induced mimetic phenomenon of participation – an imagined experience of total activity" (1991: 26) and therefore uniquely placed to challenge the political status quo and effect both intellectual and emotional engagement with the political process.

It was crucial, therefore, to introduce the company to some of the established principles of political non-naturalistic theatre and re-examine their efficacy in relation to the *E3* project.

For example, the basic principles that Brecht first laid out in his programme notes for his operatic satire "The Rise and Fall of the City of Mahagonny" (1930) that tabulated the contrasting characteristics of dramatic theatre (naturalistic) and epic theatre were discussed and modified. Key amongst these principles was Brecht's assertion that epic theatre presents scenarios where the performer's character (and by extension the spectator) is forced to face something through argument and both are brought to a point of recognition. These key signposts often directed the *E3* improvisations towards a conclusion that aroused the character's capacity for action and forced him/her to take decisions.

Paradoxically, the large amount of detailed research the performers undertook was equivalent to the weight of work expected from the Stanislavskian-inspired Method actor in their search for naturalistic truth. In *E3*, the actors' research suggested the key narrative, polemic monologues, jokes, poems, visual effects, dance routines, and music.

There were other lessons for the *E3* Project the company needed to take on board from, for example, the *Lehrstucke* plays. Importantly, the rotation of the actors through various roles created a multi-dimensionary ensemble company. All the students played teachers and pupils. This practice reinforced the notion of ensembled individualism (Sampson 1988) in the production and created a coherent company philosophy.

SHAPING THE SCRIPT

The draft script was shaped by Lloyd Peters following an exhaustive process of viewing all the recorded improvisations, formalising the areas of interest, and script editing the essential narrative and character drivers. He was aware that despite all the substantial material researched and improvised, the narrative needed to be clearly constructed so as to yield the essential narrative conflict – namely, the presentation of the teacher's dilemma for the character (and the audience) to resolve. Would she accept the bribe offered by the manipulative pupil?

The political argument "for" and "against" needed to be finely and fairly balanced. In an education system that is so skewed against the poor and under-privileged why shouldn't the pupil play the system; and in a system that is so skewed against the poor and under-privileged why shouldn't the concerned teacher help the disadvantaged pupil? There were echoes of Mother Courage here, selling arms to both sides to feed her children—in a bourgeois system not of her making, needs must.

But on the other side of the argument, compromising professional and ethical integrity is corrosively corrupt and provides a cynical model for those the teacher is employed to provide moral guidance. There is an interesting duality here that mirrored deliberately the dilemmas presented in the *Lehrstucke* plays and which, commenting on one such play: *"Die Massnahme" (1930)*, Frederick Jameson describes as "the dramatization of the dialectic" (Jameson 2000: 63).

Many Brecht plays represent, on the one hand, a polemic against an individualism born of a bourgeois culture and, then on the other, focus on the characters "centred" and informed analysis to deconstruct the dilemmas presented. It was no accident that we (the performer playing Valerie, the vulnerable teacher and Lloyd Peters) constructed Valerie's back-story to be one of intelligence, high morals, and privilege.

As Jameson states: "dualism in Brechtian theatrical practice is that of a simple affirmation or denial. This is the most obvious space of Brechtian freedom, since in it a single gesture aims to project not only what will shortly have been done—that is to say, what is being done in front of us—but what might just as well not have been done, what might have been something else altogether, or simply have been omitted" (Jameson 2000: 58).

It was this constructed dualism that informed, but did not constrict, the structural shape of the final *E3* script. To illustrate this duality and the ways that the *E3* company developed archetypal Brechtian performance models, we reproduce below the pivotal scene where Valerie presented the binary dissonance that she, and the audience, needed to confront and resolve. The performer (Sarah Mills) delivered the prose-verse in the (characteristically Brechtian) third person while performing an (un-characteristically Brechtian) choreographed dance sequence comprising of tap and balletic elements. This was intended to complement and, simultaneously, heighten the anguish of the character's dilemma. In other words, the dance acted as an additional layer of *gestus* – a stylised metaphor to reinforce the dialectical conflict. This (non-purist) synthesis of Brechtian methodologies with dance, movement, and physical theatre skills created a dynamic non-naturalistic performance fusion – in itself a duality of binary style.

SCENE 26:ALBION HIGH SCHOOL
NARRATOR:
Valerie Linneker wrestles with her conscience.
VALERIE LINNEKER:
Normally she'd go straight to the Headmaster.
But Valerie doesn't trust him.
Besides, it would get Jodie into trouble.
And she's just a frightened little girl
Who's desperate.
Fear makes you do some terrible things.

So why not help Jodie
When the odds are so stacked against her?
A poor girl from a sink estate
In the bottom set
In a school with too few books
And half a roof.
Is it such a terrible crime
To amend the spreadsheet?
B instead of F.
Worse mistakes happen all the time.
And in return?
The promise of
Tranquillity
Co-operation.
A lesson of joy
Like those at Oxford
In leafy cloisters
Over ten years ago.
And the Inspector
Would reward Miss Linneker
With a B and not an F.
And she would carry on
With the job she loves
Even though she knows
In her heart of hearts –
That the game is up.
LIGHTS DOWN
(Peters 2002)

In the same way that later Brechtian plays moved away from the *Lehrstucke* model of simply proposing a dilemma of equal opposites, so the climactic scenes of *E3* presented a resolution to the quandary Valerie outlined above. In the final scene of *E3*, the consequences of action – Valerie rejecting the bribe—were depicted through the violent revolt of the disadvantaged pupils who symbolically destroyed the school and turned on the educators who had failed them.

We had come full circle as, in true Brechtian style, the audience were left with the "images of judgement" (Jameson 2000: 119) and, hopefully, a sense that imperfect norms could not be reaffirmed but justly challenged through radical activity.

OUTCOMES AND CONCLUSIONS

It is only now that we can calmly reflect on the conclusions of the *E3* project—some six years after the event. To be truthful, audience reaction was mixed. Most spectators who provided feedback felt the piece too polemical. One audience member commented that it was "too in your face." Is this a sign that people are so disconnected from political issues?

Also, whilst there was a great deal of admiration for the multi-media presentation, and the technical virtuosity of the performers, many could not adjust to the heightened performance style. Has naturalism such a total monopoly on spectator's expectations and imagination?

One possible explanation is the parallel between the move to naturalism in theatre and the realist empiricist discourse which has come to dominate developmental psychology. This pervasive realist discourse has sought to strip developmental psychology of its political and socio-economic context. The rhetoric of experimentation and statistical significance has claimed to provide the essential truth of development, free of ideology and political ascription.

The effect of this has been to simply obscure the ideology realist psychology maintains. Its conventions maintain the status quo and contemporary political and socio-economic contexts which support it (Cushman 1991). Similarly naturalism maintains the political status quo, obscuring the hegemony of commodity-fetishism which Cushman (1991) argues is the drug which placate the angst of the "empty-self" produced by a political and socio-economic context which individualises and isolates its members.

Non-naturalistic political performance challenges this status quo and the discomfort which this can affect in audience members may be ameliorated through the process of cognitive dissonance in which the challenging concepts are dealt with by a focus on other more easily criticised performative elements. That the performative style rather than the content of the performance provided the focus for negative post-production evaluations may indicate that the messenger rather the message is easier to shoot down in metaphorical flames.

In discursive terms, by accounting for dissatisfaction in terms of unfamiliar performance styles rather than the political message contained in the performance enables the audience to avoid potential accusations of supporting an unpopular or weak political position.

However there was a great deal of positive feedback also. The fact thirty schoolchildren were integrated into the narrative was applauded as the successful culmination of an ambitious cross-institution collaborative event.

A number of spectators—especially teachers it has to be said—who saw their life experiences presented on the stage were grateful that the crucial issues of teacher stress, standards inspection and pupil testing were raised so publicly. (The production was featured in a BBC Radio Manchester feature).

The aims of the *E3* project outlined at the beginning of the article, namely 1) to examine the determinants that define education, 2) to investigate young people's engagement with political theatre, and 3) to develop an appropriate performance style were, in large part, accomplished successfully. Through the rehearsal, production and performance process we were able to formulate highly original effective practice-as-research methodologies and consequently propose newly composed definitions of political theatre templates.

For example, we suggest an amendment to Colleran and Spencer's (2001) definition of political theatre, which should strive to be a theatre that is both "engaged and engaging" combining "pleasure and instruction" that activates its audience, stages movements of history *and*, we would add, *"examines and critiques contemporary government policy"* (our emphases). Many political theatre practitioners would shrink from subscribing something so specific, local or contemporary—rather favouring "The Grand Vision" or The Internationalist approach. Our belief, confirmed by the *E3* experience, is that "the contemporary" is essential to motivate research—and as Education, Education, Education was top of Tony Blair's political agenda, we felt that it needed to be top of ours—especially as it provided young performers an immediate connection.

The six student performers had all recently been though the education system and were still involved in higher education—they all had a story to tell. This helped to establish an ethos of reflexivity and reflexive practice as one of the core values of the production process.

Whilst reflexivity has a long history as part of the performance process, the concept of reflective practice as part of the production process is less well documented. Political performance by its nature seeks to go beyond entertainment to effect engagement with issues and normative values, in order to achieve these ends performances and performers need to engage with their own ideological foundations, to challenge and reflect on their own motivations and intents. In order to effect audience engagement it is not the suspension of disbelief in the performance but rather the active belief of performers and the performance to engage in a community of change and challenge which should be evidenced in the production. Having experienced the education system and ethos of target setting and inspections, student performers were able to utilise and reflect on their own experiences and those of their peers to add layers of experiential reflection to their performances.

The western model of the self as individual and bounded by the physicality of the flesh can provide a cultural barrier to effective political and community engagement. To achieve the key aim of politicising the performers, *E3* utilised a model of "ensembled individualism" (Sampson 1988) innate to non- western cultures where notions of the self are embedded in community identity and linguistic dissociations of the "self" as a unitary phenomenon are not available, so for example it is not possible to describe oneself as "I" in the Japanese language; rather individuals formulate their identities in terms of social relationships as in "I the daughter/son of . . ." (Harre 1997: 160).

This notion of the distributed self works to foster community cohesion and breaks down barriers between notions of individual and societal good, in contrast western individualist constructions of the self work to confirm boundaries and isolate the individual from notions of communal and social responsibilities and obligations. In effect this works to depoliticise western societies one member at a time through the process of socialisation and language development.

In order to work to counter the hegemony of the individualistic notion of the self in the audience, work had to begin in the members of the production themselves. In effect in order for performers to engage in political performance it necessary to begin with a bottom up process of reflective practice to re-engage with the notion of selfhood as a social construct and one not bounded by physicality and self aggrandisement. The practical production and performance techniques which enabled this have already been discussed. The intended outcome of this focus on "ensembled individualism" was to dissolve the boundaries between the performers both with their own community of practice, i.e. the production and the wider local community from which the eventual audience would come and which the production aimed to engage. Direct exposure to the inner city schools of Salford did indeed engage the performer and changed hearts and minds. Whether it was as successful at engaging with the audiences we played before is, admittedly, not so certain. But one of the major aims was to engage and excite young performers in the business of Politics and this was certainly realised.

As a result of the performances, a number of conclusions occur to us now about the nature of political theatre: There must be INTENTION—aesthetics should not swamp the resolve to SAY something important and by that we mean, it should contain content of contemporary relevance. It should also provide a platform that offers a voice for the dispossessed, the disenfranchised, the victim of injustice. Political theatre should always strive to promote an authentic democracy for the "working class" – a Marxist term that has become outmoded even in class-ridden Britain. If the term appears outdated let us agree that in our society, there are those who have and those who have not – the latter still represent the vast majority of people in Britain and it is with this group that political theatre should strive to engage and seek alliance.

An alternative outcome for political performance may be to engage in the process of "deliberative democracy" (Pellizzoni 2001). Deliberative democracy has been viewed as a counterpoint to traditional and elitist models of the democratic process in which the external power of language and force of argument has been criticised as reinforcing elitism by which those elements of the "community" whose arguments are deemed to be less eloquent or literate are effectively disenfranchised from political debate and in which effective participation is replaced by the hegemony of "expert groups" and increased bureaucracy (Pellizzoni 2001).

The process of deliberative democracy takes the position that all positions and arguments should be considered and avoids engaging in either a top down approach in which "experts" educate those less able to articulate their positions or a bottom up approach in which "lay experts" are "educated and informed" in order to be enabled to take part in effective political dialogue. The endpoint of a process of deliberative democracy is to produce a community of practice in which the boundaries between expert and lay person; orator and audience are redefined and issues become jointly managed through a recognition of discrete competencies. The model of deliberative democracy appears to dovetail discretely with the aims of community arts engagement, the aim of which is to mobilise and solidify the community transforming membership into a practice rather than an experiential phenomenon (Adkins, 2000).

Political theatre then aims to re-politicise individuals and embed this in a collectivist sense of identity in which local issues and barriers become contextualised in the broader political and socio-economic contexts which inform and shape them and which traditional forms of democratic participation often serve to obfuscate and locate as issues of individual responsibility rather than collective action.

In conclusion, we find we are generally in accord with John McGrath—founder of Socialist Theatre Company 7:84 ("7% of the population own 84% of the Wealth")—who in his book "Naked thoughts that roam about—Reflections on Theatre" (2002) lists the attributes that a concerned political company should possess and that an audience demands. It is no coincidence that many featured in epic theatre philosophy and most were proven to be effective during the *E3* production, especially McGrath's call for, "Immediacy," Subject matter should be "much closer to the audience's lives and experiences than, say, plays at the Royal Shakespeare Company are to their middle-class audiences" (2002: 125). He maintains that audiences respond best if they have "a sense of identity" with the material and a "Localism […] the best response among working-class audiences comes from characters and events with a local feel" (2002: 126). However, it needs to be said that McGrath's desire for directness and polemic address, by speaking straight to the audience—"they like to hear what your mind is" (2002: 123)—was less successfully received by the *E3* spectators.

We sense that there is a new impetus to develop a political theatre in Britain. The challenge is to create a grass-roots theatre that truly reflects the issues that matter or as McGrath puts it, to demand:

> [A] sharp, satirical theatre to scrutinise our values, to contest the borders of our democracy, to give voice to the excluded, to the minorities, to guard against the tyranny of the majority, to criticise without fear, to seek true and multifaceted information, to combat the distorting power of the mass media, to define and re-define freedom for our age, to demand the equality of all citizens for the short time we have on this earth before we die. (2002: 239)

REFERENCES

Adkins, Jackie. (2000) *Contact Connection, a National Newsletter About Contact Improvisation* 19, 1. Quoted in: Bryan, Cordelia and Debbie Green. (2002) "How Guided Reflective Practice Can Enhance Group Work in the Performing and Creative Arts." Abstract for Symposium Oxford Centre for Staff and Learning Development: *Improving Student Learning Theory and Practice—10 years on.*

Armstrong, Derrick. (2005) "Reinventing 'Inclusion:' New Labour and the Cultural Politics of Special Education." *Oxford Review of Education* 31 (1), 135-151.

Arnold, Nicholas. (1991) "The Manipulation of the Audience by Director and Actor." in Glenn Daniel Wilson, ed. *Psychology and the Performing Arts.* Amsterdam: Swets & Zeitlinger.

Boal, Augusto. (1992) *Games for Actors and Non-actors.* London: Routledge.

Brecht, Bertolt. John Willet and Ralph Manheim, eds. (1994) *Collected plays 2* London: Methuen Drama.

Brecht, Bertolt. (1976) *The Rise and Fall of the City of Mahagonny.* Toronto: Oxford University Press.

Colleran, Jeanne and Jenny S. Spencer. (2001) *Staging Resistance.* Michigan: University of Michigan Press.

Cushman, Phillip. (1991) "Ideology Obscured: Political Uses of the Self in Daniel Stern's Infant." *American Psychologist* 46 (3), 206-13.

Dixon, Steve and Lloyd Peters,. (2003): "Big is Beautiful: Emphasizing Scale in Community Arts." *Studies in Theatre and Performance* 23 (3), 150.

Eagleton, Terry. (1996) *The Illusions of Postmodernism.* London: Blackwell Publishing.

Eisner, Lotte H. (1973) *The Haunted Screen.* London: Secker and Warburg.

Headliners. (1998) "Would you put Ridings on your CV?" <http://www.headliners.org/storylibrary/stories/1998/wouldyouputridingson yourcv.htm> [Accessed 1 December 2008].

Harré, Rom. (1997) *The Singular Self: An Introduction to the Psychology of Personhood.* London: Sage.

Kershaw, Baz. (2002) "Performance, Memory, Heritage, History, Spectacle: The Iron Ship." *Studies in Theatre and Performance* 21. (3), 138-139.

Jameson, Frederic. (2000) *Brecht and Method.* London: Verso.

McGrath, John. (2002) *Naked Thoughts That Roam About: Reflections on Theatre, 1958-2001.* London: Nick Hearn Books.

Pellizzoni, Luigi. (2001*)* "The Myth of Best Argument: Power, Deliberation and Reason." *British Journal of Sociology* 52 (1), 56-86.

Peters, Lloyd. (2002) *E to the Power 3: Education, Education, Education.* The Robert Powell Theatre (25 April—27 April). Salford, UK.

Phillips, Robert and John Furlong, eds. (2001) *Education, Reform and the State: Twenty-Five Years of Politics, Policy and Practice.* London: Routledge-Falmer.

Richard, Lionel. (1984) *The Concise Encyclopaedia of Expressionism.* Hertfordshire: Omega.

Sampson, E. E.. (1988) "The debate on individualism: Indigenous psychologies of the individual and their role in personal and societal functioning." *American Psychologist,* 43, 15-22.

Sokal, Alan and Jean Bricmont. (1998) *Intellectual Imposters.* London: Profile Books.

Styan, J. L. (1981) *Modern Drama in Theory and Practice: Volume 3, Expressionism and Epic Theatre.* Cambridge: Cambridge University Press.

GAY MUSLIMS AND SALTY MEAT PIES:
THE LIMITS OF PERFORMING COMMUNITY

SONJA ARSHAM KUFTINEC

In *Utopia in Performance* (2005) Jill Dolan writes eloquently about performative utopias—moments in which a theatrical production both imagines and manifests hope via the sociality of public engagement. Dolan's proposition resonates with some of my experience in the theatre—those mythic moments that animate and elaborate the conditions for collective action and progressive social transformation. What I'd like to detail here, however, are some of the limits of performance, particularly community-based performance. I do so not to negate moments of hope, but to discern when and how community-based performance might allow for productive dissent—ruptures that make systems of difference and exclusion visible but also potentially allow for their renegotiation. This renegotiation occurs within what Chantal Mouffe refers to as democratic or pluralistic "agonism," productive struggles around difference as opposed to consensus that elides dissent or polarization that prevents engagement.[1]

In several articles and a book, it has been my contention that the process of community-based theatre-making animates the complexity of community as something more than a homogenous site of shared heritage and values.[2] Also, that focusing attention only on the production itself can elide the more fascinating movements in the process that wrestle with difference and ambiguity. Since 1986 Cornerstone Theatre has grappled with how to honour the communities with which they work—defined variously by location, age, culture, belief, and labour—without erasing differences within that community. This negotiation becomes more fraught when the company produces "bridge shows" that bring together participants from several distinct communities as well as when the company collaborates with regional theatres that do not necessarily see theatre-making as a process of exchange between community members and "professional artists."

I'd like to concretize this investigation of productive dissent by introducing two community participants in recent Cornerstone productions. First, Ramy Eletreby reflects on his experience as a gay Muslim performing in a bridge show that brought together eight distinct communities of faith. He notes, "It was the first time such a sensitive and personal issue [as 'homosexuality'] had been discussed so openly with members of the Muslim community" (TCG 2005). I am particularly struck here, not only by the tensions between "gay" and "Muslim," but also by how Eletreby's comment foregrounds the negotiation of a private "personal issue" in an "open" public space. This interpenetration of private and public, of what is conventionally concealed coming into view, marks a radical double movement of an embodied sentiment. Eletreby shared his views after Cornerstone's production had closed, at a Theatre Communications Group National conference in 2005. Speaking on a panel alongside other Muslims who had left the bridge show because of its representation of homosexuality and Islam, Eletreby staged the possibility of his presence within the Muslim community. As I elaborate below, his enunciation both occurs in and reshapes the public sphere.

The second voice emerges from a letter written by a community performer after a first reading of *The Falls*, a play representing stories and individuals from six neighbourhoods close to the new Guthrie Theatre in Minneapolis. A congregant of a local church, cast in the first staged reading of *The Falls*, wrote the letter to playwright Jeffrey Hatcher and former Cornerstone Artistic Director Bill Rauch, and copied it to approximately fifty others including civic leaders and officiates in the local Catholic diocese. The congregant asserted that she planned to "resign" from the play for what she cited (in capital letters) as "MORAL REASONS." She added that she would do all she could to prevent audience members from attending the play, to remove any references to her congregation from the play, and to ensure that the play would not be produced at all. Though the order of events seems skewed, the intention is clear.

In contrast to Eletreby's publicly spoken statement that staged the negotiation of difference *within* a faith community, this written expression of dissent suggests a conflict between the lived experience of faith and its theatrical representation. Among the reasons cited for the author's response was the script's focus on the amount of salt included in meat pies prepared by the churchgoers, a scenario that the author felt mocked and trivialized the activities of her faith. She thus performs a speech act of resignation and threatens to shut down the production (and any further dialogue), because she feels that her Catholic self-definition and the faith itself have been threatened through its theatrical representation. It is an act designed to prevent discourse in a public theatrical space. The nature of the second communication—a "private" letter copied to leaders in a faith community—also points towards polarizing ruptures that the communicant experienced, as opposed to the more agonistic expressions of dissent featured in the TCG panel.

By highlighting these two voices, and attending to the difference in their modes of enunciation and dissent, I am hoping to foreground several proposals about how community-based theatre-making operates as public forum. I concur with many scholars who assert that community-based performances animate narratives of self and community, engaging in what Barbara Myerhoff has termed "definitional ceremonies," in which marginalized individuals appear before others to profess their own self-interpretations (1980: 185-90). At the same time, the process can productively foreground a more Foucauldian understanding of the subject as an unstable effect of discourse. This destabilization occurs when narratives of self or group encounter conflicting definitions and representation. These moments of productive dissent mark the limits of community-based performance in serving not only as public space, but as public sphere, determining how we relate to and shape each other ideologically as well as socially.

In order to explore these proposals I discuss three Cornerstone performance events. I first focus on the possibilities of civic dialogue in two collaborations with communities of faith: *You Can't Take it With You: An American Muslim Remix* (2003) and the faith-based bridge show, *A Long Bridge Over Deep Waters* (2005). I then comment on *The Falls* (2006), which inaugurated the laboratory space in the Guthrie Theatre's new multi-million dollar building.

As with many of their projects, Cornerstone's faith-based cycle emerged from a desire to explore community inclusion and exclusion. Cornerstone initiated the cycle in partnership with the Ford Foundation's Animating Democracy Initiative, which supported projects designed to promote public conversation through the arts. Focused more on producing theatre than dialogue, the Guthrie/Cornerstone collaboration also animated and negotiated difference, but these negotiations mostly remained outside of the project's intent. To further explore what could be learned about the dialogue through community-based theatre it is useful to briefly examine the notion of public sphere as described by Jürgen Habermas and his interlocutors.

In *The Structural Transformation of the Public Sphere* (1989), Habermas defines the public sphere as a virtual or actual space of discourse located between the private realm of domestic life and work (where individuals often un-reflexively practice beliefs and behaviours and enact faith and sexuality) and the arena of state power (where this individual behaviour is often regulated). The principles of the public sphere involve an open discussion within an ideal speech situation where all parties have the opportunity to freely speak and bear witness to each other. Habermas has been criticized by Nancy Fraser (1992) and Michael Warner (2003), among others, for initially downplaying how cultural institutions and practices shape public discourse, and for seeming to ignore the multiplicity of public spheres, or counterpublics existing outside of the dominant sphere. These counterpublics—which can range from transvestites, to tattooed downtown hipsters, to polygamous Mormons—define themselves, in part, by virtue of their distinction from the norm. Yet, despite the critiques of public sphere theory and the clear presence of counterpublics, the critical-rational model of individuals engaging in free dialogue and debate still underlies dominant thinking about democratic practices and social movement theory. There's a sense that all that's required for coalition-building in civil society is consciousness and space.

In a *Christian Science Monitor* article referencing Cornerstone's faith-based cycle, inter-denominational minister Robert Franklin notes, "We've demonstrated [since Sept. 11] that we can work together, that we can collaborate. Groups that didn't know each other in the past are now going to regard each other as colleagues if not friends" (quoted in Terry 2001). In a more local California paper, *The Daily Breeze,* an article focusing on Cornerstone's bridge show reiterates the myth of free assembly as an aspect of American exceptionalism. "What could be considered miraculous by other countries frequently is taken for granted in America. Everyday people representing practically every spiritual belief coexist peacefully. Christians and Muslims brave traffic jams together. Buddhists and atheists ride the subway. No matter what their faith—everyone stands in line at the post office" (Favre 2005). These principles of free assembly (as long as people are locked in their cars or buying stamps) and rational discourse also seem to guide the Animating Democracy Initiative's desire to enhance arts-based civic dialogue, all of which undergirded Cornerstone's faith-based project.

The four-and-a-half year-long faith-based cycle certainly emphasized free assembly. The program brought together individuals from diverse religious groups including Jewish Angelenos, Catholic immigrants, Black Baptists, diasporic Hindus, Buddhists, Muslims, Iranian Baha'i, and GLBT people of faith. Each group performed in its own original or adapted production then came together for the bridge show. Over fifty-three community partners included The Center for Jewish Culture and Creativity, Holy Name of Jesus Catholic Church, International Society for Krishna Consciousness,

Figure 1. *Body of Faith* (2003), Cornerstone's collaboration with GLBT members of faith. The photo features Leslie Sloan, Ruben Marquez, Adina Porter, and Pierre L. Chambers. Photograph by Craig Schwartz, courtesy of Cornerstone Theater Company.

and People of Leather Among You. Clearly there was room for expressed difference as well as connection, and Cornerstone entered into the project guided by the core question "How does faith unite *and* divide us?" (emphasis mine). Working with the National Conference for Community and Justice, which specializes in interfaith dialogue, the company structured the faith-based cycle to engage this question. NCCJ worked with Cornerstone to develop dialogue sessions— Weekly Wednesday meetings on topics of faith that allowed for the "reasoned exchange of ideas."

The principle that bringing reasoned individuals together into a public space for arts-prompted dialogue guided all aspects of the faith-based cycle. As did the principle that performance conjures definitional ceremonies for others to bear witness to. Yet, definition necessarily includes an expression of distinction—a proposition in tension with the secular humanist principles underlying ADI and classical public sphere theory. In speaking about their collaboration, Cornerstone members emphasize the process of encountering other cultures. Ensemble member Shishir Kurup attests, "In the work we do at Cornerstone, you learn the specifics of a culture in ways that you could never get—even from reading a book. It's incredibly powerful. It allows you to have a semi-membership in a community" (quoted in Henderson 2004: 38). But in the past several years, the company has experienced the limitations of difference experienced at the moment when core identities come into direct conflict with each other.

Six years prior to the faith-based bridge show Cornerstone's ensemble had faced another dilemma of difference. An African American Christian woman working for the company confessed to Artistic Director Bill Rauch that she believed he and his male partner were eternally damned. The company had to confront their principles of diversity and inclusion asking, "What happens when [individuals'] core values are in direct contradiction with one another? What happens when tolerance leads to a betrayal of one's own beliefs?" (quoted in Atlas).

This revelatory question would come as no surprise to cultural critic Stanley Fish. In "Boutique Multiculturalism" Fish argues that tolerance and difference are mutually exclusive. Multiculturalism stops short of approving other cultures at a point where some value at their centre offends against a deeper humanist "we're all the same at our core" principle. Even those who Fish terms "strong multiculturalists" fall prey to the limitations of tolerance. "The trouble with stipulating tolerance as your first principle," Fish argues, "is that you cannot possibly be faithful to it because sooner or later the culture whose core values you are tolerating will reveal itself to be intolerant at that same core" (Fish 1997: 382-3). Or as Cornerstone puts it, "What happens when tolerance leads to a betrayal of one's own beliefs?" This question and Fish's conundrum challenge principles of civic dialogue dependent upon a belief in what Habermas and other Liberal philosophers term rational individuals. Public sphere principles are ultimately a secular humanist philosophy that relies upon the belief that religion, ethnicity, and cultural practices are surface attributes laid atop a common humanity. This belief is perhaps best articulated by Ibrahim Saba, discussing his experience performing in *A Long Bridge over Deep Waters*. "[The production] accentuated something I'd been trying to articulate to myself—seeing each other as whole human race, not seeing just class, race, religion or sexual orientation. First you're human, then other aspects are secondary or tertiary" (quoted in Freya 2006: 12).

This proposition may seem self-evident. But for individuals who have a deep commitment to faith, their humanity is not *prior to* and *separate from* but *defined by* their religious beliefs and practices. Tolerance is limited to that which does not threaten those core beliefs and principles. This tension between the assumptions underlining the Animating Democracy Initiative and the need for a community to define its difference via definitional ceremony may help to explain Cornerstone's negotiations with the Islamic community in producing a play that both valued Islamic culture and attempted to present an alternative, consumable image of that culture to a community of insiders and outsiders—a play that provided both definitional ceremony and cross-cultural ethnographic encounter, even without allusion to gay Muslims.

In conversations and story circles with the Islamic community of Los Angeles, Cornerstone heard repeated requests for a representation that would situate American Muslims as tolerable to the mainstream, to "tell the untold story" of their culture as something other than "*hijabs* and hijackers" (Valdez quoted in TCG 2005). After September 11th in particular, Muslims felt increasingly isolated and misunderstood. According to Peter Howard, when asked how they wanted to be represented they unanimously responded, "do a comedy

Figure 2. *You Can't Take It With You: A Muslim American Remix* (2003) featuring Albena Dodeva and Ibrahim Saba. Photograph by Craig Schwartz, courtesy of Cornerstone Theater Company.

[…] we want people to see that we are regular Americans, like everyone else." Yet, the desire to appear "like everyone else" (or at least like "regular Americans") proved to be in tension with the need to embody the specificity of Islamic culture. Through the process of producing an "American Muslim remix" of Kauffman and Hart's *You Can't Take it With You*, these tensions played out in numerous public and private arenas. Peter Howard's powerful and poetic "remix" encountered intriguing challenges in its attempt to amalgamate Islamic culture with mid-twentieth century American romantic comedy. Lead community actress, Sondos Kholoki-Kahf, explains, "There were a number of scenes with my love interest that involved touching and flirting. First of all, in [Islam] there's no such thing as dating […] [And] as a Muslim woman, I couldn't have Amir Hussain (the actor playing her father) come over and hug me […] If the guy is not my real dad." (quoted in Henderson 2004: 37.)

In the process of public representation, private cultural codes—the unconscious habitus of embodied behaviours—became more visible. Somewhat paradoxically, cross-cultural negotiation becomes more possible. Director Mark Valdez observed that he needed to confront his own prejudices about Kholoki-Kahf's inability to touch or dance with someone not her husband. At the same time, while certain modes of physical behaviour were restricted, Koloki-Kahf celebrated the more idiosyncratic representation of a spirited *hijab*-wearing Muslim woman. She notes the pleasure she felt in being witnessed by other Muslim women in the audience wearing the *hijab*. "It was great joy that I felt to be able to represent them for once in a really positive and wonderful light" (TCG 2005). The representations of Selma also caused Koloki-Kahf to engage in further negotiations with her community. "I had long conversations with [people troubled by the character's behavior] over dinner tables" (TCG 2005). When represented publicly, "proper" Islamic behaviour came into the sphere of discourse, rather than remaining as unreflexive private practice. But the limits of discourse about appropriate Islamic behaviour were quickly reached through the proposed representational existence of gay Muslims. This representation seemed to many members of the community outside of debate or even intelligibility. According to Howard, the cast responded with several comments including: "There's no such thing as a gay Muslim." "You can't be gay *and* be Muslim." Within this group, homosexual behaviour was not tolerable as part of Muslim self-definition. Yet, this very articulation—the enunciated negation of Islamic homosexuality—enacted a more complex public discourse within three moments of representational crisis in Cornerstone's residency.

Cornerstone had at first commissioned an original play for the Muslim community from Yussef El Guindi. His play, *Ten Acrobats*, confronted Muslim homosexuality directly. At a script reading community members objected to the inclusion of an unrepentant gay son, noting that they were not ready to deal with this issue, or that it was outside the realm of the discussable, even that it disrespected the codes of collaboration. Explained cast member Baraa Kahf, "The idea is to do a collaboration with the Muslim community [...] and if there is something that immediately offends the community then obviously there's no room for collaboration" (quoted in Weingarten 2005). It's a somewhat tautological point, as Kahf limits "the Muslim community" to anyone who would be offended by the depiction of homosexuality. Though, according to Peter Howard, many in the community expressed dissent from this opinion, responding to the notion that it was "not the right time" to engage this issue with the comment, "It's been 1200 years, when do you think the right time will be?" In any case, for a number of reasons (including Cornerstone's own discomfort with the scripts' judgmental representation of gay sexuality) the company chose not to produce El Guindi's play. Peter Howard's replacement adaptation of *You Can't Take it With You* at first included a subtle reference to a gay couple which the community again resisted. Explained Howard, "They felt that any representation of homosexuality in the play, however incidental, would turn off the Muslim community and keep them from coming to the play." (Again "the Muslim community" is marked as those who would be offended by depictions of homosexuality.)

Yet, despite the erasure of gay Muslim characters in the community production, the issue entered into discourse via the rehearsal process. Notes Howard, "We had engaged members of the Muslim community in a series of conversations about a difficult topic and the people who had stayed involved in the project were doing so knowing that they were collaborating with at least one 'out' gay man." Conversations in the public sphere continued during "shared meals or in the greenroom." On opening night when cast members gathered to share a meaningful moment from the play or rehearsal, a gay Muslim participant spoke about his self-exile. Once again, private experience entered into the realm of the public. Within this same ritual—a new kind of definitional ceremony for this particular Islamic community— one of the actors who had been opposed to homosexuality, and to including gay characters in the script, apologized for her behaviour, noting that she had also spoken out at a dinner conversation with friends who had condemned gay Muslims.

In both situations, debate about gay Muslims remained off-stage. In the final bridge show, however, gay Muslim representation moved to the center, informed by Arthur Schnitzler's *La Ronde*, the bridge show brought together fifty-seven members of the eight communities with whom Cornerstone had worked, including the GLBT members of faith and the Islamic community. Wrestling with how to substantively include all of the faith communities and stories (in addition to indigenous Tongva and atheists), playwright James Still decided to introduce each community in order of its founding in the LA basin. This brought the GLBT and Islamic communities together in one of the final scenes. After having deferred to the dominant Islamic community's wishes in two productions, Cornerstone members felt beholden to the gay Muslims who they had met during the faith-based cycle, including Ramy Eletreby. Director Bill Rauch decided that the company needed to directly confront the issue in as sensitive a manner as possible. After initially agreeing to be part of the bridge show, however, non-gay Muslims dropped out when they realized how directly the representation of gay Muslims would be addressed.

Eletreby's theatrical embodiment of "gay" *and* "Muslim" animated both the limits of discursive tolerance and of the Habermasian model of critical-rational discourse, which relies, in part, on disembodiment. Sondos Kholoki-Kahf explains that she found it impossible to place her body—one that actively and publicly represented Islam through "a lot of different organizations"—on stage next to that of a real and representational gay Muslim (TCG 2005). She also felt that the script as written did not provide her with any opportunity to voice her concerns. At the same time, Kholoki-Kahf and her husband Baraa remained committed to off-stage dialogue. Baraa organized a four-hour community meeting with a diverse Islamic community that included both gay and straight Muslims and continued conversations over "long lunches." Yet, he too could not place his body on stage publicly next to Eletreby's. As Eletreby notes in an article he wrote for the *LA Magazine* just prior to the show's opening, "1200 people sitting in a theatre watching a Muslim declare himself as also a homosexual, and thus condoning his existence, was unthinkable [for the Muslim community]." By this point in the process, Eletreby has effectively written himself out of "the Muslim community."

The production evoked a different kind of crisis and opportunity for Eletreby to confront his own discursive subjectivity. In the same *LA Magazine* article Eletreby both enacts and reflects upon his own "outing." He begins by citing the warning of a friend in regards to the production, "You know you're going to be outed now" to which Eletreby responds in print, "I know. I don't care. It's about time." Eletreby's decision to "come out" in print prior to the production engages with the complex public/private dynamics of the closet illuminated by Eve Kosofsky Sedgwick. As Michael Warner notes, "We blame people for being closeted. But the closet is better understood as the culture's problem not the individual's [...] it feels private. But in an important sense it is publicly constructed" (Warner 2003: 52). By reflecting publicly on his own "outing" Eletreby makes visible not only his homosexuality but also the systems of containment that define that presence as pathological. In the process of reflecting on the impact of his performance as a gay Muslim Eletreby also begins to redefine his own subjectivity. He notes how a meeting with Muslims discussing the legitimacy of homosexuality caused him to re-examine his *religious* identity. He left the meeting feeling "disturbed and incomplete." Within the article, he ultimately re-narrates himself as an artist, defined by his capacity to refuse acceptance of the status quo. "Whether it's a portrayal on stage or a story in a magazine [artists] have the tremendous power to change people's minds by our words. We have a duty to do our part in improving this world, to promote tolerance and acceptance."

Eletreby again speaks within the rhetoric of social movement and public sphere theory, where change is sought through appeals to public opinion. But as Michael Warner points out, movements around gender and sexuality do not fully conform to a rational-critical model, because of their necessary emphasis on embodiment. In fact, counterpublics call for the animation of either a discrete lifeworld or for the fundamental inclusion of different styles of embodiment and social relations that are bracketed by a more rational Habermasian model. Counterpublics rely on a politics of visibility and distinction that can ultimately illuminate a discomfort in the normative social order with deliberately marked difference.

James Still's script for *Long Bridge* wrestles with these tensions around belonging and difference, though he does so mainly through psychologically realistic dramaturgy. Most of Still's ten scenes play out in the conventionally private spaces of the home where he conjures dramatic situations that follow a model of confrontation and resolution through rational dialogue. In one particular scene, Still alludes to the politics of visibility in religious identity formation. Two South Asian students, Sangita and Jayanti, return to their UCLA dorm room to study for a Spanish test. There they encounter Jayanti's Muslim roommate, Shama (played by a Christian Arab). Jayanti's friend Sangita is disturbed by Shama's *hijab* as both a concealment, "it's like she's *hiding* something" and an open expression of public difference, "it's like she's got to *announce* it to everyone." Sangita wants to fold Shama into her own somewhat troubled feminist

Figure 3. A rehearsal photo from *A Long Bridge Over Deep Waters* (2005) featuring Meena Serendib (Sangita) and Natasha Atalla (Shama). Ramy Eletreby, now Cornerstone's Communication Director, notes that in the actual production Atalla wore a shirt that covered her arms, consistent with the character of Shama. Photograph by Craig Schwartz, courtesy of Cornerstone Theater Company.

framework—"There's no reason for a woman in the 21st c. to cover herself up like that"—which ultimately excuses Shama by eliminating her agency, "I bet her father makes her do it."

Where Sangita serves as a representation of intolerance; her commitment to a particular set of (non-Muslim) values prevents her from seeing Shama's *hijab* as anything other than either an anti-social gesture or an unacceptable violation of Shama's *human* rights. In contrast, Jayanti operates as the signifier of acceptance through confrontation avoidance. "She's my roommate. We get along. There's no reason to make things more complicated." What allows the two roommates to co-exist in this model of American exceptionalism— where so many religions co-exist as long as they're in the post-office or isolated in cars on the highway—is silence rather than speech.

In the latter part of the scene, Still makes the politics of anxiety around marked difference more visible. Shama acknowledges,

"Sometimes I don't always want to be the one who's different, you know. Sometimes I want to take it off for a day and just go to the mall and blend in." Through Shama, Still posits Islamic religious identity as something that may only be externally marked—a habit rather than a habitus. He seems to set up this notion of removable difference in contrast to Ramy Eletreby's character, Tameem, who is beaten up for his less deliberately marked appearance as homosexual. So while Still forges a dialogue-based dramaturgy, the introduction of visible habit and embodied habitus suggests that a public sphere bracketing of embodiment can not fully embrace the politics of difference in arenas of faith and sexuality. This acknowledgement potentially allows for a more nuanced negotiation of tolerance and transformation.

Cornerstone members have mixed feelings about the success of the production in animating transformative dialogue. Certainly, the process prompted increased dialogue. Yet, few members of the Islamic community with whom Cornerstone had worked—including the Kholoki-Kahfs—bore witness to the actual production. Those that did responded in a variety of ways: applauding wildly, walking out, or sitting with arms crossed during a standing ovation (Rauch quoted in TCG 2005). Thus, the bridge production *in and of itself* emerged as less of a definitional ceremony for the Islamic community or as public sphere of discourse around tolerance. It inhabited the terrain Habermas describes as a "staged display," inviting acknowledgement (clap) or dis-identification (arms crossed). Yet, even this staged display foregrounded the importance of embodiment, of the signs produced by the body in engaging response. And as James Still asserts, this staged display, the least nuanced scenario in the production, still manifested the miraculous. "The surprise to me has to be that it exists at all. That in 2005 would have to be enough. That for eight nights on a stage on the planet Earth there was a gay Muslim in a scene" (TCG 2005). At least for some portion of the witnessing audience, and for Eletreby himself, the scene manifested a different poetic lifeworld of being and caring—a qualified performative utopia. For others, the production prompted an agonistic struggle to come to terms with differences around faith and sexuality.

In the faith-based shows I discussed, Cornerstone strove to represent and negotiate through civil dialogue ongoing tensions between sameness and difference within the Muslim community. In *The Falls*, Cornerstone's desire to represent communal difference ran up against the Guthrie Theatre's desire to market itself as quintessentially "Minnesotan" and to maintain control over the production's artistic elements. Indeed, the Cornerstone/Guthrie collaboration indicates divergent ideas of what community and artistry is in the first place.

In *Against the Romance of Community* (2002), Miranda Joseph asserts that "community" is often deployed as a means to retain social hierarchies within a capitalist economy. "Community" is often evoked in order to "sell something" whether that something is a car, a government program, or a theatrical production. What is ultimately reproduced in the evocation of community, however, is not a renewed but a reiterated social order. As a somewhat marginalized consultant in the Cornerstone/Guthrie collaboration I can attest to the many ways that *The Falls* primarily worked to reproduce "Guthrie culture" and to elide communal differences despite some fascinating and revelatory ruptures in the performance-making process.

I have written elsewhere of how collaborations between Cornerstone and professional regional theatres illuminate methodological differences between the two, differences that structure models of theatrical production and consumption against which Cornerstone initially formulated itself. "I think when we started there was kind of a 'burn down the house' mentality," elaborates ensemble member Christopher Liam Moore. "The company evolved because of a growing dissatisfaction we had with [professional] theatre, being really upset by the audience [...]it just didn't look like the world. It didn't even look like our classrooms at Harvard" (quoted in Kuftinec 2003: 145). Despite ongoing educational outreach efforts, most regional professional theatres still hail a population primarily attending the theatre as a practice of class "distinction." I have also suggested that many regional theatres obscure this fact through rhetorical adherence to principles of humanism that—in their enactment—prove exclusionary. The Guthrie mission statement claims to "illuminate the common humanity connecting Minnesota to the peoples of the world," but ignores the cultural and logistical constraints that prevent local Somalis from telling their own stories on the Guthrie stage. (For example, composing *The Falls* script in English through character-based storytelling.) Instead the company casts Somali students who provide an appearance of difference while operating within the Guthrie's storytelling and production conventions. Marked by the staff as "professional protocol" I contend that these conventions primarily worked to preserve artistic hierarchies and fold participants into Guthrie culture.

In one teleconference in which I participated, community consultants asked the Guthrie's liaison how she would mark the project's success. She responded that it would mean people would feel like they "belong at the Guthrie." The staff member also encouraged a vertical communication structure that adhered to the Guthrie's administrative hierarchy. "It's the way things work [...] artistically the lines of the communication are clearly defined [...] We have to live in the culture of the Guthrie and we bring in the community." Though asserting a desire for exchange, Guthrie staff continuously referenced "professional values," conventions within which power and voice always moved through individual artistic leaders rather than through the community asserting, "Everyone involved in this project is [ultimately] working for the Guthrie." In this process, community workshops focused on "skill building" within the terms of Guthrie's expertise.

This kind of "skill building" tended to perform a pedagogy of acquisition rather than exchange, where "artistic experts" laid a particular embodied vocabulary—such as harmonic song-singing and instrumentation—atop the "unskilled bodies" of community performers. Movement was trained into rather than emergent from participants, choreography rehearsal in particular iterated an ethos of repetition rather than discovery, and thus the community actors in these numbers often felt and appeared mechanized. The Guthrie's professional culture tended to dominate Cornerstone's more collaborative ethos.

Yet, fascinating ruptures continuously emerged in the rehearsal process in addition to the church congregant's disgruntled letter. Jeffrey Hatcher's original script for *The Falls* individualized only the white adult characters in the script. He referred to other characters as "Native Woman," "Black Preacher," or "Marcy Student #3." Clara Niiska, an Ojibwe cast as "Native Woman," worked with Hatcher to resingularize her representation and to add the specificity of Ojibwe historiography (which includes genocide and cultural erasure) to the progressive civilizing history narrated by Hatcher. Another cast member publicly marked the privileging of white normativity through scathing humour. In the first full cast reading, Korean-Canadian actress Jeany Park introduced herself as playing "White Woman #9." Hatcher conscientiously worked to include these critiques in his scripted revisions.

However, the singularity of histories that emerged from the rehearsal process were potentially elided by a final full group choreographed sing-along. In this staging, Ukrainian immigrant, Romana (playing a version of herself), shares a folk tune on the *bandura* for actors representing the Kramarczuk family, owners of a sausage factory near the Guthrie. The character of Mrs. Kramarczuk (in skillfully rendered Ukrainian accent) thanks Romana, but asks for a song that is "more Minnesota." The song selected to represent "something more Minnesota" was *Our State Fair* from the Oscar Hammerstein musical set in Iowa. Within *The Falls*, the Iowa State Fair song linked together Minnesota difference. Characters from various time periods and cultures—and even the Assistant Stage Manager—emerge onto the stage (a giant picnic blanket) singing and dancing together in fully synchronized musical choreography. Instruments including the *bandura,* tuba, and African *djembe* appear to signify a multicultural tapestry of difference. Yet instead of texturing the number with, for example, the polyrhythmic syncopation that marks most African drumming, the instrumentation was subsumed into the 4:4 regularity of the State Fair song. If one watched carefully, Clara Niiska seemed persistently unable to take this regulated choreography into her body. She always seemed "out of step" with the others, in a way that marked her body as either "unskilled" or deliberately differentiating.

The script and staging grappled with how to relate multiple narratives of arrival in Minnesota, struggling to resist the dominant historiographic framing of European settlement. The figure of Father Hennepin (a French minister who "discovered" and settled the area around the St. Anthony Falls) was initially staged standing outside of the final full-cast group with an overhead view from the balconies above, as though he were ordaining the scene's existence. Recognizing the way that this staging might be read as privileging Hennepin's viewpoint, director Michael John Garcés restaged the scene. Yet, the narrative of Fatherly origin and authority still occasionally surfaced in the script. In one early scene, a young Somali immigrant girl encounters Father Hennepin across time and insists that he continue in his explorations and documentation so that she will be able to exist in Minnesota in the future. "If you leave here, no one from your world will know you were here. Then the people you told won't know and the people they told won't know and none of this will happen." The written archive here organizes a logic of events culminating in immigrant settlements, a narrative that risks suppressing the traumatic nature of that settlement in relation to indigenous occupants. Following further conversations between Jeffrey Hatcher and Clara Niiska, an added monologue in the play's second act highlights an indigenous narrative of genocide through Niiska's portrayal of a contemporary Minneapolis tour guide.

Miranda Joseph notes the persistent return of community as an uncritically positive formation, one that elides the production of consensus as an exclusionary process that also participates in historiographic erasure. While foregrounding productive dissent and rupture, it is important to be alert to moments of false unity—compressions of difference that return multiplicity and counterpublic embodiment into a normative assimilationist model. This model is contained not only by the Guthrie culture but also by the Guthrie building, a site that intriguingly manifests and hides its own self-production. Located in a former industrial zone, the new Guthrie building's silhouette echoes that of a factory. Yet the somewhat postmodern "smokestacks" produce not manufactured waste but advertisements of itself in flickering flames of light. The building itself features gigantic images of theatrical artists such as Tyrone Guthrie, Anton Chekhov, and Arthur Miller. The two black artists represented—Lorraine Hansberry and August Wilson—are tucked into the buildings interior folds. Inside the building, production images ghost the walls—an archive of the Guthrie looking in on itself. As one of the African American actors in *The Falls* pointed out to me, however, the sole black actress represented had been initially covered over by a fire alarm. Attempts to transform the interior space with images from the community-based process had been further contained by the French architect who had designed the space with the stipulation that nothing be placed on public walls without his express consent. When confronted with this absence of community representation, a Guthrie staff member suggested displaying the archive in the community partners' spaces proposing, "Do it in the schools. It will be good advertisement for the Guthrie."

It's all too easy to lob potshots at the Guthrie, and to do so enacts its own problematic erasures; there were in fact numerous moments of encounter that disrupted the theatre's culture; moments of dissent such as those introduced by Niiska that resulted in individual as well as in limited structural transformation. Several Guthrie artistic staff members, including dramaturg Michael Dixon, also pushed for more collaboration between Guthrie and Cornerstone practices. But within a context dominated by the Guthrie's institutional culture, it is not surprising that productive dissent emerged less in lengthy community dialogues and more in privately expressed dissatisfactions such as the congregant's letter. Ironically, this conflict seems to end more happily; after several private conversations with concerned parties Hatcher rewrote his script to place the focus less on salty meat pies and more on the church's inclusion of a Korean immigrant. The congregant composed a new letter expressing her support for the project.

Is this a preferred, happier ending than that focused on the public "tolerability" of gay Muslims? Or does this situation merely foreground the ease with which the representations of more normative religious beliefs—where tolerance by the dominant culture is less at stake—can be negotiated?

Community-based performance has such noble and important goals: animating and reflecting community. We seek this social connection, the *communitas* provided by a live event witnessed together—those moments of performative utopia that conjure more progressive lifeworlds. We seek to know and to be known to others as well as to ourselves. Performance, particularly performance located in self-defined communities of belief, belonging, or place, offers a reflective space where we can bear witness to each other. But outside the realm of this self-definition—in rehearsal spaces, dinner tables, and green-room conversations open to difference and dissent—the process may contain the possibility not for unity and agreement, nor for manifestations of human commonality, but for the containment of colliding truths.

The faith-based bridge show offers two compelling moments for this possibility. At the end of *Long Bridge Over Deep Waters*, all fifty-seven actors re-emerge. They appear upon and outside of the boundaries of the stage against a starlit sky. Each one introduces him/herself by name and by attachments to faith. Here are a few:

I was raised Catholic, but I am Tongva/Gabrielino. What are you?
I am African Methodist Episcopalian.
I am Chinese Christian.
I am a mystic and a Jew.
I became a Jew.
I'm a Jew too! But I played a Christian.
I'm a Los Angeles Christian. But I played a Jew.
(Jonathan) I was raised a Catholic boy.
(Stephanie) So was I.
I am a born-again Hindu.
I am Baha'i.
I am an ardent atheist.
I was raised a Christian
I like all religions, but was raised Hindu.
I was raised straight.
I am a Rakshasi and a Hindu goddess.
I am a Hindu drag nun.
I am cosmic dust.
I am Jew-ish.
I am beyond a Muslim.
I am a saved Catholic.
I am Catholic and Chumash.
I am Cherokee and Christian.
I am Muslim and a gay man.
I am still Muslim.

In this final moment, the actors mark their difference from each other and from the representational stories they have staged. I find it a profoundly beautiful moment of being and becoming, of communal and self-definition, of coalitional difference (though absent of non-gay Muslims).

The other moment returns to my original quotation from Ramy Eletreby and occurs after the production's formal closing, at the Theatre Communications Group Conference. It does not have the poetic force of the production's staged display. But Eletreby's body finally emerges alongside those of other Muslims in a public space where he enunciates his faith *and* his sexuality, his difference articulated within and thus transforming the public sphere. Both moments propose a different kind of possible future, one marked by shared and embodied difference that occurs within the process and ongoing ripples of performance. It is a kind of production of difference and dissent that may point the way towards a coalition beyond enforced consensus or mere co-existence. These are moments of true hope and more democratic agonism.

___

NOTES
[1] Mouffe writes about the concept of agonism across a number of sources, most explicitly in *The Democratic Paradox* (2000).
[2] See "A Cornerstone for Rethinking Community Theatre" (1996), "Cornerstone's Community *Chalk Circle*" (1997), "Fighting Fences: Theatrical Rule-Breaking in Former Yugoslavia" (1999), "Staging the City with the Good People of New Haven," (2001), *Staging America: Cornerstone and Community-Based Theatre* (2003), and "Bridging Haunted Places: Performance and the Production of Mostar" (2005).

REFERENCES

Atlas, Caron. (n.d.) Introduction to "The Faith-Based Cycle Case Study: Cornerstone Theater Company"
   <http://ww3.americansforthearts.org/AnimatingDemocracy/pdf/labs/corners tone_case_study.pdf> [Accessed 10 November 2008].
Body of Faith. (2003) Written by Luis Alfaro. Directed by Christopher Liam Moore. Produced by Cornerstone Theater Company (20 February - 22 March). Los Angeles, CA.
Dolan, Jill. (2005) *Utopia in Performance: Finding Hope at the Theater.* Ann Arbor: University of Michigan Press.
Eletreby, Ramy. (2005) "Crossing the Bridge: a Young, Gay Muslim Confronts His Community by Coming Out on the Stage." *IN Los Angeles* 8 (8), 126-127. <http://www.inlamagazine.com/808/features/808_gaymuslim.html> [Accessed 6 February 2008].
The Falls. (2006) Written by Jeffrey Hatcher. Directed by Michael John Garcés and Bill Rauch. Produced by the Guthrie Theatre in collaboration with Cornerstone Theater Company (19 August - 10 September). Minneapolis, MN.
Favre, Jeff. (2005) "New Work at Ford Explores Encounters Between Faiths." *The Daily Breeze* (27 May), <http://www.aldrichpr.com/BridgeReviews.htm> [Accessed 13 November 2008].
Fish, Stanley. (1997) "Boutique Multiculturalism, or Why Liberals are Incapable of Thinking about Hate Speech." *Critical Inquiry* 23, 378-95.
Fraser, Nancy. (1992) "Rethinking the Public Sphere: A Contribution to the Critique of Actually Existing Democracy" in Craig Calhoun, ed. *Habermas and the Public Sphere.* Cambridge, MA: MIT Press, 109-42.
Freya, Jan. (2006) "Cornerstone's Faith-based Theater Cycle: How Does Faith Unite and Divide Us?" *Community Arts Network Reading Room.* (10 January) <http://www.communityarts.net/readingroom/archivefiles/2006/01/cornerst one_the.php> [Accessed 10 November 2008].
A Long Bridge Over Deep Waters. (2005) Written by James Still. Directed by Bill Rauch. Cornerstone Theater Company (2 June - 12 June). Los Angeles, CA.

Habermas, Jürgen. (1989) *The Structural Transformation of the Public Sphere: An Inquiry into a Category of Bourgeois Society.* Trans. Thomas Burger with assistance from Frederick Lawrence. Cambridge, MA: MIT Press.

Henderson, Evan. (2004) "Cornering the Faith." *Stage Directions.* (December), 36-38.

Howard, Peter. (2006) Personal interview (8 September).

Joseph, Miranda. (2002) *Against the Romance of Community.* Minneapolis: University of Minnesota Press.

Kuftinec, Sonja. (1996) "A Cornerstone for Rethinking Community Theater." *Theatre Topics* 6 (1), 91-104.

——. (1997) "Cornerstone's Community *Chalk Circle.*" *The Brecht Yearbook* 22, 239-51.

——. (1999) "Fighting Fences: Theatrical Rule-Breaking in Former Yugoslavia." *Slavic and Eastern European Performances* (Summer), 50-57.

——. (2001) "Staging the City with the Good People of New Haven." *Theatre Journal:* 197-222

——. (2003) *Staging America: Cornerstone and Community-Based Theater.* Carbondale, IL: Southern Illinois University Press.

——. (2005) "Bridging Haunted Places: Performance and the Production of Mostar" in Judith Hamera, ed. *Opening Acts: Performance in/as Communication.* Thousand Oaks, CA: Sage Publications.

Mouffe, Chantal. (2000) *The Democratic Paradox.* New York: Verso.

Myerhoff, Barbara. (1980) *Number Our Days.* New York: Touchstone.

Theatre Communications Group. (2005) "Cornerstone Theater Panel" TCG National Conference. (17 June) <http://www.tcg.org/events/conference/2005/Cornerstone.cfm> [Accessed 13 November 2008].

Terry, Sara. (2001) "Under Construction: More-connected Communities." *Christian Science Monitor.* (5 December) <http://www.csmonitor.com/2001/1205/p15s1-lihc.html> [Accessed 9 February 2008].

Warner, Michael. (2003) *Publics and Counterpublics.* Cambridge, MA: Zone Books.

Weingarten, Toni. (2005) "Theater Seeks Common Ground for Intersecting Faiths." *New York Times.* (11 June) <http://www.nytimes.com/2005/06/11/national/11religion.html> [Accessed 9 February 2008].

You Can't Take it With You: An American Muslim Remix. (2003) By Moss Hart and George S. Kaufman, adapted by Peter Howard. Directed by Mark Valdez. Cornerstone Theater Company (9 October - 26 October). Los Angeles, CA.

ABOUT THE CONTRIBUTORS

Sue Becker is a social psychologist who completed her PhD at Loughborough University looking at the ways in which arguments around child contact arrangements are negotiated and managed discursively. She specialises in the use of qualitative data corpora (e.g. naturally occurring talk and text, visual images, and haptics boxes) to explore and unpack participants' understandings of sensitive and abstract topics such as masturbation, health, and happiness. Her research interests are in qualitative psychology including social stigma and the use of laughter and humour to ameliorate and manage both perceived and enacted stigma in interaction. Sue is a member of the British Psychological Society's Qualitative Methods in Psychology Section. She is also part of Teeside University's Institute of Design, Culture and the Arts.

Paola Botham (née Sotomayor) was born in Chile, where she worked as a cultural journalist and later as a writer for the Ministry of Education. Since moving to the UK in 2001, she has been researching and lecturing in drama at the University of Worcester, where she is currently completing her doctoral thesis *Redefining Political Theatre in Post-Cold War Britain (1990-2005): An Analysis of Contemporary British Political Plays*. Her research interests include twentieth-century British and Latin American drama, new writing for the theatre, and critical theory. Recent publications are "From Deconstruction to Reconstruction: A Habermasian Framework for Contemporary Political Theatre," which appeared in *Contemporary Theatre Review* in 2008, and "Beyond the Anger and the Barking: Modernity and Identity in 1950's Chilean and English Theatre," which was published in *Cátedra de Artes* in 2005.

Sydney Cheek O'Donnell is Assistant Professor of Theatre History and head of the Theatre Studies program at the University of Utah in Salt Lake City. Her reviews and articles have been published in *Theatre Journal*, *New Theatre Quarterly*, and *Seattle Opera*

Magazine. In addition to on-going scholarly work in the areas of feminist performance analysis and Italian theatre, Dr. Cheek O'Donnell works as a production dramaturg in professional and academic theatre. She earned a B.A. at Carleton College and a Ph.D. in Theatre History and Criticism at the University of Washington.

Wendy Clupper is a performance theorist and practitioner who teaches global contemporary performance and visual arts at Maryland Institute College of Art (MICA). Wendy received her bachelor's degree in Women's Studies from Rutgers University, her master's degree from New York University, Tisch School of the Arts, in Performance Studies, and her doctoral degree from the University of Maryland at College Park in Theatre History and Performance Studies. Her dissertation, entitled *The Performance Culture of Burning Man*, is representative of her ongoing scholarship, where she considers outdoor sites for artistic presentation, as well as participatory, political, and experimental art and performance. She was previously published in the 2007 Rodopi Press book *Festivalising!: Theatrical Events, Politics and Culture*. In 2008, she was a Visiting Professor in the Florida State University School of Theatre and a guest director for the New Horizons Original Works Playwrights Festival. Wendy has performed as a solo artist in New York City, San Francisco, and in 2007, at the Transmodern Festival of performance art in Baltimore. She has been nominated four years consecutively to the Maryland State Arts Council.

David Grant has enjoyed a varied career in theatre throughout as a critic, director, and teacher. He has been Managing Editor of *Theatre Ireland* magazine, Programme Director of the Dublin Theatre Festival, and Artistic Director of the Lyric Theatre, Belfast. He has directed more than a hundred theatre productions in contexts ranging from Her Majesty's Prison Maghaberry to London's Royal National Theatre and has a special interest in community-based drama and theatre by, with, and for young people. He is currently Head of Drama Studies at Queen's University, Belfast.

Susan C. Haedicke is Associate Professor in the School of Theatre, Performance, and Cultural Policy Studies at University of Warwick. Recently, she has published extensively on European Street Theatre and is currently finishing a book, entitled *Contemporary European Street Theatre: Aesthetics and Politics*, for Palgrave Macmillan. Her other research interests include Franco-Algerian drama and community-based theatre. She is co-editor of *Performing Democracy: International Perspectives on Urban Community-Based Performance* and has published chapters in anthologies including, *Performance and Violence: Local Roots and Global Routes of Conflict* and *Staging Nationalism: Essays of Theatre and National Identity*, and articles in several journals, including *Text and Performance Quarterly*, *Theatre Topics*, *Journal of Dramatic Theory and Criticism* and *Essays in Theatre*. She has also worked as a professional dramaturg in France and the United States.

Bérénice Hamidi-Kim, PhD in Theatrical Studies, is the author of a dissertation entitled *The Cities of Political Theatre in France - 1989-2007* (Université Lyon 2, 2007) to be published in 2010 by L'Entretemps editions, and of articles about political theatre. (For a full list of the articles, see the bio-bibliography on the Group website: http://theatrespolitiques.free.fr/spip.php?article5).
She is a former student of the Ecole Normale Supérieure de Fontenay-Saint-Cloud and has held the positions of Assistant Lecturer at the Institut d'Etudes Théâtrales at the Sorbonne Nouvelle (Université Paris 3), and Associate researcher at the Groupe de Sociologie politique et Morale, Ecole des Hautes Etudes en Sciences Sociales. She is a member of the Groupe Théâtres Politiques, a research group at Nanterre University.

Deirdre Heddon is a Reader in the Department of Theatre, Film and Television Studies, University of Glasgow. She has published widely on the use of auto/biography in performance. Previous publications include *Autobiography and Performance* (Palgrave Macmillan, 2008) and, with Jane Milling, *Devising Performance: A Critical History* (Palgrave Macmillan, 2005). Forthcoming research includes *Walking, Writing and Performance: Autobiographical Texts by Deirdre Heddon, Carl Lavery and Phil Smith*, edited by Roberta Mock (Intellect, 2009) and *Live Art (UK): Histories and Practices*, edited by Deirdre Heddon and Jennie Klein (Palgrave Macmillan 2010).

Tal Itzhaki graduated from the College of Art Teachers and the Department of Theatre, Tel Aviv University. She taught theatre design at Tel Aviv University; the College of Art Teachers; the Wizo-Canada College of Design. She created the Theatre Design program at the Department of Theatre, University of Haifa, and served as its Head for nine years. She was a Visiting Professor of Theatre for three years at Columbia University, where she co-authored and designed productions such as *Neighbors* and *Xandra*. She now teaches at Sapir Academic College. Itzhaki designed sets, costumes, and puppets for over 130 shows for all major theatre and dance companies in Israel. She also translated plays from English and is the secretary of the Israeli Association of Stage Designers. Itzhaki has designed and curated design exhibitions, among them the five Israeli exhibitions of Stage Design at the Prague Quadrennial between 1991 and 2007 and the major theatre costume exhibition in Jerusalem in 2008, and served as referee in local and international design competitions. She delivered papers on theatre and scenography at professional and academic conferences, among others in Seoul, Jaipur, Maryland, Helsinki, and Prague. She was also one of the founders of the "Fringe Centre" in Tel Aviv.

Sonja Arsham Kuftinec is Associate Professor of Theatre at the University of Minnesota. She has published widely on community-based theatre including *Staging America: Cornerstone and Community-Based Theater* (2003), which received honourable mention for the Barnard Hewitt Award in theatre history. Since 1995 she has developed collaborative theatre projects with youth in the Balkans and Middle East. Her co-production *Where Does the Postman Go When all the Street Names Change?* won an ensemble prize at the 1997 Youth Theatre Festival in Mostar. Since 2000 Professor Kuftinec has worked as a facilitator with Seeds of Peace with youth from the Middle East and Balkans. Her book, *Theatre, Facilitation and Nation Formation in the Balkans and Middle East*, will be published by Palgrave Macmillan Press in 2009.

Carl Lavery teaches Theatre and Performance at Aberystwyth University. He is co-editor of *Jean Genet: Performance and Politics* (2006) and co-author of *Sacred Theatre* (2007) and *Walking, Writing and Performance* (2009). His monograph *The Politics of Jean Genet's*

Theatre: Spaces of Revolution will appear later this year, as will his co-edited collection *Contemporary French Theatre and Performance.* He is currently working with David Williams on a volume on the performance company Lone Twin.

Shimon Levy is Full Professor at the Tel Aviv University Department of Theatre Arts, and was its chair for five years (2000-05). His publications include three books on Samuel Beckett's drama (McMillan; Sussex Academic, Hakibutz Hameuchad); *Theatre and Holy Script*, [Ed.], Sussex Academic Press 1999), and on Hebrew drama [ed.], *Hanoch Levin: The Man with the Myth in the Middle.* He has published *The Bible as Theatre* (Sussex Academic Press 2002) and *The Israeli Theatre Canon* (2002) and numerous articles in Hebrew, English, and German. His book on Israeli drama and theatre appeared in Arabic (Madar, Ramalla 2007). Dr. Levy was artistic director of the Akko Theatre Festival and presently on its board. He has been theatre critic for Israeli journals and radio, dramaturge for the Habimah and Khan Theatre, and has translated over 140 plays into Hebrew. He has directed plays for theatre and radio. He is Chief Editor of *Assaph/Plays* and *Assaph/Theatre* Research series. His translation into Hebrew of *Beckett's Collected Dramatic Works* was published in 2007.

Tom Maguire is a Senior Lecturer in Drama and Distinguished Teaching Fellow at the University of Ulster. He teaches and researches in the areas of contemporary British and Irish theatre, applied theatre, theatre practice, and storytelling. He has published and presented widely on contemporary Irish theatre in particular. His *Making Theatre in Northern Ireland Through and Beyond the Troubles* was published by the University of Exeter Press in 2006. He is the Chair of the Board of Big Telly Theatre Company, Northern Ireland and of the Standing Conference of University Drama Departments, the UK subject association. He is a member of the Advisory Board of PALATINE, the United Kingdom's Higher Education Academy's subject centre for performing arts.

Sanja Nikčević is an associate professor and the head of the Drama Department and The Academy of Arts in Osijek, and a two-time Fulbright recipient. She teaches courses on American and British drama, theatre criticism, and the history of theatre. She is the editor of *Anthology of American Plays, Theatre Criticism Today* (a collection of essays in English), and *Anthology of Contemporary Croatian Drama.* She has also published three books on American drama: *The Subversive American Drama or Sympathy for Losers* (1994), *Affirmative American Drama or Long Live the Puritans* (2003), and *Losers' Genius in Our Town* (Zagreb, 2006). Her book on Croatian drama, *What is Croatian drama to us?* was published in Zagreb last year. Her book *New European Drama or Great Deception* (2005) received the Croatian award and was translated into several languages, including Slovak, Hungarian, Polish, and part of it was translated into English for the *New Theater Quarterly* in 2005. Sanja was the founder of the Croatian Centre of ITI. She has twice served as board member for ITI Worldwide and is a member of numerous associations of scholars and critics. Currently, she is the secretary of a national theatre critics' organization and adviser for the European Theatre Award.

Avraham Oz holds degrees from Tel Aviv University and The University of Bristol. He was Head of the Department of Theatre, Tel Aviv University, and founder and Head of the Department of Theatre, University of Haifa. He taught at Beit Zvi School of Dramatic Art, Hakibbutzim Seminar College, and Sapir Academic College, was a visiting lecturer at The Hebrew University in Jerusalem, served as associate artistic director at The Cameri Theatre, as dramaturg at the Haifa Municipal Theatre, as a theatre critic for major papers and the National Radio, and as a theatre editor for the magazine *Akhshav.* Oz has edited shows on radio and TV and served as president of the Israeli Association for Theatre Research (IATR). He founded and edited the publications *Assaph Theatre Studies—JTD, Journal of Theatre and Drama,* and *Mofa.* Oz has published books and articles on Shakespeare, Marlowe, political theatre, theatre and nationhood, and is completing a book on Israeli drama and Zionist narrative. Oz is the general editor of the Hebrew edition of the works of Shakespeare, and his numerous Hebrew translations of plays and operas have been performed by all major theatre companies in Israel and the Israeli Opera including nine Shakespearean plays, as well as plays by Brecht, Pinter, Turini, and many others.

Lloyd Peters has lectured at the University of Salford since 1992. In that time he became a Senior Lecturer, Head of Performance and a member of the School Executive committee. Lloyd was responsible for executive producing the award-winning documentary *Carefree* (2009) and is currently programme leader of the MA Fiction Film Production course. Lloyd's specialist research areas focus on practice-as-research projects examining non-naturalistic modes of screen and theatre performance. He co-wrote the e-article "Big is Beautiful: Emphasising Scale in Community Arts" (2003) published in *Studies in Theatre and Performance*. Lloyd has been a professional actor, director and writer and for thirty-three years. He has worked with many of the UK's leading writers, directors, and producers including Mike Leigh, Alan Bleasedale (twice), Ken Russell, Michael Wearing, and Philip Saville. He formed his own production company *Red-Roar Films* and has written, produced and directed many films that have been screened at cinemas and on television. Lloyd's writing work includes commissions for BBC television and radio. His first play for BBC Radio 4 entitled *A Higher Education* was Pick of the Day when it was transmitted on June 20, 2000 and received universally favourable reviews.

Beverly Redman is an assistant professor in Theatre and Dance at Ursinus College. Having recently completed her dissertation with the University of California, Irvine, on the history and politics of the San Francisco Mime Troupe, she specializes in radical theatre and performance, with particular interest in directing and writing about community-based projects. She also holds an MFA in directing from Irvine and an MA in Composition and Rhetoric from Georgetown University. At Ursinus Redman teaches advanced acting styles, voice and speech, theatre history, and a series of world drama courses. She directs professionally and at the college level frequently.

Kerrie Schaefer is Senior Lecturer in the Department of Drama at Exeter University. Dr. Schaefer joined the Exeter Drama Department in April 2007 after eight years in the Drama Department at the University of Newcastle, NSW. She completed her Ph.D. in Performance Studies at the University of Sydney, Australia. Her dissertation documented the performance-making practices of The Sydney Front, a contemporary Australian performance ensemble, and interrogated the company's notion of performance as seduction. In Newcastle she developed further research interests in place, history, memory, and performance-based community cultural development, which were explored through the practice-based research group Performance, Community Development and Social Change. She currently coordinates the Applied Drama programme at Exeter University, which includes the tri-annual international conference on Research in Applied Drama, Theatre and Performance. The 2008 Conference theme was Performance, Cross-Cultural Dialogue and Co-existence. She has published work in edited collections and journals including *The Drama Review, Australasian Drama Studies, About Performance, Studies in Theatre and Performance, The Senses in Performance*, edited by Sally Banes and André Lepecki (Routledge, 2006), and *Unstable Ground: Performance and the Politics of Place*, edited by Gay McAuley (Peter Lang, 2006).

David Watt is an Associate Professor in Drama at the University of Newcastle, NSW. His central area of interest has been in "political," popular, and community-based performance and the theory and practice of community cultural development. His research has ranged from archival work on precursors of contemporary community-based theatre, (such as Charles Parker, John McGrath, and Peter Cheeseman) to accounts of more recent practice, and practice as research on oral history-based and site specific performance. He has published on this work in journals and anthologies since the 1980s, and in a book, *Workers' Playtime: Theatre and the Labour Movement Since 1970*, jointly written with Canadian scholar Alan Filewood.

E.J. Westlake is an Assistant Professor of Theatre & Drama at the University of Michigan and the author of *Our Land is Made of Courage and Glory: Nationalist Performance in Nicaragua and Guatemala* (2005). She has written several articles on Latin American and community-based theatre, which have appeared in *Latin American Theatre Review, The Drama Review*, and books such as Haedicke and Nellhaus' *Performing Democracy* (2001), Lengel and Warren's *Casting Gender* (2005), and the forthcoming anthology edited by Bial and Magelssen *Theatre Historiography: Critical Questions* (2010). She is currently working on a book-length study of the Nicaraguan national dance-drama *El Güegüence* as it has evolved from anthropological artifact to national symbol to queer icon. Dr. Westlake has taught theatre history, dramatic literature, playwriting, and cultural anthropology at Auburn and Bowling Green State Universities. She was cofounder and Managing Director of Stark Raving Theatre in Portland, Oregon, where she worked as a director and playwright. She won the Oregon Book Award in 1992 for her play *A.E.: The Disappearance and Death of Amelia Earhart.*